# Film Review

# 1994-5

**James Cameron-Wilson** became a committed film buff when he moved to London at the age of seventeen. After a stint at the Webber Douglas Academy of Dramatic Art he joined *What's On in London*, and took over from F. Maurice Speed as cinema editor. Later, he edited the trade newspaper *Showbiz*, was commissioning editor for *Film Review*, was a presenter of 'The Movie Show' on BSkyB and a frequent presenter of the Radio 2 'Arts Programme'. He is also the author of the books *Young Hollywood* and *The Cinema of Robert De Niro*. He now writes regularly for *Film Review*, *Flicks*, *Now!* and *The Times*, and is syndicated in the *What's On* magazines.

**F. Maurice Speed** began his working life as an apprentice on the *Harrow Observer*. From early on, his work reflected an interest in the cinema, and he calculates that he has now spent well over seven years watching films. He has contributed to many newspapers, journals and magazines in both Britain and America, and his books include the pre-war *Movie Cavalcade* and the later *Western Film and TV Annual*. His position as the grand old man of British film criticism was confirmed when the London Film Critics' Circle presented him in 1991 with a special award in recognition of his lifetime achievement and the half-century for which he has now edited *Film Review*.

# Film Review

# 1994-5

## Including Video Releases

James Cameron-Wilson
and
F. Maurice Speed

Virgin

First published in Great Britain in 1994 by
VIRGIN BOOKS
*an imprint of Virgin Publishing Ltd*
332 Ladbroke Grove, London W10 5AH



*A catalogue record for this book is available
from the British Library*

ISBN 0 86369 842 5

Designed by Fred Price

Phototypeset by Intype Ltd, London

Printed in Great Britain by
Butler & Tanner Ltd, Frome and London

# Contents

# Introduction

## F. Maurice Speed

WHEN, fifty years ago, the first *Film Review Annual* was published (at 12*s*. 6*d*. old money, with numerous full-colour plates and with a scene from *Kismet* on the dust-jacket) I don't think anyone involved thought that fifty years on the annual would still be flourishing.

The years have seen changes of course, in size, format and style, but the aim of the book has been and is constant: to give in an entertaining way a complete coverage of the year in the cinema, including a detailed review of every film released during the period covered.

I had the idea for the annual long before it was first published. Invalided out of the Army and back looking after *What's On in London* I one day mentioned my idea for the book to a friend, Robbie Lantz, who later became the Hollywood agent-manager. Robbie enthusiastically gave me introductions to several publishers, most of whom were interested and prepared to publish as soon as paper ceased to be so strictly rationed. Macdonald, however, had some spare paper supplies and signed a contract to publish as soon as I could deliver the copy. That initial 1944–5 book sold some 80,000 copies to a book-starved public and the second annual reached a dizzy 250,000 print order (incidentally earning me enough in royalties to buy and lavishly furnish my first country cottage!). There was no competition in those paper-rationed days, and although there have been rivals since, all were short-lived.

What has remained constant through the years has been my dislike of needless foul language in films, and of the self-indulgent length of too many movies. The ideal length for a movie has to be 90–100 minutes: to exceed that a film must be very good indeed, while to reach and exceed two hours a film must be something of a masterpiece. (Yes, it can be done; I've seen *Gone With the Wind* at least six times and it has never bored me for a minute.) Constant, too, has been my antipathy to the mad film finances which make it possible for not over-talented stars to earn (or at least be paid) enough money on a single film to retire and live comfortably for the rest of their lives.

Although a large number of films still depend mainly on the money they earn at the cinema box-offices, more and more productions rely upon subsidiary income, including of course the valuable video market. For instance, Disney sold 10½ million copies of *Aladdin* in the US during the first three days of its release. And it is no exaggeration to say that the whole future of the Disney Empire depends on video sales – films only represent 35 per cent of Disney income.

Disney, for instance, now has some 250 outlets – shops etc. – for their merchandise: T-shirts, caps, jackets, toys etc. Warner, too, are developing this idea with some 60 outlets, while

Sony, having just opened their first store, are planning to launch many more.

One of the happiest stories of the year has been the success of the modestly budgeted British film in America and worldwide. Without any government help (which the cinema gets in nearly every other country) British filmmakers have raised the money and by sheer talent kept the box-offices busy: prime examples are *Four Weddings & a Funeral, The Crying Game* and *Much Ado About Nothing*. The British film studios have been busy too: after a long time away, American productions are at last beginning to return to the UK.

We've had a £40 million film at Shepperton (*Judge Dredd* with Sylvester Stallone), and a £13 million production at Pinewood (*Mary Riley*, with Julia Roberts and John Malkovich), following the £34 million film *Interview With the Vampire* with Tom Cruise and Brad Pitt. The dollar/pound rate has a lot to do with the current Hollywood invasion of the British studios, but reinforcing the decision of producers is the awareness that Britain's film technicians are some of the best in the world.

Production costs in America are still rising steadily year by year (apart from 1991 when they actually fell!). This rise is due at least in part to the ludicrous earnings of the stars, and partly also to the equally ridiculous sums paid to writers for sometimes less than inspired manuscripts. These fantastic amounts are in contrast to the wages of the lesser players and the technicians, neither having been allowed to board the gravy-trains. Just as an example of these rising budgets, five years ago the official average production cost of a major Hollywood movie was $23 million dollars; today it is $30 million.

Incidentally it isn't the film that *takes* the most money that is the most financially successful. For instance, *Jurassic Park* has earned over $900 million in a year, heading the all-time money-making list. But percentage-wise the real success of the period was a largely unsung minor effort, *The Wedding Banquet*, which was made for a million dollars and has so far earned its makers $23 million.

This year's 'In Memoriam' feature is as long and as sad as ever, with the maestro Federico Fellini heading the list. (I am always a little surprised to find this feature one of the most popular in the annual.)

Finally I'm handing you over to James Cameron-Wilson (who, incidentally, was born long after the annual first became established). James joined as a contributor but is now my hard-working co-editor, and he will in due course be taking over the sole direction of the annual – for the next fifty years, I'm sure!

---

# James Cameron-Wilson

HI. My name is James Cameron-Wilson and I'm a film buff. I admit it. That's why I put unseemly hours into this august publication year in and year out. But, truth be known, I would probably compile most of the following information whether it was published or not. Because, as an addicted cine-disciple, I need that data to feed my habit. And so what began as an honour bestowed on me by my mentor F. Maurice Speed (the 'F' stands for film-buff) has evolved into a marriage of love and discipline. As no other publication offers such a complete package of reviews, credits, box-office tallies, quotes, gossip and awards of the year, I write it myself. So, should I need to remind myself of the name of Demi Moore's latest offspring, I can look it up in the 'Film World Diary' (I did, and it's Tallulah Belle Willis). And should I need to know what are the best recent films from Canada, a quick glance at the 'Genies' in the 'Awards and Festivals' chapter will give me a pretty good idea (this year *Thirty-Two Short Films About Glenn Gould* was the clear favourite).

For me, F. Maurice Speed's *Film Review* annual is indispensable. It is an honour, then, that I have been working on it for the last seventeen years and have co-edited the last eight issues. I hope that my own contributions and innovations (such as the 'Video Releases', the aforementioned 'Diary' and this year's embryonic 'Film Soundtracks') have enhanced rather than diminished what has become a unique publishing phenomenon. Any complaints or suggestions (hell, even praise will do) are always welcome.

# Top Twenty Box-Office Hits

1. Jurassic Park
2. Mrs Doubtfire
3. Four Weddings & a Funeral
4. Aladdin
5. The Fugitive
6. Schindler's List
7. Indecent Proposal
8. Philadelphia
9. Sleepless in Seattle
10. Cliffhanger
11. Cool Runnings
12. The Firm
13. In the Line of Fire
14. Wayne's World 2
15. Addams Family Values
16. Demolition Man
17. Naked Gun 33⅓: The Final Insult
18. Free Willy
19. Groundhog Day
20. Beethoven's 2nd

*Richard Attenborough, Jeff Goldblum, Sam Neill and Laura Dern gaze at the impossible in Steven Spielberg's* Jurassic Park

*The incomparable Robin Williams as* Mrs Doubtfire

*Harrison Ford is* The Fugitive

*Instant star Hugh Grant contemplates romance in the surprise box-office smash* Four Weddings & a Funeral

# Top Ten Box-Office Stars

STAR OF THE YEAR
Robin Williams

Robin Williams never does anything by halves. One minute his career looks like it's in a tailspin, the next he's the star of two of the four hottest pictures of the year. OK, so the cocky Robin never actually *appeared* in *Aladdin*, but his presence was certainly felt. And it was he – as the voice of the genie – who enticed parents back to watch the *bons mots* they missed the first time round. It was also a fantastic year for Tom Hanks, whose AIDS drama *Philadelphia* surprisingly beat the feel-good *Sleepless in Seattle* at the UK box-office. And then there were such old favourites as Harrison, Cruise, Clint, Murray, Whoopi and Demi. Runners-up this year include Emma Thompson, Robert Redford, Meg Ryan and Michael Douglas.

**2** Tom Hanks

**3** Sylvester Stallone

**4** Harrison Ford

**5** Tom Cruise

**6** Clint Eastwood

**7** Whoopi Goldberg

**8** Demi Moore

**9** Bill Murray

**10** Andie MacDowell

# Releases of the Year

In this section you will find details of all the films released in Great Britain from 1 July 1993 to the end of June 1994 – the period covered by all the reference features in the book.

The normal abbreviations operate as follows: Dir – for Director; Pro – for Producer; Assoc Pro – for Associate Producer; Ex Pro – for Executive Producer; Pro Ex – for Production Executive; Pro Sup – for Production Supervisor; Co-Pro – for Co-Producer; Pro Co-Ord – for Production Co-ordinator; Ph – for Photographer; Ed – for Editor; Art – for Art Director; Pro Des – for Production Designer; M – for Music; and a few others which will be obvious.

Abbreviations for the names of film companies are also pretty obvious when used, such as Fox for 20th Century-Fox, Rank for Rank Film Distributors, and UIP for Universal International Pictures. Where known, the actual production company is given first, the releasing company last.

When it comes to nationality of the film, you will find that this is noted wherever possible – those films without any mention of country of origin can usually be taken as being American – but in these days of increasing international co-productions between two, three or even four countries it is sometimes difficult to sort out where the premier credit is due.

Unless otherwise specified (i.e. black-and-white), it can be taken that the film is made in Technicolor or a similar process.

Censorship certificates: U represents films suitable for persons of any age; PG (Parental Guidance) represents films which some parents might consider unsuitable for their children; 12 or 15 means no persons under that age will be admitted; and films certified with an 18 (approximately the old 'X' certificate) means that nobody under that age will be admitted to the cinema while that film is showing. 'No cert' means that no certificate has been issued by the initial showing of the film but this does not mean that one will not subsequently be issued.

***Films are reviewed by James Cameron-Wilson, with Charles Bacon, Ewen Brownrigg, Henry Palmer and Simon Rose. Each review is followed by its writer's initials.***

### Accion Mutante – Mutant Action

'Accion Mutante' is a terrorist group of the future, composed of the physically disadvantaged (and one moron) who attack the world's mineral water-drinking 'beautiful people'. However, when the group kidnaps the daughter of a doughnut tycoon its carefully laid plans go terribly awry. The first film from Pedro Almodóvar's new production company, El Deseo, *Accion Mutante* is a lively, outrageous and tongue-in-cheek schlock fest for which nothing is too obscene or violent. Probably one of the ten grossest films ever to get past the British censor. Label it Abbott and Costello for the terminally sick. [JC-W]

Cast: Antonio Resines (Ramon Yarritu), Frederique Feder (Patricia Orujo), Alex Angulo (Alex), Juan Viadas (Juanito), Saturnino Garcia (Quimicefa), Fernando Guillen, Enrique San Francisco, Karra Elejalde, Jon Gabella, Alfonso Martinez.

Dir: Alex de la Iglesia. Pro: Agustín Almodóvar, Pedro Almodóvar and Esther Garcia. Ex Pro: Agustín Almodóvar. Screenplay: de la Iglesia and Jorge Guerricaechevarria. Ph: Carles Gusi. Ed: Pablo Blanco. Art: José Luis Arizabalaga. M: Juan Carlos Cuello. Costumes: Estibaliz Garcia. Sound: Ricardo Steinberg and Daniel Goldstein. Make-up FX: Hipolito Cantero. (El Deseo/CIBY 2000–Feature Film Co.) Rel: 17 September 1993. 90 mins. Cert 18.

*The smile that launched a thousand sheep: Superstar Jim Carrey, with Courteney Cox, in Tom Shadyac's crazy* Ace Ventura: Pet Detective *(from Warner)*

### L'Accompagnatrice – The Accompanist

1942; Paris. Slow-moving character study in which Sophie Vasseur, a poor, 20-year-old pianist, is asked to accompany the beautiful, wealthy singer Irène Brice, and is subsequently drawn inextricably into the latter's world of high-living, double-dealing and treachery. *L'Accompagnatrice* works best when it unveils the complex relationship between pianist and singer, revealing a burgeoning storm of empathy, resentment and jealousy, and is particularly well played by Elena Safonova as the glowing yet tortured diva. Elsewhere, melodrama and banality lurk. [JC-W]

*Accomplice or accompanist? Romane Bohringer in the title role of Claude Miller's* L'Accompagnatrice *(from Gala)*

Cast: Richard Bohringer (Charles Brice), Elena Safonova (Irène Brice), Romane Bohringer (Sophie Vasseur), Bernard Verley (Jacques Ceniat), Samuel Labarthe (Jacques Fabert), Nelly Borgeaud (Madame Vasseur), Julien Rassam, Claude Rich, Neils Dubost, Barbara Hicks.

Dir: Claude Miller. Pro: Jean-Louis Livi. Ex Pro: Jean-José Richer. Screenplay: Miller and Luc Béraud. Ph: Yves Angelo. Ed: Albert Jurgenson. Pro Des: Jean-Pierre Kohut Svelko. M: Beethoven, Mozart, Richard Strauss, Schumann, Schubert, Berlioz, Massenet and Gay-Furber-Rose. Costumes: Jacqueline Bouchard. Sound: Paul Laine and Gerard Lamps. (Film Par Film/Canal Plus–Gala.) Rel: 12 November 1993. 111 mins. Cert PG.

### Ace Ventura: Pet Detective

Miami; 1994. When the cetacean mascot of the Miami Dolphins football team is stolen, eccentric private eye 'Ace' Ventura leaps into action – with mixed results. Unlike Frank Drebin and Inspector Clouseau, Ventura is a detective of some savvy and considerable instinct ('I'm *tired* of being right!') – but who behaves like a consummate idiot. TV comic Jim Carrey (*In Living Color*) spares no tics as he launches his big-time career with this outrageous creation, a rubber-faced, multi-limbed goon with a passion for animals. While the film rests or falls on whether or not you find Carrey's antics funny, first-time director Tom Shadyac keeps the pace going and notably restrains the rest of the cast. [JC-W]

Cast: Jim Carrey (Ace Ventura), Courteney Cox (Melissa Robinson), Sean Young (Lt Einhorn), Tone Loc (Emilio), Dan Marino

(Dan Marino), Udo Kier (Ronald Camp), Noble Willingham, Troy Evans, Raynor Scheine, Frank Adonis, David Margulies, John Capodice, Bill Zuckert, Alice Drummond, Rebecca Ferratti, Mark Margolis, Randall 'Tex' Cobb.

Dir: Tom Shadyac. Pro: James G. Robinson. Ex Pro: Gary Barber. Co-Pro: Bob Israel. Screenplay: Shadyac, Jack Bernstein and Jim Carrey. Ph: Julio Macat. Ed: Don Zimmerman. Pro Des: William Elliott. M: Ira Newborn; numbers performed by Steve Stevens, Aerosmith, Cannibal Corpse, Boy George, Tone Loc, etc. Costumes: Bobbie Read. Sound: Russell C. Fager. (Morgan Creek–Warner.) Rel: 29 April 1994. 86 mins. Cert 12.

### Addams Family Values

While the 1991 hit based on Charles Addams' morbid cartoon family exercised a degree of deadpan nonchalance (to hilarious effect), this clumsy follow-up opts for seismic farce. It is also all over the place. Morticia and Gomez have a new baby (Pubert, with moustache), Fester falls in love (with a buxom gold-digger) and Wednesday and Pugsley go to summer camp. In this case 'more' is definitely a case of 'less'. Excruciating. [JC-W]

Cast: Anjelica Huston (Morticia Addams), Raul Julia (Gomez Addams), Christopher Lloyd (Fester Addams), Joan Cusack (Debbie Jelinsky), Christina Ricci (Wednesday Addams), Jimmy Workman (Pugsley Addams), Carel Struycken (Lurch), David Krumholtz (Joel Glicker), Christopher Hart (Thing), Carol Hankins (Dementia), Dana Ivey, Peter MacNicol, Christine Baranski, Kaitlyn & Kristin Hooper, Mercedes McNab, Sam McMurray, Harriet Sansom Harris, Julie Halston, Barry Sonnenfeld, Nathan Lane, John Franklin, Charles Busch, Cynthia Nixon, David Hyde Pierce, Peter Graves, Tony Shalhoub.

Dir: Barry Sonnenfeld. Pro: Scott Rudin. Ex Pro: David Nicksay. Screenplay: Paul Rudnick; based on characters created by Charles Addams. Ph: Donald Peterman. Ed: Arthur Schmidt and Jim Miller. Pro Des: Ken Adam. M: Marc Shaiman; numbers performed by Julie Andrews, The Brady Bunch, Village People, Tag Team, Shabra Ranks, etc. Costumes: Theoni V. Aldredge. Sound: Cecelia Hall. (Paramount–UIP.) Rel: 10 December 1993. 94 mins. Cert PG.

### The Adventures of Huck Finn

Numbingly pedestrian screen version (the eighth) of Mark Twain's classic 1884 novel about the spirited orphan and his best friend, Jim, a runaway slave. The trouble is that the normally reliable Elijah Wood is wildly miscast as Huck, while some frantic editing constantly seems to want to get to the next scene. Worse still, Bill Conti's desperately jovial music is a real irritant. Charmless. [JC-W]

*Baby love: Christina Ricci as Wednesday and baby Pubert steal the acting honours in Barry Sonnenfeld's unruly* Addams Family Values *(from UIP)*

Cast: Elijah Wood (Huckleberry Finn), Courtney B. Vance (Jim), Robbie Coltrane (the Duke of Bilgewater), Jason Robards (the King of Bilgewater), Ron Perlman (Pap Finn), Anne Heche (Mary Jane Wilks), Dana Ivey, James Gammon, Paxton Whitehead, Tom Aldredge, Laura Bundy, Curtis Armstrong, Mary Louise Wilson, Frances Conroy, Daniel Tamberelli, Leon Russom, Garette Ratliff Henson, Richard Anders, Dion Anderson, Paul Dewees.

Dir and Screenplay: Stephen Sommers. Pro: Laurence Mark. Ex Pro: Barry Bernardi and Steve White. Ph: Janusz Kaminski. Ed: Bob Ducsay. Pro Des: Richard Sherman. M: Bill Conti. Costumes: Betsy Faith Heimann. (Walt Disney Pictures–Buena Vista.) Rel: 27 May 1994. 108 mins. Cert PG.

### The Age of Innocence

New York; the 1870s. Poised to marry the sweet, conventional May Welland, New York socialite and lawyer Newland Archer finds himself increasingly drawn towards the unorthodox Ellen Olenska, the estranged wife of a Polish

*Pap scared: Elijah Wood, as Huck, escapes from the clutches of his evil father, Pap Finn, in Disney's mundane* The Adventures of Huck Finn

count. However, by daring to live on her own terms, Ellen represents everything that is disdained by high society. While perfectly capturing the unspoken passions and subtextual nuances of Edith Wharton's celebrated 1920 novel, Martin Scorsese's sumptuous adaptation works best as a bloated commercial for the book, rather than as a good film in itself. Scorsese outdoes himself in his attention to the detail of the times (both an etiquette consultant and a table decoration consultant are credited), but great silverware does not a movie make. [JC-W]

Cast: Daniel Day-Lewis (Newland Archer), Michelle Pfeiffer (Ellen Olenska), Winona Ryder (May Welland), Alec McCowen (Sillerton Jackson), Geraldine Chaplin (Mrs Welland), Mary Beth Hurt (Regina Beaufort), Stuart Wilson (Julius Beaufort), Miriam Margolyes (Mrs Mingott), Carolyn Farina (Janey Archer), Michael Gough (Henry van der Luyden), Alexis Smith (Louisa van der Luyden), Jonathan Pryce (Riviere), Richard E. Grant, Sian Phillips, Norman Lloyd, Thomas Gibson, Domenica Scorsese, Joanne Woodward (narrator).

Dir: Martin Scorsese. Pro: Barbara De Fina. Screenplay: Jay Cocks and Scorsese. Ph: Michael Ballhaus. Ed: Thelma Schoonmaker. Pro Des: Dante Ferretti. M: Elmer Bernstein; Beethoven, Mendelssohn, Charles F. Gounod, Johann Strauss I, Johann Strauss II; *Marble Halls* performed by Enya. Costumes: Gabriella Pescucci. Sound: Tod Maitland. Title sequence: Elaine and Saul Bass. (Cappa–Columbia TriStar.) Rel: 28 January 1994. 139 mins. Cert U.

*Dangerous liaison: Michelle Pfeiffer and the tableware in Martin Scorsese's ravishing, barren* The Age of Innocence *(from Columbia TriStar)*

*Tall story: Kevin Bacon (right) encounters Charles Gitonga Maina and diarrhoea in Africa – in Paul Michael Glaser's diverting* The Air Up There *(from Buena Vista)*

### The Air Up There

When basketball coach Jimmy Dolan loses a star recruit, he goes on a wild goose chase to Africa to sign up a Winabi warrior. An agreeable enough Disney sports comedy, which manages to sidestep some obvious stereotyping of the tribesmen it portrays, here played by the Samburu people of Kenya. There are, however, too many pratfalls and too much toilet humour for this critic, but next to *Cool Runnings* this is a really decent movie. Filmed in Toronto, Vancouver, Kenya and South Africa. [JC-W]

Cast: Kevin Bacon (Jimmy Dolan), Charles Gitonga Maina (Saleh), Yolanda Vazquez (Sister Susan), Winston Ntshona (Urudu), Mabutho 'Kid' Sithole (Nyaga),

*Walk this way: The carpet,* Aladdin *and capuchin in Disney's most successful cartoon to date (until* The Lion King, *that is)*

Sean McCann (Ray Fox), Dennis Patrick (Father O'Hara), Ilo Mutombo, Nigel Miguel, Eric Menyuk, Keith Gibbs, Miriam Owiti, Douglas Leboyare, John Matshikiza, Ken Gampu, Jomo Lewarani.

Dir: Paul Michael Glaser. Pro: Ted Field, Rosalie Swedlin and Robert W. Cort. Ex Pro: Lance Hool and Scott Kroope. Co-Pro: Conrad Hool. Screenplay: Max Apple. Ph: Dick Pope. Ed: Michael E. Polakow. Pro Des: Roger Hall. M: David Newman; numbers performed by The Mahotella Queens, Nkuku & Jopie Sisters, The Mint Juleps, Matthew Wilder, etc. Costumes: Hope Hanafin. (Hollywood Pictures/ Interscope/PolyGram/Nomura Babcock & Brown/Longview Entertainment–Buena Vista.) Rel: 10 June 1994. 108 mins. Cert PG.

## Aladdin

Disney's highest-grossing cartoon yet – and the top earner of 1992 – *Aladdin* is a big, spectacular fantasy, the success of which hinges on the comic improvisations of Robin Williams. Williams, with his quick-fire repartee, gives the Disney animators a genuine challenge as his amorphous genie of the lamp mixes off-the-cuff impersonations of Robert De Niro and Jack Nicholson with more relevant references to the Orient. While adults can relish the verbal pyrotechnics, children should be suitably entertained by the vivid animation, even if much of it is crude and charmless (although technically polished). Also, the magic carpet must rank as one of Disney's most ingenious and endearing characters. Winner of two Oscars, for best score and best song ('A Whole New World'). [JC-W]

Voices: Scott Weinger (Aladdin), Robin Williams (Genie), Linda Larkin (Jasmine), Jonathan Freeman (Jafar), Frank Welker (Abu), Gilbert Gottfried (Iago), Douglas Seale (Sultan).

Dir and Pro: John Musker and Ron Clements. Co-Pro: Donald W. Ernst and Amy Pell. Screenplay: Clements, Musker, Ted Elliott and Terry Rossio. Ed: H. Lee Peterson. Pro Des: R. S. Vander Wende. M: Alan Menken. Songs: Menken, Howard Ashman and Tim Rice. (Walt Disney–Buena Vista.) Rel: 19 November 1993. 91 mins. Cert U.

*Staying alive: Jeff Bridges and Edward Furlong hang on to each other in Martin Bell's moving* American Heart *(from Entertainment)*

## American Heart

Seattle; 1992. Fresh out of prison, retired bank robber Jack Kelson has enough problems without his 15-year-

*With friends like these . . . Joseph Lindsey struts his testosterone in Rob Weiss's accomplished, hard-nosed* Amongst Friends *(from Rank)*

old son, Nick, hanging on his coattails. Besides, Jack reasons, he doesn't want his dead-end life to rub off on his son. But Nick needs his father back and he's prepared to pay any price . . . After English filmmaker Martin Bell won an Oscar nomination for his documentary *Streetwise*, an uncompromising look at kids on the streets of Seattle, he was approached by producer Jon Peters to make a fictionalised excursion into the same territory. The result is a work of enormous integrity, deftly realised by an outstanding cast and atmospherically photographed by James Bagdonas. Grim viewing at times, but the film never strikes a false note. [JC-W]

Cast: Jeff Bridges (Jack Kelson), Edward Furlong (Nick Kelson), Lucinda Jenney (Charlotte), Don Harvey (Rainey), Tracey Tyla Kapisky (Molly), Maggie Welsh (Freddie), Christian Frizzell (Rollie), Melvyn Hayward (Normandy), Jayne Entwistle, Kit McDonough, Shareen Mitchell.

Dir: Martin Bell. Pro: Rosilyn Heller and Jeff Bridges. Assoc Pro: Mary Ellen Mark. Co-Pro: Neil Koenigsberg. Ex Pro: Cary Brokaw. Screenplay: Peter Silverman; from a story by Bell, Mark and Silverman. Ph: James Bagdonas. Ed: Nancy Baker. Pro Des: Joel Schiller. M: James Newton Howard; numbers performed by Tom Waits, John Lee Hooker, The Pointer Sisters, Joan Jett and The Blackhearts, Jeff Bridges, etc. Costumes: Beatrix Aruna Pasztor. Sound: Hamilton Sterling. (World Films/Avenue Entertainment/AsIs–Entertainment.) Rel: 10 December 1993. 114 mins. Cert 15.

### Amongst Friends

Long Island, New York; early 1980s–92. Close since childhood, three rich boys find their friendship strained when they become involved with the local Mafia. From-the-hip dialogue and edgy performances help brighten this trek into well-trodden territory, shot for a mere $370,000 (partly financed by gamblers) by first-time director Rob Weiss. Mira Sorvino, the female lead, is the daughter of actor Paul Sorvino. [JC-W]

Cast: Steve Parlavecchio (Andy), Joseph Lindsey (Billy), Patrick McGaw (Trevor), Mira Sorvino (Laura), David Stepkin (Jack Trattner), Michael Artura (Michael), Ford Sorvino (Fish), Richard Magnogna, Brett Lambson, Michael Ringer, Frank Medrano, Louis Lombardi, Rob Weiss, Stan Schwartz, Sybil Temtshine.

Dir, Ex Pro and Screenplay: Rob Weiss. Pro: Matt Blumberg. Co-Pro: Mark Hirsch. Ph: Michael Bonvillain. Ed: Leo Trombetta. Pro Des: Terrence Foster. M: Mick Jones; numbers performed by Big Audio Dynamite II, Beastie Boys, LL Cool J, The Stranglers, Lemonheads, AMG, Red Hot Chili Peppers, Ministry, T–99, Redmen, T–42, Act of Mercy, Mott the Hoople, Tony Bennett, Dramarama, Judy Cole, The Band, etc. Costumes: Traci Digesu and Danielle Hollywood. Sound: Leo Trombetta. (PolyGram/Fine Line Entertainment/Islet/Last Outlaw–Rank.) Rel: 26 November 1993. 88 mins. Cert 18.

### Anchoress

Set in a remote English village in the 14th century, British director Chris Newby's remarkable first film tells the true story of a 14-year-old peasant girl. Because of her fixation on a wooden statue of the Virgin Mary and her refusal to marry the steward of the manor, the innocent provokes a battle of wills between the Church and the State. An Anglo-Belgian co-production magnificently filmed in black-and-white, *Anchoress* has much to say about the exploitation of women today, while vividly capturing the nuances of a bygone world. Filmed in Belgium. [CB]

Cast: Natalie Morse (Christine Carpenter), Eugene Bervoets (Reeve), Toyah Willcox (Pauline Carpenter), Peter Postlethwaite (William Carpenter), Christopher Eccleston (priest), Michael Pas, Brenda Bertin, Annette Badland, Veronica Quilligan, Julie T. Wallace, Ann Way.

Dir: Chris Newby. Pro: Paul Breuls and Ben Gibson. Ex Pro: Angela Topping. Screenplay: Judith Stanley-Smith and Christine Watkins. Ph: Michel Baudour. Ed: Brand Thumim. Pro Des: Niek Kortekaas. Costumes: Annie Symons. Sound: Andre Patrouillie. (Corsan Prods–BFI.) Rel: 10 September 1993. 108 mins. Cert 12.

### And the Band Played On

Fascinating, stirring docudrama based on Randy Shilts's best-selling 1987 book, chronicling the early discovery and spread of the AIDS virus. Matthew Modine heads an all-star cast as Don Francis, a pioneering researcher at Atlanta's Center for Disease Control. It is from there that Francis struggles to raise funds for research and to show the world that AIDS is neither a political nor gay issue, but a health and human one. Although some of the star cameos (Richard Gere, Anjelica Huston, Steve Martin) detract from the story's sense of reality, they do enliven the stretches of medical verbiage. Shilts, himself a gay journalist for *The San Francisco Chronicle* and the first reporter to be signed full time to the AIDS story, reportedly objected to the film's soap-operatic approach and homosexual stereotyping. Nevertheless, the picture *is* accessible and will undoubtedly stimulate more awareness. [JC-W]

Cast: Matthew Modine (Don Francis), Alan Alda (Robert Gallo), Glenne Headly (Mary Guinan), Donal Logue (Bobbi Campbell), Richard Masur (Bill Darrow), Ian McKellen (Bill Kraus), Peter McRobbie (Max Essex), Saul Rubinek (Jim Curran), Charles Martin Smith (Harold Jaffe), Lily Tomlin (Selma Dritz), Patrick Bachau, Nathalie Baye, Christian Clemenson, David Clennon, Phil Collins, Alex Courtney, David Dukes, Richard Gere, David Marshall Grant, Ronald Guttman, Anjelica Huston, Ken Jenkins, Richard Jenkins, Tcheky Karyo, Swoosie Kurtz, Jack Laufer, Howie Mandel, Steve Martin, Dakin Matthews, Lawrence Monoson, Jeffrey Nordling, B. D. Wong, Clyde Kusatsu,

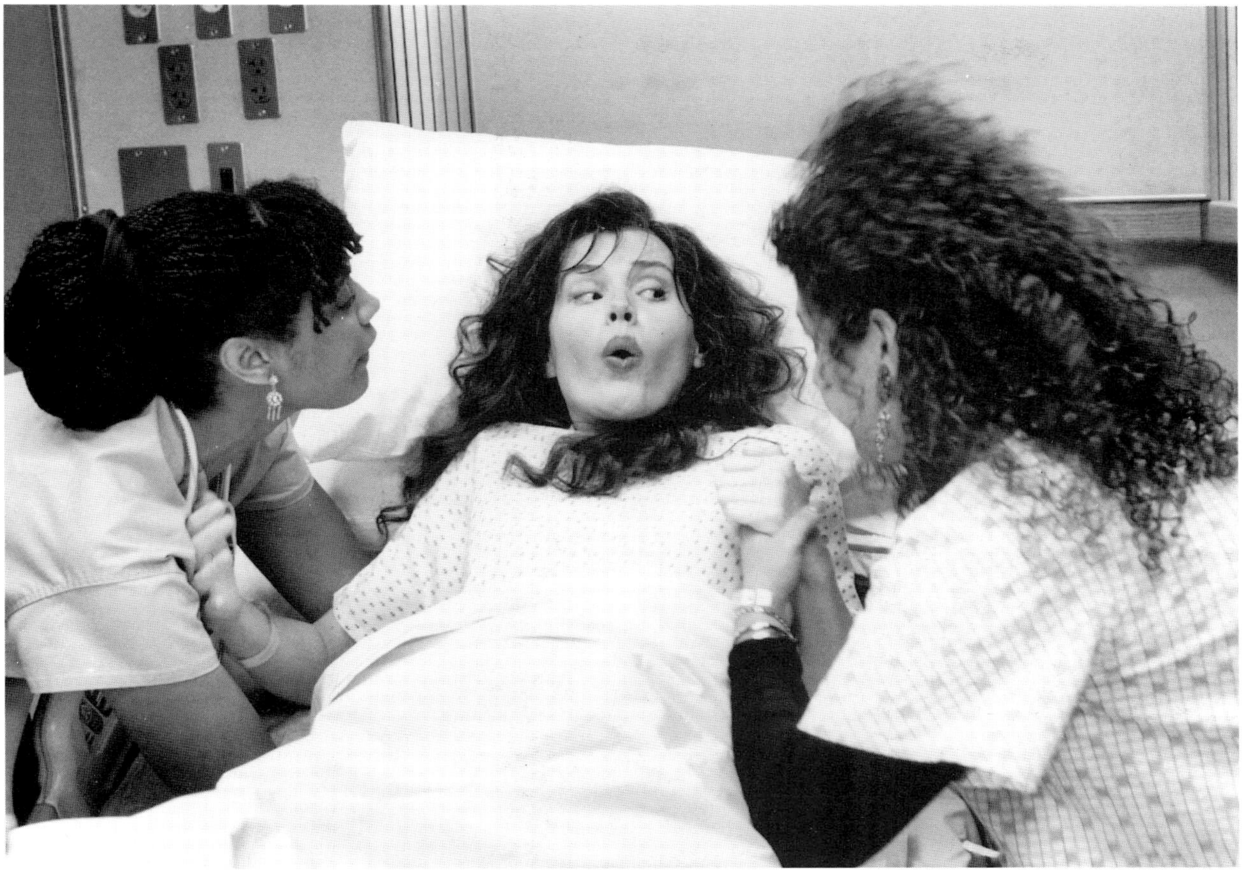

*The birthday party: Geena Davis struggles with her pelvis in Martha Coolidge's endearing* Angie *(from Buena Vista)*

Rosemary Murphy, Richard Fancy, Laura James, Angela Paton.

Dir: Roger Spottiswoode. Pro: Midge Sanford and Sarah Pillsbury. Ex Pro: Aaron Spelling and E. Duke Vincent. Screenplay: Arnold Schulman. Ph: Paul Elliott. Ed: Lois Freeman-Fox. Pro Des: Victoria Paul. M: Carter Burwell; numbers performed by Elton John, Queen, etc. Costumes: Patti Callicott. Sound: Walt Martin. (Odyssey Entertainment/HBO–ITC.) Rel: 8 April 1994. 143 mins. Cert 12.

*Plague dogs: Alan Alda and Matthew Modine fight politics as the AIDS epidemic flourishes in Roger Spottiswoode's gripping* And the Band Played On *(from ITC)*

## Angie

Bensonhurst, Brooklyn; 1972–94. For Angie Scacciapensieri, her present and future are inexorably tied to her past. But her past lies in murky waters. Her mother vanished when she was three and, growing up with her father and stepmother, she never felt she belonged. When she gets pregnant by her neighbourhood boyfriend she undergoes a dramatic change of focus. *Angie* is a hilarious, insightful and terribly moving character study deftly adapted from Avra Wing's novel *Angie I Says* by actor-turned-screenwriter Todd Graff. Originally tailored for Madonna (who lost the role over 'creative differences'), the film seems an odd choice for Geena Davis, a statuesque and striking WASP. After all, Angie is an average Italian-American girl trapped in mediocrity. But Davis's immersion into the role is so extraordinary that we soon forget the actress and end up crying for the character. Stephen Rea seems a little off-kilter as the long-haired lawyer who offers Angie dreams of a better life, and there's an unfortunate jump in narrative halfway through. Nevertheless, the film's warmth, wit and insight soon eradicate any shortcomings. A little gem. [JC-W]

Cast: Geena Davis (Angie Scacciapensieri), James Gandolfini (Vinnie), Aida Turturro (Tina), Philip Bosco (Frank Scacciapensieri), Stephen Rea (Noel), Jenny O'Hara (Kathy Scacciapensieri), Michael Rispoli (Jerry), Ray Xifo (Dr Gould), Betty Miller, Susan Jaffe, Jeremy Collins, Rosemary De Angelis, Rae Allen, Ida Benardini, Frank Pellegrino, Michael Laskin, Adam LeFevre, Matt Hofherr, John Toles-Bey.

Dir: Martha Coolidge. Pro: Larry Brezner and Patrick McCormick. Ex Pro: Joe Roth and Roger Birnbaum. Screenplay: Todd Graff. Ph: Johnny E. Jensen. Ed: Steven Cohen. Pro Des: Mel Bourne. M: Jerry Goldsmith; numbers performed by The Staple Singers, Louie Louie, Freda Payne, Kate Bush, Staxx, Rosanne Cash, etc. Costumes: Jane Robinson. (Hollywood Pictures/Morra–Brezner–Steinberg–Tenenbaum–Buena Vista.) Rel: 17 June 1994. 108 mins. Cert 15.

### Another Stakeout

When ace surveillance cops Chris Lecce and Bill Reimers are asked to stake out an elegant waterfront house in Washington, they move in next door. However, this time – with the interference of assistant DA Gina Garrett and her inquisitive Rottweiler – they become the new neighbours from hell. While the original *Stakeout* (1987) was a taut thriller with some nice touches of humour, this clodhopping sequel blows the humour into farcical proportions to produce an icky *Abbot & Costello Meet the Neighbours* circus. Only Miguel Ferrer as a hired assassin retains his dignity. [JC-W]

Cast: Richard Dreyfuss (Chris Lecce), Emilio Estevez (Bill Reimers), Rosie O'Donnell (Gina Garrett), Dennis Farina (Brian O'Hara), Marcia Strassman (Pam O'Hara), Cathy Moriarty (Lu Delano), Madeleine Stowe (Maria), John Rubinstein, Miguel Ferrer, Sharon Maughan, Christopher Doyle, Sharon Schaffer, Gene Allison, Dan Lauria, Larry B. Scott, Sammy Jackson, Blu Mankuma, Thomas Mitchell, Scott Anderson, Michael DeLano, Taylor Estevez, John Badham.

Dir and Ex Pro: John Badham. Pro: Jim Kouf, Cathleen Summers and Lynn Bigelow. Co-Pro: D. J. Caruso. Screenplay: Kouf. Ph: Roy H. Wagner. Ed: Frank Morris. Pro Des: Lawrence G. Paull. M: Arthur B. Rubinstein; 'Love Has a Mind of Its Own' sung by Ray Charles. Costumes: Stephanie Nolin. Sound: William L. Manger. (Touchstone Pictures–Buena Vista.) Rel: 31 December 1993. 109 mins. Cert PG.

*A new life for more deaths: Gabriel Byrne teaches Bridget Fonda the hard way in John Badham's* The Assassin *(from Warner)*

### Après l'Amour

Paris; 1992. Lola is an independent novelist having an affair with two married men with children. The eldest man, David, an architect, is himself involved with his secretary, Rachel, who is also attracted to David's half-brother, Romain, who is thinking of marrying Anne. And so it goes on, a chain of *amour fou* that fails to gather any comic or tragic (or even ironic) momentum as the film meanders from one romantic and/or argumentative clinch to the next. It left me cold. [JC-W]

Cast: Isabelle Huppert (Lola), Bernard Giraudeau (David), Hippolyte Girardot (Tom), Lio (Marianne), Yvan Attal (Romain), Ingrid Held (Anne), Laure Killing (Elizabeth).

Dir: Diane Kurys. Pro: Jean-Bernard Fetoux. Ex Pro: Robert Benmussa. Screenplay: Kurys and Antoine Lacomblez. Ph: Fabio Conversi. Ed: Herve Schneid. Art: Tony Egry. M: Yves Simon. Costumes: Mic Cheminal. Sound: Bernard Bats. (Alexandre Films/TFI/Sofiarp/Investimage 3/Canal Plus–Mayfair Entertainment.) Rel: 13 August 1993. 104 mins. Cert 15.

### The Assassin

(US: *Point of No Return.*) What if you were at an all-time low and you did something inexcusable? And what if, for your sins, you were given a choice – death, or life as a government assassin? And what if, on accepting the second offer, you were trained to fit in anywhere and with anybody? And what if, released into ordinary life once more, you finally had the self-confidence to return someone else's love? And yet you could never reveal who you really were? This heart-wrenching predicament was the central theme of Luc Besson's brilliant *Nikita* (written specially for Besson's wife Anne Parillaud). Unpredictable, stylish and frighteningly naturalistic, *Nikita* was one of the most popular French films of 1990. Here, the film is not so much adapted for an American audience as translated – scene for scene (even most of the names are the same). The predominant difference is that *The Assassin* is a *stylised*, detached and humourless thriller, whereas *Nikita* was a black comedy with style and an underlying tenderness. Nevertheless, the story still punches a wallop, although only Harvey Keitel (as an emotionless killer) is equal to his French counterpart (Jean Reno). [JC-W]

Cast: Bridget Fonda (Maggie/Nina), Gabriel Byrne (Bob), Dermot Mulroney (J.P.), Anne Bancroft (Amanda), Harvey Keitel (Victor the Cleaner), Miguel Ferrer

(Kaufman), Olivia d'Abo (Angela), Lorraine Toussaint (Beth), Richard Romanus, Geoffrey Lewis, Michael Rapaport, John Capodice, Calvin Levels.

Dir: John Badham. Pro: Art Linson. Co-Pro: James Herbert. Screenplay: Robert Getchell and Alexandra Seros. Ph: Michael Watkins. Ed: Frank Morriss. Pro Des: Philip Harrison. M: Hans Zimmer; numbers performed by Nina Simone, L7, Vikki Carr, Buckwheat Zydeco, etc. Costumes: Marlene Stewart. Sound: Willie D. Burton. (Warner.) Rel: 2 July 1993. 108 mins. Cert 18.

*Macon rouge: Nils Dorando and Julia Ormond in Peter Greenaway's provocative* The Baby of Macon *(from Electric)*

### Assassin of the Tsar

Powerfully acted, but somewhat heavy-handed Anglo-Russian psychological drama partially based on Chekhov's 'The Patient in Room 9'. Malcolm McDowell, in his best role for years, plays a schizophrenic Muscovite who believes he was responsible for the assassination of Nicholas II and his family in 1918. The celebrated Russian actor Oleg Yankovsky plays the physician who takes part in McDowell's fantasies in order to cure his patient. [CB]

Cast: Malcolm McDowell (Timofeyev/Yurovsky), Oleg Yankovsky (Smirnov/Tsar Nicholas II), Armen Dzhigarkhanian (Alexander Yegorovich), Yuri Sherstnyov, Angela Ptashuk, Victor Seferov.

Dir: Karen Shakhnazarov. Pro: Christopher Gawor, Erik Vaisberg and Anthony Sloman. Ex Pro: Benjamin Brahms and Vladimir Dostal. Screenplay: Shakhnazarov and Alexander Borodyansky. Ph: Nikolai Nemolyaev. Ed: Sloman. Art: Ludmila Kusakova. M: John Altman. Costumes: Vera Romanova. Sound: Igor Mayorov. (Spectator Film International/Mosfilm/Courier–Blue Dolphin.) Rel: 1 October 1993. 103 mins. Cert 12.

### Atlantis

In September of 1988, the French director Luc Besson (*Subway*, *Nikita*) set sail from the south of France to spend the next three years recording the wonders of marine life. Aided by an underwater film crew and state-of-the-art technology, Besson travelled from the North Pole to the Great Barrier Reef, from the Red Sea to the Seychelles, to capture on film a beautiful, alien world before it is lost to us forever. The result is quite elevating. [CB]

Dir: Luc Besson. Ph: Christian Petron. M: Eric Serra. (Warner.) Rel: 3 September 1993. 76 mins. Cert U.

### The Baby of Macon

More blood, sex and beautiful costumes from Peter Greenaway, in a baroque allegory about the abuse of innocence. Set in a provincial theatre in 1659, the film's play-within-a-play format is at first bewildering, then fascinating, as the audience is subjected to a horrific tale in which a baby boy is born on stage (to a hideous old woman) and then exploited – first, by the boy's older sister (who claims she is a virgin mother), and secondly by the Catholic Church. As the play progresses, the audience becomes increasingly involved in the drama and soon reality starts overlapping with fiction. A courageous, ferociously original work thick with symbolism, theatrical illusion and religious allusion, which demands to be seen more than once – if you can stomach the gorier passages. [JC-W]

Cast: Julia Ormond (the daughter), Ralph Fiennes (the bishop's son), Philip Stone (the bishop), Jonathan Lacey (Cosimo

Medici), Frank Egerton (the prompter), Tony Vogel (the father), Nils Dorando (the baby of Macon), Don Henderson, Celia Gregory, Jeff Nuttall, Jessica Stevenson, Kathryn Hunter, Gabrielle Reidy, Anna Niland, Graham Valentine, Diana van Kolck.

Dir and Screenplay: Peter Greenaway. Pro: Kees Kasander. Ex Pro: Denis Wigman. Co-Pro: Yves Marmion. Ph: Sacha Vierny. Ed: Chris Wyatt. Pro Des: Ben Van Os and Jan Roelfs. M: Henry Purcell, Matthew Locke, John Blow, Andreas Clamer, Archangelo Corelli, Claudio Monteverdi, Giralamo Frescobaldi and Thomas Tallis. Costumes: Dien van Straalen. Sound: Garth Marshall. (Allarts/UGC/Cine Electra/Channel 4/Filmstiftung Nordrhein Westfalen/La Sept Cinéma–Electric.) Rel: 17 September 1993. 120 mins. Cert 18.

## Back in the USSR

On his last day in Moscow, American teenager Archer Sloan decides he wants to experience 'the real Russia' – beyond the Kremlin, the Bolshoi and all the usual tourist traps. However, when he befriends local prostitute Lena (Natalya Negoda, indigenous star of the controversial *Little Vera*), he inadvertently becomes involved in a seedier, more violent side of Russia than you'd hope to encounter this side of Ivan the Terrible. While the locations are never less than alluring, the film's unevenness gets on one's nerves as it lunges from black comedy to thriller to routine spy caper with sloppy abandon. Still, Roman Polanski (in a rare acting appearance) makes a memorable villain, whispering icily to Archer Sloan, 'What is it about you that makes me want to hurt you?' as he casually smears food all over the latter's face. Made in 1991. [JC-W]

Cast: Frank Whaley (Archer Sloan), Natalya Negoda (Lena), Roman Polanski (Kurilov), Dey Young (Claudia), Ravil Issyanov (Georgi), Brian Blessed (Chazov), Andrew Divof, Harry Ditson, Constantine Gregory, Alexei Yevdokimov, Boris Romanov, Yuri Sarantsev, Oleg Anofriev, Yladimir Druzhnikov.

Dir: Deran Sarafian. Pro and Screenplay: Lindsay Smith and Ilmar Taska. Ex Pro: Louis A. Stroller. Ph: Yuri Neyman. Ed: Ian Crafford. Pro Des: Vladimir Philippov. M: Les Hooper; 'Back in the USSR' sung by Special Arrangement. Costumes: Cynthia Bergstrom. Sound: Gary Cunningam. Special KGB liaison: John Plateroti. (Largo International/Mosfilm–Warner.) Rel: 22 April 1994. 90 mins. Cert 15.

*Minority interests: Chinaman David Chung and man-woman Suzy Amis let down their guard in Maggie Greenwald's arresting* The Ballad of Little Jo *(from Rank)*

## Backbeat

Liverpool/Hamburg; 1960–2. Totally unconvincing look at the early days of The Beatles, in particular the triangular relationship between Stuart Sutcliffe, John Lennon and the fashionable German photographer Astrid Kirchherr. Unfortunately, there is so little chemistry between Stephen Dorff (as Stu) and Sheryl Lee (very dull as Astrid), that even Ian Hart's spirited turn as Lennon cannot save the film. Moreover, the actors here look nothing like the original Beatles, which strains credibility even further. [JC-W]

Cast: Sheryl Lee (Astrid Kirchherr), Stephen Dorff (Stuart Sutcliffe), Ian Hart (John Lennon), Gary Bakewell (Paul McCartney), Chris O'Neill (George Harrison), Scot Williams (Pete Best), Kai Wiesinger (Klaus Voormann), Jennifer Ehle (Cynthia Powell), Paul Duckworth (Ringo Starr), Finola Geraghty, Rob Spendlove, Freida Kelly, Paul Humpoletz, Christina Uriarte, Abigail Wrapson, Galit Hershkovitz, Manuel Harlan, Wolf Kahler, James Doherty. The Backbeat Band: Greg Dulli, Don Fleming, Dave Grohl, Mike Mills, Thurston Moore, Dave Pirner.

Dir: Iain Softley. Pro: Finola Dwyer and Stephen Woolley. Ex Pro: Nik Powell. Line Pro: Paul Cowan. Screenplay: Softley, Michael Thomas and Stephen Ward. Ph: Ian Wilson. Ed: Martin Walsh. Pro Des: Joseph Bennett. M: Don Was. Costumes: Sheena Napier. Sound: Glenn Freemantle. (PolyGram/Scala Prods/Channel Four Films/Forthcoming Prods–Rank.) Rel: 1 April 1994. 100 mins. Cert 15.

## The Ballad of Little Jo

1867–1904; Idaho. When Josephine Monaghan disgraced herself by having a baby out of wedlock, she headed West to start a new life. But out in Idaho a woman was either a wife or a whore, so Josephine Monaghan became a man. Cutting her hair and disfiguring her face with a cutthroat razor, Miss Monaghan became Little Jo, and learned to handle sheep, pack a gun, ride a horse and stand up for herself and others. And, amazingly, she managed to keep her real gender secret. A 'true' story pieced together from newspaper cuttings and letters, *The Ballad of Little Jo* is a fascinating tale beautifully brought to life by Maggie Greenwald's economic, poetic direction, aided by a frisky score from David Mansfield and some unforgettable photography. There are good performances, too, notably Suzy Amis's comically tenacious hero/heroine, Bo Hopkins's craggy, charismatic landowner, Ian McKellen's unpredictable mine superintendent and David Chung's ailing, dignified Chinaman. [JC-W]

Cast: Suzy Amis (Josephine 'Little Jo' Monaghan), Bo Hopkins (Frank Badger), Ian McKellen (Percy Corcoran), David Chung (Tinman Wong), Carrie Snodgrass (Ruth Badger), Heather Graham (Mary), Anthony Heald (Henry Grey), Melissa Leo (Mrs Grey), Rene Auberjonois, Sam Robards, Tom Bower, Ruth Malaczech, Olinda Turturro, Irina Pasmur, Sean Murphy.

Dir and Screenplay: Maggie Greenwald. Pro: Fred Berner and Brenda Goodman. Ex Pro: John Sloss and Ira Deutchman. Assoc Pro: Anne Dillon. Ph: Declan Quinn. Ed: Keith Reamer. Pro Des: Mark Friedberg. M: David Mansfield. Costumes: Claudia Brown. Sound: Felipe Borero. (PolyGram/Fineline Features/Joco–Rank.) Rel: 4 March 1994. 121 mins. Cert 15.

*A new, old world: A Kayapo child peers out of the Brazilian rainforest in Ron Fricke's remarkable* Baraka *(from Mayfair Entertainment)*

## Baraka

A wordless testament to the world we live in, *Baraka* is quite simply a series of images conjuring up the diversity of our planet. A sort of *National Geographic* set to music, Ron Fricke's ambitious, awe-inspiring project was filmed in 24 countries and has managed to infiltrate areas other cameras have failed to reach. Whether probing the deep, undisturbed thought of a Japanese monk, or the wise sorrow of a snow monkey, whether documenting the belching oil fires of Kuwait, or the stark, endless space of Alaska, the film stares unflinchingly at a world that is full of pain, wonder, horror and beauty. And all this on 70mm. [JC-W]

Locations: Aguaca Falls in Argentina, Alaska, Arizona, Auschwitz, Ayers Rock, Bali, Bangkok, Calcutta, Cambodia, Chartres Cathedral, Colorado, Ecuador, Egypt, Empire State Building, the Ganges at Varanasi, Grand Central Terminal in New York, Hawaii, Hong Kong, Iran, Istanbul, Java, Kenya, Kathmandu, Kuwait, Los Angeles, Madras, Mecca, Mount Everest, Mount Fuji, New Mexico, Reims Cathedral, Rio de Janeiro, São Paulo, Tanzania, Tiananmen Square, Tokyo, Utah, Vatican City, the Wailing Wall of Jerusalem, World Trade Centre, Xi'an (Terracotta Warriors and Horses of Qin Shi Huang), etc.

*Puppy love: Bonnie Hunt, Nicholle Tom, Christopher Castile and Sarah Rose Kerr – with whelps – in Rod Daniel's* Beethoven's 2nd *(from UIP)*

Dir and Ph: Ron Fricke. Pro: Mark Magidson. Supervising Pro: Alton Walpole. Concept and Scenario: Fricke, Magidson and Bob Green; from a treatment by Fricke, Genevieve Nicholas and Constantine Nicholas. Ed: Fricke, Magidson and David E. Aubrey. M: Michael Stearns; and Dead Can Dance, Somei Satoh, The Harmonic Choir, Anugama & Sebastiano, Kohachiro Miyata, L. Subramaniam, Monks of the Dip Tse Ling Monastery, Ciro Hurtado, and Brother. (Mayfair Entertainment.) Rel: 16 July 1993. 96 mins. Cert PG.

## Beethoven's 2nd

Serviceable follow-up to the 1992 hit, in which the eponymous canine falls in love and fathers four puppies. Of course, the Newton children want to keep the mutts, but Dad has other ideas – until he's emotionally bludgeoned. Enter comic-book villains Debi Mazar and Chris Penn who are intent on stealing the puppies for monetary gain. Predictability and buffoonery prevail, but things are kept at a brisk pace and younger children will probably love it. Director Rod Daniel was

*Lock up your daughters: Maribel Verdu and Jorge Sanz in Fernando Trueba's cosy, Oscar-winning* Belle Epoque *(from Mayfair Entertainment)*

previously responsible for the James Belushi–Alsatian caper *K–9*. [JC-W]

Cast: Charles Grodin (George Newton), Bonnie Hunt (Alice Newton), Debi Mazar (Regina), Chris Penn (Floyd), Nicholle Tom (Ryce Newton), Christopher Castile (Ted Newton), Sarah Rose Kerr (Emily Newton), Ashley Hamilton (Taylor Devereaux), Danny Masterson (Seth), Catherine Reitman, Maury Chaykin, Hea-

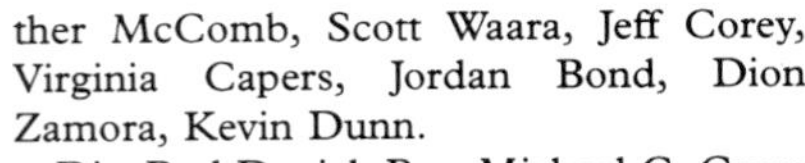

ther McComb, Scott Waara, Jeff Corey, Virginia Capers, Jordan Bond, Dion Zamora, Kevin Dunn.

Dir: Rod Daniel. Pro: Michael C. Gross and Joe Medjuck. Ex Pro: Ivan Reitman. Co-Pro: Gordon Webb. Screenplay: Len Blum. Ph: Bill Butler. Ed: Sheldon Kahn and William D. Gordean. Pro Des: Lawrence Miller. M: Randy Edelman; numbers performed by Dolly Parton and James Ingram, His Boy Elroy, Spin Doctors, The Contours and Paul Shaffer. Costumes: April Ferry. Sound: Gene S. Cantamessa. (Universal–UIP.) Rel: 25 March 1994. 89 mins. Cert U.

## Belle Epoque

Spain; 1931. When a young army deserter takes refuge in the home of an old painter, he becomes irrevocably involved with the painter's four comely daughters. Played with wide-eyed incredulity by Jorge Sanz (a dead ringer for Robert Downey Jr) and with splendid abandon by the four daughters, *Belle Epoque* cannot fail to delight, however slight its premise. On a scale of yawn to belly laugh, this rates a smile. It's astonishing that the film scooped nine Goya awards (including citations for best film and director) and won the Oscar for best foreign film of 1993, which made the Academy look very silly (particularly as *Farewell My Concubine*, *The Scent of Green Papaya* and *The Wedding Banquet* were also nominated). Filmed in Portugal. [JC-W]

Cast: Penelope Cruz (Luz), Miriam Díaz-Aroca (Clara), Gabino Diego (Juanito), Fernando Fernán Gómez (Manolo), Ariadna Gil (Violeta), Jorge Sanz (Fernando), Maribel Verdú (Rocio), Michel Galabru, Agustin González, Chus Lampreave, Mary Carmen Ramírez, Juan Jose Otegui.

Dir: Fernando Trueba. Ex Pro: Andrés Vicente Gómez. Line Pro: Cristina Huete. Screenplay: Rafael Azcona; from a story by Azcona, Trueba and José Luis Garcia Sanchez. Ph: José Luis Alcaine. Ed: Carmen Frías. Pro Des: Juan Botella. M: Antoine DuHamel. Sound: Georges Prat. (Lola Films/Animatografo/Sogepaq/Eurimages–Mayfair Entertainment.) Rel: 1 April 1994. 108 mins. Cert 15.

## Benefit of the Doubt

When 12-year-old Karen Braswell testified against her father for the murder of her mother, Frank Braswell went to prison for 22 years. Now Karen is a parent herself and is none

*Come to Daddy!: Amy Irving and Rider Strong cower in Jonathan Heap's formulaic* Benefit of the Doubt

too thrilled that her father is a free man. But all Frank Braswell wants is his family back . . . After a promising start, this first film from MTV director Jonathan Heap derails and then rattles along the well-worn tracks of many a made-for-video thriller. Still, Amy Irving makes a feisty heroine and the Arizona scenery is a treat. [JC-W]

Cast: Donald Sutherland (Frank Braswell), Amy Irving (Karen Braswell), Graham Greene (Calhoun), Christopher McDonald (Dan), Rider Strong (Peter Braswell), Gisela Kovach (Susanna), Theodore Bikel, Ferdinand Mayne, Shane McCabe, Margaret Johnson.

Dir: Jonathan Heap. Pro: Michael Spielberg and Brad M. Gilbert. Co-Pro: Dieter Geissler. Ex Pro: Bob Weinstein and Harvey Weinstein. Screenplay: Jeffrey Polman and Christopher Keyser; from a story by Michael Lieber. Ph: Johnny E. Jensen. Ed: Sharyn L. Ross. Pro Des: Marina Kieser. M: Hummie Mann. Costumes: Marsha Perloff. Sound: Gregory King. (Miramax/CineVox/Monument–Warner.) Rel: 26 November 1993. 91 mins. Cert 18.

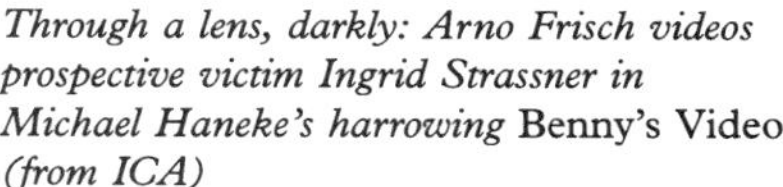

*Through a lens, darkly: Arno Frisch videos prospective victim Ingrid Strassner in Michael Haneke's harrowing* Benny's Video *(from ICA)*

## Benny & Joon

'Don't underestimate the mentally ill,' Joon warns her brother, Benny – and she's right. Joon paints pictures of enormous vitality, speaks like a poet and reads voraciously. But she has a problem with setting things on fire . . . And then Joon meets Sam, a genuine innocent and eccentric, a Chaplinesque figure who mashes potatoes with a tennis racket and irons his sandwiches. They're both unique and maybe were made for each other . . . *Benny & Joon* is a genuine original, replete with lyrical moments, unexpected pleasures and an extraordinary turn from Johnny Depp, who seems to have been born to play Sam. Mary Stuart Masterson, too, is outstanding in a difficult part, a role that was to have been played by Laura Dern (who, it is said, turned the film down after she was refused top-billing). [JC-W]

Cast: Johnny Depp (Sam), Mary Stuart Masterson (Juniper 'Joon' Pearl), Aidan Quinn (Benjamin 'Benny' Pearl), Julianne Moore (Ruthie), Oliver Platt (Eric), C. C. H. Pounder (Dr Garvey), Dan Hedaya, Joe Grifasi, William H. Macy, Liane Alexandra Curtis, Eileen Ryan.

Dir: Jeremiah Chechik. Pro: Susan Arnold and Donna Roth. Ex Pro: Bill Badalato. Screenplay: Barry Berman; from a story by Berman and Leslie McNeil. Ph: John Schwartzman. Ed: Carol Littleton. Pro Des: Neil Spisak. M: Rachel Portman; numbers performed by Joe 'Pinetop' Perkins, Temple of the Dog, John Hiatt and Joe Cocker. Costumes: Aggie Guerard Rodgers. Sound: James Thornton. (MGM–UIP.) Rel: 9 July 1993. 99 mins. Cert 12.

*Madly in love: Johnny Depp and Mary Stuart Masterson are not only special, but special to each other – in Jeremiah Chechik's luminous* Benny & Joon *(from UIP)*

## Benny's Video

*Benny's Video* opens with the graphic killing of a pig. The scene is then rewound and played in slow motion. In

*Fair cop: Eddie Murphy repeats his winning formula (seen here with Timothy Carhart) in John Landis's mediocre sequel* Beverly Hills Cop III *(from UIP)*

all, we are shown the pig dying four times. At first, the scene is shocking, but by the fourth viewing the incident has lost its impact. And that is precisely the film's point: repeated viewing of violence numbs our sensibilities. Benny, a quiet, retiring teenager, is addicted to violent videos. Consequently he has arrived at the point where he cannot separate real life from his TV screen, and in an attempt to experience something deeper he casually shoots a young girl dead. The act is committed off-screen, but in its aural realism is far more chilling than anything witnessed on Benny's videos. Made in Austria in 1992. [JC-W]

Cast: Arno Frisch (Benny), Angela Winkler (mother), Ulriche Muhe (father), Ingrid Stassner (young girl), Stephanie Brehme, Stefan Polasek, Christian Pundy.

Dir and Screenplay: Michael Haneke. Pro: Veit Heiduschka and Bernard Lang. Ph: Christian Berger. Ed: Marie Homolkova. Pro Des: Christoph Kanter. M: Johann Sebastian Bach. Costumes: Erika Navas. Sound: Karl Schlifelner. (Wega Film Wien/Austrian Film Fund–ICA.) Rel: 27 August 1993. 105 mins. Cert 18.

## Beverly Hills Cop III

Looking more like *Die Hard* than ever, this spectacular sequel follows the formula of the first Eddie Murphy vehicle with alarming fidelity (Axel Foley's friend is shot in Detroit, he tracks down the killer to LA, then embarrasses the LAPD with his unorthodox police procedure, etc). Only when Foley uncovers a counterfeit money operation using an amusement park as its cover does the film flip into a whole different movie. It is at Wonder-World, with its unending theme song and tireless happy faces, that the film gathers satirical momentum and where the bad guys look even badder. And, consumer jabs aside, the train rides, rollercoasters, dinosaurs and jungles are a spectacular backdrop for a good ol' shoot-out. It's just a shame that the pre-programmed jokes can't keep up. [JC-W]

Cast: Eddie Murphy (Axel Foley), Judge Reinhold (Billy Rosewood), Hector Elizondo (Jon Flint), Theresa Randle (Janice), Bronson Pinchot (Serge), Timothy Carhart (Ellis DeWald), Stephen McHattie (Steve Fulbright), John Saxon (Orrin Sanderson), Alan Young (Uncle Dave Thornton), Jon Tenney, Joey Travolta, Jimmy Ortega, Rick Avery, Gil Hill, Fred Asparagus, Louis Lombardi, Michael Bowen, Al Green, Hattie Winston, Tracy Lindsey, Steven Banks, George Lucas, Martha Coolidge, George Schaefer, Joe Dante, Helen Martin, Elaine Kagan, Peter Medak, Arthur Hiller, Ray Harryhausen, Robert Sherman, Barbet Schroeder, John Singleton.

Dir: John Landis. Pro: Mace Neufeld and Robert Rehme. Co-Pro: Leslie Belzberg. Ex Pro: Mark Lipsky. Screenplay: Steven E. de Souza; based on characters created by Danilo Bach and Daniel Petrie Jr. Ph: Marc Ahlberg. Ed: Dale Beldin. Pro Des: Michael Seymour. M: Nile Rodgers, numbers performed by Nile Rodgers, The Supremes, INXS, Tony Toni Tone, Eazy-E, Jerry Lewis, Shai, Patti LaBelle, Terence Trent D'Arby, Inner Circle, etc. Costumes: Catherine Adair. (Eddie Murphy Prods/ Paramount–UIP.) Rel: 24 June 1994. 104 mins. Cert 15.

## Beyond Bedlam

Friern Barnet, London; 1993. It's hard to decode the plot of this affront to logic, but it would seem that a serial killer is being treated with experimental drugs, enabling him to enter the minds of whomever he pleases and causing them to take their own lives. Alternative comedian Keith Allen appears to be enjoying his part as the mind rapist, but the token hunk (Craig Fairbrass, from *Cliffhanger*) and bimbo (Elizabeth Hurley, from *Passenger 57*) are poor substitutes for actors. The sound, photography, editing, music and direction are all abominable, too. Voted most promising British newcomer by the London Film Critics' Circle (for co-directing and co-producing *Leon the Pig Farmer*), Vadim Jean has let the side down. [JC-W]

Cast: Craig Fairbrass (Terry Hamilton), Elizabeth Hurley (Stephanie Lyell), Keith Allen (Marc Gilmour), Anita Dobson (Judith Hamilton), Jesse Birdsall (Scott), Craig Kelly (Matthew Hamilton), Faith Kent (Miss Coope), Georgina Hale, Samantha Spiro, Stephen Brand, Zoe Heyes, Annette Badland, Paul Brooks.

Dir: Vadim Jean. Pro: Paul Brooks. Ex Pro: Alan Martin. Co-Ex Pro: Alec Georgiadis and Tony Georgiadis. Assoc Pro: Simon Brooks. Screenplay: Jean and Rob Walker. Ph: Gavin Finney. Ed: Liz Webber. Pro Des: James Helps. M: David Hughes and John Murphy. Costumes: Jayne Gregory. Sound: Richard Flynn. (Metrodome Films–Feature Film Co.) Rel: 22 April 1994. 96 mins. Cert 18.

*Pier pressure: Peter Cellier romances Lalita Ahmed at the seaside in Gurinder Chadha's bewitching* Bhaji on the Beach *(from First Independent)*

## Bhaji on the Beach

Nothing could be more English than a day out at Blackpool. And yet an outing of potential jollity for members of the Saheli Asian Women's Centre is constantly marred by racial abuse as white strangers order the women to 'go home'. Nevertheless, 'home' for these women is Britain, complete with all its racism, sexism and lousy weather. Director Gurinder Chadha could well have made her debut feature a hard-hitting, depressing drama, but has opted to highlight the humour of her story, relishing the comic contrast between East and West and young and old. After a confusing start, Chadha manages to juggle several story strands with some aplomb, bringing depth, perception and humanity to her colourful characters. [JC-W]

Cast: Kim Vithana (Ginder), Jimmi Harkishin (Ranjit), Sarita Khajuria (Hashida), Mo Sesay (Oliver), Lalita Ahmed (Ahsa), Shaheen Khan (Simi), Souad Faress (Rekha), Peter Cellier (Ambrose Waddington), Zohra Segal, Nisha Nayar, Renu Kochar, Tanveer Ghani, Akbar Kurtha, Rudolph Walker, Fraser James, Dean Gatiss, Shireen Shah, Gurdial Sira, Adlyn Ross, Moti Makan.

Dir: Gurinder Chadha. Pro: Nadine Marsh-Edwards. Line Pro: Paul Sarony. Screenplay: Meera Syal; from a story by Chadha and Syal. Ph: John Kenway. Ed: Oral Ottley. Pro Des: Derek Brown. M: John Altman, Craig Pruess and Kuljit Bhamra. Costumes: Annie Symons. Sound: Ronald Bailey. (Umbi Films/Channel Four–First Independent.) Rel: 21 January 1994. 101 mins. Cert 15.

## Black Diamond Rush

Believe it or not, this is Warren Miller's 44th feature film. Recipient of the prestigious AT&T Skiing Award and an inductee in the Ski Hall of Fame, Miller knows all about the world's most famous pistes, but it's unlikely that anybody but snow fanatics will take to this skiing documentary. Filmed all over the shop, in the US, Canada, Russia, Iceland, Romania and Chile. [CB]

Dir and Pro: Kurt Miller and Peter Speek. Assoc Pro: Max Bervy, Jr. Screenplay and Narrator: Warren Miller. Ph: Don Brolin. Ed: Katie Hedrich and Kim Schneider. M: Tom Windrif, David Levita, Anthony Johnson and Middleman; numbers performed by Kirsty MacColl, General Public, The Alarm, Spooky Organization, Nevins, Love Games, etc. Sound: Mark Rozett. (Warren Miller Entertainment–Black Diamond Films.) Rel: 5 November 1993. 90 mins. No cert.

## Blink

Chicago; 1994. Blind for twenty years, folk violinist Emma Brody receives a corneal transplant that enables her to start recovering her sight. Although her vision is initially blurred and distorted, Emma can see clearly 'after the event', a condition called 'retroactive hallucination' – a phenomenon in which the eyes take in an image which the brain cannot process until much later. So, when Emma 'sees' the man who killed her neighbour, she doesn't visualise him until the following morning. This makes her an iffy witness for

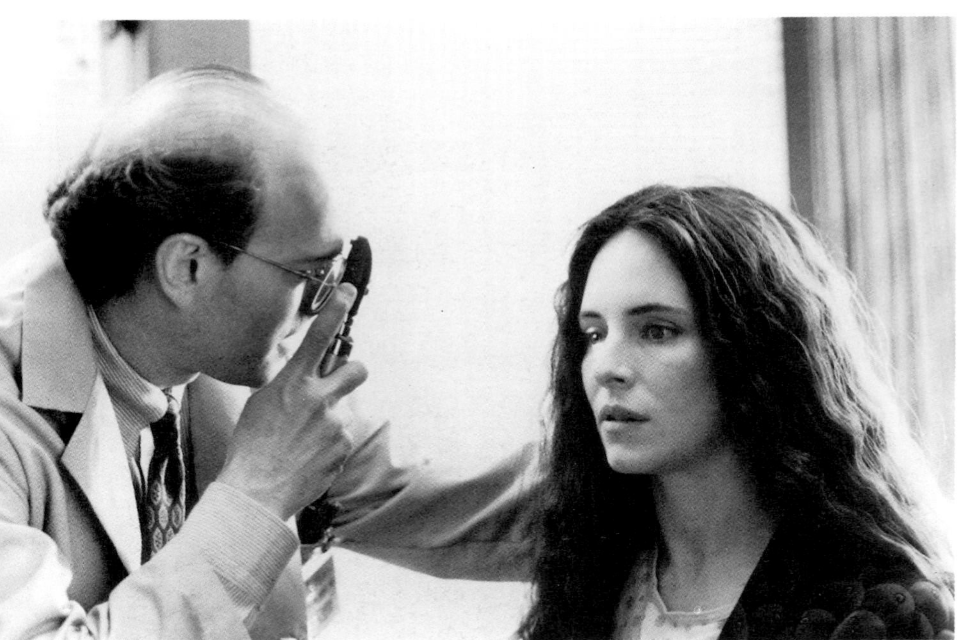

*Blindsided: Madeleine Stowe is examined by Dr Peter Friedman in Michael Apted's intriguing* Blink *(from Guild)*

*Mexican graffiti: Damian Chapa in Taylor Hackford's epic perspective of Mexican Americana,* Blood In Blood Out *(from Buena Vista)*

the police, but then they've got nothing else to go on. Besides, she could be in mortal danger herself . . . Madeleine Stowe is on terrific form as the no-bull heroine, while Aidan Quinn injects his customary Irish charm as the jaded detective assigned to her case. A taut, literary and photogenic thriller, *Blink* is abetted by a wry sense of humour with an attention-grabbing premise. In a genre as well-trodden as a copper's shoes, it is a joy to behold. P. S. Stowe and Quinn previously co-starred in *Stakeout*. [JC-W]

Cast: Madeleine Stowe (Emma Brody), Aidan Quinn (John Hallstrom), James Remar (Thomas Ridgely), Peter Friedman (Dr Ryan Pierce), Laurie Metcalf (Candice), Bruce A. Young, Matt Roth, Paul Dillon, Michael P. Byrne, Anthony Cannata, Greg Noonan.

Dir: Michael Apted. Pro: David Blocker. Ex Pro: Robert Shaye and Sara Risher. Screenplay: Dana Stevens. Ph: Dante Spinotti. Ed: Rick Shaine. Pro Des: Dan Bishop. M: Brad Fiedel; numbers performed by The Drovers, etc. Costumes: Susan Lyall. (New Line–Guild.) Rel: 13 May 1994. 106 mins. Cert 18.

**Blood In Blood Out**

1972–84; East Los Angeles. Three-hour epic about three *hombres* from the Hispanic quarter of LA who part company, one becoming a painter, one a cop and one a gangster. Labelled a Chicano *Godfather*, this artless melodrama is far south of Coppola's majestic epic, hamstrung by acting of the eye-bulging variety and corn as high as it gets. Nevertheless, a film of this scope is bound to unearth some fascinating insights (such as the *modus operandi* of the Mexican Mafia from within San Quentin prison) – but none of it is convincing. Like *American Me* (directed by and starring Edward James Olmos), this film was inspired by a real-life Hispanic gang leader called Cheyenne and is also co-scripted by Floyd Mutrux. [JC-W]

Cast: Damian Chapa (Miklo Velka), Jesse Borrego (Cruz), Benjamin Bratt (Paco), Enrique Castillo (Montana), Victor Rivers (Magic Mike), Delroy Lindo (Bonafide), Tom Towles (Red Ryder), Carlos Carrasco (Popeye), Lanny Flaherty (Big Al), Karmin Murcelo (Dolores), Gary Cervantes (Smokey), Thomas F. Wilson (Rollie McCann), Teddy Wilson, Raymond Cruz, Valente Rodriguez, Billy Bob Thornton, Geoffrey Rivas, Jenny Gago, Noah Verduzco, Lupe Ontiveros, Ray Oriel, Mike Genovese, Natalija Nogulich, Ving Rhames, Art Snyder, Richard Masur.

Dir: Taylor Hackford. Pro: Hackford and Jerry Gershwin. Ex Pro: Jimmy Santiago Baca and Stratton Leopold. Screenplay: Santiago Baca, Jeremy Iacone and Floyd Mutrux; from a story by Ross Thomas. Ph: Gabriel Beristain. Ed: Fredric Steinkamp and Karl F. Steinkamp. Pro Des: Bruno Rubeo. M: Bill Conti; numbers performed by Chelo Silva, WAR, Santana, The Isley Brothers, James Brown, Al Green, Jimi Hendrix, Malo, Rick James, etc. Costumes: Shay Cunliffe. Sound: Edward Tise. (Hollywood Pictures–Buena Vista.) Rel: 1 October 1993. 181 mins. Cert 18.

### Blue

The colour blue is not only used as the basis for a series of metaphors, but is the colour of the screen throughout this extraordinary film. Director Derek Jarman, who was diagnosed HIV-positive six years ago and died in 1994, utilised his failing sight to make a film without images, employing a blank blue screen as a sounding board for his rich, poetic soundtrack. Using actors' voices to explore the ramifications of his disease, Jarman here produced a challenging, difficult and painfully personal work that stretches the boundaries of experimental cinema. But is it cinema at all? [CB]

Voices: John Quentin, Nigel Terry, Derek Jarman, Tilda Swinton.

Dir and Screenplay: Derek Jarman. Pro: James Mackay and Takashi Asai. M: Simon Fisher Turner. Sound: Marvin Black. (Chanel Four/Arts Council of Great Britain/Opal/BBC Radio 3–Basilisk Communications/Uplink.) Rel: 27 August 1993. 76 mins. No cert.

*Altered images: Four people in search of their lives, namely* (from top left, clockwise) *Eric Stoltz, Bridget Fonda, Tim Roth and Phoebe Cates – in Michael Steinberg's* Bodies, Rest and Motion *(from Electric)*

### Blue

See *Three Colours Blue.*

### Bodies, Rest and Motion

In the dead-end desert town of Enfield, Arizona, three young people find their lives altered by the sudden decision of a local TV salesman to move to Montana. Borrowing Newton's First Law of Motion for its inspiration ('a body at rest or in motion will remain in that state unless acted upon by an outside force'), the film itself seems more at rest than in motion. Nonetheless, there are some wonderful moments and a lot of good talk, although the latter betrays the film's origins as a stage play. The young cast is uniformly good. [JC-W]

Cast: Phoebe Cates (Carol), Bridget Fonda (Beth), Tim Roth (Nick), Eric Stoltz (Sid), Alicia Witt (Elizabeth), Sandra Lafferty, Sidney Dawson, Jon Proudstar, Peter Fonda.

Dir: Michael Steinberg. Pro: Allan

*Barely simmering: Dennis Hopper as yet another villain in James B. Harris's lethargic* Boiling Point *(from Guild)*

Mindel, Eric Stoltz and Denise Shaw. Co-Pro: Roger Hedden and Jeffrey Sudzin. Ex Pro: Joel Castleberg. Screenplay: Hedden; from his own play. Ph: Bernd Heinl. Ed: Jay Cassidy. Pro Des: Stephen McCabe. M: Michael Convertino. Costumes: Isis Mussenden. Sound: Walt Martin. (Fine Line/ August Entertainment–Electric.) Rel: 4 February 1994. 94 mins. Cert 15.

**Boiling Point**

Los Angeles; now. Seeking to illustrate the thin line that separates the lifestyles of the law enforcers and the law breakers, writer-director James B. Harris (*Cop*) has produced a surprisingly bland piece of *film noir*. While employing the framework of an action-thriller, Harris dashes our expectations (not helped by the potboiling title) with a film that lacks suspense, humour and atmosphere, but is loaded with cliché. Wesley Snipes plays a US treasury agent whose bull-headed quest to unmask a counterfeit money-dealer has cost him a divorce and the death of his partner. If that doesn't sound familiar, how about the casting of Dennis Hopper as the villain? [JC-W]

Cast: Wesley Snipes (Jimmy Mercer), Dennis Hopper (Red Diamond), Lolita Davidovich (Vikki), Viggo Mortensen (Ronnie), Dan Hedaya (Brady), Seymour Cassel (Leach), Christine Elise (Carol), Valerie Perrine (Mona), Lorraine Evanoff (Connie), Tobin Bell (Freddy Roth), Jonathan Banks, Tony Lo Bianco, James Tolkan, Paul Gleason, Stephanie Williams, Bobby Hosea, Mark Phelan.

Dir and Screenplay: James B. Harris; from the novel *Money Men* by Gerald Petievich. Pro: Marc Frydman and Leonardo De La Fuente. Ex Pro: Rene Bonnell and Olivier Granier. Co-Pro: Patrick Beaufront. Ph: King Baggot. Ed: Jerry Brady. Pro Des: Ron Foreman. M: Cory Lerios and John D'Andrea. Costumes: Molly Maginnis. Sound: David Lewis Yewdall. (Hexagon Films–Guild.) Rel: 24 September 1993. 93 mins. Cert 15.

**Bound and Gagged: A Love Story**

When Elizabeth meets the husband of her bisexual lover at gunpoint, she decides to kidnap her girlfriend for her own good. A sort of lesbian *Thelma & Louise* played for laughs, *Bound and Gagged* was filmed in Minnesota over a period of two-and-a-half years. Obviously a labour of love, the film's offbeat humour is a little too staged while its bizarre set of characters are just that: *characters*, not people. However, newcomer Elizabeth Saltarrelli (as Elizabeth) is a real find. [JC-W]

Cast: Ginger Lynn Allen (Leslie), Christopher Denton (Cliff), Elizabeth Saltarrelli (Elizabeth), Karen Black (Carla), Mary Ella Ross (Lida), Chris Mulkey (Steve), Abdul Salaam El Razzac, Andrea Scarpa, Phyllis Wright, Bill Schoppert, Randy Schmidt, Sarah Todd, Travis James, Garth Schumacher, Lisa Jensen.

Dir and Screenplay: Daniel Appleby. Pro: Dennis J. Mahoney. Ex Pro: Mahoney and Jay Harjula. Ph: Dean Lent. Ed: Kaye Davis. Pro Des: Dane Pizzuti Krogman. M: William Murphy; numbers performed by Tango Project, Boiled in Lead, Jill Holly, Carol Pope, Lou Reed, Buckwheat Zydeco, etc. Costumes: Deborah Fiscus. (Cinescope–Metro Tartan.) Rel: 3 December 1993. 95 mins. Cert 18.

**A Bronx Tale**

New York; 1960–8. A kid growing up in the Bronx has to decide between the values of his hard-working father (a bus driver) and the local Godfather who adopts him. Crafted with enormous panache and love, *A Bronx Tale* marks Robert De Niro's directorial debut, and a work of art it is, too. Superbly orchestrated and beautifully paced, it shows the actor has paid attention to his directors (Scorsese, Leone, Coppola, Bertolucci). However, the size of the picture (costing a pretty $24m) and the expectations set up by the early scenes fail to serve the simplicity of the film's heart (based on Chazz Palminteri's one-man show). Besides, by playing it safe and choos-

*From* Taxi Driver *to bus driver: Robert De Niro explores his roots in* A Bronx Tale, *his directorial debut – with Francis Capra (from Rank)*

*Emotional bondage: Elizabeth Saltarrelli, Ginger Lynn Allen and Chris Mulkey in Daniel Appleby's erratic* Bound and Gagged: A Love Story *(from Metro Tartan)*

ing such familiar territory, De Niro has produced a film of enormous *déjà vu*. Ultimately, it's like watching *GoodFellas* without the excitement. [JC-W]

Cast: Robert De Niro (Lorenzo Anello), Chazz Palminteri (Sonny), Lillo Brancato (Calogero Anello, aged 17), Francis Capra (Calogero Anello, aged 9), Taral Hicks (Jane Williams), Kathrine Narducci (Rosina Anello), Clem Caserta (Jimmy Whispers), Joseph D'Onofrio (Slick, aged 17), Alfred Saucgelli Jr, Frank Pietrangolare, Joe Pesci, Robert D'Andrea, Eddie Montanaro, Fred Fischer, Dave Salerno, Luigi D'Angelo, Louis Vanaria, Dominik Rocchio, Tommy A. Ford, Louis Gioia, Mitch Kolpan, Richard DeDomenico.

Dir: Robert De Niro. Pro: De Niro, Jane Rosenthal and Jon Kilik. Ex Pro: Peter Gatien. Screenplay: Chazz Palminteri. Ph: Reynaldo Villalobos. Ed: David Ray and R. Q. Lovett. Pro Des: Wynn Thomas. M: numbers performed by Cool Change, Dion & The Belmonts, The Cleftones, Frank Sinatra, Della Reese, Dean Martin, Miles Davis, Aaron Neville, The Rascals, The Flamingos, Wilson Pickett, Tony Bennett, John Coltrane, The Beatles, The Moonglows, Otis Redding, The Moody Blues, The Four Tops, The Kinks, The Jimi Hendrix Experience, Cream, James Brown, etc. Costumes: Rita Ryack. Sound: Dan Sable. (Mario & Vittorio Cecchi Gori and Silvio Berlusconi/Price Entertainment/ Tribeca–Rank.) Rel: 18 February 1994. 121 mins. Cert 18.

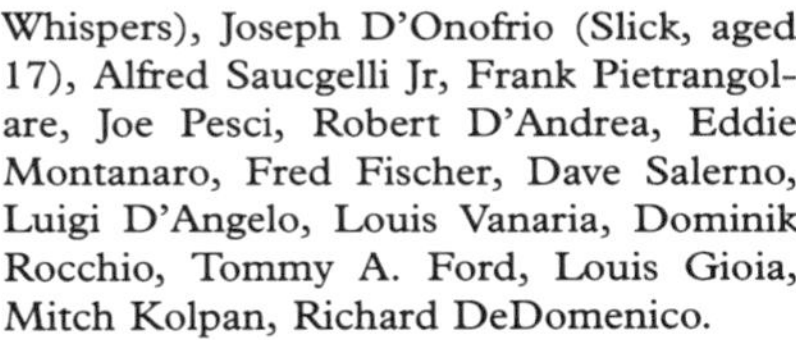

## A Business Affair

London; 1993. Kate Swallow, the loving French wife of Alec Bolton, a well-regarded, hard-up, mentally constipated and spectacularly vain writer,

*The gangster and the stripper: Al Pacino and Penelope Ann Miller in Brian DePalma's polished but unexciting* Carlito's Way *(from UIP)*

decides to pen her own novel. He, of course, is furious, and becomes downright hysterical when his own publisher decides to print his wife's tome. Worse still, the publisher would seem to have more than a professional interest in the beauty . . . After a promising, very funny start, this playful romantic comedy loses steam halfway through, in spite of some sprightly dialogue and game playing from its four principals. [JC-W]

Cast: Christopher Walken (Vanni), Carole Bouquet (Catherine Swallow/Kate Bolton), Jonathan Pryce (Alec Bolton), Sheila Hancock (Judith), Anna Manahan (Bianca), Fernando Guillen Cuervo (Angel), Tom Wilkinson (Bob), Marisa Benlloch, Bhasker, Annabel Leventon, Patti Love, Robert Swan, Jerome Willis, Jonathan Cecil.

Dir: Charlotte Brandstrom. Pro: Clive Parsons, Davina Belling and Xavier Larere. Ex Pro: Martha Wansborough and Willi Baur. Assoc Pro: Diana Costes Brook. Screenplay: William Stadiem; from a story by Stadiem and Brandstrom, inspired by the books *Tears Before Bedtime* and *Weep No More* by Barbara Skelton. Ph: Willy Kurant. Ed: Laurence Méry-Clark. Pro Des: Sophie Becher. M: Didier Vasseur. Costumes: Tom Rand. (Film and General/ Osby Films/Connexion Films/Canal Plus–Entertainment.) Rel: 27 May 1994. 101 mins. Cert 15.

## Carlito's Way

New York; 1975. Al Pacino is Carlito Brigante, a Puerto Rican gangster fresh out of jail and determined to go straight. But every crook has his debts, and bad friends stick to Carlito like flies to a corpse. And not even Carlito's good woman (Penelope Ann Miller mixing grit with vulnerability) can veer him away from the odious, lying, thieving, cheating, coke-snorting lawyer played by Sean Penn. It's all terribly familiar, but Pacino is as magnetic as ever and DePalma refrains from over-directing this time out. He does, however, exhibit some of his old flair for elaborate, suspenseful set-pieces, in particular a drug deal that goes wrong and a climactic chase through the New York subway. If you like gangster movies, this is a good one. [JC-W]

Cast: Al Pacino (Carlito Brigante), Sean Penn (David Kleinfeld), Penelope Ann Miller (Gail), John Leguizamo (Benny Blanco), Luis Guzman (Pachanga), Ingrid Rogers (Steffie), James Rebhorn (Norwalk), Viggo Mortensen (Lalin), Joseph Siravo, Richard Foronjy, Jorge Porcel, Frank Minucci, Adrian Pasdar, Angel Salazar, Al Israel, Rick Aviles, Jaime Sanchez, Edmonte Salvato, Paul Mazursky, Tera Tabrizi, Christopher Bregman.

Dir: Brian DePalma. Pro: Martin Bregman, Willi Baer and Michael S. Bregman. Ex Pro: Louis A. Stroller and Ortwin Freyermuth. Screenplay: David Koepp; based on the novels *Carlito's Way* and *After Hours* by Edwin Torres. Ph: Stephen H. Burum. Ed: Bill Pankow and Kristina Boden. Pro Des: Richard Sylbert. M: Patrick Doyle; 'Lakme' by Leo Delibes; numbers performed by Jellybean, Santana, Sinoa, Joan Sutherland, The Three Degrees, The O'Jays, The Bee Gees, Cheryl Lynn, KC and The Sunshine Band, Rozalla, Joe Cocker, Ed Terry, Labelle, Celia Cruz, Hector Lavoe, Willie Colon, etc. Costumes: Aude Bronson-Howard. Sound: Les Lazarowitz. (Universal/Epic Prods–UIP.) Rel: 7 January 1994. 141 mins. Cert 18.

## 'CB4'

A wild and wacky satire on rap culture that is so off-the-wall, so hip-hop-centric and downright offensive that it comes off like an extended, X-rated *Saturday Night Live* revue sketch. This, however, is not entirely suprising as the movie is the brainchild of Chris Rock (star, co-scriptor, co-producer and co-inspiration), the 26-year-old luminary (comic, writer) of *Saturday Night Live* itself. His film, the story of the rise of the controversial 'gangsta rappers' CB4 (short for Cell Block 4), is a slam-bang affair bursting with promise, although you'd have to be a rap junky to understand half of it. Director Tamra Davis brings much vitality to the proceedings. [JC-W]

Cast: Chris Rock (Albert Brown/MC Gusto), Allen Payne (Euripides Smalls/Dead Mike), Deezer D (Otis O. Otis/Stab Master Arson), Chris Elliott (A. White), Phil Hartman (Virgil Robinson), Charlie Murphy (Gusto), Khandi Alexander (Sissy), Arthur Evans (Albert Brown Snr), Theresa Randle (Eve Edwards), Willard E. Pugh (Trustus), Rachel True (Daliha), J. D. Daniels (Ben Robinson), Tyrone Granderson Jones, Victor Wilson, Richard Gant, Stoney Jackson, La Wanda Page, Sharisse Jackson, John Walcutt, Ice-T, Ice Cube, Halle Berry, Butthole Surfers, Flavor Flav, Eazy E and Shaquille O'Neal.

Dir: Tamra Davis. Pro: Nelson George. Co-Pro: William Fay and Chris Rock. Ex Pro: Sean Daniel and Brian Grazer. Screenplay: Rock, George and Robert LoCash. Ph: Karl Walter Lindenlaub. Ed: Earl Watson. Pro Des: Nelson Coates. M: John Barnes; numbers performed by Public Enemy, MC Ren, Hurricane and The Beastie Boys, LL Cool J, PM Dawn, CB4, etc. Costumes: Bernie White. Sound: Sandy Gendler and Val Kuklowsky. (Universal–UIP.) Rel: 26 November 1993. 88 mins. Cert 18.

*Just like Eddie: Charlie Murphy, older brother of a well-known superstar, knuckles in on the music business in Tamra Davis's* 'CB4' *(from UIP)*

## The Cement Garden

When their father dies and their mother takes to her bed, four children act out their most private fantasies immune from adult censure. Alas, what should have been a shocking and compelling adaptation of Ian McEwan's sensuous and disturbing short novel turns out to be nothing but ponderous and awkward. For the record, director/screenwriter Andrew Birkin is the boyfriend of the film's producer (Bee Gilbert), the uncle of the film's star (Charlotte Gainsbourg), and the father of the boy who plays Gainsbourg's little brother (Ben Birkin). [JC-W]

Cast: Charlotte Gainsbourg (Julie), Andrew Robertson (Jack), Sinead Cusack (mother), Alice Coulthard (Sue), Ned Birkin (Tom), Hanns Zischler (father), Jochen Horst (Derek), Gareth Brown (William), William Hootkins (Commander Hunt).

*Kids' stuff? Charlotte Gainsbourg and Andrew Robertson break the rules in Andrew Birkin's chilling* The Cement Garden *(from Metro Tartan)*

*As time goes by: Clive Owen and Miranda Richardson struggle with the realities of a new age – and more – in Stephen Poliakoff's exhilarating, thought-provoking* Century *(from Electric)*

Dir and Screenplay: Andrew Birkin. Pro: Bee Gilbert and Ene Vanaveski. Co-Pro: Steve O'Rourke. Ex Pro: Bernd Eichinger and Martin Moszkowicz. Ph: Stephen Blackman. Ed: Toby Tremlett. Pro Des and Costumes: Bernd Lepel. M: Edward Shearmur. Sound: Andy Kennedy. (Constantin Film/Canal Plus–Metro Tartan.) Rel: 22 October 1993. 105 mins. Cert 18.

## Century

1900; London. Innovative ideas, fresh horizons and new dangers conspire to transform the lives of three people: the preeminent head of a medical research institute, an arrogant, idealistic young doctor and a self-possessed laboratory assistant with a past. Stephen Poliakoff, one of England's most brilliant playwrights, had long dreamed of making a period film, 'a movie that wasn't either nostalgic about the past, or makes you look at it like a picture,' he explained. After much academic excavation, the writer-director has fashioned a vivid, mesmerising document of a time when the future had never looked so exciting, with the arrival of moving pictures, the horseless carriage and the first moving staircase at Harrods. But Poliakoff's *coup de main* is to people his intellectual carnival with credible, complex and modern characters, thereby transforming the celebration of a new era into an articulate, potent human drama that takes us by surprise. [JC-W]

Cast: Charles Dance (Professor Mandry), Clive Owen (Paul Reisner), Miranda Richardson (Clara), Robert Stephens (Mr Reisner), Joan Hickson (Mrs Whiteweather), Lena Headey (Miriam), Neil Stuke (Felix), Carlton Chance (James), Fiona Walker (Mrs Pritchard), Liza Walker, Joseph Bennett, Graham Loughbridge, Alexis Daniel, Ian Shaw, Bruce Alexander, Dail Sullivan, Trevor Cooper, Allie Byrne.

Dir and Screenplay: Stephen Poliakoff. Pro: Therese Pickard. Ex Pro: Mark Shivas and Ruth Caleb. Ph: Witold Stok. Ed: Michael Parkinson. Pro Des: Michael Pickwoad. M: Michael Gibbs. Costumes: Anushia Nieradzik and Daphne Dare. Sound: Hugh Strain. (BBC/Beambright–Electric.) Rel: 31 December 1993. 114 mins. Cert 15.

## Chain of Desire

New York; 1992. Weaving such themes as adultery, masochism, homosexuality, male prostitution, virginity, voyeurism and masturbation into a chain of 14 erotic encounters, this is an AIDS-infected *La Ronde* for the '90s. A gimmicky, styleless and depressing film. [JC-W]

Cast: Linda Fiorentino (Alma), Elias Koteas (Jesus), Tim Guinee (Ken), Grace Zabriskie (Linda), Assumpta Serna (Cleo), Patrick Bauchau (Jerald), Seymour Cassel (Mel), Malcolm McDowell (Hubert), Angel Aviles (Isa), Jamie Harrold (Keith), Dewey Weber (David), Holly Marie Combs (Diana), Kevin Conroy (Joe), Suzanne Douglas (Angie).

Dir and Screenplay: Temistocles Lopez. Pro: Brian Cox. Ex Pro: Anant Singh. Ph: Nancy Schreiber. Ed: Suzanne Fenn. Pro Des: Scott Chambliss. M: Nathan Birnbaum. Costumes: Pilar Limosner. Sound: Joe Romano. (Distant Horizon–Mainline.) Rel: 30 July 1993. 107 mins. Cert 18.

## Champions

(US: *The Mighty Ducks.*) Gordon Bombay is a smug, workaholic lawyer who will stoop to any depths to hold on to his unchallenged record of successful court cases. Then, one night, he is arrested for drunken and reckless driving and is forced to serve 500 hours community service coaching a delinquent ice hockey team that has never won a game. Bombay hates ice hockey and children, the kids hate him and so you know exactly what'll happen. However, the film throws a few interesting obstacles into the path of its predictable outcome, and the energy seldom (if ever) lets up. A surprise hit for Disney, this, but then not so startling when you consider the sure-fire box-office ingredients of slapstick (plenty of prat falls in ice hockey), schmaltz, sport, kids, and the sort of humour that thinks farting and dog-do is funny. [JC-W]

Cast: Emilio Estevez (Gordon Bombay), Joss Ackland (Hans), Lane Smith (Coach Reilly), Heidi Kling (Casey), Josef Sommer (Gerald Ducksworth), Joshua Jackson (Charlie Conroy), Elden Ratliff (Fulton Reed), Vincent A. Larusso (Adam Banks),

Claudia Wilkens (principal), Shaun Weiss, M. C. Gainey, Matt Doherty, Brandon Adams, J. D. Daniels, Aaron Schwartz, Garette Ratliff Henson, Marguerite Moreau, Robert Pall, George Coe, Mark Bradley.

Dir: Stephen Herek. Pro: Jordan Kerner and Jon Avnet. Screenplay: Steven Brill. Ph: Thomas Del Ruth. Ed: Larry Bock and John F. Link. Pro Des: Randy Ser. M: David Newman; numbers performed by The Poorboys, Southside Johnny, Marky Mark and the Funky Bunch, Dr John, Queen and The Outfield. Costumes: Grania Preston. Sound: Ed Novick. (Walt Disney–Buena Vista.) Rel: 2 July 1993. 104 mins. Cert PG.

*Gordon the Duck: Emilio Estevez (*bottom right*) and hapless co-stars in Stephen Herek's decidedly juvenile* Champions *(from Buena Vista)*

## The Chase

California; 1994. Extra-lite romantic action comedy in which executive producer Charlie Sheen plays a wrongfully convicted Nice Guy who kidnaps a beautiful young woman to escape the police. The cops turn out to be hard to shake off and Sheen's hostage the daughter of the richest man in the universe. Cue for the usual quota of disposable squad cars and an uninspired plot which will have you gasping at its predictability. Still, it is an immensely likeable diversion, even if the high-speed chase seldom seems to accelerate past the speed limit of a tricycle. [JC-W]

Cast: Charlie Sheen (Jack Hammond), Kristy Swanson (Natalie Voss), Henry Rollins (Officer Dobbs), Josh Mostel (Officer Figus), Wayne Grace (Chief Boyle), Rocky Carroll (Byron Wilder), Ray Wise (Dalton Voss), Marshall Bell, Joe Segal, Claudia Christian, Wirt Cain, Brian Chessney, Joe Berryman, Natalija Nogulich, Chamblee Ferguson, Paul Dandridge, Flea, Anthony Kiedis, Cary Elwes, Cassian Elwes.

Dir and Screenplay: Adam Rifkin. Pro: Brad Wyman and Cassian Elwes. Ex Pro: Eduard Sarlui and Charlie Sheen. Ph: Alan Jones. Ed: Peter Schink. Pro Des: Sherman Williams. M: Richard Gibbs: numbers performed by Offspring, The Rollins Band, Suede, NOFX, Rancid, Bad Religion, Down by Law, etc. Costumes: Yvette Correa. (Capitol Films–Fox.) Rel: 17 June 1994. 89 mins. Cert 15.

## The Concierge

Manhattan, New York; 1993. Douglas Ireland is the genie of the hotel business. He can get you last-minute tickets to the hottest show in town or an overpriced watch at two-thirds of the price. He'll even babysit your mistress . . . Michael J. Fox, America's lightest of light romantic comedians, is in his element here as the answer to everybody's dreams but who has no time for his own. Britain's Gabrielle Anwar provides some very alluring romantic interest. Thanks to a sharp script, some considerable visual flair and a fascinating insight into the world of hotel business, *The Concierge* is a class-A souffle. [JC-W]

Cast: Michael J. Fox (Doug Ireland), Gabrielle Anwar (Andy Hart), Anthony Higgins (Christian Hanover), Michael Tucker (Mr Wegman), Bob Balaban (Mr Drinkwater), Isaac Mizrahi (Julian Russell), Patrick Breen (Gary Taubin), Dan Hedaya (Gene Salvatore), Fyvush Finkel (Milton), Douglas Seale (Freddy), Udo Kier, Simon Jones, Dianne Brill, Mike G, Saverio Guerra, Daniel Hagen, La Chanze, Paula Laurence, Donna Mitchell, Nicole Beach, John Cunningham, Alice Playten, Le Clanche du Rand, Bobby Short, Richard B. Shull.

*Blame it on the bellhop: Michael J. Fox reaping big tips from small turns – in Barry Sonnenfeld's* The Concierge *(from UIP)*

*Strangers in purgatory: Patrick Timsit and Vincent Lindon in Coline Serreau's charmingly offbeat* La Crise *(from Electric)*

Dir: Barry Sonnenfeld. Pro: Brian Grazer. Ex Pro: David T. Friendly. Screenplay: Mark Rosenthal and Lawrence Konner. Ph: Oliver Wood. Ed: Jim Miller. Pro Des: Peter Larkin. M: Bruce Broughton; numbers performed by Ray Charles, The Singing Nun, Gabrielle Anwar, Big Mountain, Little Sister, Bobby Short, Army of Lovers, etc. Costumes: Susan Lyall. Sound: Skip Lievsay. (Imagine/Universal–UIP.) Rel: 19 November 1993. 95 mins. Cert PG.

## Cool Runnings

Lame comedy 'inspired' by the true story of the Jamaican bobsleigh team that competed in the 1988 Winter Olympics at Calgary. When ace sprinter Derice Bannock is tripped up in his qualifying race to compete in the Olympics, he turns to down-at-heel bobsleigh coach Irv Blitzer to help him contend in an alternative sport. The only problem is that Bannock doesn't know what a bobsleigh is and there's no snow in Jamaica. Besides, there's no time and Blitzer isn't interested. Yet, against impossible odds, four unlikely Jamaicans make it to Calgary. A good story in search of a comedy, *Cool Runnings* goes for obvious laughs and aggravates matters with clumsy doses of sentimentality and banality. [JC-W]

Cast: Leon (Derice Bannock), Doug E. Doug (Sanka Coffie), Rawle D. Lewis (Junior Bevil), Malik Yoba (Yul Brenner), John Candy (Irv Blitzer), Raymond J. Barry (Kurt Hemphill), Peter Outerbridge, Paul Coeur, Larry Gilman, Charles Hyatt, Winston Stona, Bertina Macauley, Pauline Stone Myrie, Jay Brazeau, Campbell Lane, David Lovgren, Al Trautwig, John Morgan.

Dir: Jon Turteltaub. Pro: Dawn Steel. Ex Pro: Christopher Meledandri and Susan B. Landau. Screenplay: Lynn Siefert, Tommy Swerdlow and Michael Goldberg; from a story by Siefert and Michael Ritchie. Ph: Phedon Papamichael. Ed: Bruce Green. Pro Des: Stephen Marsh. M: Hans Zimmer; numbers performed by Wailing Souls, Tiger, Diana King, Jimmy Cliff, etc. Costumes: Grania Preston. Sound: Mark Mangini. (Walt Disney–Buena Vista.) Rel: 25 February 1994. 99 mins. Cert PG.

## La Crise

Victor, a high-flying company lawyer, is having a bad day. His wife has left him and when he turns up at work he finds he has no job. It transpires that having engineered a masterful coup for his company, he is no longer needed. Desperate to spill his troubles on to a sympathetic shoulder, Victor finds that everybody else is too tied up in their own problems to give him the time of day. Whether it's the credibility of the situations or just the subtitles, this is a farce that seems as real as life itself. Coline Serreau keeps the story going at a breathless pace, and even when Victor's comic sidekick keeps falling over (three times?), it just feels like an extension of the picture's comic urgency. True, the film is neither as funny nor as moving as Serreau's *Three Men and a Cradle* or *Romuald et Juliette*, but it is a genuine hoot with a canny ring of truth. The scene in which Victor's mother 'retires' from her maternal duties to start her own life elicits painful smiles. [JC-W]

Cast: Vincent Lindon (Victor), Patrick Timsit (Michou), Zabou (Isabelle), Annick Alame (Mamie), Valerie Alane (Therese), Gilles Privat (Laurent), Nanoue Garcia (Sophie), Christian Benedetti (Paul), Didier Flaman (Monsieur Laville).

Dir and Screenplay: Coline Serreau. Pro: Alain Sarde. Ph: Robert Alazraki. Ed: Catherine Renault. Pro Des: Guy Claude Francois. M: Sonia Wieder-Atherton. Costumes: Karen Serreau. Sound: Guillaume Sciama. (TFI Films/Canal Plus–Electric.) Rel: 18 February 1994. 95 mins. Cert 15.

## The Crow

Eight days before the film's completion, the scene in which Brandon Lee is shot down by hoodlums cost the star his life. The tip of a real bullet, jammed in the barrel of a gun loaded with a blank, lodged itself in the actor's spine and killed him. The scene has been deleted from the film, but nevertheless there is a ghoulish air that accompanies this ugly, violent 'thriller'. For a start, Lee plays a man who returns from the dead to wreak vengeance on the men who killed him and his girlfriend, and the picture is dedicated to Lee and Eliza Hutton, the woman Lee was to have married immediately after *The Crow* completed production. Sadly, the movie that cost the actor his life is a despicable pile of junk, a chaotic, noisy, ugly shambles that barely resembles a film as we know it. If its star had not died, it never would have been released. And now there's talk of a sequel . . . [JC-W]

Cast: Brandon Lee (Eric Draven), Ernie Hudson (Albrecht), Michael Wincott (Top Dollar), David Patrick Kelly (T-Bird), Angel David (Stank), Rochelle Davis (Sarah) Jon Polito (Gideon), Bai Ling, Lawrence Mason, Michael Massee, Bill Raymond, Marco Rodriguez, Sofia Shinas, Anna Thomson, Tony Todd, Kim Sykes, Rock Taulbee.

Dir: Alex Proyas. Pro: Edward R. Pressman and Jeff Most. Ex Pro: Robert L.

Rosen and Sherman L. Baldwin. Screenplay: David J. Schow and John Shirley; based on the comic book series by James O'Barr. Ph: Dariusz Wolski. Ed: Dov Hoenig and Scott Smith. Pro Des: Alex McDowell. M: Graeme Revell; numbers performed by The Cure, Stone Temple Pilots, Nine Inch Nails, Medicine, Helmet, Violent Femmes, Rage Against the Machine, Jesus and Mary Chain, Pantera, Jane Siberry, etc. Costumes: Arianne Phillips. (Entertainment.) Rel: 10 June 1994. 101 mins. Cert 18.

## The Crush

What if a 14-year-old prodigy decided to hide her precocity in order to cover her dirty deeds? Darian Forrester does just that, playing up her childish charms while shrewdly plotting against the 28-year-old journalist who spurns her advances. *Lolita* meets *Fatal Attraction* and gives birth to a thriller that's so derivative it's not funny. Hell has a growing membership but its resident child prodigy can't act. [JC-W]

Cast: Cary Elwes (Nick Eliot), Jennifer Rubin (Amy Maddik), Kurtwood Smith (Cliff Forrester), Alicia Silverstone (Darian Forrester), Amber Benson (Cheyenne), Gwynyth Walsh (Liv Forrester), Matthew Walker (Michael), Deborah Hancock, Beverley Elliott, Andrew Airlie.

Dir and Screenplay: Alan Shapiro. Pro: James G. Robinson. Ex Pro: Gary Barber. Ph: Bruce Surtees. Ed: Ian Crafford. Pro Des: Michael Bolton. M: Graeme Revell; numbers performed by Starclub, Chris Kowanko, Auto & Cherokee, etc. Costumes: Sharon Purdy. Sound: Michael T. Williamson. (Morgan Creek–Warner.) Rel: 17 September 1993. 89 mins. Cert 15.

## The Cure Show

Punk satirists The Cure star in their second concert movie (following *The Cure in Orange*), this time filmed over two nights at The Palace in Detroit. Cure fans should enjoy. [CB]

The Cure: Robert Smith, Simon Gallup, Porl Thompson, Boris Williams, Perry Bamonte.

Dir: Aubrey Powell and Leroy Bennett. Pro: Steve Swartz. Ex Pro: Chris Parry, Marcus Peterzell and Veronica Gretton. Ph: Jeff Zimmerman. Ed: Nick Wickam, Robert Smith, Ian Mallet and Liam Hall. M: The Cure hits 'The Walk', 'In Between Days', 'Just Like Heaven', 'Lullaby', 'Never Enough', etc. Sound: Bryan 'Chuck' New and Robert Smith. (Fiction Films/PolyGram Video–Rank.) Rel: 2 July 1993. 97 mins. Cert 12.

*Life imitating art: Harvey Keitel as Abel Ferrara directs Madonna as Madonna in Ferrara's astonishing* Dangerous Game *(from Rank)*

## The Custodian

Taut, engrossing Australian thriller from first-time director John Dingwall examining corruption in the Sydney police force. Expat Anthony LaPaglia stars as James Quinlan, a cop on the verge of self-destruction who can no longer turn a blind eye to the moral decay around him. In spite of a few 'first film' bumps, *The Custodian* develops into an intriguing drama that pulls few punches. Essie Davis, in her film debut, is particularly effective as the angelic waitress who tempers Quinlan's nerves. Only Hugo Weaving's theatrical performance as a snarling villain and a melodramatic score impair the proceedings. [JC-W]

Cast: Anthony LaPaglia (James Quinlan), Hugo Weaving (Frank Church), Kelly Dingwall (Tony Reynolds), Barry Otto (Ferguson), Essie Davis (Jilly), Skye Wansey (Claire), Gosia Dobrowolska (Josie), Wayne Pygram, Tim McKenzie, Richard Hill, Russell Newman, Joy Smithers, Christina Totos, Naomi Watts, Steven Grives, Bill Hunter, Norman Kaye.

Dir and Screenplay: John Dingwall. Pro: Adrienne Read. Ex Pro: Gary Hamilton and Mikael Borglund. Co-Pro: Dingwall and Dimitra Meleti. Ph: Steve Mason. Ed: Michael Honey. Pro Des: Philip Warner. M: Philip Houghton. Costumes: Terry Ryan. Sound: Ben Osmo. (J.D. Prods–NFT.) Rel: 13 May 1994. 109 mins. No cert.

## Daens

Powerful, handsomely mounted drama adapted from Louis Paul Boon's novel *Pieter Daens*, itself based on the true story of a 19th-century priest who fought for the rights of Belgian workers. A surprisingly assured work from the cinematic wasteland of Belgium, this, which should give that country's industry a much-needed shot in the arm. Nominated for an Oscar for best foreign film of 1992. [EB]

Cast: Jan Decleir (Adolf Daens), Gerard Desarthe (Charles Woeste), Antje De Boeck (Nette Scholliers), Michael Pas (Jan De Meeter), Johan Leysen, Idwig Stephane, Linda Van Dijck.

Dir: Stinjn Coninx. Pro: Dirk Impens. Ex Pro: Szymon Zaleski. Screenplay: Coninx and Francois Chevallier. Ph: Wather Vanden Ende. Ed: Ludo Troch. Pro Des: Allan Starski. M: Dirk Brosse. Costumes: Yan Tax. Sound: Henri Morelle and Jean-Paul Loublier. (Favourite Films/Investco/Kredietbank Luxembourg–Mayfair Entertainment.) Rel: 25 March 1994. 134 mins. Cert 15.

## Dangerous Game

As the director of a scorching drama detailing the self-destruction of an upper-middle class couple, Harvey Keitel berates his leading actress, a world-famous star played by

*Honest trouble: Debra Winger as Martha Horgan, who cannot tell a lie, in Stephen Gyllenhaal's mesmerising* A Dangerous Woman *(from First Independent)*

Madonna. Madonna's reaction to Keitel's verbal abuse is almost beyond acting. In fact, the 'acting' in this searing portrait of the LA film scene seems to go beyond mere performance. One is made to fear not just for the characters themselves, but for those who play them. But then, this film-within-a-film that spills over into reality is a stunning example of life imitating art. Abel Ferrara, who gave us the numbing *Bad Lieutenant*, excels himself here, unnerving his audience as he stretches and emotionally dismantles his cast. Madonna has never been better, while the director's own wife, Nancy Ferrara, is excellent as Keitel's betrayed wife, adding even more reality to the uncomfortable stew. Previously known as *Snake Eyes*. [JC-W]

Cast: Harvey Keitel (Eddie Israel), Madonna (Sarah Jennings/Claire), James Russo (Francis Burns/Russell), Nancy Ferrara (Madlyn), Reilly Murphy (Tommy), Victor Argo, Leonard Thomas, Christina Fulton, Heather Bracken, Glenn Plummer.

Dir: Abel Ferrara. Pro: Mary Kane. Ex Pro: Freddy DeMann and Ron Rotholz. Screenplay: Nicholas St John. Ph: Ken Kelsch. Ed: Anthony Redman. Pro Des: Alex Tavoularis. M: Joe Delia. Costumes: Marlene Stewart. Sound: Greg Sheldon. (Mario & Vittorio Cecchi/Maverick–Rank.) Rel: 3 June 1994. 109 mins. Cert 18.

## A Dangerous Woman

Southern California; 1993. Debra Winger, one of America's finest screen actresses, gives another career-spinning performance as a woman who cannot tell a lie – to the detriment of not only others, but herself. Honest to a fault, Martha Horgan is one of life's misfits. Awkward and clumsy, she has led a sheltered existence, supervised at arm's length by her young, snobbish aunt. For Martha, an invitation to a Tupperware party embodies the apogee of excitement. Then, after years of inactivity, two events conspire to transform her life: she is accused of stealing money at work and a stranger arrives in town . . . As Winger brings a remarkable gaucheness, strength and vulnerability to her role, Barbara Hershey registers equally strongly in the less showy and sympathetic part of the aunt, while Gabriel Byrne is a revelation as the Irish stranger. But then everybody is excellent down the line, well served by Stephen Gyllenhaal's intelligent, claustrophobic direction and Naomi Foner's daring, fluid writing. This marks the first time that husband and wife Gyllenhaal and Foner have worked together. [JC-W]

Cast: Debra Winger (Martha Horgan), Barbara Hershey (Frances Beecham), Gabriel Byrne (Colin Mackey), John Terry (Steve Bell), Laurie Metcalf (Anita Bell), Brad Blaisdell (Wesley), Breon Gorman (Heidi), Maggie Gyllenhaal, Jacon Gyllenhaal, Myles Sheridan, Richard Riehle, Viveka Davis, Paul Dooley, Warren Munson, Jan Hooks.

Dir: Stephen Gyllenhaal. Pro and Screenplay: Naomi Foner; from the novel by Mary McGarry Morris. Ex Pro: Kathleen Kennedy. Line Pro: Patricia Whitcher. Ph: Robert Elswit. Ed: Harvey Rosenstock. Pro Des: David Brisbin. M: Carter Burwell. Costumes: Susie DeSanto. (Amblin/World Films/Gramercy/Rollercoaster–First Independent.) Rel: 13 May 1994. 110 mins. Cert 15.

## The Dark Half

Castle Rock, Maine; 1991. When a blackmailer discovers that the respected writer Thad Beaumont is in fact the sensationalist novelist George Stark, Beaumont decides to kill off his alter ego and go public. But George Stark is taking no crap from anybody . . . As with most Stephen King stories, this one is blessed with an intriguing premise. It is also well executed by horror director George A. Romero and exceptionally well acted by the principal cast. However, because it *is* so naturalistically played, the story's outrageous concept is even harder to swallow than usual. I, for one, found myself scrambling for a logical conclusion to all the mayhem. Filmed in 1991. [JC-W]

*Split image: Timothy Hutton as renowned author Thad Beaumont surveying* The Dark Half *(from Columbia TriStar)*

Cast: Timothy Hutton (Thad Beaumont/George Stark), Amy Madigan (Liz Beaumont), Julie Harris (Reggie DeLesseps), Michael Rooker (Alan Pangborn), Tom Mardirosian (Rick Cowley), Kent Broadhurst (Mike Donaldson), Glenn Colerider (Homer Gamache), Chelsea Field (Annie Pangborn), Patrick Brannan, Beth Grant, Robert Joy, Rutanya Alda, Royal Dano, William Cameron.

Dir, Ex Pro and Screenplay: George A. Romero. Pro: Declan Baldwin. Assoc Pro: Christine Romero. Ph: Tony Pierce-Roberts. Ed: Pasquale Buba. Pro Des: Cletus Anderson. M: Christopher Young; 'Are You Lonesome Tonight?' performed by Elvis Presley. Costumes: Barbara Anderson. (Orion–Columbia TriStar.) Rel: 20 May 1994. 121 mins. Cert 18.

## Dave

If you were president of the United States, what one thing would you do to make the world a better place? Dave Kovic, employment agent and sometime presidential impersonator, finds himself in the White House when the real man suffers a stroke during a bout of adultery. A villainous Chief of Staff (Frank Langella, superbly brutal and oily) wants the lookalike in office until he can disqualify the vice-president and engineer a takeover for himself. Meanwhile, Dave takes to the job like a duck to water and finds that he *can* make the world a better place. This is a concept movie that builds on its premise and never lets up, providing genuine belly laughs, excitement and snuffles, while artfully juggling its political smarts with a romantic, sentimental outlook. Tapping into the feel-good, home-grown philosophies of the old Frank Capra comedies (cf. *Mr Smith Goes to Washington*), *Dave* is a delight from beginning to end. [JC-W]

*The distinguished gentleman: Kevin Kline (on pig) impersonates the US president and finds that he's better than the real thing – in Ivan Reitman's warming* Dave *(from Warner)*

Cast: Kevin Kline (Dave Kovic/Bill Mitchell), Sigourney Weaver (Ellen Mitchell), Frank Langella (Bob Alexander), Kevin Dunn (Alan Reed), Ving Rhames (Duane Stevensen), Ben Kingsley (Vice-President Nance), Charles Grodin (Murray Blum), Laura Linney, Bonnie Hunt, Charles Hallahan, Tom Dugan, Alba Oms, Larry King, Jay Leno, Thomas P. 'Tip' O'Neill, Arnold Schwarz-

*Corrupt counsel: Jane Horrocks finds blood on her hands in Mandie Fletcher's wickedly enjoyable* Deadly Advice *(from Mayfair Entertainment)*

enegger, Senator Paul Simon, Oliver Stone, Stephen Root, Catherine Reitman, George Martin, Jason Reitman, Robin Gammell, Bonnie Bartlett.

Dir: Ivan Reitman. Pro: Reitman and Lauren Shuler-Donner. Ex Pro: Joe Medjuck and Michael C. Gross. Screenplay: Gary Ross. Ph: Adam Greenberg. Ed: Sheldon Kahn. Pro Des: J. Michael Riva. M: James Newton Howard; 'Don't' performed by Elvis Presley. Costumes: Richard Hornung. Sound: Robert Grieve. (Northern Lights Entertainment–Warner.) Rel: 5 November 1993. 110 mins. Cert 12.

## Deadly Advice

Hay-on-Wye, Wales; today. Delicious black comedy in which the sublime Jane Horrocks stars as Jodie, a sweet, mousey bookshop assistant dominated by her puritanical mother. Haunted by the ghosts of waxworks from the Chamber of Horrors, Jodie finally decides to take decisive action to rid her life of maternal aggro. A beautfully judged comedy, rife with good performances, witty dialogue, sprightly music and some scrumptious photography of the Welsh countryside. But towering above all is Ms Horrocks, whose comic reactions to everything are a joy to behold. Mandie Fletcher, best known for directing TV's *Blackadder*, makes her feature film debut with aplomb. [JC-W]

Cast: Jane Horrocks (Jodie Greenwood), Brenda Fricker (Iris Greenwood), Imelda Staunton (Beth Greenwood), Jonathan Pryce (Dr Ted Philips), Edward Woodward (Major Herbert Armstrong), Billie Whitelaw (Kate Webster), Hywel Bennett (Dr Hawley Crippen), Jonathan Hyde (George Joseph Smith), John Mills (Jack the Ripper), Ian Abbey (Bunny the stripper), Eleanor Bron, Roger Frost, Gareth Gwyn-Jones, Richard Moore, Alison Burrows, Sarah Blackburn, Dillie Keane, Sue Jones-Davies.

Dir: Mandie Fletcher. Pro: Nigel Stafford-Clark. Assoc Pro: Charles Salmon. Screenplay: Glenn Chandler. Ph: Richard Greatrex. Ed: John Jarvis. Pro Des: Christopher Hobbs. M: Richard Harvey; numbers performed by The Yardbirds, Dusty Springfield, Long John Baldry, etc. Costumes: Emma Porteous. (Zenith–Mayfair Entertainment.) Rel: 29 April 1994. 91 mins. Cert 15.

## Decadence

Woefully misguided attempt to turn Steven Berkoff's outrageous theatrical two-hander into a film. Even with the glossy presence of Joan Collins gamely throwing herself into the dual roles of a sexually active aristocrat and an East End wife, this fiasco is a terrible bore. Berkoff's uncontrolled satire on the excesses of the rich (complete with rhyming dialogue) makes its point long before the blaspheming, farting and vomiting is over. Berkoff, who makes his screen directing debut here, shows an extraordinary ineptitude for the medium. [CB]

Cast: Joan Collins (Helen/Sybil), Steven Berkoff (Steve/Les Titorelli), Michael Winner, Christopher Biggins, Marc Sinden, Edward Duke, Robert Longdon, David Alder, Susannah Morley, Veronica Lang.

Dir and Screenplay: Steven Berkoff. Pro: Lance Reynolds. Ex Pro: Fred Bestall, Frank Henschke and Romain Schroder. Ph: Denis Lenoir. Ed: John Wilson. Pro Des: Yolanda Sonnabend and Simon Holland. M: Stewart Copeland. Costumes: David Blight. Sound: George Richards. (Vendetta/Schlemmer/Delux–Mayfair Entertainment.) Rel: 28 January 1994. 108 mins. Cert 18.

## Demolition Man

The year is 1996 and Los Angeles is a war zone. Only one man, John Spartan, can stem the flow of violence. However, when Spartan's ambush of a ruthless killer backfires and 30 innocent hostages are killed, both he and his prey – Simon Phoenix – are sentenced to the CryoPenitentiary. Thirty-six years later, LA – now known as San Angeles – has become a crime-free zone in which nicotine, caffeine, meat, contact sports and 'fluid transfer activities' (sex) have been outlawed. There are even on-the-spot fines for 'violations of verbal morality' (swearing). It's a perfect world for Phoenix to rise from the ashes, break parole and wreak havoc. And only one man can stop him . . . Thanks to a massive injection of humour, some breakneck editing and a great physical look, this mammoth collision of stunts and special effects sets the head spinning. The acting is below par, but it's hard to find time to notice. [JC-W]

Cast: Sylvester Stallone (John Spartan), Wesley Snipes (Simon Phoenix), Sandra Bullock (Lenina Huxley), Nigel Hawthorne (Dr Raymond Cocteau), Benjamin Bratt (Alfredo Garcia), Bob Gunton (Chief George Earle), Glenn Shadix (Associate Bob), Denis Leary (Edgar Friendly), Grand L. Bush, Pat Skipper, Steve Kahan, Andre Gregory, Troy Evans, Bill Cobbs, Lara Harris.

Dir: Marco Brambilla. Pro: Joel Silver, Michael Levy and Howard Kazanjian. Co-Pro: James Herbert and Jacqueline George. Ex Pro: Steven Bratter and Faye Schwab. Assoc Pro: Tony Munafo. Screenplay: Daniel Waters, Robert Reneau and Peter M. Lenkov. Ph: Alex Thomson and Matthew F. Leonetti. Ed: Stuart Baird. Pro Des: David L. Snyder. M: Elliot Goldenthal; 'Demolition Man' sung by Sting. Costumes: Bob Ringwood. Sound: Robert G. Henderson. (Silver Pictures–Warner.) Rel: 12 November 1993. 115 mins. Cert 15.

### Dennis

(US: *Dennis the Menace.*) *Home Alone* meets *Problem Child* in this artless, contrived cinematic reincarnation of Hank Ketcham's classic cartoon featuring the mischievous 5-year-old. Here, Dennis is portrayed as a moronic kid plagued by his own wayward curiosity and misguided attempts to please. Add a saccharine subplot about the grumpy neighbour's deep-seated love for the boy, and you have a film that insults the young and gags the even older. At least Kevin McCallister in the *Home Alone* films was bursting with charm and ingenuity. [JC-W]

Cast: Walter Matthau (Mr Wilson), Mason Gamble (Dennis Mitchell), Christopher Lloyd (Switchblade Sam), Joan Plowright (Martha Wilson), Lea Thompson (Alice Mitchell), Robert Stanton (Henry Mitchell), Amy Sakasitz, Kellen Hathaway, Paul Winfield, Natasha Lyonne, Devin Ratray, Billie Bird, Bill Erwin, Arnold Stang, Casey Gamble.

Dir: Nick Castle. Pro: John Hughes and Richard Vane. Ex Pro: Ernest Chambers. Screenplay: Hughes; based on characters created by Hank Ketcham. Ph: Thomas Ackerman. Ed: Alan Heim. Pro Des: James Bissell. M: Jerry Goldsmith; numbers performed by Jo Stafford, Glenn Miller, and The Orions. Costumes: Ann Roth and Bridget Kelly. Sound: Jim Alexander. (Warner.) Rel: 30 July 1993. 96 mins. Cert PG.

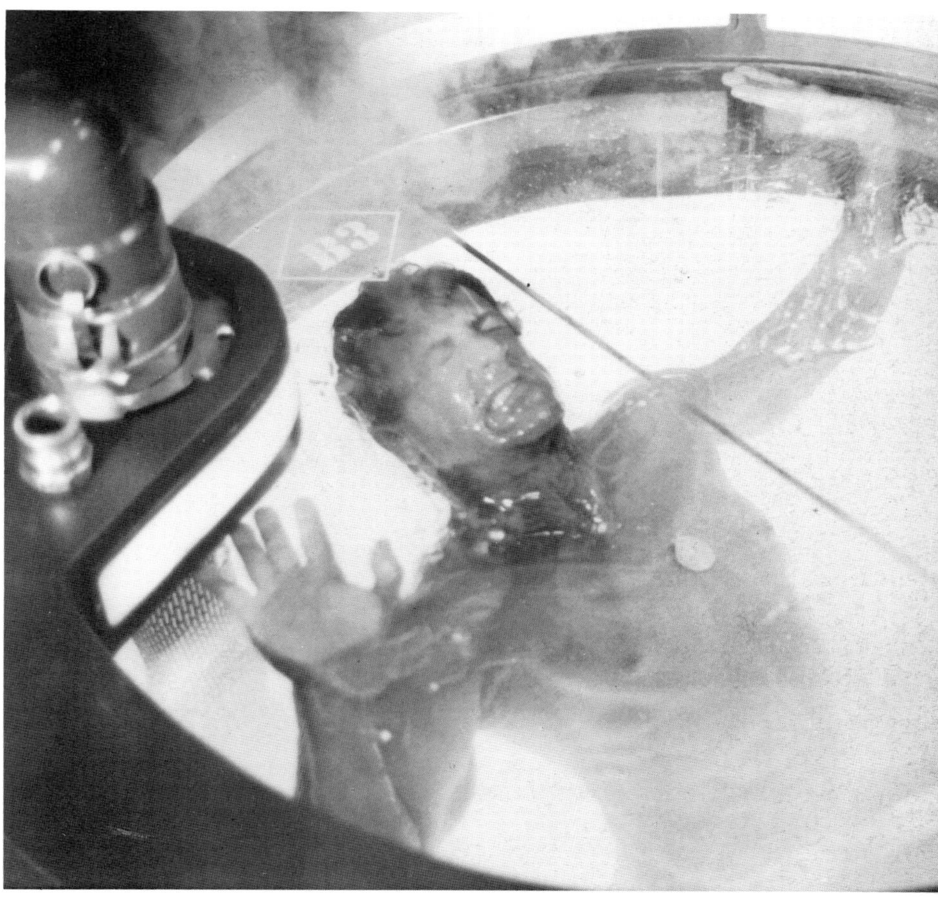


*Frozen asset: Supercop Sylvester Stallone is cryogenically detained in Marco Brambilla's crackerjack sci-fi comedy* Demolition Man, *the cinema's first satire on political correctness (from Warner)*

### Dennis the Menace

See *Dennis.*

### Desperate Remedies

A genuine original, this, a highly camp New Zealand melodrama aimed squarely at the gay crowd. However, it is injected with such flair and energy

*The brat attack: Walter Matthau succumbs to the good-natured mayhem of Mason Gamble – in Nick Castle's* Dennis *(from Warner)*

*Kung fu fighting: Jason Scott Lee (*right*) on the attack – with John Cheung – in Rob Cohen's enjoyable* Dragon: The Bruce Lee Story *(from UIP)*

that it should appeal to a much larger audience. Set in the mythical seaport of Hope somewhere in the 19th century, the film follows the crossed attractions of a variety of outrageously dressed characters as a beautiful draper plots to rescue her younger sister from the clutches of an evil opium dealer. [CB]

Cast: Jennifer Ward-Lealand (Dorothea Brook), Kevin Smith (Lawrence Hayes), Lisa Chappell (Anne Cooper), Cliff Curtis (Fraser), Michael Hurst (William Poyser), Kiri Mills (Rose), Bridget Armstrong, Timothy Raby, Helen Steemson, Geeling Ching.

Dir and Screenplay: Stewart Main and Peter Wells. Pro: James Wallace. Assoc Pro: Trishia Downie. Ph: Leon Narby. Ed: David Coulson. Pro Des: Michael Kane. M: Peter Scholes. Costumes: Glenis Foster. Sound: Graham Morris. (New Zealand Film Commission/NZ On Air/Avalon-NFU Film Studios–Electric.) Rel: 24 December 1993. 92 mins. Cert 15.

## The Diary of Lady M – Le Journal de Lady M

Paris/Barcelona/Catalonia; 1992. Following a passionate and unconventional affair with a Spanish painter, the actress Myriam Mezières set about recording the event in a screenplay. Teaming up with Alain Tanner – who directed her in the 1987 *A Flame in My Heart* (which she co-wrote with him) – Mezières plays herself and persuasively re-enacts many of her sexual escapades with actors. All this would have been fascinating viewing were it not for Tanner's drab, deadly photography and Mezières' penny-dreadful voice-over. The line between *cinéma vérité* and amateur dramatics can be perilously thin. A Swiss-Belgian-Spanish-French co-production. [JC-W]

Cast: Myriam Mezières (Lady M), Juanjo Puigcorbe (Diego), Felicité Wouassi (Nuria), Nanou, Marie Peyrucq-Yamou, Gladys Gambie.

Dir: Alain Tanner. Pro: Tanner, Jacques De Clercq, Dimitri De Clercq, Gerardo Herrero, Marta Esteban and Christophe Rossignon. Ex Pro: Gerard Ruey. Screenplay: Myriam Mezières. Ph: Denis Jutzeler. Ed: Monica Goux. M: Arie Dzierlatka. (Filmograph/Nomad Film/Messidor Films/Lanzennec/Cab Prods–Mainline.) Rel: 8 April 1994. 113 mins. Cert 18.

## Dirty Weekend

What better way for Michael Winner to head off his critics than to make a vigilante movie from a *feminist* viewpoint? Furthermore, he got writer Helen Zahavi to adapt her own acclaimed novel in which put-upon Bella (Lia Williams) tops any man who's beastly to her. Unfortunately, Winner's heavy-handed direction throttles the life out of the drama, which ends up as flat and lifeless as a bad 1960s training film. This rather distasteful *Dirty Weekend* is less a romantic affair with roses and champagne at Brighton's Metropole Hotel, than a seedy fling consummated in a run-down bed and breakfast. [SR]

Cast: Lia Williams (Bella), David McCallum (Reggie), Rufus Sewell (Tim), Sylvia Syms (Mrs Crosby), Ian Richardson (Nimrod), Matthew Marsh (Bascombe), Christopher Ryan, Sean Pertwee, Jack Galloway, Mark Burns, Matthew Long, Neil Norman.

Dir: Michael Winner. Pro: Winner and Robert Earl. Ex Pro: Jim Beach. Screenplay: Winner and Helen Zahavi. Ph: Alan Jones. Ed: Arnold Crust (Winner). Pro Des: Crispian Sallis. M: David Fanshawe. Sound: Roy Baker and Bill Trent. (Scimitar Films–UIP.) Rel: 29 October 1993. 102 mins. Cert 18.

## Dragon: The Bruce Lee Story

And a fascinating story it is, too. Although born in San Francisco, Lee Yuen Kam was raised in Hong Kong but dreamed of an America that, for him, meant 'James Dean, French fries and "the sky's the limit".' However, America mistreated Lee and provided him with nothing – apart from his wife, Linda. It is the latter's book, *Bruce Lee: The Man Only I Knew*, that provides the foundation of this biography, a surprisingly old-fashioned love story at heart. In fact, Lee's reign as martial arts superstar is only sketchily filled in, while the kung fu fighting itself is cornily choreographed and undermined by naff sound effects. The film is further sabotaged by some irritating fantasy sequences in which Lee fights his personal demons (personified by a giant samurai knight). However, Jason Scott Lee (no relation) is suitably charismatic in the title role and displays an appropriately muscular physique for the part. [JC-W]

Cast: Jason Scott Lee ('Bruce' Lee Yuen Kam), Lauren Holly (Linda Lee), Robert Wagner (Bill Krieger), Michael Learned (Vivian Emery), Nancy Kwan (Gussie Yang), Ric Young (Bruce's father), Sterling Macer (Jerome Sprout), Iain M. Parker (Brandon Lee), Forry Smith (Van Williams, star of *Green Hornet*), Ed Parker

Jr (Ed Parker), Kay Tong Lim, Luoyong Wang, Sven-Ole Thorsen, John Cheung, Ong Soo Han, Clyde Kusatsu, Kong Kwok Keung, Johnny Cheung, Van Williams, Shannon Lee (Bruce's daughter), Louis Turenne, Paul Mantee, Rob Cohen.

Dir: Rob Cohen. Pro: Raffaella De Laurentiis. Ex Pro: Dan York. Screenplay: Edward Khmara, John Raffo and Cohen. Ph: David Eggby. Ed: Peter Amundson. Pro Des: Robert Ziembicki. M: Randy Edelman. Costumes: Carol Ramsey. Fight Choreography: John Cheung. Sound: John Nutt. (Universal–UIP.) Rel: 22 October 1993. 119 mins. Cert 15.

## El Mariachi

See *Mariachi, El.*

## Equinox

Two men, physically identical but poles apart emotionally, strive to improve their lot in an unnamed American city. Henry Petosa, a timid garage mechanic, despairs that 'my whole life seems to be taking place without me in it'. Freddy Ace, a chauffeur for the Mob, is getting ideas above his station and isn't afraid to carry them out. The two men's lives are inextricably drawn together as their respective personalities strengthen. That, at least, is just one interpretation of this multi-textured, complex, funny and fascinating piece of cinema. Alan Rudolph, a man who obviously enjoys the labyrinthine potential of his medium, spins the strands of his narrative with the skill of a magician, conjuring up an array of vivid performances and startling moments. Interestingly, for a film dealing primarily with duality, *Equinox* was filmed in the twin cities of Minneapolis-St Paul. [JC-W]

Cast: Matthew Modine (Henry Petosa/Freddy Ace/Immanuel), Lara Flynn Boyle (Beverly Franks), Tyra Ferrell (Sonya Kirk), Marisa Tomei (Rosie Copa), Tate Donovan (Richie Nudd), Kevin J. O'Connor (Russell Franks), Lori Singer (Sharon Ace), Gailard Sartain (Dandridge), M. Emmet Walsh (Pete Petosa), Fred Ward (Paris), Tony Genaro (Eddie Gutierrez), Angel Aviles (Anna Gutierrez), Dirk Blocker, Pat Clemons, Debra Dusay, Les Podewell, Megan Lee Ochs, Carlos Sanz, Lenora Finley, Tom Kasat, Dana Wheeler-Nicholson, Shirley Venard, Mark Modine.

Dir and Screenplay: Alan Rudolph. Pro: David Blocker. Ex Pro: Nicolas Stiliadis, Syd Cappe and Sandy Stern. Ph: Elliot Davis. Ed: Michael Ruscio. Pro Des: Steven Legler. M: Rachmaninov; numbers performed by Roger Eno, Terje Rypdal, The Tango Project, etc. Costumes: Sharen Davis. Sound: Susumu Tokunow. (SC Entertainment International–Metro Tartan.) Rel: 9 July 1993. 103 mins. Cert 15.

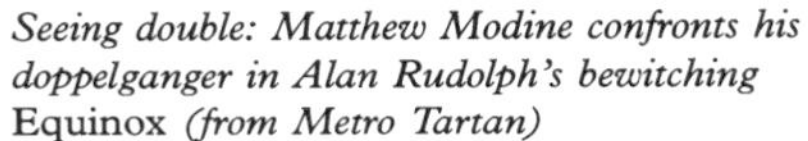

*Seeing double: Matthew Modine confronts his doppelganger in Alan Rudolph's bewitching* Equinox *(from Metro Tartan)*

## Ethan Frome

Faithful, earnest and beautifully photographed adaptation of Edith Wharton's 1911 novella, filmed in the snowy countryside of Vermont. Far from the moneyed classes of New York – as detailed in the film version of Wharton's *The Age of Innocence* – a community of hard-working people struggles to survive in the harsh climate of turn-of-the-century New England. There, a young farmer, Ethan Frome, finds himself trapped in a loveless marriage while longing for the attentions of his young housekeeper. While some might find it all a bit austere, the film does encapsulate the nuances of Wharton's story of frustrated passion with disciplined exactness. However, it is probably the visuals that one will remember. Once

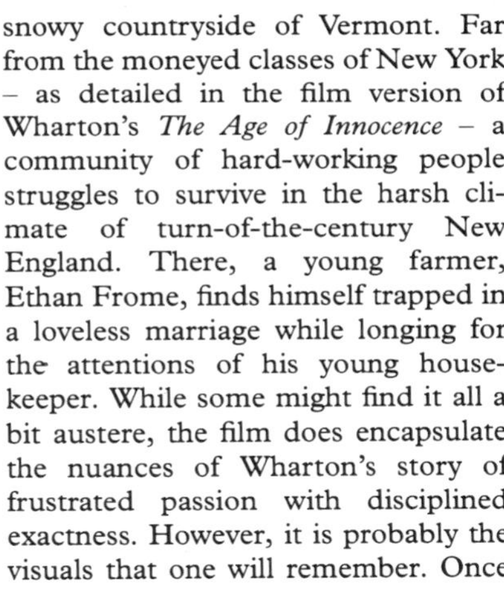

*Winter of discontent: Liam Neeson and Tate Donovan in John Madden's* Ethan Frome *(from BFI)*

*Fitting in with nature: Reese Witherspoon, Ethan Randall and Sarel Bok secure the assistance of some elephants in Mikael Salomon's captivating* A Far Off Place *(from Buena Vista)*

*Banging the gong for China: Gong Li in Chen Kaige's multi-award winning* Farewell My Concubine *(from Artificial Eye)*

planned as a vehicle for Gary Cooper and Bette Davis in the 1940s, the novel was almost filmed on two further occasions (by Warner Brothers and MGM). [JC-W]

Cast: Liam Neeson (Ethan Frome), Patricia Arquette (Mattie Silver), Joan Allen (Zeena), Tate Donovan (Reverend Smith), Katharine Houghton (Ruth Hale), Stephen Mendillo (Ned Hale), George Woodard (Jotham), Phil Garran, Virginia Smith, Annie Nessen, Debbon Ayer, Rob Campbell.

Dir: John Madden. Pro: Stan Wlodkowski. Ex Pro: Lindsay Law and Richard Price. Assoc Pro: Johlyn Dale. Screenplay: Richard Nelson. Ph: Bobby Bukowski. Ed: Katherine Wenning. Pro Des: Andrew Jackness. M: Rachel Portman. Costumes: Carol Oditz. (American Playhouse/ BBC–BFI.) Rel: 11 February 1994. 108 mins. No cert.

## A Far Off Place

When two American teenagers find themselves hunted by poachers, they flee into the Kalahari Desert with the help of a young Bushman and discover a new affinity with the mysterious powers of nature. Adapted from the novels *A Story Like the Wind* and *A Far Off Place* by Laurens van der Post, this is more than just an exciting and heart-warming children's adventure. By updating the stories to contemporary Africa and by swapping the mercenary bad guys for poachers, the film brings a new urgency and depth to its message of a disappearing world. As Robert Burke says, Africa is 'the only country left with a soul'. The film is also blessed with a luminary performance from Reese Witherspoon (*The Man in the Moon*, *Jack the Bear*) as the spunky heroine, as well as by some devastatingly beautiful landscapes, a great soundtrack and superlative widescreen cinematography. Filmed in Zimbabwe and Namibia. [JC-W]

Cast: Reese Witherspoon (Nonnie Parker), Ethan Randall (Harry Winslow), Jack Thompson (John Ricketts), Maximilian Schell (Col Mopani Theron), Sarel Bok (Xhabbo), Robert Burke (Paul Parker), Patricia Kalember, Daniel Gerroll, Miles Anderson, Fidelis Cheza, Kessia Randall.

Dir: Mikael Salomon. Pro: Eva Monley and Elaine Sperber. Ex Pro: Kathleen Kennedy, Frank Marshall and Gerald R. Molen. Screenplay: Robert Caswell, Jonathan Hensleigh and Sally Robinson. Ph: Juan Ruiz-Anchia. Ed: Ray Lovejoy. Pro Des: Gemma Jackson. M: James Horner. Costumes: Rosemary Burrows. Sound: Colin Charles. (Walt Disney/Amblin–Buena Vista.) Rel: 13 August 1993. 116 mins. Cert PG.

### Farewell My Concubine – Ba Wang Bie Ji

1925–77; China. Episodic, hugely symbolic and visually striking epic about two opera singers and a woman whose interchanging relationship reflects the political turmoil in China over fifty years. Cast for life in the parts to which they are most suited, two students of the Peking Opera take on the role of the king and his concubine in the tragic, popular piece of the title, and to which Douzi, as the concubine, identifies to the point of political myopia. A brave, complex work, *Concubine* won the Palme d'Or at the 1993 Cannes Festival and was subsequently banned in its native country. A must for all lovers of the Peking Opera, although others might find it rather heavy going. [JC-W]

Cast: Leslie Cheung (Douzi/Cheng Dieyi), Zhang Fengyi (Shitou/Duan Xiaolou), Gong Li (Juxian), Lu Qi (Master Guan Jifa), Ge You (Master Yuan), Lei Han (Xiao Si as an adult), Ying Da, Tong Di, Yin Zhi, Zhao Hailong, Li Dan, Jiang Wenli, Zhi Yitong.

Dir: Chen Kaige. Pro: Hsu Feng. Ex Pro: Hsu Bin and Jade Hsu. Screenplay: Lilian Lee and Lu Wei; from the novel by Lee. Ph: Gu Changwei. Ed: Pei Xiaonan. Art: Chen Huaikai. M: Zhao Jiping. Costumes: Chen Changmin. Sound: Tao Jing. (Tomson (HK) Films/China Film Co-Pro. Corp./Beijing Film Studio–Artificial Eye.) Rel: 7 January 1994. 156 mins. Cert 15.

*Building bridges in the air: Jeff Bridges as Max Klein in Peter Weir's intelligent drama* Fearless *(from Warner)*

### Fausto

Fausto Barbarico is a 17-year-old orphan in 1960s Paris. After being expelled from one institution for convincing fellow inmates that he'd poisoned them, Fausto settles down at a new orphanage where he befriends Raymond, an overweight hedonist who can fart in tune. With the help of the latter, Fausto builds up his self-confidence and as an apprentice to the dour gentleman tailor Mietek Breslaur begins a promising career as fashion designer. While capturing the joy of *Cinema Paradiso* and matching it with the sensual ambience of *The Hairdresser's Husband*, this romantic fantasy is a delight from start to finish. From Jean Yanne's priceless performance as the gruff tailor, to the uplifting score, the film is a genuine tonic. First-time director Rémy Duchemin has a lot to live up to. [JC-W]

*Designing magic: Florence Darel and Ken Higelin in Remy Duchemin's enchanting* Fausto *(from Mayfair Entertainment)*

Cast: Jean Yanne (Mietek Breslaur), Ken Higelin (Fausto Barbarico), Francois Hautesserre (Raymond), Florence Darel (Tonie Rosengarten), Maurice Bénichou (Lucien), Arthur H (Max the Cat), Bruce Myers, Marianne Groves, Maité Nahyr, François Chattot.

Dir: Rémy Duchemin. Pro: Joël Foulon and Daniel Daujon. Screenplay: Duchemin and Richard Morgiève; based on the novel by Morgiève. Ph: Yves Fafaye. Ed: Maryline Monthieux. Pro Des: Fouillet et Wieber. M: Denis Barbier. Costumes: Philippe Guillotel and Annie Périer. (Lili Prods/BBD Prods/France 2 Cinema/Canal Plus–Mayfair Entertainment.) Rel: 10 June 1994. 81 mins. Cert 15.

### Fearless

San Francisco; 1993. A man who's afraid of flying is one of a handful of survivors of a massive aeroplane crash. Transformed, Max Klein now believes he is invulnerable and becomes progressively alienated from his family. In

*Sword dance: Omero Antonutti and Assumpta Serna in Pedro Olea's* The Fencing Master *(from Mayfair Entertainment)*

turn, he is increasingly drawn to a young boy and a woman, two other survivors of the crash. They have their own ghosts to live with, but Max Klein is becoming a breed apart. No longer afraid of dying, he is living a life of his own . . . Director Peter Weir, returning to his theme of ordinary people remoulded by extraordinary circumstances, has created another powerful, thought-provoking work, magnificently realised. His use of sound (and sometimes lack of it) as a dramatic device is particularly effective. [JC-W]

Cast: Jeff Bridges (Max Klein), Isabella Rossellini (Laura Klein), Rosie Perez (Carla Rodrigo), Tom Hulce (Brillstein), John Turturro (Dr Bill Perlman), Benicio Del Toro (Manny Rodrigo), Deirdre O'Connell (Nan Gordon), John De Lancie (Jeff Gordon), Spencer Vrooman (Jonah Klein), Daniel Cerny (Byron Hummel). Eve Roberts, Robin Pearson Rose, Debra Monk, Cynthia Mace, Randle Mell, Craig Rovere, Doug Ballard, Molly Cleator, Rance Howard, Sally Murphy, Stephanie Erb, Elsa Raven.

Dir: Peter Weir. Pro: Paula Weinstein and Mark Rosenberg. Co-Pro: Robin Forman and William Beasley. Ph: Allen Daviau. Ed: William Anderson. Pro Des: John Stoddart. M: Maurice Jarre; Górecki, Maraire, Beethoven; numbers performed by U2 and Gipsy Kings. Costumes: Marilyn Matthews. Sound: Lee Smith. (Spring Creek–Warner.) Rel: 15 April 1994. 122 mins. Cert 15.

*French leave: Béatrice Dalle takes control of her life in Maroun Bagdadi's exciting* La Fille de l'Air *(from Metro Tartan)*

## The Fencing Master – El Maestro de Esgrima

Don Jamie De Astarloa, Madrid's undisputed fencing maestro, steers clear of sex and politics at a time (1868) when Queen Isabel II flaunts her promiscuity and faces dethronement at the hands of the republican hardliners. Don Jaime's sole love and consuming interest is fencing, a combat which he considers a sacred art. He then meets the beautiful Adela de Otoro, a nobleman who is as skilled with a foil as she is with the craft of seduction . . . A handsomely mounted tale of intrigue, passion and treachery, *The Fencing Master* basks in the poetry of fencing and the sport's innate *double entendres* (the feint, the parry, the thrust), but degenerates into melodrama in its final act. [JC-W]

Cast: Omero Antonutti (Don Jaime De Astarloa), Assumpta Serna (Adela de Otoro), Joaquim De Almeida (Luis De Ayala), Jose Luis Lopez Vazquez (Campillo), Miguel Rellan (Argapito Carceles), Alberto Closas, Elisa Matilla, Ramon Goyanes.

Dir: Pedro Olea. Pro: Antonio Cardenal. Screenplay: Olea, Obdulia Beringola, Francisco Prada and Arturo Perez Reverte; based on the novel by Reverte. Ph: Alfredo Mayo. Ed: Jose Salcedo. Art: Luis Valles, M: Jose Nieto. Costumes: Javier Artinano. Sound: Eduardo Fernandez. (Origen/Altube/ICAA–Mayfair Entertainment.) Rel: 2 July 1993. 88 mins. Cert 12.

## La Fille de l'Air

When the father of her unborn child was arrested and condemned to 36 years in prison for armed robbery, Nadine Vaujour could not see beyond the injustice of his sentence. Child-killers, she argued, got less than that. But because Michel Vaujour committed his crimes on the run, his prison terms had to be served consecutively. Such was the law in France. So, after years of scrimping and saving, waiting, planning and investing all her spare money in learning to fly a helicopter, on 26 May 1986 Nadine Vaujour rescued her husband from the Santé prison in Paris and seized the imagination of the tabloids. This is her story, a slick, lean and highly dramatic retelling of a recent (and true) event in French history. By capturing the humanity of his protagonists, director Maroun Bagdadi (*Hors la Vie*) stacks the sympathy heavily in favour of the criminals while making a laughing stock of France's penal system. It's a fascinating tale, and extremely well told at that. N.B. Nadine Vaujour gave birth to both Michel's children behind bars. [JC-W]

Cast: Béatrice Dalle (Brigitte Roubiot, based on Nadine Vaujour), Thierry Fortineau (Daniel Loic Barnier, based on Michel Vaujour), Hippolyte Girardot (Phillipe Roubiot, based on Nadine's brother Gille), Roland Bertin (M Lefort), Jean-Claude Dreyfus (Marcel), Jean-Paul Roussillon (Raymond), Catherine Jacob (Rose), Liliane Rovere (mother), Arnaud Chevrier (Micky), Louise-Laure Mariani, Elisabeth Macocco, Isabelle Candelier.

Dir: Maroun Bagdadi. Line Pro: Faroud Chaouche. Ex Pro: Jean-Claude Fleury. Screenplay: Bagdadi and Florence Quentin; 'inspired' by Nadine Vaujour's book. Ph: Thierry Arbogast. Ed: Luc Bernier. Art: Michel Vandestien. M: Gabriel Yared; numbers performed by Toto Cotugno, Roxy Music, and Culture Club. Costumes: Cecile Balme. Sound: Jean-Pierre Duret and Stéphanie Granel. (CIBY 2000/TFI Films/Canal Plus–Metro Tartan.) Rel: 5 November 1993. 106 mins. Cert 15.

## The Firm

Mitch McDeere is a bright, ambitious Harvard law student from a poor family. When an exclusive tax firm in Memphis (Bendini, Lambert & Locke) offers him 20 per cent more than his previous highest offer – and throws in a Mercedes and mortgage *and* pays off his student loans – Mitch is hitched. But his wife, Abby, is not so enamoured. She is told that the firm doesn't 'forbid' wives to work and that offspring are 'encouraged'. What does the firm think it is, anyway? Mitch is about to find out – and it could cost him his life. Based on the mega-bestseller by John Grisham (paperback sales: 7 million), this is a slick, competent version of the book, with a few surprises of its own. The giddy attraction of obscene wealth and power still packs a wallop, although the one-dimensional characters are left wilting in the slipstream. [JC-W]

Cast: Tom Cruise (Mitchell Y. McDeere), Jeanne Tripplehorn (Abby McDeere),

*Beyond the bar exam: Tom Cruise as ambitious law student Mitchell Y. McDeere in Sydney Pollack's savvy* The Firm *(from UIP)*

Gene Hackman (Avery Tolar), Ed Harris (Wayne Tarrance), Holly Hunter (Tammy Hemphill), Hal Holbrook (Oliver Lambert), David Strathairn (Ray McDeere), Terry Kinney (Lamar Quinn), Wilford Brimley (William Devasher), Gary Busey (Eddie Lomax), Steven Hill (F. Denton Voyles), Barbara Garrick (Kay Quinn), Jerry Weintrub (Sonny Capps), Paul Sorvino (Mr Morolto), Tobin Bell, Jerry Hardin, Paul Calderon, Sullivan Walker, Karina Lombard, Margo Martindale, John Beal, Tommy Cresswell, David Kimball, Mark Johnson, Jonathan Kaplan, Terri Welles.

Dir: Sydney Pollack. Pro: Pollack, Scott Rudin and John Davis. Ex Pro: Michael Hausman and Lindsay Doran. Screenplay: David Rabe, Robert Towne and David Rayfiel. Ph: John Seale. Ed: William Steinkamp and Fredric Steinkamp. Pro Des: Richard MacDonald. M: Dave Grusin; numbers performed by Robben Ford and The Blue Line, Charlie Rich, T-Bone Walker, Lyle Lovett, Ollie Nightingale, Jimmy Buffett, Nanci Griffith, etc. Costumes: Ruth Myers. Sound: David MacMillan. (Mirage/Paramount–UIP.) Rel: 10 September 1993. 155 mins. Cert 15.

## Fixing the Shadow

Although inspired by the true story of an undercover sheriff responsible for 200 arrests, *Fixing the Shadow* plays like a sex/drugs/rock 'n' roll programmer. Having said that, its exposé of biker gangs and their lifestyle should prove irresistible to Hell's Angels fantasists. Charlie Sheen adopts a beard (and frequently sheds his shirt) as the real-life Dan Saxon, who joins the leather and chrome set to uncover a gun-running ring. Trouble is, as a kid Dan was abused by his uncle – a cop – and, in the words of girfriend Linda Fiorentino, he is unable 'to tell the knife from the wound'. Michael Madsen, as the meanest mother on a Harley, rides away with the film. [JC-W]

Cast: Charlie Sheen (Dan 'Sid' Saxon), Linda Fiorentino (Renee), Michael Madsen (Blood), Courtney B. Vance (Conroy Price), Leon Rippy (Virgil 'Dildo'), Dennis Burkley (Oatmeal), Rip Torn (Prescott), Larry Ferguson (Kelly, Chief of Police), Lyndsay Riddell, Rino Thunder, Holly Chamberlain, Richard Madsen, John Schwer, Dan Saxon.

Dir and Screenplay: Larry Ferguson. Pro: John Fielder and Mark Tarlov. Ex Pro: Ronna B. Wallace and Richard N. Gladstein. Co-Ex Pro: Joe Caracciolo, Jr. Ph: Robert Stevens. Ed: Robert C. Jones and Don Brochu. Pro Des: James L. Schoppe. M: Cory Lerios and John D'Andrea; numbers performed by Chris Rea, Cory Lerios, Juice Newton & Silver Spur, Diamondback, Asphalt Ballet, Robbie Robertson, etc. Costumes: Ileane Meltzer. Sound:

*Near miss: Kristin Scott Thomas and Hugh Grant in Mike Newell's hilarious* Four Weddings & a Funeral *(from Rank)*

John Nutt. (Polar Entertainment/Capitol Films–Columbia TriStar.) Rel: 10 June 1994. 101 mins. Cert 18.

### Flight of the Innocent – La Corsa dell' Innocent

On second thoughts it's easy to see why Hollywood embraced Carlo Carlei, the 31-year-old Italian director, on the strength of this, his first film. The saga of a photogenic 10-year-old Calabrian boy running for his life after his family is massacred, the film is stunning to look at but snowballs into melodrama after a promising start. Carlei has a good eye, but he's also obviously spent too much time watching over-directed movies by Sam Peckinpah and Martin Scorsese. Very bloody, very OTT. Next, Carlei directed the thriller *Fluke* for MGM. [CB]

Cast: Manuel Colao (Vito), Francesca Neri (Marta Rienzi), Jacques Perrin (Davide Rienzi), Federico Pacifici (Scarface), Sal Borgese (Vito's father), Lucio Zagaria (Orlando), Giusi Cataldo (Giovanna), Massimo Lodolo (Rocco), Anita Zagaria (Vito's mother).

Dir: Carlo Cerlei. Pro: Franco Cristaldi and Domenico Procacci. Ex Pro: Massimo Cristaldi and Bruno Ricci. Screenplay: Carlei and Gualtiero Rosella. Ph: Raffaele Mertes. Ed: Carlo Fontana and Claudio Di Mauro. Pro Des: Franco Ceraolo. M: Carlo Siliotto. Costumes: Mariolina Bono. (Rocket Pictures/Raitre/Fildebroc–Buena Vista.) Rel: 18 February 1994. 105 mins. Cert 18.

### For Love or Money

See *The Concierge*.

### Four Weddings and a Funeral

London/the Home Counties/Scotland; the 1990s. A group of firm friends find that their lives seem to revolve around other people's weddings. Very silly at times, and the odd joke is pushed way too far, but so much *is* genuinely funny that to nitpick would be churlish. Hugh Grant, as the flustered, bespectacled perennial bachelor, is a comic revelation. And the final gag at the expense of Kristin Scott Thomas (or rather her sister, Serena – remember her 'starring' role in *Diana – The True Story*?) is a scream. The first British film to reach No. 1 at the US box office since *A Fish Called Wanda*. [JC-W]

Cast: Hugh Grant (Charles), Andie MacDowell (Carrie), Kristin Scott Thomas (Fiona), Simon Callow (Gareth), James Fleet (Tom), John Hannah (Matthew), Charlotte Coleman (Scarlett), David Bower (David), Corin Redgrave (Hamish), Rowan Atkinson (Father Gerald), Anna Chancellor (Henrietta), Timothy Walker, Sara Crowe, Ronald Herdman, Elspet Gray, Philip Voss, Rupert Vansittart, Nicola Walker, Paul Stacey, Simon Kunz, Robin McCaffrey, Michael Mears, Kenneth Griffiths, David Haigh, Sophie Thompson, Donald Weedon, Nigel Hastings, Emily Morgan, Amanda Mealing, Melissa Knatchbull, Polly Kemp, Hannah Taylor Gordon, Bernice Stegers, Robert Lang, Jeremy Kemp, Rosalie Crutchley, Ken Drury, Struan Rodger, Lucy Hornack, Pat Starr, Richard Butler.

Dir: Mike Newell. Pro: Duncan Kenworthy. Ex Pro: Tim Bevan and Eric Fellner. Screenplay and Co-Ex Pro: Richard Curtis. Ph: Michael Coulter. Ed: Jon Gregory. Pro Des: Maggie Gray. M: Richard Rodney

Bennett; numbers performed by Wet Wet Wet, Elton John, Barry White, Nu Colours, Gloria Gaynor, Swing Out Sister, 1 To 1, Gladys Knight and The Pips, Squeeze, Lena Fiagbe, and Sting. Costumes: Lindy Hemming. (PolyGram/Channel Four/ Working Title–Rank.) Rel: 13 May 1994. 117 mins. Cert 15.

*A boy and his cetacean: Jason James Richter and Keiko in Simon Wincer's enthralling* Free Willy *(from Warner)*

### Free Willy

Portland, Oregon; 1993. With a boy in care, a whale in captivity and a title song by Michael Jackson, you have the potential for something pretty icky. However, *Free Willy* is so well directed, acted, photographed and scored that the tears flow without guilt. Newcomer Jason James Richter overcomes his predictable photogenia with conviction as the 12-year-old who never had anybody to love, while Keiko as Willy, the three-and-a-half-ton, 22-foot-long orca killer whale, never puts a foot wrong. The story may be a tad weak, but the emotional impact is no less for that. [JC-W]

Cast: Jason James Richter (Jesse), Lori Petty (Rae), Jayne Atkinson (Annie), August Schellenberg (Randolph), Michael Madsen (Glen), Michael Ironside (Dial), Richard Riehle (Wade), Mykelti Williamson (Dwight), Michael Bacall (Perry), Danielle Harris, Isaiah Malone.

Dir: Simon Wincer. Pro: Jennie Lew Tugend and Lauren Shuler-Donner. Ex Pro: Richard Donner and Arnon Milchan. Co-Pro: Penelope L. Foster, Richard Solomon and Jim Van Wyck. Screenplay: Keith A. Walker and Corey Blechman. Ph: Robbie Greenberg. Ed: Nicholas Brown. Pro Des: Charles Rosen. M: Basil Poledouris; 'Will You Be There' performed by Michael Jackson. Costumes: April Ferry. Sound: Tim Chau. (Le Studio Canal Plus/ Regency Enterprises/Alcor Films–Warner.) Rel: 11 February 1994. 112 mins. Cert U.

### Friends

Sophie Gordon, a white librarian from a privileged family, doubles as a terrorist for the African National Congress. Thoko, a black teacher, abhors violence and strives to live a balanced life amongst whites and blacks. Aninka, a working-class Afrikaans archaeologist, disapproves of apartheid but is unable to express her feelings. As different from each other as they could be, Sophie, Thoko and Aninka befriended each other at university and now share a suburban house in Johannesburg as the racist violence of the late 1980s erupts around them. A self-acknowledged examination of the friendship of three women, *Friends* fails to summon a sense of camaraderie or even to convey why such disparate characters should be soul mates. Nevertheless, Kerry Fox (*An Angel at My Table*) is terrific as Sophie and the myriad Johannesburg locations are atmospherically captured. [JC-W]

*Humanity vs. politics: Michele Burgers, Dambisa Kente and Kerry Fox struggle to hold on to their friendship in turbulent times – in Elaine Proctor's* Friends *(from Metro Tartan)*

*The Running Man: Harrison Ford as Richard Kimble in Andrew Davis's breathless* The Fugitive *(from Warner)*

Cast: Kerry Fox (Sophie Elizabeth Gordon née Cummings), Dambissa Kente (Thoko), Michele Burgers (Aninka), Marius Weyers (Johan), Tertius Meintjes (Jeremy), Dolly Rathebe (Innocentia), Wilma Stockenstrom, Carel Trichardt, Anne Curteis, Ralph Draper.

Dir and Screenplay: Elaine Proctor. Pro: Judith Hunt. Ph: Dominique Chapuis. Ed: Tony Lawson. Pro Des: Carmel Collins. M: Rachel Portman. Costumes: Moira Meyer. Sound: Rodney Glenn. (Chrysalide Films/Rio/Channel Four Films/British Screen/Canal Plus–Metro Tartan.) Rel: 14 January 1994. 109 mins. Cert 15.

## The Fugitive

Dr Richard Kimble, an eminent vascular surgeon, has it all: a job that gives him enormous satisfaction, a comfortable house in the Chicago suburbs and a beautiful, loving wife. Then, one night, he returns home from work to find his wife dead and a one-armed intruder in his house. The intruder escapes, and Kimble – the sole beneficiary to his wife's considerable fortune – is sentenced to death by lethal injection. On his way to Death Row Kimble escapes (following a spectacularly staged bus-and-train crash), and spends the rest of the movie trying to find his wife's killer. He's also relentlessly pursued by US Marshal Samuel Gerard who's obsessed with catching his man – innocent or not. Based on the cult 1963–7 TV series which starred David Janssen, this is a pulse-accelerating thriller that manages to flesh out its characters while never losing a moment's momentum. Harrison Ford seems born to play the role of the doctor who uses brain instead of brawn to stay alive, while Tommy Lee Jones steals the show as his merciless adversary. A real seat-gripper, superbly oiled by action director Andrew Davis (*The Package, Under Fire*). [JC-W]

Cast: Harrison Ford (Dr Richard Kimble), Tommy Lee Jones (Samuel Gerard), Sela Ward (Helen Kimble), Julianne Moore (Dr Anne Eastman), Joe Pantoliano (Cosmo Renfro), Andreas Katsulas (Sykes), Jeroen Krabbe (Dr Charles Nichols), Daniel Roebuck (Biggs), Tom Wood (Newman), Ron Dean (Det. Kelly), Jane Lynch (Dr Kathy Wahlund), L. Scott Caldwell, Joseph Kosala, Joseph Guzaldo, Dick Cusack, Andy Romano, Richard Riehle, Eddie 'Bo' Smith Jr, Danny Goldring, Nick Searcy, Bill Cusack, Lillie Richardson, Monika Chabrowski, Lonnie Sima.

Dir: Andrew Davis. Pro: Arnold Kopelson. Ex Pro: Keith Barish and Roy Huggins. Co-Pro: Peter MacGregor-Scott. Screenplay: Jeb Stuart and David Twohy; based on characters created by Huggins. Ph: Michael Chapman. Ed: Dennis Virkler and David Finfer. Pro Des: Dennis Washington. M: James Newton Howard; numbers performed by B. B. King and Bobby Bland, Voyage, and Wayne Shorter. Costumes: Aggie Guerard Rodgers. Sound: Scott D. Smith. (Warner.) Rel: 24 September 1993. 140 mins. Cert 12.

## Germinal

The 1870s; Northern France. When Etienne Lantier, an unemployed mechanic (the satirical singer Renaud in his film debut), finds work in the Montsou coal mine, he is appalled by the working conditions. His colleagues have barely enough to eat, are forced to timber their own mine shafts (at their expense) and live in constant danger of losing their lives. Although a newcomer to the terrible poverty and injustice of Montsou, Lantier sets about changing the miners' lives for ever – but for better or worse? The most expensive French film ever made (at a cost of 172 million francs), *Germinal* is a striking, earnest and detailed realisation of Emile Zola's acclaimed 1885 novel. It is, however, unrelenting in its grimness, and although Gérard

Depardieu is as persuasive as ever, he really is too fat to play a starving miner. Photography, music and production design are all top notch. [JC-W]

Cast: Miou-Miou (Maheude), Renaud (Etienne Lantier), Gérard Depardieu (Maheu), Jean Carmet (Bonnemort), Judith Henry (Cathérine Maheu), Jean-Roger Milo (Chaval), Gerard Croce (Paul Negrel), Thierry Levaret (Zacharie Maheu), Albano Guaetta (Jeanlin Maheu), Celine Bois (Cécile Grégoire), Laurent Terzieff, Jean-Pierre Bisson, Bernard Fresson, Jacques Dacqmine, Anny Duperey, Pierre Lafont, Annik Alane, Frédéric Van Den Driessche.

Dir and Pro: Claude Berri. Ex Pro: Pierre Grunstein. Screenplay: Berri and Arlette Langmann. Ph: Yves Angelo. Ed: Hervé De Luze. Pro Des: Thanh At Hoang and Christian Marti. M: Jean-Louis Roques. Costumes: Sylvie Gautrelet, Caroline De Vivaise and Bernadette Villard. Sound: Michel Klochendler. (Renn Productions/France 2 Cinema/Alternative Films/Canal Plus–Guild.) Rel: 6 May 1994. 158 mins. Cert 15.

*Heavy duty: Miou-Miou (holding Judith Henry) curses the upper classes in Claude Berri's costly* Germinal *(from Guild)*

## Golden Balls – Huevos de Oro

Africa/Spain/Miami; today. Raunchy, picturesque tale of greed, ants, breasts and erections – from the director of *Jamon Jamon*. Benito Gonzalez dreams of erecting the tallest skyscraper in Benidorm and of marrying the girl of his dreams. However, his obsession proves to be his undoing as compromise and lust collide on his ruthless climb to the top. No amount of heavy panting, bouncing breasts or cheap symbolism can make up for such an unpleasant protagonist or the lack of a decent storyline. Still, the film is an excellent showcase for some fine Spanish actresses, none of whom have any problem in revealing their assets. P.S. *Golden Balls* must be the first film in which the closing credits reveal the weight of the cast! [JC-W]

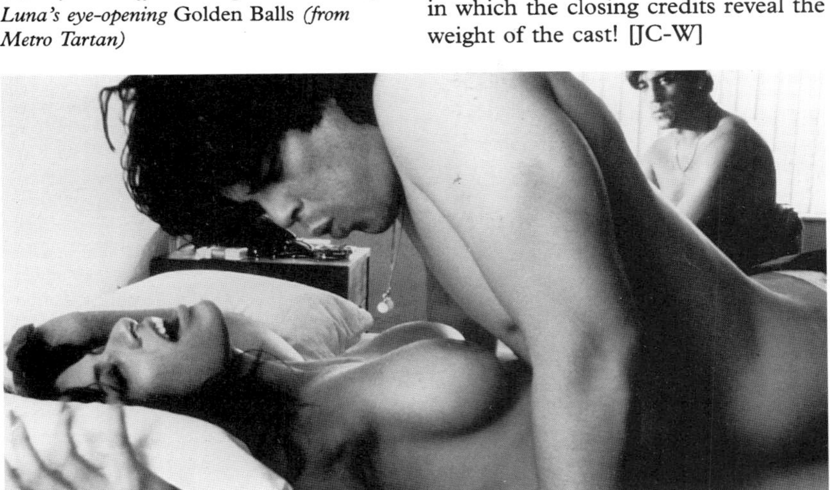

*Lust in the translation? Javier Bardem* (far right) *looks on as his girlfriend (Rachel Bianca) has it off with the gardener – in Bigas Luna's eye-opening* Golden Balls *(from Metro Tartan)*

Cast: Javier Bardem (Benito Gonzalez), Elisa Touati (Rita), Maria de Medeiros (Marta), Maribel Verdú (Claudia), Rachel Bianca (Ana), Alessandro Gassman (Miguel), Francesco M. Dominedo, Albert Vidal, Ángel de Andrés López, Benico del Toro.

Dir: Bigas Luna. Ex Pro: Andres Vicente Gómez. Screenplay: Luna and Cuca Canals. Ph: José Luis Alcaine. Ed: Carmen Frias. Art: Antxon Gómez. M: Nicola Piovanni; 'Por el amor de una mujer' performed by Julio Iglesias. Costumes: Neus Olivella. (Lolafilms/Ovideo TV–Metro Tartan.) Rel: 24 June 1994. 95 mins. Cert 18.

## Grief

Los Angeles; 1993. It is all too easy to treat the subject of AIDS with a respect and gravity that obscures its human context. Here, first-time writer-director Richard Glatzer addresses the bereavement of Mark, a gay story editor, in a comedy that never loses sight of its humanity. And, whenever things look like they may get too morose, Glatzer injects scenes from an outrageous TV soap opera that Mark and his colleagues are

*Couch potatoes: Alexis Arquette and Carlton Wilborn in Richard Glatzer's gently satirical* Grief *(from ICA Projects)*

*Dirty old men: Jack Lemmon and Walter Matthau vie for the attentions of Ann-Margret in Donald Petrie's witless comedy,* Grumpy Old Men *(from Warner)*

working on (involving anything and everything from leprosy to 'circus lesbians'). While sending up TV with some wit (Glatzer actually worked on *Divorce Court*), the film never loses touch with reality, even though one character notes: 'There are a million ways to tell a story – and realism is the dullest.' *Grief*, thankfully, is anything but. [JC-W]

Cast: Craig Chester (Mark Levy), Jackie Beat (aka Kent Fuher) (Jo/Harvey), Illeana Douglas (Leslie), Alexis Arquette (Bill Blake), Carlton Wilborn (Jeremy), Lucy Gutteridge (Paula), Robin Swid (Kelly), Shawn Hoffman (Ben), Mickey Cottrell, Catherine Connella, Mary Woronov, Paul Bartel.

Dir and Screenplay: Richard Glatzer. Pro: Ruth Charny and Yoram Mandel. Ex Pro: Marcus Hu. Line Pro: Nancy Nickerson. Ph: David Dechant. Ed: Robin Katz and William W. Williams. Pro Des: Don Diers. M: Tom Judson. Costumes: Laser N. Rosenberg. Sound: Thomas Jones. (ICA Projects.) Rel: 1 April 1994. 87 mins. No cert.

## Grumpy Old Men

Minnesota; winter. Jack Lemmon, who's transformed the fusion of pathos and sentimentality into a fine art, here achieves a new glutinosity with his portrayal of a lonely, embittered widower waging war on his neighbour. Mercifully, the latter is played by none other than Walter Matthau, Lemmon's old sparring partner (this is their sixth film together), who brings some welcome cynicism to the proceedings. However, when the cantankerous old farts start vying for the romantic attentions of new neighbour Ann-Margret, the syrup builds up faster than the ubiquitous snow. [JC-W]

Cast: Jack Lemmon (John Gustafson), Walter Matthau (Max Goldman), Ann-Margret (Ariel Truax), Kevin Pollak (Jacob Goldman), Ossie Davis (Chuck), Daryl Hannah (Melanie Gustafson), Burgess Meredith (Grandpa Gustafson), Buck Henry (Elliott Snyder), Christopher McDonald (Mike), Steve Cochran (weatherman).

Dir: Donald Petrie. Pro: John Davis and Richard C. Berman. Ex Pro: Dan Kolsrud. Screenplay: Mark Steven Johnson. Ph: John E. Jensen. Ed: Bonnie Koehler. Pro Des: David Chapman. M: Alan Silvestri; numbers performed by Ella Fitzgerald, Otis Redding, Right Said Fred, The Young Rascals, Bing Crosby, Nat King Cole, The Skinny Boys, etc. Costumes: Lisa Jensen. (Lancaster Gate–Warner.) Rel: 27 May 1994. 104 mins. Cert 12.

## Guilty as Sin

Chicago; now. When brilliant attorney Jennifer Haines accepts the challenge of representing a sleazy wife-killer, she finds herself defending him to save her own life. This is actually a superb story, but is so blandly directed and so flabbily edited that the whole thing looks like a mediocre TV movie. It's hard to believe that Sidney Lumet is the director responsible. [JC-W]

Cast: Rebecca De Mornay (Jennifer Haines), Don Johnson (David Hector Greenhill), Stephen Lang (Phil Garson), Jack Warden (Moe), Dana Ivey (Judge D. Tompkins), Ron White (Diangelo), Norma Dell'Agnese (Emily), Christina Baren (Miriam Langford), Sean McCann, Luis Guzman, Robert Kennedy, James Blendick, Tom Butler, Lynne Cormack, John Kapelos, Harvey Atkin.

Dir: Sidney Lumet. Pro: Martin Ransohoff. Ex Pro: Don Carmody and Bob Robinson. Screenplay: Larry Cohen. Ph: Andrzej Bartkowiak. Ed: Evan Lottman. Pro Des: Philip Rosenberg. M: Howard Shore. Costumes: Gary Jones. Sound: Ron Bochar. (Hollywood Pictures–Buena Vista.) Rel: 12 November 1993. 107 mins. Cert 15.

*A law of averages: Rebecca De Mornay and Don Johnson in Sidney Lumet's unforgivably pedestrian* Guilty as Sin *(from Buena Vista)*

### Gunhed

Tacky slice of mega-schlock set on a Pacific island in the year 2038, where an outsize computer has declared war on humanity. A Japanese mechanic called Brooklyn and a female Texas Ranger in a rubber suit join forces to save the world. Corny, cheap and cheerful. Made in Japan in 1989. [CB]

Cast: Masahiro Takashima (Brooklyn), Brenda Bakke (Nim), Yukin Harada (Seven), Kaori Mizushima (Eleven), Aya Enjyoji, Micky Curtis, James B. Thompson.

Dir: Masato Harada. Pro: Gunhed Production Committee. Ex Pro: Tomoyuki Tanaka and Eiji Yamamura. Screenplay: Harada and James Bannon. Ed: Fumio Ogawa. M: Toshiyuki Honda. SF/X: Koichi Kawakita. (Toho Co./Sunrise–Manga Entertainments.) Rel: 18 March 1994. 101 mins. Cert 12.

*Happiness is a warm gun: Tony Leung holds his own in John Woo's dynamic display of action* – Hard Boiled *(from Metro Tartan)*

### Hard Boiled – Lashou Shentan

Although this is Chinese director John Woo's 20th film, *Hard Boiled* is the first to win an official British release – due, no doubt, to the praise and controversy heaped on his last three pictures, *The Killer, Bullet in the Head* and *Once a Thief*. This entry continues the snowballing bodycount and must be one of the bloodiest, most bullet-packed movies ever made. Woo regular Chow Yun-Fat stars as Inspector Yuen (nicknamed 'Tequila'), an aggressive, dedicated Hong Kong cop on the trail of a gang of gun-runners. Both police and villains seem to swap their dispositions as the inevitable climax approaches, but not before a string of spectacular shoot-outs have left half the population of Kowloon dead. However, even these bloody and epic distractions cannot prepare us for the showdown in a Triad-owned hospital, where Woo's knack for inventive action choreography comes into its own. While pushing his stuntmen on to ever-greater feats of balletic exertion

*Pitiless prey: Jean-Claude Van Damme calls the shots in John Woo's stylish, trashy* Hard Target *(from UIP)*

and showering his action with ballistic blood, Woo brings a brutal poetry to his carnival of carnage. [JC-W]

Cast: Chow Yun-Fat (Inspector Yuen, 'Tequila'), Tony Leung (Tony), Teresa Mo (Teresa), Philip Chan (Superintendent Chan), Anthony Wong (Johnny Wong), Kwan Hoi-Shan (Hoi), Bowie Lam (A-Lung), Philip Kwok, Bobby Au Yuen, Ng Shui-Ting, John Woo.

Dir: John Woo. Pro: Linda Kuk and Terence Chang. Assoc Pro: Amy Chin. Screenplay: Barry Wong; from a story by Woo. Ph: Wong Wing-Heng. Ed: Woo, Kai Kit-Wai and David Woo Jack. Art: James Leung and Joel Chong. M: Michael Gibbs and James Wong. Costumes: Bruce Yu and Janet Chun. Sound: Brian Schwegmann and Ching Siu-Lung. (Golden Princess/Milestone Pictures–Metro Tartan.) Rel: 8 October 1993. 126 mins. Cert 18.

## Hard Target

For action fans, the teaming of the world's fastest rising action star with the world's fastest rising action director must seem like a heady prospect. The result is a non-stop express train of noisy effects, extreme violence and contrived set-pieces that look like expensive commercials for death. Jean-Claude Van Damme plays an unemployed merchant sailor who agrees to help a young woman find her father, apparently lost in the wasteland of New Orleans's vagrant population. But it soon transpires that the missing man was an unwitting 'volunteer' in an illegal human safari, played out by the sadistic rich of Louisiana. When Van Damme becomes the next prey, the hunters realise that they have taken on more than they can handle . . . In the tradition of director John Woo's cult Hong Kong thrillers, *Hard Target* offers undiluted exploitation, like a state-of-the-art video game. Inspired by the 1932 film *The Most Dangerous Game*. [JC-W]

Cast: Jean-Claude Van Damme (Chance Boudreaux), Lance Henriksen (Emil Fouchon), Yancy Butler (Natasha Binder), Arnold Vosloo (Pik Van Cleaf), Kasi Lemmons (Carmine Mitchell), Wilford Brimley (Uncle Douvee), Chuck Pfarrer (Douglas Binder), Willie Carpenter (Elijah Roper), Eliott Keener (Randal Poe), Marco St John, Ted Raimi, Sven Thorsen.

Dir: John Woo. Pro: James Jacks and Sean Daniel. Ex Pro: Moshe Diamant, Sam Raimi and Robert Tapert. Screenplay and Co-Pro: Chuck Pfarrer. Ph: Russell Carpenter. Ed: Bob Murawski. Pro Des: Phil Dagort. M: Graeme Revell, Kodo and Beethoven; numbers performed by Buckwheat Zydeco and Creedence Clearwater Revival. Costumes: Karyn Wagner. Sound: John Dunn and George Simpson. (Universal/Alphaville/Renaissance–UIP.) Rel: 26 November 1993. 95 mins. Cert 18.

## The Hawk

Kept on a tight leash by the demands of raising a family, housewife Annie Marsh is led to believe she has a happy marriage. Then one day she starts piecing together fragments of a puzzle too horrific to contemplate. Is the man she lives with a serial killer? Based on the novel by Peter Ransley, itself inspired by the case of the Black Panther – the Yorkshireman who, unbeknownst to his wife, kept a woman down a mineshaft – *The Hawk* is never sure what it wants to be. At times the film verges on becoming an interesting character study of domestic blindness and then veers into cheap thriller territory, complete with gratuitous, misleading close-ups and melodramatic thunderclaps on the soundtrack. Ultimately, David Hayman's gimmicky direction distances us from his characters, rendering this potentially fascinating film impotent. [JC-W]

Cast: Helen Mirren (Annie Marsh), George Costigan (Stephen Marsh), Rosemary Leach (Mrs Marsh), Owen Teale (Ken Marsh), Melanie Hill (Norma), Clive Russell (Chief Inspector Daybury), Marie Hamer (Jackie Marsh), Christopher Madin (Matthew Marsh), Daryl Webster, David Harewood, Pooky Quesnel, Helen Ryan, John Duttine, Caroline Paterson, Jayne MacKenzie, Nadim Sawalha.

Dir: David Hayman. Pro: Ann Wingate and Eileen Quinn. Ex Pro: Mark Shivas, Eric Fellner, Larry Kirstein and Kent Walwin. Screenplay: Peter Ransley; from his own novel. Ph: Andrew Dunn. Ed: Justin Krish. Pro Des: David Myerscough-Jones. M: Nick Bicat. Costumes: Pam Tait. Sound: Kant Pan and Ian Fuller. (BBC/Initial/Screen Partners–Feature Film Company.) Rel: 3 December 1993. 88 mins. Cert 15.

*Helen Mirren points out her intentions to brother-in-law Owen Teale in David Hayman's tricksy thriller* The Hawk *(from The Feature Film Company)*

## Hear No Evil

Following the sensorally-deprived heroines of *The Spiral Staircase*, *Wait Until Dark*, *Blind Terror* and *Jennifer Eight* comes this mediocre re-tread starring the genuinely hearing-impaired Marlee Matlin. Marlee is a deaf fitness trainer in Portland, Oregon, who unknowingly has the world's most valuable coin hidden in her bleeper. Corrupt cop Martin Sheen, shady reporter John C. McGinley and an unknown assailant all go to enormous lengths to get it, while handsome restaurant manager D. B. Sweeney steps into the fray as Marlee's knight in shining armour. Few surprises and a host of lost opportunities conspire to cancel out any acting honours. Marlee may be deaf, but this movie is just dumb. [JC-W]

Cast: Marlee Matlin (Jillian Shananhan), D. B. Sweeney (Ben Kendall), Martin Sheen (Lt Philip Brock), John C. McGinley (Mickey O'Malley), Christina Carlisi (Grace), Greg Elam (Cooper), Charley Lang, Marge Redmond, Billie Worley, George Rankins, Karen Trumbo.

Dir: Robert Greenwald. Pro: David Matalon. Ex Pro: David Streit. Screenplay: R. M. Badat and Kathleen Rowell; from a story by Badat and Danny Rubin. Ph: Steven Shaw. Ed: Eva Gardos. Pro Des: Bernt Capra. M: Graeme Revell; excerpts from Mascagni's *Cavalleria Rusticana*, Ottorino Respighi's *La Fiamma*; numbers performed by Dub Squad. Costumes: Fleur Thiemeyer. Sound: Mark Ulano. (Fox.) Rel: 14 January 1994. 91 mins. Cert 15.

## Heaven and Earth

The final entry in Oliver Stone's Vietnam trilogy (following *Platooon* and *Born on the Fourth of July*), *Heaven and Earth* is the harrowing, virtually unbelievable but true story of a Vietnamese girl. Based on the dual

*The killing field: Hiep Thi Le in Oliver Stone's shocking epic* Heaven and Earth *(from Warner)*

*The incomparable Bruce Spence sounds off in David Parker's genuinely very funny* Hercules Returns *(from Metro Tartan)*

memoirs of Le Ly Hayslip – *When Heaven and Earth Changed Places* and *Child of War, Woman of Peace* – the picture is a tour-de-force of filmmaking, but often self-consciously so. The story itself needs no dramatic flourishes, and works best when left to its own devices. There are some wonderful set-pieces, however, particularly Le Ly's first encounter with an American supermarket (right up there with Kubrick's 'Blue Danube' sequence from *2001*). There are also some shining performances, with 22-year-old boat refugee Hiep Thi Le making a striking acting debut in the central role, and Tommy Lee Jones and Joan Chen excellent in support, as, respectively, Le Ly's husband and mother. [JC-W]

Cast: Tommy Lee Jones (Sgt Steve Butler), Joan Chen (Mama), Haing S. Ngor (Le Ly's father), Hiep Thi Le (Le Ly), Debbie Reynolds (Eugenia), Conchata Ferrell (Bernice), Vivian Wu (Madame Lien), Dale Dye (Larry), Long Nguyen (Anh, Le Ly's aristocratic lover), Thuan Le (Kim, Le Ly's bargirl sister), Dustin Nguyen, Liem Whatley, Robert Burke, Michael Paul Chan, Timothy Carhart, Tim Guinee, Catherine Ai, Lan Nguyen Calderon, Vinh Dang, Tuan Tran, Chau Mau Doan, Michelle Lee, Mai Nguyen, Michael Lee, Annie McEnroe, Marshall Bell, Le Ly Hayslip, Jeffrey Jones.

Dir and Screenplay: Oliver Stone. Pro: Stone, Arnon Milchan, Robert Kline and A. Kitman Ho. Ex Pro: Mario Kassar. Co-Pro: Clayton Townsend. Ph: Robert Richardson. Ed: David Brenner and Sally Menke. Pro Des: Victor Kempster. M: Kitaro; numbers performed by Hiep Thi Le, Kitaro, Monks of the Dip Tse Chok Ling Monastery, Frankie Valli, B. B. and The Screaming Buddha Heads, Donovan, Wilson Pickett, The Eric Gales Band, Procol Harum, The Archies, etc. Costumes: Ha Nguyen. Sound: Wylie Stateman. (Regency Enterprises/Le Studio Canal Plus/Alcor Films/Ixtlan/New Regency/Todd-AO/TAE–Warner.) Rel: 21 January 1994. 141 mins. Cert 15.

## Hercules Returns

Proclaiming itself 'sexier than *The Little Mermaid*' and 'funnier than *Gandhi*', this outrageous spoof adds a distinctive Australian slant to the gimmick Woody Allen patented with his 1966 *What's Up, Tiger Lily?* Taking the 1963 Italian-Spanish sword-and-sandal epic *Hercules, Samson, Maciste and Ursus Are Invincible* as its visual dartboard, the Melbourne-based comic act Double Take (i.e. Des Mangan and Sally Patience) sends the film up rotten. Dubbing in their own impromptu, often profane dialogue over the original Italian, the result is initially hilarious. Whether or not it can sustain this hilarity is up to the perseverance of the audience, but the irreverent ad-libs and the inanity of the original movie offer many choice moments. [JC-W]

Cast: David Argue (Brad McBain), Michael Carman (Sir Michael Kent), Mary Coustas (Lisa), Bruce Spence (Sprocket), Brendon Suhr, Nick Polites, Laurie Dobson. Voices: Des Mangan, Sally Patience.

Dir: David Parker. Pro: Philip Jaroslow. Ex Pro: Peter Winter. Screenplay: Des Mangan. Ph: David Connell. Ed: Peter Carrodus. Pro Des: Jon Dowding. M: Philip Judd. Costumes: Aphrodite Kondos. (Philm Prods–Metro Tartan.) Rel: 17 June 1994. 80 mins. Cert 15.

*Bothered and bewildered: Thora Birch is captured by 17th century witch Bette Midler – in Kenny Ortega's dreadful* Hocus Pocus *(from Buena Vista)*

## Hocus Pocus

In spite of the combined comedic talents of Bette Midler, Sarah Jessica Parker and Kathy Najimy, not to mention the computer technology, the real star of this Disney shambles is 11-year-old Thora Birch, who steals the honours from everybody and everything. Midler, Parker and Najimy play three grotesque witches hanged in 1683 for practising sorcery, only to turn up three hundred years later (on Hallowe'en) to steal the lives of all the children in Salem, Massachusetts. However, they hadn't reckoned on the tenacity of three local youngsters (including Miss Birch), who attempt to thwart their evil plan. While Midler and her cohorts prove to be a numbing disappointment (resembling The Three Stooges in make-up), the film is otherwise a hotchpotch of banality and unpleasantness. It all leaves one with the icky feeling of having spent too much time in a cut-price toy shop. [JC-W]

Cast: Bette Midler (Winifred Sanderson), Sarah Jessica Parker (Sarah Sanderson),

Kathy Najimy (Mary Sanderson), Omri Katz (Max Dennison), Thora Birch (Dani Dennison), Vinessa Shaw (Allison), Amanda Shepherd, Larry Bagby III, Tobias Jelinek, Stephanie Faracy, Charlie Rocket, Doug Jones, Sean Murray, Kathleen Freeman, Don Yesso, Michael McGrady, Garry Marshall, Penny Marshall.

Dir: Kenny Ortega. Pro: David Kirschner and Steven Haft. Co-Pro: Bonnie Bruckheimer. Ex Pro: Ralph Winter. Screenplay: Mick Garris and Neil Cuthbert; from a story by Kirschner and Garris. Ph: Hiro Narita. Ed: Peter E. Berger. Pro Des: William Sandell. M: John Debney; numbers performed by Bette Midler and Joe Malone. Costumes: Mary Vogt. Sound: George Watters II. Choreography: Ortega and Peggy Holmes. (Walt Disney–Buena Vista.) Rel: 29 October 1993. 97 mins. Cert PG.

*Pet fantasy: Shadow, Ben and Sassy head for the hills in Disney's engaging* Homeward Bound – The Incredible Journey

### A Home of Our Own

Los Angeles/Hankston, Idaho; 1962. Loosely based on truth, this is another weepy from Tony Bill (*Untamed Heart*, *Six Weeks*), the story of a widow and her six kids who try to build their own home in a backwater Idaho town. In spite of a script dotted with some unbelievable dialogue, Bill's direction skilfully sidesteps melodrama and sentimentality to produce a work of genuine pathos and warmth. Filmed in Utah. [JC-W]

Cast: Kathy Bates (Frances Lacey), Edward Furlong (Shayne Lacey), Clarissa Lassig (Lynn Lacey), Miles Feulner (Murray Lacey), Soon-Teck Oh (Mr Munimura), Tony Campisi (Norman), Sarah Schaub, Amy Sakasitz, T. J. Lowther, Dave Jensen, H. E. D. Redford, Melvin Ward, Michael Flynn, Don Re Simpson, Rosalind Soulam.

Dir: Tony Bill. Pro: Dale Pollock and Bill Borden. Assoc Pro: Helen Bartlett. Ex Pro and Screenplay: Patrick Duncan. Ph: Jean Lepine. Ed: Axel Hubert. Pro Des: James Schoppe. M: Michael Convertino. Costumes: Lynn Bernay. (PolyGram/A&M Films–Rank.) Rel: 20 May 1994. 104 mins. Cert PG.

### Homeward Bound: The Incredible Journey

An American bulldog puppy, an ageing golden retriever and a prissy Himalayan cat cross the Oregon mountains in search of their human family. A re-make of Disney's 1963 classic, this winning wilderness family drama borrows the voice-over gimmick from *Look Who's Talking* with mixed results. Sally Field's catty asides as the feline hiker come off best, but the script is on the corny side (chased by a puma, the bulldog quips, 'It's an Arnold Schwarzen-kitten!'). Still, the animal stunts are convincing, the scenery wonderful and the schmaltz suit-

*Family ties: Edward Furlong, Clarissa Lassig, Miles Feulner, Sarah Schaub and Amy Sakasitz in Tony Bill's poignant* A Home of Our Own *(from Rank)*

*Contrary captives: Denis Leary (centre) gets more than he bargained for when he kidnaps Judy Davis and Kevin Spacey in Ted Demme's priceless* Hostile Hostages *(from Buena Vista)*

ably thick. Young children should love it. [JC-W]

Cast: Robert Hays (Bob Burnford), Kim Greist (Laura Burnford), Jean Smart (Kate), Veronica Lauren (Hope), Kevin Chevalia (Jamie), Benj Thall (Peter), Ed Bernard, Anne Christianson, Ted D'Arms, Woody Eney, Rich Hawkins, Jane Jones, Frank Roberts. Voices: Michael J. Fox (Ben, the bulldog), Sally Field (Sassy, the cat), Don Ameche (Shadow, the golden retriever).

Dir: Duwayne Dunham. Pro: Franklin R. Levy and Jeffrey Chernov. Ex Pro: Donald W. Ernst and Kirk Wise. Screenplay: Caroline Thompson and Linda Woolverton; based on Sheila Burnford's novel *The Incredible Journey*. Ph: Reed Smoot. Ed: Jonathan P. Shaw. Pro Des: Roger Cain. M: Bruce Broughton. Costumes: Karen Patch. Sound: Bayard Carey. Animal Coordinator: Joe Camp. (Walt Disney Pictures–Buena Vista.) Rel: 22 October 1993. 85 mins. Cert U.

*Love and bullets: Charlie Sheen and Valeria Golino are reunited – in his dreams – in Jim Abrahams' wild and woolly* Hot Shots! Part Deux *(from Fox)*

## Hostile Hostages

(US: *The Ref*.) The suburbs, Connecticut; Christmas Eve. Lloyd and Caroline Chasseur are on the precipice of a divorce and Lloyd's family is coming for dinner – *tonight*. The fact that Lloyd and Caroline have just been taken hostage by an angry, gun-wielding maniac is the least of their problems. For the maniac, however, his worst nightmare has just begun . . . While bearing all the hallmarks of a farce, *Hostile Hostages* is actually a potent drama trapped inside a very funny comedy. By casting good actors in the roles of the bickering protagonists, the comedy develops an additional layer of reality which, in turn, fuels the humour. An unexpected delight. [JC-W]

Cast: Denis Leary (Gus), Judy Davis (Caroline Chasseur), Kevin Spacey (Lloyd Chasseur), Robert J. Steinmiller Jr (Jesse Chasseur), Glynis Johns (Rose), Raymond J. Barry (Lt Huff), Richard Bright (Murray), Christine Baranski (Connie), Adam LeFevre (Gary), Phillip Nicoll (John), Ellie Raab (Mary), Bill Raymond, John Scurti, Jim Turner, Rutanya Alda, Herbie Ade, Kenneth Utt, Robert Ridgely, Caroline Yeager.

Dir: Ted Demme. Pro: Ron Bozman, Richard LaGravenese and Jeff Weiss. Ex Pro: Don Simpson and Jerry Bruckheimer. Screenplay: LaGravenese and Mary Weiss. Ph: Adam Kimmel. Ed: Jeffrey Wolf. Pro Des: Dan Davis. M: David A. Stewart; numbers performed by Lou Ann Barton, Burl Ives, David A. Stewart, Nat King Cole, etc. Costumes: Judianna Makovsky. (Touchstone Pictures–Buena Vista.) Rel: 27 May 1994. 93 mins. Cert 15.

## Hot Shots! Part Deux

Another gag-fest from the director of *Airplane!*, *Big Business* and *Hot Shots!*, with Charlie Sheen repeating his turn as Topper Harley, now transformed from a Tom Cruise flyboy to a Stallonian hunk rescuing MIAs from Iraq. The jokes are as scattershot and silly as ever, but this time more of them seem to hit the mark. Sheen, Golino, Bakke, Crenna and Ferrer all play their roles with commendable restraint, while only Lloyd Bridges makes a horse's ass of himself. [JC-W]

Cast: Charlie Sheen (Sean 'Topper' Harley), Lloyd Bridges (Tug Benson), Valeria Golino (Ramada Rodham Hayman), Brenda Bakke (Michelle Rodham Huddleston), Richard Crenna (Col Denton Walters), Miguel Ferrer (Harbinger), Rowan Atkinson (Dexter Hayman), Jerry Haleva (Saddam Hussein), Rosemary Johnston (Lavinia Rodham Benson), Dian Kobayashi (Mrs Rodham Soto), David Wohl, Mitchell Ryan, Ryan Stiles, Gregory Sierra, Andreas Katsulas, Clyde Kusatsu, Nancy Abrahams, Charlie Abrahams,

*Hog wild: Colin Firth and Lysette Anthony in Leslie Megahey's medieval jape,* The Hour of the Pig *(from Mayfair)*

Karen 'Boom Boom' Proft, Jamie Abrahams, Joseph 'Bambi' Abrahams, Alison Anne Abrahams, Siren, Zap, Martin Sheen.

Dir: Jim Abrahams. Pro: Bill Badalato. Ex Pro: Pat Proft. Screenplay: Abrahams and Proft. Ph: John R. Leonetti. Ed: Malcolm Campbell. Pro Des: William A. Elliott. M: Basil Poledouris; 'I'm So Excited' sung by The Pointer Sisters. Costumes: Mary Malin. Sound: Thomas Causey. (Fox.) Rel: 20 August 1993. 87 mins. Cert 12.

## The Hour of the Pig

Between the years 1403 and 1506 in France, 90 animals were charged with crimes ranging from bestiality to murder. Loosely basing this film on recorded facts, writer-director Leslie Megahey has fashioned an extraordinary tale of a Parisian lawyer who moves to a small rural community in order to serve the people better. There, he encounters a web of intrigue, corruption and sex as he ends up defending a pig accused of the murder of a young Jewish boy. If played straight, this could have been a fascinating medieval curio, like an anthropomorphic *The Name of the Rose.* Unfortunately, Megahey can't resist emphasising the story's inherent humour which reduces the whole thing to broad farce. Nevertheless, there is plenty to enjoy, not least the period detail, Ian Holm's performance as a lascivious priest and some surprising revelations of medieval sexuality. [JC-W]

Cast: Colin Firth (Richard Courtois), Ian Holm (Albertus), Donald Pleasence (Pincheon), Nicol Williamson (Seigneur Jehan d'Auferre), Lysette Anthony (Filette), Amina Annabi (Samira), Jim Carter (Mathieu), Sophie Dix (Maria), Justin Chadwick, Michael Gough, Harriet Walter, Michael Cronin, Elizabeth Spriggs, Emil Wolk, Vincent Grass, Jean-Pierre Stewart, Dave Atkins, Vernon Dobtcheff, Joanna Dunham, Roy Evans, Robert Putt, Ralph Nossek.

Dir and Screenplay: Leslie Megahey. Pro: David Thompson. Ex Pro: Michael Wearing and Claudine Sainderichin. Ph: John Hooper. Ed: Isabelle Dedieu. Pro Des: Bruce Macadie. M: Alexandre Desplat. Costumes: Anna Buruma. Sound: Joe Walker. (BBC/CiBy 2000/British Screen–Mayfair.) Rel: 21 January 1994. 117 mins. Cert 15.

## House of Angels – Anglagard

Nestled at the edge of shaded woodland and green pastures lies a picturesque village, an idyllic hamlet straight out of Chekhov. However, the quiet existence of the community is turned on its head when the local vicar (while listening to Abba) runs over the landlord of a local estate, killing him instantly. Believed to have had no heirs, the victim turns out to have a granddaughter, who turns up unexpectedly at his funeral on a motorbike – accompanied by a leather-clad figure in Alice Cooper mode. Trouble can only follow . . . A huge success in its native Sweden, this moral comedy is full of surprises and is a constant delight. Directed by England's Colin Nutley, now a Swedish resident. [JC-W]

Cast: Helena Bergstrom (Fanny), Rikard Wolff (Zac), Sven Wollter (Axel Flogfalt), Viveka Seldahl (Rut Flogfalt), Per Oscarsson (Erik Zander), Ernst Gunther (Gottfried Petersson), Tord Petterson (Ivar Petersson), Ing-Marie Carlsson (Eva Agren), Jan Mybrand (Per-Ove Agren), Peter Andersson, Gorel Crona, Jacob Eklund, Gabriella Boris.

Dir and Screenplay: Colin Nutley. Pro: Lars Jonsson. Ph: Jens Fischer. Ed: Perry Schaffer. Pro Des: Ulla Herdin. M: Bjorn Isfalt. Costumes: Sven Lundgren and Britt Marie Larsson. Sound: Eddie Axeberg and

*Fanny and Alice Cooper: Rikard Wolff and Helena Bergstrom shake up Bergman country in Colin Nutley's* House of Angels *(from Mayfair Entertainment)*

Lasse Liljeholm. (Memfis Film–Mayfair Entertainment.) Rel: 9 July 1993. 119 mins. Cert 15.

### The House of the Spirits

Spanning three generations of a Chilean family and the love, tragedy and spirituality that infects it, this is an ambitious if foolhardy attempt to bring Isabel Allende's epic, intricate best-selling novel to the screen. Had Coppola or Bertolucci attempted the same material and devoted two three-hour films to it (in the spirit of *Jean de Florette* and *Manon des Sources*), this could have been powerful cinema. As it is, it is an embarrassing mess. Just because the Danish film-maker Bille August has directed two Palme d'Or-winning films (*Pelle the Conqueror*, *The Best Intentions*), does not make him the prime candidate to direct (and write!) a South American *Gone With the Wind*. A Danish-German-Portuguese co-production with an American-English-Spanish-German-Venezuelan-Indian cast (all playing Chileans), this version of *The House of the Spirits* looks like a ten-hour miniseries cut to shreds (with just the melodramatic bits left in). [JC-W]

Cast: Meryl Streep (Clara Trueba), Glenn Close (Ferula Trueba), Jeremy Irons (Esteban Trueba), Winona Ryder (Blanca Trueba), Antonio Banderas (Pedro), Armin Mueller-Stahl (Severo), Maria Conchita Alonso (Transito), Sarita Choudhury (Pancha), Vanessa Redgrave (Nivea), Jan Niklas (Satigny), Vincent Gallo (Esteban Garcia), Teri Polo (Rosa), Edith Clement, Miriam Colon, Fran Fullenwider, Sasha Hanau, Denys Hawthorne, Joaquim Martinez.

Dir and Screenplay: Bille August. Pro: Bernd Eichinger. Co-Pro: Martin Moszkowicz. Ex Pro: Edwin Leicht, Paula Weinstein and Mark Rosenberg. Ph: Jorgen Persson. Ed: Janus Billeskov Jansen. Pro Des: Anna Asp. M: Hans Zimmer. Costumes: Barbara Baum. Sound: Niels Avild. (Neue Constantin Film/Spring Creek/ Costa do Castelo–Entertainment.) Rel: 18 March 1994. 150 mins. Cert 15.

*Irons in the mire: Jeremy Irons dons stetson and an intriguing accent in Bille August's ill-conceived* The House of the Spirits *(from Entertainment)*

### In Custody

Madhya Pradesh, north central India; 1993. Although teaching Hindi in a small provincial college, Deven is a staunch devotee of Urdu, a language fast disappearing in his native India. So, when he's given the chance to interview Nur, his country's greatest poet still writing in the language, he jumps at the opportunity. But Deven's mission is fraught with problems. His wife objects to his long hours away, he cannot afford to purchase a tape recorder and Nur himself has deteriorated into an alcoholic slob. And that's just for starters. *In Custody* has been praised for its use of vibrant colours, invisible editing and structural confidence, but compared to the deft and poetic humanistic cinema of Satyajit Ray, it is very heavy going indeed. Still, there is much to admire in this poignant fable, the first film directed by producer Ismail Merchant (of Merchant Ivory fame) since his little-seen *The Courtesans of Bombay* back in 1983. The performances are all first-rate, and the music quite hypnotic. [JC-W]

Cast: Shashi Kapoor (Nur), Shabana Azmi (Imtiaz Begum), Om Puri (Deven), Sushma Seth (Safiya Begum), Neena Gupta, Tinnu Anand, Prayag Raj, Ajay Sahni, Maza Bi.

Dir: Ismail Merchant. Pro: Wahid Chowhan. Ex Pro: Paul Bradley and Donald Rosenfeld. Screenplay: Anita Desai and Shahrukh Husain; from the novel by Desai. Ph: Larry Pizer. Ed: Roberto Silvi. Pro Des: Suresh Sawant. M: Zakir Hussain and Ustad Sultan Khan. Costumes: Lovleen Bains. (Merchant Ivory–Mayfair Entertainment.) Rel: 3 June 1994. 120 mins. Cert PG.

### In the Line of Fire

Although Clint Eastwood has a field day poking fun at his image *and* his encroaching years (he's 62), it is John Malkovich's ruthless, brilliant madman who steals this picture. Eastwood is a Secret Service bodyguard who failed JFK in Dallas and is determined to make up for it when Malkovich starts threatening the life of the present (fictitious) US leader. Pitting the latest government technology against Malkovich's cunning and ingenuity is where the film comes into its own, although the whole thing is so efficiently packaged that there's never a dull moment. As far as genre thrillers go, this is in the top league. [JC-W]

Cast: Clint Eastwood (Frank Horrigan), John Malkovich (Mitch Leary), Rene Russo (Lilly Raines), Dylan McDermott (Al D'Andrea), Gary Cole (Bill Watts), John Mahoney (Sam Campagna), Jim Curley (President), Fred Dalton Thompson, Greg Alan-Williams, Clyde Kusatsu, Tobin Bell, Elsa Raven, Patrika Darbo, John Heard, Anthony Peck, William G. Schilling.

Dir: Wolfgang Petersen. Pro: Jeff Apple. Ex Pro: Petersen, Gail Katz and David Valdes. Screenplay: Jeff Maguire. Ph: John Bailey. Ed: Anne V. Coates. Pro Des: Lilly Kilvert. M: Ennio Morricone; 'All Blues' performed by Miles Davis. Costumes: Erica Edell Phillips. Sound: Wylie Stateman and Gregg Baxter. (Castle Rock/Apple Rose–Columbia TriStar.) Rel: 27 August 1993. 129 mins. Cert 15.

### In the Name of the Father

Incredible but (essentially) true, the extraordinary story of the Guildford Four brought vividly to life by director Jim Sheridan and his magnificent trio of actors, Daniel Day-Lewis, Pete Postlethwaite and Emma Thompson. Using Gerry Conlon's book *Proved Innocent* as its source, the film follows Conlon's early clashes with the IRA in Belfast, his trip to London (and a whole new world of free love and drugs), and his eventual arrest by British police. Accused of bombing two army pubs in Guildford, Conlon is forced to sign a statement proclaiming

*The executioner's song: John Malkovich running rings around the White House in Wolfgang Petersen's gripping* In the Line of Fire *(from Columbia TriStar)*

his guilt and is sentenced to life imprisonment. And to make the case stick, authorities doctor the evidence . . . Day-Lewis went to extraordinary lengths to bring credibility to his performance, including bouts of starvation and sleep deprivation, but it is the supporting turns of Postlethwaite and Thompson that charge the film with its human strength. Shocking cinema, superbly executed, with nary a false note sounded. [JC-W]

Cast: Daniel Day-Lewis (Gerry Conlon), Emma Thompson (Gareth Peirce), Pete Postlethwaite (Giuseppe Conlon), John Lynch (Paul Hill), Mark Shepard (Paddy Armstrong), Beatie Edney (Carol Richardson), Marie Jones (Sarah Conlon), Britta Smith (Annie Maguire), Corin

*Jail debate: Daniel Day-Lewis as Gerry Conlon in Jim Sheridan's scorching* In the Name of the Father *(from UIP)*

*Here's looking at Isabella, Tony: Isabella Rossellini on a foreign runway, with Anthony Hopkins looking on – in John Schlesinger's* The Innocent *(from Entertainment)*

Redgrave (Robert Dixon), Don Baker (Joseph McAndrew), Patterson Joseph, John Benfield, Frank Harper, Anna Meegan, Leah McCullagh, Saffron Burrows, Peter Sheridan Snr, Rob Spendlove, Philip Davis, Rachael Dowling, Tina Kellegher, Ronan Wilmot, Peter Howitt, Daniel Massey, Bosco Hogan, Malcolm Tierney, Peter Sheridan, Denys Hawthorne, Tom Wilkinson.

Dir and Pro: Jim Sheridan. Co-Pro: Arthur Lappin. Ex Pro: Gabriel Byrne. Screenplay: Sheridan and Terry George. Ph: Peter Biziou. Ed: Gerry Hambling. Pro Des: Caroline Amies. M: Trevor Jones; numbers performed by Bono and Gavin Friday, The Jimi Hendrix Experience, The Kinks, Bob Marley and The Wailers, Thin Lizzy, and Sinead O'Connor. Costumes: Joan Bergin. Sound: Ron Davis. (Hell's Kitchen/Universal–UIP.) Rel: 11 February 1994. 133 mins. Cert 15.

## The Innocent

Berlin; 1955. This is a classic case of a film sabotaged by miscasting. Adapted by Ian McEwan from his own chilling novel, *The Innocent* tells of a callow English technician enlisted to help tap into the 'classified telephone traffic' running between Berlin and Moscow. However, the young and impressionable Leonard Marnham is soon distracted by the charms of Maria, a seductive and flirtatious German girl. Boasting such ingredients as sex, subterfuge and murder, the film promises much, particularly with John Schlesinger behind the camera directing such a talented cast. But with Anthony Hopkins giving a slapdash impersonation of Bob Hoskins doing his American act, the 42-year-old Italian Isabella Rossellini as the coquettish German girl and the 31-year-old, New York-born Campbell Scott as the virginal Englishman, the film cannot hope for a minute of credibility. Gene Hackman, Nastassja Kinski and Clive Owen would not only have made an ideal cast, but would have enabled the audience to concentrate on the film instead of the accents. (P. S. Rossellini's mother, Ingrid Bergman, and Scott's father, George C., both appeared in the 1965 British film *The Yellow Rolls-Royce*) [JC-W]

Cast: Anthony Hopkins (Bob Glass), Isabella Rossellini (Maria Eckdorf), Campbell Scott (Leonard Marnham), Hart Bochner (Russell), Ronald Nitschke (Otto), James Grant (John MacNamee), Richard Durden, Jeremy Sinden, Corey Johnson, Richard Good, Lena Lessing, Matthew Burton.

Dir: John Schlesinger. Pro: Norma Heyman, Wieland Schulz-Kiel and Chris Sievernich. Ex Pro: Ann Dubinet. Screenplay: Ian McEwan. Ph: Dietrich Lohmann. Ed: Richard Marden. Pro Des: Luciana Arrighi. M: Gerald Gouriet. Costumes: Ingrid Zore. (Lakehart/Sievernich-Film/Defa Studios Babelsberg–Entertainment.) Rel: 24 June 1994. 118 mins. Cert 15.

*Rook of the year: Max Pomeranc, a chess prodigy himself, makes his acting debut as Josh Waitzkin in Steven Zaillian's enthralling, masterful* Innocent Moves *(from UIP)*

## Innocent Moves

(US: *Searching for Bobby Fischer.*) Josh Waitzkin has just turned seven and loves baseball, basketball, fishing and chess. He's not obsessive about chess, but he can beat his father without looking at the board and enjoys defeating veterans of the game in two minutes flat. In fact, Josh Waitzkin could be the greatest player since Bobby Fischer. However, Josh is only seven, and all his mother wants is his happiness. The pressures of becoming America's star child prodigy provide no room for a normal life, let alone contentment. But should such a talent be squandered? The subject of chess hardly lends itself to the cinema, but thanks to the basic human elements of this fascinating true story and to some deft choreography, the excitement builds from the word go. It is also an excellent piece of filmmaking, superbly realised by first-time director Steven Zaillian (who wrote the screenplays for *Awakenings*, *Jack the Bear* and *Schindler's List*), who has coaxed exemplary performances from a top-notch cast, and is aided by some luminous photography, adroit pacing and a perfectly modulated score. As Josh, eight-year-old newcomer Max Pomeranc (a chess prodigy himself) is a real find. [JC-W]

Cast: Joe Mantegna (Fred Waitzkin), Laurence Fishburne (Vinnie), Joan Allen (Bonnie Waitzkin), Max Pomeranc (Josh Waitzkin), Ben Kingsley (Bruce

Pandolfini), Michael Nirenberg (Jonathan Poe), Hal Scardino (Morgan), Robert Stephens, David Paymer, Vasek Simek, William H. Macy, Dan Hedaya, Laura Linney, Anthony Heald, Chelsea Moore, Josh Mostel, Josh Kornbluth, Tony Shalhoub, Austin Pendleton, Kamran Shirazi, Joel Benjamin, Roman Dzindzichashvili, Katya Waitzkin, Caroline Yeager.

Dir and Screenplay: Steve Zaillian; from the book *Searching for Bobby Fischer* by Fred Waitzkin. Pro: Scott Rudin and William Horberg. Ex Pro: Sydney Pollack. Co-Pro: David Wisnievitz. Ph: Conrad L. Hall. Ed: Wayne Wahrman. Pro Des: David Gropman. M: James Horner. Costumes: Julie Weiss. (Paramount/Mirage–UIP.) Rel: 6 May 1994. 110 mins. Cert PG.

*Can do: Olivier Martinez sprays his way to infamy in Jean-Jacques Beineix's playfully unpredictable* IP5 *(from Artificial Eye)*

## Intersection

Vancouver; today. A successful 42-year-old architect finds himself at an emotional crossroads when his grand design of having a daughter in the country, a girlfriend in the city and a wife in the office isn't working. Vincent Eastman must make a decision – before it's too late. In spite of good performances (particularly from Lolita Davidovich as the mistress) and a terrific ending, the film's thick coat of gloss and splintered narrative prevents any genuine emotion filtering through. For the record, this is Richard Gere's third starring role in an American remake of a French film, this one taken from the 1969 *Les Choses de la Vie* which starred Michel Piccoli, Romy Schneider and Lea Massari. [JC-W]

Cast: Richard Gere (Vincent Eastman), Sharon Stone (Sally Eastman), Lolita Davidovich (Olivia Marshak), Martin Landau (Neal), David Selby (Richard Quarry), Jenny Morrison (Meaghan Eastman), Ron White, Matthew Walker, Scott Bellis, Patricia Harras, Robyn Stevan, Suki Kaiser, Tom Heaton, Timothy Webber.

Dir: Mark Rydell. Pro: Rydell and Bud Yorkin. Ex Pro: Frederic Golchan. Co-Pro: Ray Hartwick. Screenplay: David Rayfiel and Marshall Brickman. Ph: Vilmos Zsigmond. Ed: Mark Warner. Pro Des: Harold Michelson. M: James Newton Howard; Bach. Costumes: Ellen Mirojnick. (Paramount–UIP.) Rel: 3 June 1994. 99 mins. Cert 15.

*Building bridges to burn: Richard Gere as the architect of love in Mark Rydell's* Intersection *(from UIP)*

## IP5

Any movie that starts with a pulsating rap song on a Paris bridge and ends up on the top of the Pyrenees can't be all bad. The beauty of Jean-Jacques Beineix's films (this is his fifth) is that they obey no rules of conventional narrative and transport us on journeys denied us elsewhere. Here, a graffiti artist and a young black kid go on a crime spree and end up with an old man with psychic powers. As the latter, Yves Montand is simply wonderful in his last screen performance. [JC-W]

Cast: Yves Montand (Léon Marcel), Olivier Martinez (Tony), Sekkou Sall (Jockey), Géraldine Pailhas (Gloria), Colette Renard, Sotigui Kouyate, Georges Staquet, Arlette Didier, Kléber Bouzonne, Fabien Behar, Gabriel Monnet.

Dir and Pro: Jean-Jacques Beineix. Screenplay: Beineix and Jacques Forgeas. Ph: Jean-François Robin. Ed: Joëlle Hache.

*Road to imagination: Jacob Tierney as the killer and pathological liar with a heart of gold – in Billy Weber's fresh and offbeat* Josh and S.A.M. *(Rank)*

Pro Des: Dan Weil. M: Gabriel Yared; rap songs by Beineix. Costumes: Emmanuelle Steunou. Sound: Pierre Befve. (Cargo Films/Gaumont–Artificial Eye.) Rel: 26 November 1993. 119 mins. Cert 15.

## Jack Be Nimble

When New Zealand siblings Jack and Dora are separated in their youth, they are psychologically transformed by their respective foster parents – but never lose their longing for one another. Dora, a psychic, is adopted by a kind, comfortably well-off couple, but Jack ends up with a family from hell. Mocked by his four step-sisters and whipped with barbed wire by his 'father', Jack gradually turns into a time bomb of pent-up violence. When they are reunited as adults, Dora and Jack find they are no longer compatible and cannot escape their inevitable fate. New Zealander Garth Maxwell's first film as director is played so broadly that one secretly hopes it's a black comedy, but soon it becomes all too apparent that *Jack Be Nimble* is no such animal. A Gothic horror story unrelieved by humour, it is so badly acted and directed that it's a wonder it was ever released. [JC-W]

Cast: Alexis Arquette (Jack), Sarah Smuts-Kennedy (Dora), Bruno Lawrence (Teddy), Tony Barry (Clarrie), Elizabeth Hawthorne (Bernice), Brenda Simmons (Mrs Birch), Tricia Phillips (Anne), Gilbert Goldie, Paul Minifie, Kristen Seth, Amber Woolston, Tracey Brown, Wendy Adams, Bridget Armstrong, Bridget Donovan.

Dir and Screenplay: Garth Maxwell. Pro: Jonathan Dowling and Kelly Rogers. Ex Pro: Murray Newey and John Barnett. Assoc Pro: Judith Trye. Ph: Donald Duncan. Ed: John Gilbert. Pro Des: Grant Major. M: Chris Neal. Costumes: Ngila Dickson. Sound: Cethin Creagh. (Essential Productions/New Zealand Film Commission–Metro Tartan.) Rel: 4 February 1994. 93 mins. Cert 18.

## Josh and S.A.M.

Seven-year-old Sam Whitney is good at football but little else, and when his older brother, Josh, teases him that he's a genetically engineered 'Strategically Altered Mutant' he believes it. This leads to no end of trouble as the two boys head for the Canadian border, Sam to escape the Pentagon guard, Josh to flee the police after killing a drunkard. On one level this is a fresh, original morality tale (in which both boys, from a broken home, are actually running away from themselves), yet on another is a laboured road movie conspicuously striving for eccentricity. Take your pick. [JC-W]

Cast: Jacob Tierney (Josh Whitney), Noah Fleiss (Sam Whitney), Joan Allen (Caroline Whitney), Stephen Tobolowsky (Thom Whitney), Chris Penn (Derek Baxter), Martha Plimpton (Alison, 'The Liberty Maid'), Ronald Guttman (Jean-Pierre), Maury Chaykin, Udo Kier, Sean Baca, Jake Gyllenhaal, Anne Lange, Ann Hearn, Christian Clemenson, Allan Arbus, Kayla Allen, Brent Hinkley, Amy Wright, Annie McEnroe, Harry Caesar.

Dir: Billy Weber. Pro: Martin Brest. Ex Pro: Arne L. Schmidt. Co-Pro: Frank Deese and Alex Gartner. Screenplay: Deese. Ph: Don Burgess. Ed: Chris Lebenzon. Pro Des: Marcia Hinds-Johnson. M: Thomas Newman; 'Hot Mocking Bird' performed by Chet Atkins. Costumes: Jill M. Ohanneson. (Castle Rock/New Line/City Lights–Rank.) Rel: 27 May 1994. 98 mins. Cert 12.

## The Joy Luck Club

The much-acclaimed film version of Amy Tan's 1989 No. 1 best-seller, which gave an astounding shot in the arm to Chinese-American literature, is

*The guilt of innocence: Ming-Na Wen bathes her child for the last time in Wayne Wang's emotionally dense* The Joy Luck Club *(from Buena Vista)*

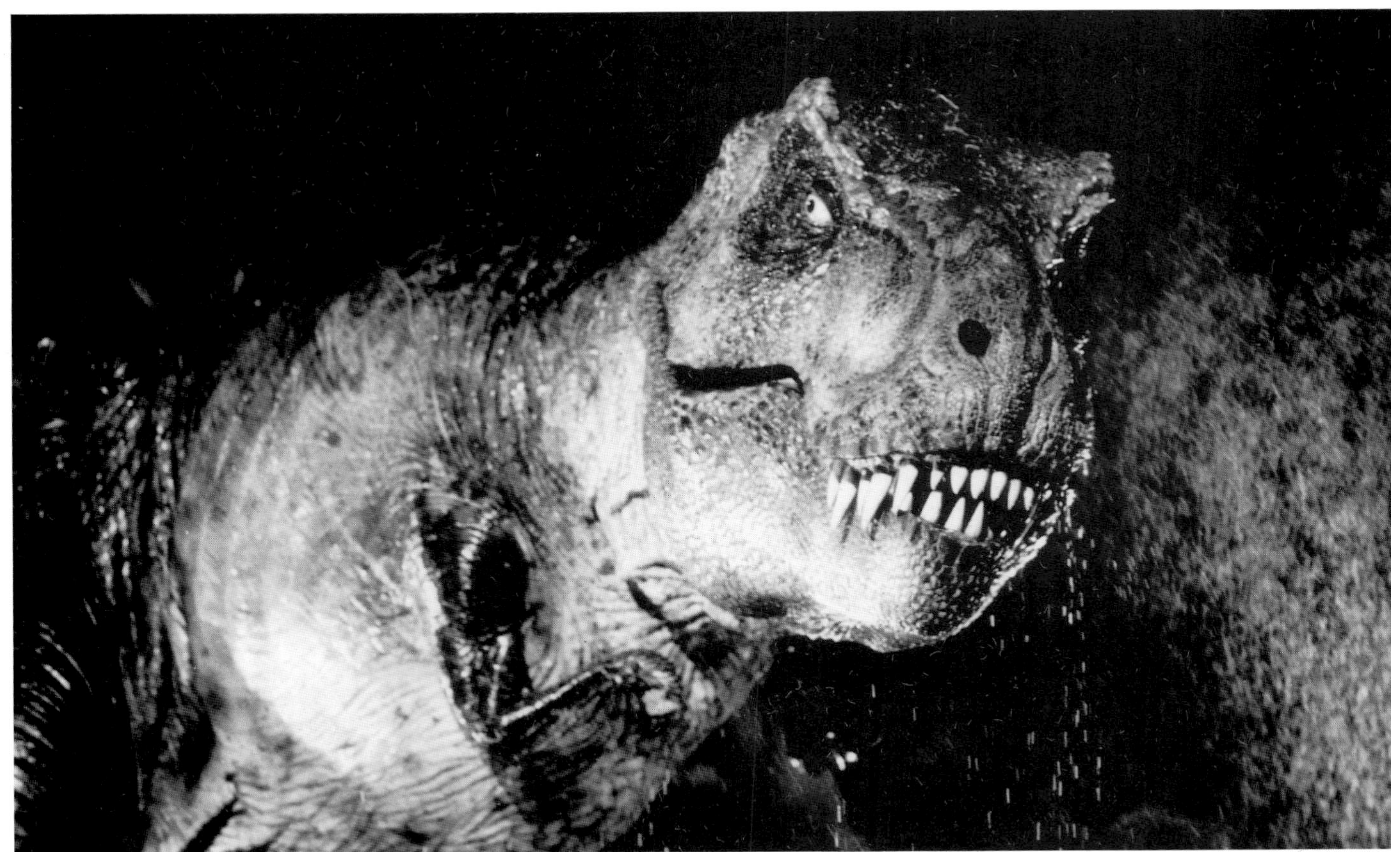

*The dino soars:* That *Tyrannosaurus Rex, hungry for box-office records – in Steven Spielberg's* Jurassic Park *(from UIP)*

both a miracle and a disappointment. Chronicling the lives of four Chinese women living in San Francisco and their ambiguous relationships with their American-born daughters, the film takes on a heavy load, but director Wayne Wang interweaves the stories and liaisons with some deftness. However, by faithfully adhering to the book's myriad story strands, the picture cannot hope to engage the viewer in quite the same emotional depth as the book did. And, while the actresses are uniformly good, their interaction is not always convincing (or clear). Nevertheless, the film is always sumptuous to look at, although Rachel Portman's score dictates to the emotions far too blatantly. [JC-W]

Cast: Kieu Chinh (Suyuan), Tsai Chin (Lindo), France Nuyen (Ying Ying), Lisa Lu (An Mei), Ming-Na Wen (June), Tamlyn Tomita (Waverly), Lauren Tom (Lena), Rosalind Chao (Rose), Melanie Chang (June, aged 9), Vu Mai (Waverly, aged 6–9), Guo-Rong Chen (Huang Tai Tai), Irene Ng (Lindo, aged 15), Christopher Rich (Rich), Yu Fei Hong (Ying Ying, aged 16–25), Michael Paul Chang (Harold), Vivian Wu (An Mei's mother), Andrew McCarthy (Ted Jordan), Diane Baker (Mrs Jordan), Chao-Li Chi, Mei Juan Xi, Hsu Ying Li, Qugen Cao, William Gong, Nicholas Guest, Ya Shan Wu, Russell Wong, Grace Chang, Phillip Moon, Melissa Tan, Yi Ding, Jack Ford.

Dir: Wayne Wang. Pro: Wang, Amy Tan, Ronald Bass and Patrick Markey. Ex Pro: Oliver Stone and Janet Yang. Screenplay: Tan and Bass. Ph: Amir Mokri. Ed: Maysie Hoy. Pro Des: Donald Graham Burt. M: Rachel Portman. Costumes: Lydia Tanji. Sound: Tim Chau. (Hollywood Pictures–Buena Vista.) Rel: 11 March 1994. 139 mins. Cert 15.

## Jurassic Park

By extracting the blood from a prehistoric mosquito preserved in amber, scientists discover the DNA of dinosaurs bitten 65 million years ago. Then, by copying the DNA (or genetic code) and placing it in the cell of a frog, they are able to hatch a dinosaur embryo in laboratory conditions. Dotty Scottish billionaire John Hammond (Richard Attenborough) capitalises on the idea by masterminding an epic theme park populated by brachiosauruses, triceratops, a tyrannosaurus rex and whathaveyou. Before revealing his secret to the public, Hammond invites a palaeontologist (Sam Neill), a palaeobotanist (leggy Laura Dern), a mathematician (a cynical Jeff Goldblum) and a financier (Martin Ferrero) to his unique zoo of a bygone era. Big mistake . . . Drawing from a budget of $60 million, Spielberg and Industrial Light & Magic produce the goods and then some, creating an astonishing range of gentle, intelligent and ferocious creatures that move, breath and attack like the real thing. Unfortunately, the prehistoric cast is introduced too soon for full dramatic effect, while the human characters are less convincing. Still, *Jurassic Park* is an exhilarating and often intensely frightening experience that should outlast the next millennium. Interestingly, the week that the film opened in the US (on 11 June 1993), scientists successfully isolated genetic material from an extinct weevil dating from 120 to 130 million years ago, providing the sort of publicity that not even Spielberg could afford to buy. [JC-W]

*Trial by terror: Ian Holm and Jeremy Irons encounter The Castle in Steven Soderbergh's plushly satirical* Kafka *(from Guild)*

Cast: Sam Neill (Dr Alan Grant), Laura Dern (Ellie Sattler), Jeff Goldblum (Ian Malcolm), Richard Attenborough (John Hammond), Bob Peck (Robert Muldoon), Martin Ferrero (Donald Gennaro), Joseph Mazzello (Tim Murphy), Ariana Richards (Alexis Murphy), Samuel L. Jackson (Arnold), Wayne Knight (Dennis Nedry), Richard Kiley (tour voice), B. D. Wong, Jerry Molen, Miguel Sandoval, Cameron Thor, Dean Cundey.

Dir: Steven Spielberg. Pro: Kathleen Kennedy and Gerald R. Molen. Screenplay: Michael Crichton and David Koepp; based on the novel by Crichton. Ph: Dean Cundey. Ed: Michael Kahn. Pro Des: Rick Carter. M: John Williams. Sound: Ron Judkins. Live Action Dinosaurs: Stan Winston. (Universal/Amblin–UIP.) Rel: 16 July 1993. 126 mins. Cert PG.

## Just Another Girl on the I.R.T.

Just another home movie from the squalid streets of Brooklyn, this time focusing on the tough, ugly life of a 17-year-old student who dreams of going to medical school. But first Chantel Mitchell must circumvent a quagmire of poverty, drugs, sex, AIDS, moral decadence and teenage pregnancy. The acting, photography and sound leave a lot to be desired, but there are moments of remarkable spontaneity, while the film is notable as the first major commercial feature to be directed by a black American woman. [JC-W]

Cast: Ariyan Johnson (Chantel Mitchell), Kevin Thigpen (Tyrone), Ebony Jerido (Natete), Jerard Washington (Gerard), Chequita Jackson, William Badget, Karen Robinson, Tony Wilkes, Johnny Roses, Shawn King, Laura Ross, Rashmella, Erwin Wilson.

Dir and Screenplay: Leslie Harris. Pro: Harris and Erwin Wilson. Ph: Richard Connors. Ed: Jack Haigis. Pro Des: Mike Green. M: Eric Sadler; numbers performed by Nikki D, Cee-Asia, Kimberly Davis, Angela Stone, Angie B, BWP, The O'Jays, etc. Costumes: Bruce Brickus. Sound: Harrison Williams. (Truth 24 FPS/Miramax—Metro Tartan.) Rel: 30 July 1993. 97 mins. Cert 15.

## Kafka

Blending themes from the works of the angst-ridden Czech writer Franz Kafka into this fictitious story of a man of the same name, director Steven Soderbergh has fashioned a work of extraordinary originality and aplomb that defies categorisation. However, for those unfamiliar with Kafka and his writings, the film should prove to be impenetrable. And, while the black-and-white photography (atmospherically capturing the shadowy, narrow cobbled streets of Prague) and some nice performances (notably from Joel Grey and Armin Mueller-Stahl) should entrance many, the end product too often resembles an intellectual acid trip. [JC-W]

*Ghetto crazy: Ariyan Johnson fighting the system in Leslie Harris's vibrant* Just Another Girl on the I.R.T. *(from Metro Tartan)*

Cast: Jeremy Irons (Kafka), Theresa Russell (Gabriela), Joel Grey (Burgel), Ian Holm (Dr Murnau), Jeroen Krabbe (Bizzlebek), Armin Mueller-Stahl (Inspector Grubach), Alec Guinness (the chief clerk), Keith Allen (Ludwig), Simon McBurney (Oscar), Vladimir Gut (Eduard Raban), Brian Glover, Robert Flemyng, Matyelok Gibbs, Ion Caramitru, Hilde Van Meighem, Jan Nemejovsky, Toon Agterberg, Maria Miles, Emil Wolk, Jerome Flynn, Ewan Stewart, David Jensen.

Dir and Ed: Steven Soderbergh. Pro: Stuart Cornfeld and Harry Benn. Ex Pro: Paul Rassam and Mark Johnson. Screenplay: Lem Dobbs. Ph: Walt Lloyd. Pro Des: Gavin Bocquet. M: Cliff Martinez. Costumes: Michael Jeffery. Sound: Mark Mangini. (Renn/Baltimore Pictures/Pricel SA–Guild.) Rel: 25 February 1994. 98 mins. Cert 15.

## Kalifornia

When *Kalifornia* opened in New York, it was reviewed by 12 major critics. Four raved, four booed and four gave it a mixed reception. Now, *that* is the sign of a great movie: one that is able to divide the critics so precisely. True, *Kalifornia* is not an easy film to like, but it is poetic, visceral and superbly acted, lurching from dark comedy to numbing drama without flinching. Brad Pitt, in yet another swerve away from typecasting, plays a piece of white trash with an 18-year-old girlfriend (Juliette Lewis, sensational) whom he won't let drink or smoke or swear and whom he beats regularly. David Duchovny, perfectly cast, is an

Ivy League journalist obsessed with the phenomenon of serial murder, who is writing a book on America's most notorious cases. Low on cash, Duchovny advertises for a passenger to share expenses for the ride from Pittsburgh to California, on which journey he and his photographer girlfriend will visit the sites of the grisliest murders in recent memory. But, with Pitt and Lewis along for the ride, Duchovny finds himself closer to his subject than he'd ever cared to get . . . With his photographic eye and talent for guiding actors, first-time director Dominic Sena should have an amazing career ahead of him. [JC-W]

Cast: Brad Pitt (Early Grayce), Juliette Lewis (Adele Corners), David Duchovny (Brian Kessler), Michelle Forbes (Carrie Laughlin), Sierra Pecheur, Gregory Mars Martin, Bill Crabbe.

Dir: Dominic Sena. Pro: Steve Golin, Sigurjon Sighvatsson and Aristides McGarry. Ex Pro: Michael Kuhn, Jim Kouf and Lynn Bigelow. Screenplay: Tim Metcalf; from a story by Metcalfe and Stephen Levy. Ph: Bojan Bazelli. Ed: Martin Hunter. Pro Des: Michael White. M: Carter Burwell; numbers performed by The Indians, East 17, Sheryl Crow, David Baerwald, Mind Bomb, Quicksand, Drivin' 'n' Cryin', Daniel O'Brien, Heather Myles, Hugh Harris, X, Pere Ubu, Asleep at the Wheel, Soup Dragons, and Therapy? Costumes: Kelle Kutsugeras. Sound: Jose Antonio Garcia. (Propaganda Films/PolyGram/Viacom-Rank.) Rel: 1 April 1994. 118 mins. Cert 18.

*Kasual Killing: Juliette Lewis in her best performance yet as the girlfriend of a serial killer (Brad Pitt) in Dominic Sena's terrific* Kalifornia *(from Rank)*

### Kickboxer III – The Art of War

Third in the series kick-started by Jean-Claude Van Damme, this one with American high-step champion Sasha Mitchell rippling his quadriceps femoris in Rio de Janeiro – both in and out of competition. Dennis Chan repeats his role as the spiritual teacher Xian Chow from the first two films. Shown in cinemas purely to give its video release extra clout. Are you sold? [EB]

Cast: Sasha Mitchell (David), Dennis Chan (Xian Chow), Richard Comar (Lane), Noah Verduzco (Marcos), Alethea Miranda (Isabella), Ian Jacklin, Milton Goncalves, Ricardo Petraglia, Gracindo Junior.

Dir: Rick King. Pro: Michael Pariser. Ex Pro: Luciana Boal Marinho. Screenplay: Dennis Pratt. Ph: Edgar Moura. Ed: Daniel Loewenthal. Pro Des: Clovis Bueno. M: Harry Manfredini. Costumes: Isabela Braga. (Kings Road/MPC–Columbia TriStar.) Rel: 27 May 1994. 91 mins. Cert 18.

### The Killer

Hong Kong; 1989. A killer with a conscience and a cop with a temper find themselves irrevocably drawn to each

*Chow Yun-Fat shows his mettle in John Woo's spectacular bloodbath,* The Killer *(from Made in Hong Kong)*

*Prince of survival: Jesse Bradford as Aaron Kurlander in Steven Soderberg's masterful* King of the Hill *(from UIP)*

other as gangland violence erupts around them. Soaked in John Woo's trademark visuals – flocks of doves, a conflagration of candles, flying corpses – *The Killer* is the movie that established the cult Chinese director's reputation abroad (see reviews of *Hard Boiled* and *Hard Target*). It's easy to see why: in spite of the corny set-ups and self-conscious 'style', *The Killer* is a well-plotted, spectacular and innovative thriller bursting with energy and ingenuity. Picked up by TriStar Pictures and Walter Hill to be re-made in an English-language version. [JC-W]

Cast: Chow Yun-Fat (Jeffrey Chow), Danny Lee (Inspector Lee), Sally Yeh (Jennie), Chu Kong (Sydney Fung), Kenneth Tsang (Sgt Randy Chang), Shing Fui-On (Johnny Weng), Ip Wing-Cho (Tony Weng), Yee Fan-Wai (Frank), Wong Kwong-Leung, Barry Wong, Parkman Wong.

Dir and Screenplay: John Woo. Pro: Tsui Hark. Ph: Wong Wing-Hang. Ed: Fan Kung Ming. Art: Luk Man Wah. M: Lowell Lowe. (Golden Princess/Magnum/Film Workshop–Made in Hong Kong.) Rel: 8 October 1993. 111 mins. Cert 18.

## King of the Hill

1933; St Louis, Missouri. Based on the memoirs of A. E. Hotchner, the friend and biographer of Ernest Hemingway, this affecting story of a 12-year-old boy struggling to hold his own in the Depression once again illustrates Steven Soderbergh's knack for directing actors. Pushing cliché and sentimentality to one side, Soderbergh has produced a story of enormous texture and truth as Aaron Kurlander fends for himself as the youngest resident of the run-down Empire Hotel. With his father away on business and his mother in the sanatorium, Aaron witnesses first-hand the misery of poverty and has only his wits for company. Jesse Bradford, already a veteran at 13, is simply superb in the central role in a film that succeeds on almost every level. Photography, editing, production design, music and costumes are all first-rate and combine to produce a work of enormous grace and vitality. [JC-W]

Cast: Jesse Bradford (Aaron Kurlander), Jeroen Krabbe (Mr Kurlander), Lisa Eichhorn (Mrs Kurlander), Karen Allen (Miss Mathey), Spalding Gray (Mr Mungo), Elizabeth McGovern (Lydia), Joseph Chrest (Ben), Adrien Brody (Lester), Cameron Boyd (Sullivan Kurlander), Katherine Heigl (Christina Sebastian), Amber Benson (Ella McShane), Kristin Griffith (Mrs McShane), Chris Samples, Peggy Frieson, John McConnell, John Durbin, Lauryn Hill, David Jensen, Sarah Mermelstein, Ron Yerxa.

Dir, Screenplay and Ed: Steven Soderbergh. Pro: Barbara Maltby, Albert Berger and Ron Yerxa. Ex Pro: John Hardy. Ph: Elliot Davis. Pro Des: Gary Frutkoff. M: Cliff Martinez. Costumes: Susan Lyall. Sound: Larry Blake (Gramercy/Wildwood/Bona Fide–UIP.) Rel: 26 December 1993. 109 mins. Cert 12.

## Lake Consequence

California; 1993. Heard the one about the bored housewife, the gardener and the untapped sexual reservoir? The consequence of this ludicrous, shameful and slick revision of *Lady Chatterley's Lover* is that bored housewives may feel free to entertain their wildest sexual fantasies so long as they return to their families afterwards. Both AIDS- and logic-free, *Lake Consequence* is the latest bout of above-the-waist erotica from the man (Zalman King) who brought us *9½ Weeks*, *Two Moon Junction* and *Wild Orchid*. [JC-W]

Cast: Billy Zane (Billy), Joan Severance (Irene), May Karasun (Grace), Whip Hubley (Jim), Courtland Mead (Christopher), Dan Reed (Xiao).

Dir: Rafael Eisenman. Pro: Avram 'Butch' Kaplan. Ex Pro: Zalman King. Screenplay: King, Melanie Finn and Henry Cobbold; from a story by MacGregor Douglas. Ph: Harris Savides. Ed: James Gavin Bedford and Curtis Edge. Pro Des: Dominic Watkins. M: George S. Clinton. Costumes: Elisabetta Rogiani. Sound: Stephen Halbert. (PolyGram–Rank.) Rel: 20 August 1993. 90 mins. Cert 18.

## Last Action Hero

The film that tainted the gold on Arnie's crown may not have lived up to expectations but is still one helluva enjoyable movie. Arnie sends up his screen image as the indestructible hero, this time as maverick cop Jack Slater, a fictitious icon battling insurmountable odds in a movie-within-a-movie (*Jack Slater IV*). When an 11-year-old film buff is magically transported into the make-believe world, he tries to tell Slater that it's 'just a movie' and, thanks to having seen the first half of the picture, knows more about the villains than Slater does. Borrowing a concept first exploited in 1924 by Buster Keaton with *Sherlock Jr* (and later by Woody Allen with *The Purple Rose of Cairo*), the film bolsters the fantasy-faction with some commendable morality (in real life violence causes pain), which allows us to enjoy the pyrotechnics of *Slater IV* with a clean conscience. Crammed with cameos, intentional continuity errors and in-jokes (Joan Plowright lecturing on Olivier's *Hamlet* is priceless), *Last Action Hero* is a treat both for *aficionados* of the action genre and for *cinéastes*. [JC-W]

Cast: Arnold Schwarzenegger (Sgt Jack Slater/Arnold Schwarzenegger), F. Murray Abraham (John Practice), Art Carney (Frank), Charles Dance (Benedict), Frank McRae (Dekker), Tom Noonan (Ripper), Robert Prosky (Nick), Anthony Quinn (Tony Vivaldi), Mercedes Ruehl (Mom), Austin O'Brien (Danny Madigan), Ian McKellen (Death), Tina Turner (the Mayor), Bridgette Wilson (Whitney/Meredith), Professor Toru Tanaka, Joan Plowright, Keith Barish, Jim Belushi, Chevy Chase, Chris Connelly, Karen Duffy, Larry Ferguson, Leeza Gibbons, Hammer, Little Richard, Robert Patrick,

*This too too solid flesh: Arnold Schwarzenegger as Hamlet in John McTiernan's wildly underrated* Last Action Hero *(from Columbia TriStar)*

Maria Shriver, Sharon Stone, Jean-Claude Van Damme, Melvin Van Peebles, Damon Wayans, Ryan Todd, John Finnegan, Anthony Peck, Sven-Ole Thorson, Rick Ducommun, Michael V. Gazzo, Colleen Camp, John McTiernan Sr.

Dir: John McTiernan. Pro: McTiernan and Steven Roth. Ex Pro: Arnold Schwarzenegger. Screenplay: Shane Black and David Arnott; from a story by Zak Penn and Adam Leff. Ph: Dean Semler. Ed: John Wright. Pro Des: Eugenio Zanetti. M: Michael Kamen; numbers performed by Alice in Chains, Tesla, AC/DC, Anthrax, Megadeth, Def Leppard, Aerosmith, Fishbone, etc. Costumes: Gloria Gresham. Sound: Lee Orloff. Visual Effects Consultant: Richard Greenberg. (Oak/Columbia—Columbia TriStar.) Rel: 30 July 1993. 131 mins. Cert 15.

## The Last Bolshevik

Slapdash documentary (out-of-focus subtitles, appalling video quality) tracing the parallel histories of Russia and its cinema in relation to the work of the little known filmmaker Alexander Ivanovich Medvedkin. A very self-indulgent home movie, eloquently narrated by British actor Michael Pennington. [JC-W]

Pro: Michael Kustow. Screenplay and Ed: Chris Marker. M: Alfred Schnittke; Michel Krasna. (Michael Kustow Prods/Epidem Oy/Les Films de L'Astrophore–ICA.) Rel: 4 August 1993. 118 mins. No cert.

## Laws of Gravity

Shot on a budget of $38,000 over 12 days, this is a compellng and authentic look at a group of losers living on the edge of violence in Brooklyn. Unreel-

*Lean streets: Edie Falco and Peter Greene live on the edge of Nick Gomez's assertive* Laws of Gravity *(from Oasis)*

*Finding freedom: Ivan Shvedov and Steffan Trevor discover themselves through each other in Endaf Emlyn's wonderful* Leaving Lenin *(from Feature Film Co.)*

ing his narrative on a short fuse, first-time director Nick Gomez allows his capable cast of unknowns enormous flexibility to develop their characters, and by so doing has created a very real atmosphere in which anything could conceivably happen. A real slice-of-life drama for audiences who want to smell the real thing. Winner of the Wolfgang Staudte prize at the 1993 Berlin Film Festival. [JC-W]

Cast: Peter Greene (Jimmy), Edie Falco (Denise), Adam Trese (Johnny Sousa), Arabella Field (Celia), Paul Schulze (Frankie), Saul Stein (Sal), Tony Fernandez (Tommy), James McCauley, Anibel Lierras, Miguel Sierra, John Gallagher, William Sage.

Dir and Screenplay: Nick Gomez. Pro: Bob Gosse and Larry Meistrich. Ex Pro: Meistrich. Ph: Jean de Segonzac. Ed: Tom McArdle. Pro Des: Monica Bretherton. M: The Poor Righteous Teachers, Run DMC, 2nd II None, Derrick Irie, Nardo Ranks/Junior Demus and Nemesis. Sound: Jeff Pullman and Jean Gilliland. (Oasis Films.) Rel: 20 August 1993. 100 mins. Cert 18.

### Leaving Lenin – Gadael Lenin

The latest nugget in a snowballing Gaelic film industry – of quality, if not quantity – *Leaving Lenin* is a charming, touching and funny Welsh film set in Russia (of all places). Seven students from the upper sixth of Maes Ifor School in Pontypridd are on a trip to St Petersburg, when they are separated from their three quarrelsome teachers. With remarkable lack of pretension the film follows the adventures of its protagonists as they react in their different ways to what Russia has to offer (or not). Particularly affecting is the story of class outsider Spike Powell, who discovers himself through the spontaneous friendship with a Russian soulmate. Drawing comedy out of real life is a fine art, and Endaf Emlyn has perfected it to a T, neither compromising his characters nor suffocating the innate humour of his scenario. One of the most unexpectedly delightful films of the year. Emlyn previously directed the award-winning *One Full Moon.* [JC-W]

Cast: Sharon Morgan (Eileen), Wyn Bowen Harries (Mostyn), Ifan Huw Dafydd (Mervyn), Steffan Trevor (Spike Powell), Catrin Mai (Rhian), Ivan Shvedov (Sasha), Richard Harrington (Charlie), Shelley Rees (Sharon), Anna Vronskaya, Nerys Thomas, Helen Louise Davies, Geraint Francis, Mikhail Maizel.

Dir: Endaf Emlyn. Pro: Pauline Williams. Screenplay: Emlyn and Sion Eirian. Ph: Ray Orton. Ed: Chris Lawrence. Art: Vera Zelinskaya. M: John Hardy. Costumes: Noelle Rees Rowlands. Sound: Jeff Mathews. (Gaucho Cyf/S4C TV/Lara Globus–Feature Film Co.) Rel: 3 June 1994. 90 mins. Cert 15.

### Leningrad Cowboys Meet Moses

Mexico/Coney Island/France/Frankfurt/Leipzig/Dresden/Poland; 1994. Most of the original members of the world's worst rock 'n' roll band have died of tequila poisoning in Mexico, and so the remaining few team up with their old mentor-cum-nemesis Vladimir (now calling himself Moses) and head for Europe. While Aki Kaurismaki's first film, *Leningrad Cowboys Go America*, was an absurdist, minimalist look at America through Scandinavian eyes (and frequently hilarious), his sequel is just absurd and minimal. The band's outrageous hairstyles and the director's self-conscious lack of style barely supported a full-length feature the first time. Now they have outstayed their welcome by 90 minutes. [JC-W]

Cast: Matti Pellonpaa (Moses/Vladimir), Twist-Twist Erkinharju, Ben Granfelt, Sakke Jarvenpaa, Jore Marjaranta, Ekke Niiva, Lyle Narvanen, Pemo Ojala, Silu Seppala, Mauri Sumén and Mato Valtonen (Leningrad Cowboys), Kari Vaananen (the mute), André Wilms (Lazar/Johnson/Elijah), Nicky Tesco, Kirsi Tykkylainen.

Dir, Pro, Screenplay and Ed: Aki Kaurismaki. Ex Pro: Paula Oinonen, Reinhard Brundig and Fabienne Vonier. Ph: Timo Salminen. Pro Des: John Ebden. M: Mauri Sumén. Sound: Jouko Lumme and Timo Linnasalo. (Sputnik Oy/Pandora Film/Pyramide/La Sept Cinema/Canal Plus–Finnish Film Institute.) Rel: 25 February 1994. 92 mins. No cert.

### The Lie – Mensonge

Paris; now. Charles and Emma have lived happily together for ten years with their 8-year-old-son, Romain. Both are successful at what they do (he an in-demand war correspondent,

*The truth of* The Lie*: Nathalie Baye gives yet another outstanding performance – in Francois Margolin's stunning debut film (from Gala)*

she extolling the virtues of lemon pie to 800,000 Parisians), and are comfortable and secure in their relationship. But when Emma decides to have another baby a cataclysmic shock rends her world apart. Her blissful adult life, she discovers, has been a lie. By humanising and concentrating Emma's pain, *The Lie* is a devastatingly credible antidote to the flash anger of Cyril Collard's *Savage Nights*, both films exposing the harsh reality of AIDS in France today. *The Lie* is supplemented by an exceptionally intelligent array of performances, never strikes a false note and is all the more astounding as it marks the directorial debut of François Margolin. One of the most moving films of the year. [JC-W]

Cast: Nathalie Baye (Emma), Didier Sandre (Charles), Hélene Lapiower (Louise), Marc Citti (Louis), Dominique Besnéhard (Rozenberg), Adrien Beau (Romain), Christophe Bourseiller (Gege), Louis Ducreux, Josiane Stoleru, Francis Girod.

Dir: François Margolin. Pro: Alain Sarde. Screenplay: Margolin and Denis Saada. Ph: Caroline Champetier. Ed: Martine Giordano. Pro Des: Julie Sfez and Arnaud de Moleron. Costumes: Catherine Meurisse. Sound: Jean-Jacques Ferran. (Les Films Alain Sarde/Cuel Lavalette Prods/France 3/Canal Plus–Gala.) Rel: 10 September 1993. 89 mins. Cert 15.

### Like Water For Chocolate – Como Agua Para Chocolate

Mexico; 1895–1934. After the spaghetti Western, the enchilada romance. A surprise success in the United States (where it grossed over $18m), the film is a culinary metaphor for the struggle of women in a society dominated by sexist tradition. The title itself refers to the local preparation for hot chocolate, an analogy for the bubbling state of sexual arousal. When young Tita is proposed to by the handsome Pedro, Tita's mother intervenes, declaring that Tita, her youngest daughter, must remain single to look after her until her death. Instead of Tita, the matriarch offers Pedro her second youngest daughter, Rosaura. Pedro agrees to marry the sister in order to be closer to the one he truly loves, thus setting the stage for a romantic epic tinged with magic realism and gastronomical metaphor. Although peppered with memorable moments and a beguiling humour, *Like Water For Chocolate* lacks the narrative drive and stylistic confidence that could have made it a minor classic. [JC-W]

Cast: Lumi Cavazos (Tita), Marco Leonardi (Pedro), Regina Torne (Mama Elena), Mario Ivan Martinez (John Brown), Ada Carrasco (Nacha), Yareli Arizmendi (Rosaura), Claudette Maille (Gertrudis), Pilar Aranda (Chencha), Farnesio De Bernal, Joaquin Garrido, Rodolfo Arias, Amado Ramirez, Arcelia Ramirez.

Dir and Pro: Alfonso Arau. Screenplay: Laura Esquivel; based on her novel. Ph: Emmanuel Lubezki and Steve Bernstein. Ed: Carlos Bolado and Francisco Chiu. Art: Mario Antonio Arteaga, Mauricio de Aguinaco and Denise Pizzini. M: Leo Brower. Costumes: Carlos Brown. Sound: Aurelio Lopez. (Arau Films International–Electric.) Rel: 1 October 1993. 114 mins. Cert 15.

*A feast of metaphor: Lumi Cavazos as the daughter who literally cooks up her revenge – in Alfonso Arau's* Like Water For Chocolate *(from Electric)*

### Little Buddha

Seattle, Washington; Bhutan; Nepal; India. Increasingly drawn to the subject of Buddhism over the years, Bernardo Bertolucci completes his 'Oriental' trilogy (following *The Last Emperor* and *The Sheltering Sky*) with

*Seeking the light: young Bhutan monks line up to greet their new lama in Bernardo Bertolucci's striking, rich philosophical journey,* Little Buddha *(from Buena Vista)*

this enthralling, epic, yet narratively flawed piece of cinema. While it never carries through its promise of emotional catharsis, falls down on some iffy casting (Chris Isaak, of all people?) and relies too much on the humanly photogenic, the film is an extraordinary celebration of cinema and life. Every image is calculated for the greatest seductive effect, every set elaborately and authentically adorned, every detail thoroughly researched. But unlike a hollow piece of well-dressed cinema like *The Age of Innocence*, *Little Buddha* does embrace some fundamental issues seldom – if ever – broached by the medium. Seeking the reincarnation of their spiritual teacher, a deputation of Tibetan Buddhist monks travel to Seattle to interview Jesse Konrad, a 9-year-old boy who fits the astrological description of their lama. At first meeting some resistance from Jesse's parents, the monks' sincerity soon wins them over. As Jesse is slowly drawn into the mysterious world of Buddhism, he learns of the spiritual journey of Siddhartha, the Indian prince who forsook his royal roots to become the first Buddha. Overflowing with astonishing sequences (the baby Siddhartha talking and walking shortly after his birth, the cremation of a corpse, the uncomprehending faces of lepers), the film constantly engages the interest even as it fails to come to a satisfying conclusion. If it doesn't change any lives, it certainly causes one to stop and think. N.B. *Little Buddha* is the first feature allowed access to the Himalayan kingdom of Bhutan. [JC-W]

Cast: Keanu Reeves (Siddhartha), Ying Ruocheng (Lama Norbu), Chris Isaak (Dean Konrad), Alex Wiesendanger (Jesse Konrad), Bridget Fonda (Lisa Konrad), Raju Lal (Raju), Greishma Makar Singh (Gita), Sogyal Rinpoche (Kenpo Tenzin), Ven. Khyongla Rato Rinpoche (Abbot), Kanika Pandey (Queen Maya), Ven. Geshe Tsultim Gyelsen, Jo Champa, Jigme Kunsang, Rajeshwaree, Santosh Bangera.

Dir: Bernardo Bertolucci. Pro: Jeremy Thomas. RPC Associate: Chris Auty. Screenplay: Rudy Wurlitzer and Mark Peploe; from a story by Bertolucci. Ph: Vittorio Storaro. Ed: Pietro Scalia. Pro Des and Costumes: James Acheson. M: Ryuichi Sakamoto. Sound: Ivan Sharrock. (Recorded Pictures Company/CIBY 2000–Buena Vista.) Rel: 29 April 1994. 123 mins. Cert PG.

*Peking turkey: Jeremy Irons (seen here with John Lone) continues his run of bad luck in David Cronenberg's implausible* M. Butterfly *(from Warner)*

### Look Who's Talking Now!

Grossly sentimental, laboured follow-up to *Look Who's Talking* and *Look Who's Talking Too*. This time young Mikey has lost his mental vocal chords and the jokey voice-over is supplied by a streetwise mutt and a pompous poodle (courtesy of Danny DeVito and Diane Keaton) who move into the chaotic household of the unbearable Ubriacco family. Yet, while Rocks and the dainty Daphne swap witty-ish put-downs, the human animals take the movie into a realm of numbing bathos. While James Ubriacco (Travolta) enjoys his new high-flying, high-paying job as private pilot to glamorous cosmetics executive Samantha D'Bonne, Mollie (Kirstie Alley) sits at home stewing in her own jealousy. Barking. [JC-W]

Cast: John Travolta (James Ubriacco), Kirstie Alley (Mollie Ubriacco), Lysette Anthony (Samantha D'Bonne), Olympia Dukakis (Rosie), David Gallagher (Mikey Ubriacco), Tabitha Lupien (Julie Ubraccio), Danny DeVito (the voice of Rocks, mutt), Diane Keaton (the voice of Daphne, poodle), George Segal, Charles Barkley, John Stocker, Elizabeth Leslie, Gerry Rousseau, Ron Gabriel, Michael Puttonen, Miriam Smith, Andrea Nemeth.

Dir: Tom Ropelewski. Pro: Jonathan D. Krane. Ex Pro: Leslie Dixon. Co-Pro: Amy Heckerling and Fitch Cady. Screenplay: Ropelewski and Dixon. Ph: Oliver Stapleton. Ed: Michael A. Stevenson and Harry Hitner. Pro Des: Michael Bolton. M: William Ross; numbers performed by Jordy, Elvis Presley, The Chipmunks, John Hiatt, PHD, etc. Costumes: Molly Maginnis and Mary E. McLeod. (Columbia TriStar.) Rel: 27 May 1994. 95 mins. Cert 12.

### Lost in Yonkers

See *Neil Simon's Lost in Yonkers*.

### M. Butterfly

While the incredible true story of the French diplomat Bernard Boursicot and his Chinese lover may have worked within the innate artifice of the theatre, it is made a laughing stock under the unflinching gaze of the movie camera. Furthermore, David Cronenberg – who brought William S. Burroughs' unfilmable novel *Naked Lunch* spluttering to the screen – has booby-trapped his latest white elephant from the word go. If the concept of a married, sexually precocious diplomat thinking he has impregnated a man is not unbelievable enough, Cronenberg has cast the quintessentially English Jeremy Irons as the Frenchman in question (with the equally British Ian Richardson as his Gallic superior). Then, at a time when judicious subtitles have finally become acceptable, Cronenberg has the Chinese talking to each other in English. And did the lay French *really* refer to Peking as Beijing back in 1968? *Au contraire*. [JC-W]

Cast: Jeremy Irons (René Gallimard), John Lone (Song Liling), Barbara Sukowa (Jeanne Gallimard), Ian Richardson (Ambassador Toulon), Annabel Leventon (Frau Baden), Shizuko Hoshi, Richard

McMillan, Vernon Dobtcheff, Margaret Ma, Tristram Jellinek, Philip McGough, David Neal, Sean Hewitt, Peter Messaline, Michael Mehlmann.

Dir: David Cronenberg. Pro: Gabriella Martinelli. Screenplay: David Henry Hwang; based on his play of the same name. Ph: Peter Suschitzky. Ed: Ronald Sanders. Pro Des: Carol Spier. M: Howard Shore. Costumes: Denise Cronenberg. (Geffen–Warner.) Rel: 6 May 1994. 101 mins. Cert 15.

*Working Boy: John Turturro in the title role of* Mac*, the actor's labour of love that took twelve years to reach fruition (from Entertainment)*

## Mac

Queens, New York; the 1950s. Intensely personal film marking the directorial debut of actor John Turturro (*Barton Fink, Miller's Crossing*) who spent 12 years bringing his project to the screen. The story of a New York builder who loves his work, *Mac* is a tribute to Turturro's father, a man who valued hard labour over the money it brought in. But for Mac Vitelli and his two brothers, Vico and Bruno, a man's hands alone can no longer provide for a family – so the brothers go into business for themselves. A beautifully sculptured drama, lovingly capturing the detail of building work (the laying of a concrete floor, the construction of a brick wall), *Mac* is also an actor's dream. Slow-moving to be sure, but an assured, stylish, bravura work. [JC-W]

Cast: John Turturro (Mac Vitelli), Michael Badalucco (Vico Vitelli), Carl Capotorto (Bruno Vitelli), Katherine Borowitz (Alice), Ellen Barkin (Oona), John Amos (Nat), Steven Randazzo (Gus), Olek Krupa (Polowski), Joe Paparone, Dennis Farina, Mike Starr, Shirley Stoler, Katherine Turturro, Aida Turturro, Amadeo Turturro, Nicholas Turturro.

Dir: John Turturro. Pro: Nancy Tenenbaum and Brenda Goodman. Screenplay: Turturro and Brandon Cole. Ph: Ron Fortunato. Ed: Michael Berenbaum. Pro Des: Robin Standefer. M: Richard Termini and Vin Tese; numbers performed by Charlie Parker, Louis Prima, Dizzie Gillespie, Xavier Cugat, Frankie Laine and Enrico Caruso. Costumes: Donna Zakowska. Sound: Don Sable. (Tenenbaum/Goodman–Entertainment.) Rel: 7 January 1994. 118 mins. Cert 18.

## Mad Dog and Glory

As a favour to a cop who saved his life, a gangster sends him a beautiful girl for a week. The cop, Mad Dog, is incensed by the audacity of the gesture, but the gangster is determined that he should be happy. And if the girl, Glory, cannot please him, then her penalty will be severe. But Glory does too good a job . . . Besides the seductive story, this film should be seen for the standard of screenwriting, for the quality of acting and for the power of its direction. Scenarist Richard Price (*The Color of Money, Sea*

*The comic and artist as gangster and cop: Bill Murray and Robert De Niro in John McNaughton's sly, intelligent* Mad Dog and Glory *(from UIP)*

*A town like* Malice*: Bill Pullman is left out in the cold (yet again) in Harold Becker's competent, topsy-turvy thriller (from Rank)*

*of Love*) loads his scenes with fascinating detail and gritty dialogue and then unleashes unexpected flashes of humour. Uma Thurman as Glory reveals new depths of vulnerability, while Bill Murray is perfect (and inspired casting) as the poetic gangster. And John McNaughton (whose first film, *Henry: Portrait of a Serial Killer*, attracted outrage and acclaim) consolidates his reputation as a filmmaker to watch, here enhancing his dark vision with an affecting humanity and eye-catching style. [JC-W]

Cast: Robert De Niro (Wayne 'Mad Dog' Dobie), Uma Thurman (Glory), Bill Murray (Frank Milo), David Caruso (Mike), Mike Starr (Harold), Kathy Baker (Lee), Derek Anunciation (Shooter), Tom Towles, Doug Hara, Evan Lionel, Anthony Cannata, J. J. Johnston, Guy Van Swearingen, Jack Wallace, Richard Belzer, Richard Price.

Dir: John McNaughton. Pro: Barbara De Fina and Martin Scorsese. Ex Pro and Screenplay: Richard Price. Ph: Robby Muller. Ed: Craig McKay and Elena Maganini. Pro Des: David Chapman. M: Elmer Bernstein. Costumes: Rita Ryack. Sound: James J. Sabat. (Universal–UIP.) Rel: 2 July 1993. 97 mins. Cert 15.

## Made in America

When a black girl learns that she is the product of artificial insemination, she breaks into a sperm bank to find out the name of her father. To her astonishment she discovers that Dad is a local car salesman who happens not only to be famous (for his crass TV commercials) but *white*. An interesting premise is bludgeoned into farce with frantic direction, moronic music and unbearable caricatures (the hip brother, the bimbo girlfriend, the cowardly TV producer) – and then, in the sentimental final reel, the film expects us to relate to its protagonists as real people. What a mess. [JC-W]

Cast: Whoopi Goldberg (Sarah Mathews), Ted Danson (Hal Jackson), Will Smith (Tea Cake Walters), Nia Long (Zora Mathews), Jennifer Tilly (Stacy), Rawley Valverde (Diego), Fred Mancuso (Bruce), Paul Rodriguez, Peggy Rea, Clyde Kusatsu, David Bowe, Jeffrey Joseph, Charlene Fernetz, Shawn Levy, Lu Leonard, Phyllis Avery, Frances Bergen, Mel Stewart.

Dir: Richard Benjamin. Pro: Arnon Milchan, Michael Douglas and Rick Bieber. Ex Pro: Nadine Schiff and Marcia Brandwynne. Co-Ex Pro: Steven Reuther. Co-Pro: Patrick Palmer. Screenplay: Holly Goldberg Sloan; from a story by Brandwynne, Schiff and Sloan. Ph: Ralf Bode. Ed: Jacqueline Cambas. Pro Des: Evelyn Sakash. M: Mark Isham; numbers performed by Gloria Estefan, Judy Garland, Ben E. King, Deep Purple, YT Style, Del Thafunkee Homosapien, etc. Costumes: Elizabeth McBride. Sound: Richard Lightstone. (Le Studio Canal Plus/Regency Enterprises/Alcor Films/Stonebridge Entertainment/Kalola Prods–Warner.) Rel: 13 August 1993. 111 mins. Cert 12.

## Malice

A series of rapes is disrupting the placid waters of a small Massachusetts university town. Around the same time a brilliant trauma surgeon is hired by the local hospital. And Dr Jed Hill is not only a caring man, but is good-looking and has charm to spare. He also has a keen sense of humour. For instance, he threatens to cut a colleague's lungs out with an ice cream scoop. When the latter observes, 'I'm not going to like you, am I?' Dr Hill retorts, 'Don't be ridiculous. Every-

*'If you prick us, do we not bleed?' Mel Gibson briefs pupil Nick Stahl on Shakespeare and the human condition in his magnificent* The Man Without a Face *(from Entertainment)*

*Detective story: Ron Rifkin, Diane Keaton, Woody Allen, Anjelica Huston and Joy Behar combine forces to trick a murder suspect in Allen's shining return to form – in* Manhattan Murder Mystery *(from Columbia TriStar)*

body likes me.' However, newlyweds Andy and Tracy Safian, who rent out the top floor of their Victorian house to him, are having second thoughts . . . A most enjoyable thriller, this, adding a few new twists to an already contorted genre. [JC-W]

Cast: Alec Baldwin (Dr Jed Hill), Nicole Kidman (Tracy Safian), Bill Pullman (Andy Safian), Bebe Neuwirth (Dana), Peter Gallagher (Dennis Riley), Josef Sommer (Lester Adams), Anne Bancroft (Ms Kennsinger), George C. Scott (Dr Kessler), Diana Bellamy (Ms Worthington), Tobin Bell, William Duff-Griffin, Deborah Farentino, Gwyneth Paltrow, David Bowe, Sara Nelson, Ann Cusack.

Dir: Harold Becker. Pro: Becker, Rachel Pfeffer and Charles Mulvehill. Ex Pro: Michael Hirsh and Patrick Loubert. Screenplay: Aaron Sorkin and Scott Frank; from a story by Sorkin and Jonas McCord. Ph: Gordon Willis. Ed: David Bretherton. Pro Des: Philip Harrison. M: Jerry Goldsmith; numbers performed by Randy Newman, Bryan Ferry, Spin Doctors, Eric Clapton and Gene Harris. Costumes: Michael Kaplan. Sound: Robert Eber. (Castle Rock/New Line Cinema–Rank.) Rel: 7 January 1994. 107 mins. Cert 15.

## The Man Without a Face

Cranesport, Maine; the 1960s. Everybody has a past, but when your face is disfigured and your nature reclusive, it's easy for people to attach their own legends to your life. Living on his own in a large waterfront house, ex-teacher Justin McLeod – the man without a face – has been branded a psycho, a homosexual, even a Kennedy. When 13-year-old Chuck Norstadt fails the entrance exam to his late father's boarding school, he approaches the fearsome McLeod in a last-ditch attempt for decent tutorship. Neither McLeod nor Chuck are willing to change their opinions of each other, but the love of learning can do strange things to people . . . A moving, intelligent translation of Isabelle Holland's novel, this marks Mel Gibson's first foray into directing, and a fine job he does, too. He is also superb in the title role, a part he reluctantly took on when William Hurt turned it down. [JC-W]

Cast: Mel Gibson (Justin McLeod), Margaret Whitton (Catherine), Fay Masterson (Gloria), Gaby Hoffman (Meg), Geoffrey Lewis (Chief Stark), Richard Masur (Carl Hartley), Nick Stahl (Chuck Norstadt), Michael DeLuise (Douglas Hall), Ethan Phillips, Jean De Baer, Jack De Mave, Viva, Justin Kanew, Sean Kellman, George Martin.

Dir: Mel Gibson. Pro: Bruce Davey. Ex Pro: Stephen McEveety. Co-Pro: Dalisa Cohen. Screenplay: Malcolm MacRury. Ph: Donald M. McAlpine. Ed: Tony Gibbs. Pro Des: Barbara Dunphy. M: James Horner. Costumes: Shay Cunliffe. Sound: Jonathan Bates. (Majestic Films/Icon Prods–Entertainment.) Rel: 19 November 1993. 114 mins. Cert 12.

## Manhattan Murder Mystery

Manhattan; 1993. After all the soul searching and intellectual angst, Woody Allen reverts to pure comedy with this wonderful return to old form, the story of a husband and wife who suspect their neighbour of murder. While the plot itself proves to be surprisingly involving (co-scripted by Marshall Brickman), the plentiful one-liners serve to decorate rather than obstruct. It's good, too, to see Allen playing so well off Diane Keaton, while Alan Alda and Anjelica Huston lend confident support. For the record, Ms Keaton last starred opposite Allen in *Manhattan* 14 years previously (not counting her cameo in *Radio Days*). [JC-W]

*For a Few Pesos Less: Reinol Martinez and Consuelo Gomez act for tortilla chips in Robert Rodriguez's sprightly* El Mariachi *(from Columbia)*

Cast: Alan Alda (Ted), Woody Allen (Larry Lipton), Anjelica Huston (Marcia Fox), Diane Keaton (Carol Lipton), Jerry Adler (Paul House), Lynn Cohen (Lillian House), Melanie Norris (Helen Moss), Marge Redmond (Mrs Dalton), Ron Rifkin, William Addy, Zach Braff, Aida Turturro, Ruth Last.

Dir: Woody Allen. Pro: Robert Greenhut. Co-Pro: Helen Robin and Joseph Hartwick. Ex Pro: Jack Rollins and Charles H. Joffe. Screenplay: Allen and Marshall Brickman. Ph: Carlo Di Palma. Ed: Susan E. Morse. Pro Des: Santo Loquasto. M: Cole Porter, Miklos Rozsa, Richard Wagner, Paul Desmond, Louis Prima, Erroll Garner, etc; numbers performed by Bobby Short, Erroll Garner, The Dave Brubeck Quartet, Bob Crosby & The Bobcats, Coleman Hawkins, Benny Goodman and His Orchestra, etc. Costumes: Jeffrey Kurland. Sound: Bob Hein. (Columbia TriStar.) Rel: 21 January 1994. 104 mins. Cert PG.

## Man's Best Friend

*Beethoven* meets *The Terminator.* By extracting the salient DNA from a number of diverse animals and cloning it all into the body of a Tibetan Mastiff, Dr Jarret has created a unique creature. But Max, the supermutt, needs his regular shots to keep him docile, so that when aspiring TV news reporter Lori Tanner adopts him as her guard dog the world of sunny San Remo is thrown into mortal danger. Ludicrous, but fun. From the director of *Child's Play 2.* [JC-W]

Cast: Ally Sheedy (Lori Tanner), Lance Henriksen (Dr Jarrett), Robert Costanzo (Det. Kovaca), John Cassini (Det. Bendetti), Fredric Lehne (Perry), Trula M. Marcus (Annie), J. D. Daniels (Rudy), William Sanderson, Robin Frates, Rick Barker, Bradley Pierce.

Dir and Screenplay: John Lafia. Pro: Charles Roven. Ex Pro: Daniel Grodnik and Robert Kosberg. Ph: Mark Irwin. Ed: Michael N. Kune. Pro Des: Jaymes Hinkle. M: Joel Goldsmith; 'Puppy Love' performed by Marty Blasick. Costumes: Beverly Hong. Sound: Harry Cohen. Creature Special Supervisor: Kevin Yagher. (New Line/Roven-Cavallo Entertainment–Guild.) Rel: 21 January 1994. 87 mins. Cert 15.

## El Mariachi

During his summer break while attending the University of Texas, film student Robert Rodriguez entered a research centre as a guinea pig for a new anti-cholesterol drug. One month later he emerged – unharmed – with a screenplay under his arm and $3000 in his wallet. For an unbelievable $7000, he then shot and bankrolled *El Mariachi,* a fast-paced, violent, contemporary Mexican Western powered with a throwaway black humour. The *mariachi* of the title (Spanish for travelling minstrel) thinks the omen of a free coconut promises a run of good luck when he enters a dusty border town – but he couldn't be further from the truth. Mistaken for a ruthless vigilante (also wearing black and carrying a guitar case), he is chased by gunmen and almost castrated by the woman he loves. Utilising an energetic editing technique, myriad close-ups and speeded-up film, Rodriguez has produced a miracle film of tremendous style and vitality. [JC-W]

Cast: Carlos Gallardo (El Mariachi), Consuelo Gómez (Domino), Jaime De Hoyos (Bigoton), Peter Marquardt (Mauricio/'Mocco'), Reinol Martinez (Azul), Ramiro Gomez, Jesus Lopez, Luis Baro, Jaime Rodriguez,

Dir, Screenplay, Ph, Ed, Camera Operator, Special Effects and Sound: Robert Rodriguez. Pro: Rodriguez and Carlos Gallardo. Assoc. Pro: Elizabeth Avellan and Carmen M. De Gallardo. M: Marc Trujillo, Alvaro Rodriguez, Juan Suarez, Cecilio Rodriguez and Eric Guthrie. (Los Hooligans–Columbia TriStar.) Rel: 20 August 1993. 80 mins. Cert 15.

## Menace II Society

Watts, Los Angeles; 1965–93. The orphaned son of a drug dealer and addict and a product of the ghetto, Caine Lawson was destined to be a bad egg. And, in spite of his attempts to keep his nose clean, Caine is sucked deeper and deeper into transgression. The most successful low-budget urban black film of 1993, *Menace II Society* explores familiar LA turf where drugs and drive-by killings are the norm. However, the film is so well directed by the 20-year-old twin brothers Allen and Albert Hughes, that it grips the attention from the word go. Of course, we've seen it all before, but the prob-

*Killing for a living: Tyrin Turner threatens Martin Davis in the Hughes brothers' powerful* Menace II Society *(from First Independent)*

lems still have to be addressed, both by social reform and the cinema itself. Compulsive, hard-hitting and authentic drama. [JC-W]

Cast: Tyrin Turner (Caine Lawson), Jada Pinkett (Ronnie), Larenz Tate (O-Dog), Arnold Johnson (grandpapa), Marilyn Coleman (grandmama), Vonte Sweet (Sharif), Glenn Plummer (Pernell), MC Eiht, Clifton Powell, Bill Duke, Samuel L. Jackson, Charles S. Dutton, Pooh Man, Jullian Roy Doster, Anthony Johnson, Khandi Alexander, Ryan Williams, Todd Anthony Shaw, Martin Davis, Mike Kelly.

Dir: Allen and Albert Hughes. Pro: Darin Scott. Ex Pro: Kevin Moreton. Line Pro: Michael Bennett. Co-Pro: Tyger Williams and the Hughes brothers. Screenplay: Williams; from a story by Williams and the Hughes brothers. Ph: Lisa Rinzler. Ed: Christopher Koefoed. Pro Des: Penny Barrett. M: QD III; numbers performed by SPICE 1, MC Eiht, R. Kelly and Public Announcement, The Cutthroats, Smooth, Too Short, Hi-Five, George Clinton, Al Green, Zapp, N.W.A., Marvin Gaye, The Isley Brothers, QD III, etc. Costumes: Sylvia Vega-Vasquez. Sound: Veda Campbell. (New Line–First Independent.) Rel: 7 January 1994. 97 mins. Cert 18.

*Making Mr Right: Matt Dillon and Annabella Sciorra search for a solution in Anthony Minghella's beguiling* Mr Wonderful *(from Buena Vista)*

### The Meteor Man

Washington DC; 1993. At last: America's black urban ghettos get their own superhero (albeit a reluctant one). Writer-director Robert Townsend (*Hollywood Shuffle, The Five Heartbeats*) dons cloak and undies in the title role, as Jefferson Reed, a timid schoolteacher who believes in flight at the first whiff of danger. However, when JR is struck by a meteorite he finds himself invested with superhuman powers. And so Meteor Man is born. Although energetic and sometimes pointed satire, the film lacks a vital street savvy that Townsend used to be able to dole out in spades. [CB]

Cast: Robert Townsend (Jefferson Reed), Marla Gibbs (Mrs Reed), Eddie Griffin (Michael), Robert Guillaume (Mr Reed), James Earl Jones (Mr Moses), Roy Fegan (Simon), Cynthia Belgrave, Marilyn Coleman, Another Bad Creation, Tiny Lister, Stephanie Williams, Jenifer Lewis, Naughty By Nature, Cypress Hill, Biz Markie, Big Daddy Kane, Frank Gorshin, Beverly Johnson, LaWanda Page, Lela Rochon, Sinbad, Nancy Wilson, Luther Vandross, Bill Cosby (as Marvin).

Dir and Screenplay: Robert Townsend. Pro: Loretha C. Jones. Ph: John A. Alonzo. Ed: Adam Bernardi. Pro Des: Toby Corbett. M: Cliff Eidelman; numbers performed by Hi-Five, Elaine Stepter, Naughty By Nature, Keith Washington, Lisa Taylor, Malaika, Technotronic and Hammer. Costumes: Ruth Carter. Sound: Mark Weingarten. (Tinsel Townsend/MGM–Electric Triangle Pics.) Rel: 17 December 1993. 100 mins. Cert PG.

### The Mighty Ducks

See *Champions*.

### Mother's Boys

Los Angeles; 1994. Inexplicably absent for three years, Jude Madigan returns to her husband and three young sons to start life anew. However, Robert Madigan is now in love with assistant school principal Callie, and wants a divorce. Of course, hell hath no fury like a woman scorned . . . Nudging into the territory of *Fatal Attraction* and *Single White Female*, *Mother's Boys* is not as superficial as it could be and does explore some serious issues. However, the old cheap shock effects are wheeled out in predictable order, although the character of Jude (played with controlled insanity by Jamie Lee Curtis) is refreshingly ambiguous. And, while the Canadian filmmaker Yves Simoneau gives his film a stylish look, the dialogue lets him down. In the end, *Mother's Boys* seems unsure whether or not it wants to be high camp or sober social commentary. [JC-W]

Cast: Jamie Lee Curtis (Jude Madigan), Peter Gallagher (Robert Madigan), Joanne Whalley-Kilmer (Callie), Vanessa Redgrave (Lydia), Luke Edwards (Kes Madigan), Colin Ward (Michael Madigan), Joey Zimmerman (Ben Madigan), Joss Ackland, Paul Guilfoyle, J. E. Freeman, John C. McGinley, Lorraine Toussaint, Mary Anne McGarry.

Dir: Yves Simoneau. Pro: Jack E. Freedman, Wayne S. Williams and Patricia Herskovic. Ex Pro: Bob Weinstein, Harvey Weinstein and Randall Poster. Screenplay: Barry Schneider and Richard Hawley; from the novel by Bernard Taylor. Ph: Elliot Davis. Ed: Michael Ornstein. Pro Des. David Bomba. M: George S. Clinton. Costumes: Deena Appel and Simon Tuke. (CBS Entertainment–Guild.) Rel: 29 April 1994. 95 mins. Cert 15.

### Mr Wonderful

Anthony Minghella, the English writer-director of *Truly, Madly, Deeply*, makes a classy American debut with this bittersweet romantic comedy. Eliciting faultless performances from his top-notch cast, Minghella explores the lives of five characters (and their respective friends) as Gus Dimarco, a New York electrician, struggles to sort out his life. Trapped in a hole (literally, as he works under the street) in order to meet his ex-wife's alimony payments, Dimarco is desperate to find extra cash to pay for his share of a dream – to open a bowling alley with his four best friends. He then embarks on a side career as matchmaker to find the perfect mate for his ex in order to eliminate his alimony debt. Matt Dillon, as Dimarco, has never exhibited a better understanding of throw-away comic timing, while Annabella Sciorra is perfectly complex, vulnerable and staunch as his ex-wife. However, the film's stand-out is Mary-Louise Parker, who plays Dimarco's shrewd, defenceless girlfriend who finds herself caught in the middle. While adding some Hollywood sugar to his dramatic stew, Minghella includes enough pepper to make this a human comedy of enormous pathos and appeal. [JC-W]

Cast: Matt Dillon (Gus Dimarco), Annabella Sciorra (Lee), Mary-Louise Parker (Rita), William Hurt (Tom), Vincent D'Onofrio (Dominic), David Barry Gray (Pope), Dan Hedaya (Harvey), Bruce Kirby (Dante), Luis Guzman (Juice), James Gandolfini (Mike Crosby), Jessica Harper, Joanna Merlin, Paul Bates, Arabella Field, Renee Lippin, Brooke Smith, Bruce Altman, Angela Hall.

Dir and Screenplay: Anthony Minghella; from an original screenplay by Amy Schor and Vicki Polon. Pro: Marianne Moloney. Co-Pro: Steven Felder. Ph: Geoffrey Simpson. Ed: John Tintori. Pro Des: Doug Kraner. M: Michael Gore. Costumes: John Dunn. Sound: Douglas Murray. (Samuel Goldwyn–Buena Vista.) Rel: 22 October 1993. 97 mins. Cert 12.

*Granny on the ball: Robin Williams (seen here with Matthew Lawrence) outdoes Mary Poppins in Chris Columbus's phenomenal hit,* Mrs Doubtfire *(from Fox)*

## Mrs Doubtfire

San Francisco; 1993. A star vehicle if ever there was one. Robin Williams plays Daniel Hillard, a gentle, caring, funny actor with a conscience who refuses to grow up. He's also a father of three, and although he provides plenty of fun for his kids, he's a little slack in the responsibility stakes. His wife, a hard-working design executive, supplies the money and ground rules and has grown tired of her husband's frivolous behaviour. Worse still, she doesn't like who she is when she's around him. Filing for divorce, Miranda Hillard successfully bars Daniel from seeing his children except under limited supervision. So, with the help of heavy-duty make-up, he takes on the persona of Mrs Doubtfire, a to-die-for Scottish nanny who transforms the Hillard household. His family may not know who he is, but at least Daniel can be close to his kids. Following in the high heels of Dustin Hoffman in *Tootsie* (his co-star from *Hook*), Williams is irresistible as the soft-spoken governess, a prim matron with an unexpected sardonic wit. The film itself is mawkish, manipulative and homiletic, but is a good deal more tenable than most Hollywood films about fractured marriages. It also refuses to take sides and is consequently quite moving. And, when not pushing the slapstick beyond credibility, *Mrs Doubtfire* is very amusing. [JC-W]

Cast: Robin Williams (Daniel Hillard/Mrs Doubtfire), Sally Field (Miranda Hillard), Pierce Brosnan (Stu), Harvey Fierstein (Frank), Robert Prosky (Mr Lundy), Polly Holliday (Gloria), Lisa Jakub (Lydia Hillard), Matthew Lawrence (Chris Hillard), Mara Wilson (Natalie Hillard), Anne Haney, Scott Capurro, Sydney Walker, Joe Bellan, Martin Mull, Terence McGovern, Rick Overton, Paul Guilfoyle, Andrew L. Prosky.

Dir: Chris Columbus. Pro: Marsha Garces Williams, Robin Williams and Mark Radcliffe. Ex Pro: Matthew Rushton. Co-Pro: Joan Bradshaw. Screenplay: Randi Mayem Singer and Leslie Dixon; from the novel *Alias Madame Doubtfire* by Anne Fine. Ph: Donald McAlpine. Ed: Raja Gosnell. Pro Des: Angelo Graham. M: Howard Shore; numbers performed by Aerosmith, The Four Seasons, Frank Sinatra, House of Pain, James Brown, and B. B. King and Albert Collins. Costumes: Marit Allen. Sound: Gary Rydstrom. Make-up: Greg Cannom. Animation: Chuck Jones. (Blue Wolf–Fox.) Rel: 28 January 1994. 120 mins. Cert 12.

## Much Ado About Nothing

Seldom has a Shakespearean text been brought to life so vividly, clearly and wittily on screen as in this exhilarating adaptation. Kenneth Branagh, aged 32, directs his fourth film with an energy and *joie de vivre* that celebrates not only the pleasures of great writing, but of love and the human condition itself. A starry, exemplary cast attack their roles with relish, but Branagh as the misogynistic Benedick towers over them all with a mesmerising performance of verbal dexterity and physical wit. Filmed in Tuscany at the 14th-century Villa Vignamaggio, once the home of Leonardo's Mona Lisa. [JC-W]

Cast: Kenneth Branagh (Benedick of Padua), Richard Briers (Leonato, governor of Messina), Michael Keaton (Dogberry), Robert Sean Leonard (Claudio of Florence), Keanu Reeves (Don John), Emma Thompson (Beatrice), Denzel Washington (Don Pedro, Prince of Arragon), Kate Beckinsale (Hero), Gerard

*All mirth and no matter: Emma Thompson and Kenneth Branagh in the latter's glorious* Much Ado About Nothing *(from Entertainment)*

Horan (Borachio), Richard Clifford (Conrade), Brian Blessed (Antonio), Jimmy Yuill (Friar Francis), Imelda Staunton (Margaret), Phyllida Law (Ursula), Ben Elton (Verges), Teddy Jewesbury, Andy Hockley, Chris Barnes, Conrad Nelson, Alex Scott, Alex Lowe, Patrick Doyle.

Dir and Screenplay: Kenneth Branagh; from the comedy by William Shakespeare. Pro: Branagh, Stephen Evans and David Parfitt. Ph: Roger Lanser. Ed: Andrew Marcus. Pro Des: Tim Harvey. M: Patrick Doyle. Costumes: Phyllis Dalton. Sound: David Crozier. (Samuel Goldwyn/Renaissance Films/BBC–Entertainment.) Rel: 27 August 1993. 111 mins. Cert PG.

## The Music of Chance

Bizarre story of two drifters who find themselves at the mercy of a pair of eccentric millionaire gamblers at the latter's palatial country retreat. Unfortunately, static direction and by-the-numbers editing slow down the action and exaggerates the film's literary conceits (from the novel by Paul Auster). And, while Mandy Patinkin brings a quiet strength to his role as the philosophical itinerant, James Spader is all over the place as his disagreeable partner. Intriguing, but no thank you. [JC-W]

Cast: James Spader (Jack Pozzi), Mandy Patinkin (James Nashe), M. Emmet Walsh (Calvin Murks), Charles Durning (Bill Flower), Joel Grey (Willie Stone), Samantha Mathis (Tiffany), Christopher Penn, Pearl Jones, Paul Auster (driver).

Dir: Philip Haas. Pro: Frederick Zollo and Dylan Sellers. Ex Pro: Miles Copeland III, Paul Colichman and Lindsay Law. Screenplay: Philip Haas and Belinda Haas. Ph: Bernard Zitzermann. Ed: Belinda Haas. Pro Des: Hugo Luczyc-Wyhowski. M: Phillip Johnston; numbers performed by Wendy White. Costumes: Rudy Dillon. Sound: Les Lupin. (IRS/Trans Atlantic/American Playhouse–Feature Film Co.) Rel: 18 March 1994. 95 mins. Cert 15.

## My Father the Hero

Paradise Island Resort, Nassau, the Bahamas; 1994. Disney re-make of the funny, enchanting 1991 French comedy *Mon Père, Ce Heros.* The twist here is that Gérard Depardieu repeats his role from the earlier film, this time playing the French father of a 14-year-old *American* girl whom he takes on holiday to the Bahamas. There, he

*Ace of Spader: James Spader deals the cards in Philip Haas's curious* The Music of Chance *(from Feature Film Company)*

*American soufflé: Gerard Depardieu and Katherine Heigl in Steve Miner's so-so* My Father the Hero *(from Buena Vista)*

attempts to win back his estranged daughter's love, while she just wants to flaunt her burgeoning sexuality and to discover boys. To impress a local beach Lothario, she pretends that her father is her lover masquerading as her father which creates no end of problems for the Frenchman. Lacking the charm and credibility of the original, this American photocopy does have its moments. Chief among these must be the scene in which Depardieu sits down at the piano in front of the entire resort and delivers a lusty impersonation of Maurice Chevalier singing 'Thank Heaven For Little Girls'. [JC-W]

Cast: Gérard Depardieu (André), Katherine Heigl (Nicole), Dalton James (Ben), Lauren Hutton (Megan), Faith Prince (Diana Blaine), Emma Thompson (Isabelle), Stephen Tobolowsky, Ann Hearn, Robyn Peterson, Frank Renzulli, Manny Jacobs, Jeffrey Chea, Stephen Burrows, Michael Robinson, Robert Miner, Betty Miner, Steve Wise, Judy Clayton.

Dir: Steve Miner. Pro: Jacques Bar and Jean-Louis Livi. Ex Pro: Edward S. Feldman. Co-Pro: Ted Swanson. Screenplay: Francis Veber and Charlie Peters. Ph: Daryn Okada. Ed: Marshall Harvey. Pro Des: Christopher Nowak. M: David Newman; numbers performed by The Baha Men. Costumes: Vicki Sanchez. (Touchstone–Buena Vista.) Rel: 6 May 1994. 90 mins. Cert PG.

## My Life

When successful PR man Bob Jones discovers he's dying of cancer, he makes a video of his life for his unborn child – only to discover he cannot remember his childhood. While the sentiments of this paean to life and death are to be admired, the heavy hand of manipulation is all too apparent. From the opening bars of John Barry's mawkish score to the spiritual blasts of ethereal light, the film pummels the tear ducts. Having said that, Michael Keaton and Nicole Kidman – as Bob and his pregnant wife – play their roles with considerable restraint, although Kidman's part is desperately underwritten. Originally to have been made as a TV movie (starring Mike Farrell), the project was upgraded to a major feature when first-time director Bruce Joel Rubin hit pay dirt with his script for *Ghost*. [JC-W]

Cast: Michael Keaton (Bob 'Robert Ivanovich' Jones), Nicole Kidman (Gail Jones), Bradley Whitford (Paul Ivanovich), Queen Latifah (Theresa), Michael Constantine (Bill Ivanovich), Rebecca Schull (Rose Ivanovich), Haing S. Ngor (Mr Ho), Mark Lowenthal, Lee Garlington, Toni Sawyer, Romy Rosemont, Kenneth Tigar, Sondra Rubin, Vasek C. Simek, James Rubin, Gary Rubin, Charlotte Zucker, Blanche Rubin, Ari Rubin.

Dir and Screenplay: Bruce Joel Rubin. Pro: Rubin, Jerry Zucker and Hunt Lowry. Ex Pro: Gil Netter. Ph: Peter James. Ed: Richard Chew. Pro Des: Neil Spisak. M: John Barry. Costumes: Judy Ruskin. Sound: John Sutton III. (Capella Films–Guild.) Rel: 11 March 1994. 117 mins. Cert 12.

*Death of a salesman: Michael Keaton grapples with the mechanics of videotaping and the complexities of regret, in Bruce Joel Rubin's glutinous* My Life *(from Guild)*

*Naked anger: Deborah MacLaren and David Thewlis in Mike Leigh's provocative, numbing and witty satire of nineties Britain (from First Independent)*

### My New Gun

Some nice lines, offbeat humour and unexpected twists cannot save the terminal stasis of this fuzzy mystery comedy. Diane Lane plays Debbie Bender, a perfect New Jersey housewife married to Gerald, an arrogant radiologist who insists that she adopt a .38 gun. Consequently, the new toy sparks off an unexpected chain of events that transforms the lives of the Benders forever (although the only time the gun is fired is when Gerald shoots himself in the foot!). Tighter pacing *might* have turned this into something special. [JC-W]

Cast: Diane Lane (Debbie Bender), James Le Gros (Skippy), Stephen Collins (Gerald Bender), Tess Harper (Kimmy Hayes), Bruce Altman (Irwin Bloom), Maddie Corman (Myra), Bill Raymond (Andrew), Phillip Seymour (Chris Hoffman), Stephen Pearlman (Al Schlyen), Suzzy Roche, Patti Chambers, Gene Canfield, Gussie Levy.

Dir and Screenplay: Stacy Cochran. Pro: Michael Flynn. Ex Pro: Miles A. Copeland III, Paul Colichman and Harold Welb. Co-Pro: Lydia Dean Pilcher. Ph: Ed Lachman. Ed: Camilla Toniolo. Pro Des: Toby Corbett. M: Pat Irwin. Costumes: Eugenie Bafaloukos. (IRS Media Inc.–Feature Film Co.) Rel: 13 May 1994. 98 mins. Cert 15.

### Naked

A 27-year-old man from Manchester finds himself on the streets of London, where he pontificates about the meaning of life and the Apocalypse, abuses those he loves and, occasionally, helps complete strangers. A man of enormous wit, self-education and cruelty, Johnny is due for a few life lessons of his own but not before he has left an indelible mark on all those he meets. Juggling scabrous black humour with doses of devastating social drama, Mike Leigh once again tramples across the narrow divide between naturalism and caricature. But whatever else you may think of this work, you cannot take your eyes – or heart – off it. A remarkable British film which won Leigh and leading actor David Thewlis the top honours at the 1993 Cannes Film Festival. [JC-W]

Cast: David Thewlis (Johnny), Lesley Sharp (Louise), Katrin Cartlidge (Sophie), Greg Cruttwell (Jeremy/Sebastian), Claire Skinner (Sandra), Peter Wight (Brian), Ewen Bremner (Archie), Susan Vidler (Maggie), Deborah MacLaren (woman in window), Gina McKee (cafe girl), Carolina Giammetta (masseuse), Elizabeth Berrington, Darren Tunstall, Robert Putt, Angela Curran.

Dir and Screenplay: Mike Leigh. Pro: Simon Channing-Williams. Ph: Dick Pope. Ed: Jon Gregory. Pro Des: Alison Chitty. M: Andrew Dickson. Costumes: Lindy Hemming. Sound: Peter Maxwell. (Film Four International/British Screen/Thin Man–First Independent.) Rel: 5 November 1993. 126 mins. Cert 18.

*Gun and games: Leslie Nielsen ingratiates himself with Kathleen Freeman, Fred Ward and Anna Nicole Smith in Peter Segal's gag-packed* Naked Gun 33⅓: The Final Insult *(from UIP)*

### Naked Gun 33⅓: The Final Insult

Frank Drebin (Leslie Nielsen) has retired from the LA police squad and is leading a life of quiet obsessional domesticity with his beautiful wife of six months, Jane Spencer-Drebin (Priscilla Presley). But when a terrorist threatens to target the Oscar ceremony in Hollywood Drebin finds himself back in action. From the opening shot of a newspaper headline screaming DYSLEXIA FOR CURE FOUND, this second

*Ill-met: Annabella Sciorra mistakes Kevin Anderson for her dream date – in Warren Leight's most bewitching* The Night We Never Met *(from Guild)*

sequel (to the movie based on an unsuccessful TV series) refuses to let up. Packing in more (mostly new) jokes per minute than the last, feeble outing, *The Final Insult* is another very silly, hit-or-miss jumble, but with a fair number of comic bullseyes. [JC-W]

Cast: Leslie Nielsen (Lt Frank Drebin), Priscilla Presley (Jane Spencer-Drebin), George Kennedy (Ed Hocken), O. J. Simpson (Nordberg), Fred Ward (Rocco), Kathleen Freeman (Muriel), Anna Nicole Smith (Tanya), Ellen Greene (Louise), Raye Birke (Papshmir), Ed Williams, Matt Roe, Earl Boen, Karen Segal, Charlotte Zucker, Doris Belack, Randall 'Tex' Cobb, Ann B. Davis, Tom Finnegan, Joe Grifasi, Vanna White, 'Weird Al' Yankovic, Mary Lou Retton, Pia Zadora, Burt Zucker, David Zucker, Peter Segal, Bill Erwin, John Capodice, Florence Henderson, Nicole Segal, Shannen Doherty, Olympia Dukakis, R. Lee Ermey, Morgan Fairchild, Elliott Gould, Mariel Hemingway, James Earl Jones, Raquel Welch.

Dir: Peter Segal. Pro: Robert K. Weiss and David Zucker. Ex Pro: Jerry Zucker, Jim Abrahams and Gill Netter. Screenplay: Pat Proft, David Zucker and Robert LoCash. Ph: Robert Stevens. Ed: James R. Symons. Pro Des: Lawrence G. Paull. M: Ira Newborn; numbers performed by Huey Lewis and The News, The Bee Gees, Johnny Mathis, Jerry Lee Lewis, Pia Zadora, Peter Segal, etc. Mr Newman's Really Sexy Cousin: Amanda. Costumes: Mary E. Vogt. Special Make-Up: David B. Miller. Too Much Make-Up: Tammy Faye Bakker. Kiss and Make-Up: Burt and Loni. (Paramount–UIP.) Rel: 20 May 1994. 83 mins. Cert 12.

### Neil Simon's Lost in Yonkers

Yonkers; 1942. Impeccably staged screen version of Neil Simon's Pulitzer prize-winning Broadway success about a dysfunctional New York family. When their father is forced to take to the road to sell scrap metal, 15-year-old Jacob and 13-year-old Arthur Kurnitz reluctantly move in with their domineering grandmother and scatty aunt Bella. There, they discover some disconcerting truths about their family and some handy life lessons from their crooked Uncle Louie. Although the dialogue bears Simon's signature insight and wit, there is an uncomfortable familiarity about it all, born – one suspects – from too much public navel-gazing. Still, Irene Worth is mesmerising as the unforgiving grandma, although the rest of the cast are frequently caught acting. [JC-W]

Cast: Richard Dreyfuss (Louie Kurnitz), Mercedes Ruehl (Bella Kurnitz), Irene Worth (Grandma Kurnitz), David Strathairn (Johnny), Brad Stoll (Jacob 'Jay' Kurnitz), Mike Damus (Arthur 'Arty' Kurnitz), Jack Laufer (Eddie Kurnitz), Susan Merson (Aunt Gert), Robert Guy Miranda, Illya Haase, Jesse Vincent.

Dir: Martha Coolidge, Pro: Ray Stark. Ex Pro: Joseph M. Caracciolo. Co-Pro: Emanuel Azenberg. Screenplay: Neil Simon. Ph: Johnny E. Jensen. Ed: Steven Cohen. Pro Des: David Chapman. M: Elmer Bernstein. Costumes: Shelley Komarov. (Rastar–Columbia.) Rel: 17 June 1994. 113 mins. Cert PG.

### Night and Day – Nuit et Jour

Julie and Jack are a young couple living in a Parisian apartment. At night Jack drives a taxi while Julie, unable to stand the loneliness, walks the streets. During the day they make love and talk of their happiness. They have no friends, no furniture and little money. But that is all they need. Then Jack introduces Julie to Joseph, a fellow taxi driver . . . Lots of talk, little action, *très ennuyeux*. [JC-W]

Cast: Guilaine Londez (Julie), Thomas Langmann (Jack), François Negret (Joseph), Nicole Colchat, Pierre Laroche (Jack's parents).

Dir and Screenplay: Chantal Akerman. Ex Pro: Martine Marignac and Maurice Tinchant. Ph: Jean-Claude Neckelbrouck, Pierre Gordower, Bernard Belville and Olivier Dessalles. Ed: Francine Sandberg and Camille Bordes-Resnais. Art: Michel Vandestien and Dominique Douret. M: Marc Herouet, Heitor Villa-Lobos, Gabriel Faure and Jean Louise Aubert. Costumes: Brigitte Nierhaus and Michele Blondeel. Sound: Alixe Comte and Pierre Tucat. (Pierre Grise/Centre National de la Cinematographie/Canal Plus/Sofinergie 2/Paradise Films/La RTBF/George Reinhart Pros–Artificial Eye.) Rel: 6 August 1993. 90 mins. Cert 15.

### The Night We Never Met

Unlike Tom Hanks and Meg Ryan in *Sleepless in Seattle* (whose romantic destiny was separated by a continent), the protagonists of *The Night We Never Met* live on top of each other. Sam and Ellen time-share an old-fashioned Greenwich Village apartment, with Sam renting the place on Saturdays and Mondays, and Ellen stopping over on Tuesdays and Thursdays. He contributes tasteful furniture and cooks gourmet meals, she sews lace curtains and paints still lifes. They were made for each other – but never meet. Matters are complicated by a third tenant, Brian, a yuppie slob who uses the apartment as a bachelor pad and regularly trashes the place. Unfortunately, he also owns the joint and there's little Sam or Ellen can do about the blip in their paradise. Matthew Broderick, always an adept comedian, brings both style and credibility to his role of a cultured bachelor; Annabella Sciorra contributes her usual blend of iron and honey; while Kevin Anderson as Brian is perfectly unbearable. Remarkably, this thoroughly delightful, very funny comedy of mistaken identity marks the film directing/writing debut of New York humourist Warren Leight. [JC-W]

Cast: Matthew Broderick (Sam Lester), Annabella Sciorra (Ellen Holder), Kevin Anderson (Brian McVeigh), Jeanne Tripplehorn (Pastel), Justine Bateman (Janet Beehan), Tim Guinee (Kenneth), Dana Wheeler-Nicholson (Inga), Louise Lasser (Mrs Winkler), Michael Mantell, Christine Baranski, Doris Roberts, Dominic Chianese, Bradley White, Greg Germann, Bill Campbell, Michelle Hurst, Lewis Black, Ranjit Chowdhry, Naomi Campbell, Katherine Houghton, Brooke Smith, Paul Guilfoyle.

Dir and Screenplay: Warren Leight. Pro: Michael Peyser. Ex Pro: Sidney Kimmel, Bob Weinstein and Harvey Weinstein. Co-Pro: Rudd Simmons. Ph: John A. Thomas. Ed: Camilla Toniolo. Pro Des: Lester Cohen. M: Evan Lurie. Costumes: Ellen Lutter. Sound: William Sarokin. (Miramax/Tribeca–Guild.) Rel: 27 August 1993. 98 mins. Cert 15.

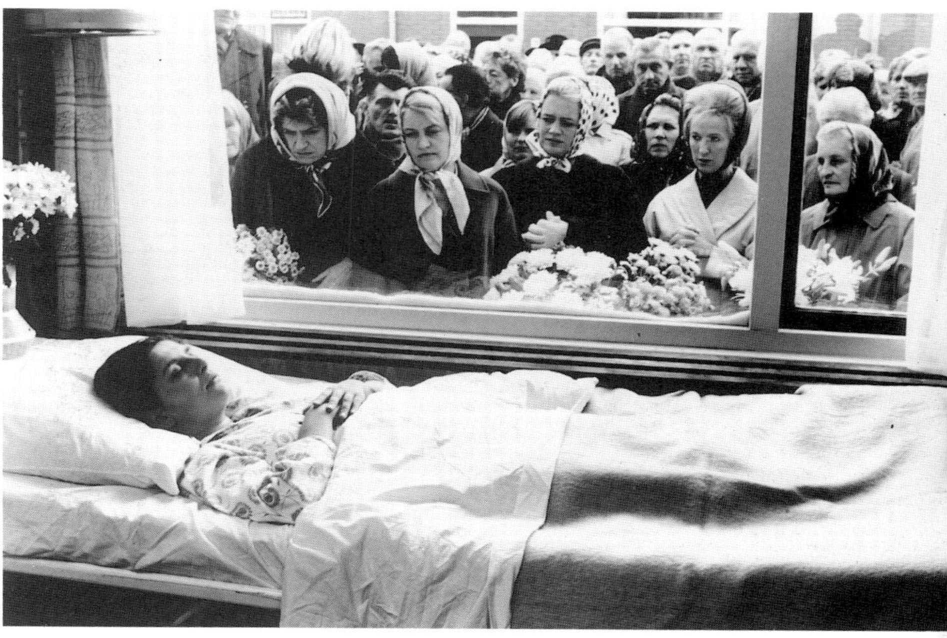

*Estate of affairs: Annet Malherbe becomes a spectacle in Alex van Warmerdam's extraordinary* The Northerners *(from Mayfair Entertainment)*

## No Escape

In the year 2022 the incarceration of dangerous criminals has become big business, but as with any industry devoted to profit (such as the policing of parking) the line between efficacy and morality has become blurred. One warder of a state-of-the-art, escape-proof penal institution looks on his job as 'the reprocessing of human garbage'; his catch phrase: 'Death is the only way out.' But new inmate John Robbins is not convinced – even after being relegated to Absolom, a tropical island governed by the most dangerous cons in the world. After setting up a fascinating premise and deftly establishing a dystopian world in the vein of *The Terminator*, *No Escape* suddenly changes gear into a sort of old-fashioned adventure in which human values vie with the law of the jungle. Still, the action sequences are terrific. *Mad Max* meets *Papillon*. [JC-W]

Cast: Ray Liotta (John Robbins, prisoner No. 2675), Lance Henriksen (The Father), Stuart Wilson (Marek), Kevin Dillon (Casey), Kevin J. O'Connor (Stephano), Don Henderson (Killian), Ian McNeice (King), Jack Shepherd (Dysart), Michael Lerner (Warder), Ernie Hudson (Hawkins), Russell Kiefel, Brian M. Logan, Cheuk-Fai Chan, Machs Colombani, David Argue.

Dir: Martin Campbell. Pro: Gale Anne Hurd. Ex Pro: Jake Eberts. Co-Pro: Michael R. Joyce and James Eastep. Screenplay: Michael Gaylin and Joel Gross; based on Richard Herley's novel *The Penal Colony*. Ph: Phil Meheux. Ed: Terry Rawlings. Pro Des: Allan Cameron. M: Graeme Revell. Costumes: Norma Moriceau. (Platinum Pictures–Guild.) Rel: 3 June 1994. 115 mins. Cert 15.

## The Northerners – De Noorderlingen

Somewhere in Holland, 1960: a solitary street stands beside a dense forest, cut off from the rest of the world. The first leg of an abandoned housing development, the street takes on an aberrant personality of its own as its inhabitants (a horny butcher, vigilant hunter, snooping postman and endless nosy housewives) strive to lead ordinary lives. A bizarre black comedy, *The Northerners* is nothing to write home about, but is executed with

*Escape-of-the-art: Kevin Dillon and Ray Liotta face impossible odds in Martin Campbell's entertaining* No Escape *(from Guild)*

*The Iceman Directeth: Steven Seagal (*right*) with John C. McGinley and Michael Caine in* On Deadly Ground*, a Seagal/Nasso production of a Steven Seagal film directed by Steven Seagal (from Warner)*

some economic flair and does cast its own peculiar spell. From the director of *Abel.* [JC-W]

Cast: Leonard Lucieer (Thomas), Jack Wouterse (Jacob, the butcher), Rudolf Lucieer (Anton, the ranger), Alex van Warmerdam (Simon Plagge, the postman), Annet Malherbe (Martha), Loes Wouterson (Elisabeth), Veerle Dobbelaere (Agnes), Dary Some, Jaques Commandeur, Janny Goslinga, Theo Van Gogh.

Dir: Alex van Warmerdam. Pro: Laurens Geels and Dick Maas. Screenplay: Van Warmerdam and Aat Ceelen. Ph: Marc Felperlaan. Ed: Rene Wiegmans. Pro Des: Rikke Jelier. M: Vincent van Warmerdam. Costumes: Leonie Polak. Sound: Bert Flantua. (First Floor Features–Mayfair Entertainment.) Rel: 14 January 1994. 108 mins. Cert 15.

### On Deadly Ground

Alaska; 1994. Ruthless industrialist Michael Caine will lose his oil franchise to the Inuit natives if he cannot meet his deadline. So he goes on pumping crude in spite of faulty equipment that could endanger lives and devastate the environment. Steven Seagal, ponytail intact, gets wind of Caine's machinations and single-handedly declares war on the tycoon's empire. Marking Seagal's debut as composite director, producer and superstar, this is a dumb, artless, spectacular and good-looking action thriller with a vital message to impart. The dialogue stinks, but then Shakespeare didn't write *The Terminator.* [JC-W]

Cast: Steven Seagal (Forrest Taft), Michael Caine (Michael Jennings), Joan Chen (Masu), John C. McGinley (MacGruder), R. Lee Ermey (Stone), Shari Shattuck (Liles), Richard Hamilton (Hugh Palmer), Billy Bob Thornton, Chief Irvin Brink, Elsie Pistolhead, Mike Starr, Sven-Ole Thorsen, Irvin Kershner, Bart the Bear.

Dir: Steven Seagal. Pro: Seagal, Julius R. Nasso and A. Kitman Ho. Ex Pro: Robert Watts and Jeffrey Robinov. Co-Pro: Edward McDonnell. Screenplay: Ed Horowitz and Robin U. Russin. Ph: Ric Waite. Ed: Robert A Ferretti. Pro Des: Wm Ladd Skinner. M: Basil Poledouris. Costumes: Joseph G. Aulisi. Sound: Edward Tise. (Seagal/Nasso–Warner.) Rel: 11 March 1994. 102 mins. Cert 15.

### Once Upon a Forest

Well-meaning but artless and charmless story about a young mouse, mole and hedgehog who go on an expedition to save their badger friend, Michelle, who is dying from poisonous gas inhalation after a tanker has crashed in the woods. While treading on the ecologically friendly heels of *Ferngully The Last Rainforest*, this latest outing from Hanna-Barbera (*The Flintstones*, *Yogi Bear*) lacks wit and depth and is an oversimplification of the issues threatening wildlife. Kids should be bored. [JC-W]

Voices of: Michael Crawford (Cornelius), Ben Vereen (Phineas), Ellen Blain (Abigail), Ben Gregory (Edgar), Paige Gosney (Russell), Elizabeth Moss (Michelle).

Dir: Charles Grosvenor. Pro: David Kirschner and Jerry Mills. Ex Pro: William Hanna and Paul Gertz. Screenplay: Mark Young and Kelly Ward; based on the Welsh story created by Rae Lambert. Ed: Pat A. Foley. Pro Des: Carol Holman Grosvenor. M: James Horner; numbers performed by Michael Crawford, Ben Vereen, and Florence Warner Jones. Sound: David Lewis Yewdall. (Hanna-Barbera/HTV Cymru/Wales–Fox.) Rel: 22 October 1993. 68 mins. Cert U.

### Painted Heart

Kenosha/Milwaukee, Wisconsin; 1992. Unusual, wry American comedy-drama set in a midwestern twilight zone in which nobody is who they seem to be. While the sandy-haired Wesley appears one spanner short of a tool set, he is a harmless good ol' boy in love with the wife of his boss. She's not sure if she's happy in her marriage, while her husband seems preoccupied with dating vagrants . . . All will be revealed in the film's memorable climax. While the premise itself borders on the simplistic, it is the everyday detail and conversational non sequiturs that make the film so endearing, like a technicolor photocopy of life at its weirdest. A rich Country soundtrack and some eloquent photography smooth out the rough edges. [JC-W]

Cast: Will Patton (Wesley), Bebe Neuwirth (Margaret), Robert Pastorelli (Willie), Casey Siemaszko (Cal), Mark Boone Jr (Tom), Richard Hamilton (Robert Tony), Jayne Haynes, Jeff Weiss, John Diehl, Dale Rehfeld, Robert Breuler, Ted Levine (Kenny the DJ).

Dir and Screenplay: Michael Taav. Pro: Marc Pollard and Randall Poster. Ex Pro: Marc Glimcher. Ph: Robert Yeoman. Ed: Nancy Richardson. Pro Des: Mark Friedberg. M: John Wesley Harding. Costumes: Wendy A. Rolfe. Sound: Brit Warner. (Second Son Entertainment–Metro Tartan.) Rel: 22 April 1994, 91 mins. Cert 15.

## The Paper

Ferociously entertaining comedy-drama set in a day of the life of a New York tabloid. Michael Keaton stars as Henry Hackett, the overworked metro editor of *The New York Sun*, an adrenaline junkie who has to make some major decisions concerning his private life, his future and the lead story in tomorrow's paper. It's a miracle that screenwriters David and Stephen Koepp (brothers) have managed to pack so many characters and subplots into one screenplay, even if the final fifth crashes into out-and-out melodrama. Bully, too, for Ron Howard, who directs with muscular grace, and to his editor and camera operator for managing to keep up. David Koepp, incidentally, was only 30 when he wrote and co-produced *The Paper* and already has *seven* screenplays to his credit (including *Jurassic Park* and *Carlito's Way*). [JC-W]

*Hold the presses! Glenn Close and Michael Keaton discuss expediency versus ethics in Ron Howard's gripping, funny* The Paper *(from UIP). Randy Quaid looks on*

Cast: Michael Keaton (Henry Hackett), Glenn Close (Alicia Clark), Marisa Tomei (Martha Hackett), Randy Quaid (Dan McDougal), Robert Duvall (Bernie White), Jason Robards (Graham Keighley), Jason Alexander (Marion Sandusky), Spalding Gray (Paul Bladden), Lynne Thigpen (Janet), Jack Kehoe (Phil), Roma Maffia (Carmen), Amelia Campbell (Robin), Jill Hennessy (Deanne White), Catherine O'Hara, Clint Howard, Geoffrey Owens, William Prince, Augusta Dabney, Bruce Altman, Jack McGee, Bobo Lewis, Edward Hibbert, Michael Countryman, Siobhan Fallon, Joe Viviani, Michael Moran, Stephen Koepp, Victor Truro, Rance Howard, Vickie Thomas, Jean Speegle Howard, Jim Meskimen, Mike Sheehan, Cheryl Howard, Bob Costas, Richard Price, Jeannie Williams.

Dir: Ron Howard. Pro: Brian Grazer and Frederick Zollo. Co-Pro: David Koepp. Ex Pro: Dylan Sellers and Todd Hallowell. Screenplay: David Koepp and Stephen Koepp. Ph: John Seale. Ed: Daniel Hanley and Michael Hill. Pro Des: Todd Hallowell. M: Randy Newman: numbers performed by Randy Newman, Mervyn Warren, Marvin Gaye, Spectrum, Beth Hooper, Tom Jones, etc. Costumes: Rita Ryack. (Imagine Entertainment/Universal–UIP.) Rel: 6 May 1994. 112 mins. Cert 15.

## Passion Fish

When soap star May-Alice Colehaine is crippled on her way to have her legs

*Bayou blues: David Strathairn, Alfre Woodard and Mary McDonnell in John Sayles' outstanding* Passion Fish *(from Mayfair Entertainment)*

*The spy who loved her: Denzel Washington in Alan J. Pakula's elaborate thriller* The Pelican Brief *(from Warner)*

waxed, she returns to her late parents' home on the edge of the Louisiana swampland. There, she is subjected to the bizarre personal problems of a string of nurses, until settling on the quiet, enigmatic Chantelle. Chantelle needs the job, and May-Alice needs Chantelle – in spite of the odd couple's apparent differences. But gradually the spoilt, alcoholic actress ('a bitch on wheels') and the reticent, emotionally damaged Chantelle discover they have more in common than they at first realised. Besides the emotions it evokes and the questions it confronts, *Passion Fish* is a masterclass in filmmaking at its finest. Boasting one of the sharpest, funniest and most humanly insightful scripts in years, the film is superbly atmospheric and acted, proving yet again that John Sayles is one of the greatest filmmakers alive. [JC-W]

Cast: Mary McDonnell (May-Alice Colehaine), Alfre Woodard (Chantelle Blades), Vondie Curtis-Hall (Sugar LeDoux), David Strathairn (Rennie), Angela Bassett (Dawn/Rhonda), Marianne Muellerleile (Drushka), Leo Burmester (Uncle Reeves), Mary Portser (Precious), Nora Dunn (Ti-Marie), Maggie Renzi, Victoria Edwards, Amanda Carlin, Elaine West, Linda Castle, Leigh Harris, Tom Wright, Jennifer Gardner, Sheila Kelley, Nancy Mette, Shauntisa Willis, John Henry.

Dir, Screenplay and Ed: John Sayles. Pro: Sarah Green and Maggie Renzi. Ex Pro: John Sloss. Ph: Roger Deakins. Pro Des: Dan Bishop and Dianna Freas. M: Mason Daring; numbers performed by Duke Levine, John Delafose and The Eunice Playboys, Willis Prudhomme and The Zydeco Express, etc. Costumes: Cynthia Flynt. Sound: Philip Stockton. (Atchafalaya-Mayfair Entertainment.) Rel: 3 September 1993. 135 mins. Cert 15.

## The Pelican Brief

A beautiful young law student in New Orleans concocts a theory behind the assassination of two supreme court judges and finds herself in deep trouble. As conspiracy thrillers go, this is an efficient condensation of John Grisham's complex, best-selling novel set in the giddy world of law, counter-intelligence and inconceivable corruption. However, you'll have to be pretty alert to follow the multiple narrative threads. While everybody concerned (cast, crew, director-scripter Alan J. Pakula) puts on a good show, they all take second place to the plot. Incidentally, Pakula covered similar terrain with far more aplomb (and suspense and credibility) with the fact-based *All the President's Men*. [JC-W]

Cast: Julia Roberts (Darby Shaw), Denzel Washington (Gray Grantham), Sam Shepard (Thomas Callahan), John Heard (Gavin Verheek), Tony Goldwyn (Fletcher Coal), James B. Sikking (Denton Voyles), William Atherton (Bob Gminski), Robert Culp (the President), Stanley Tucci (Khamel), Hume Cronyn (Justice Abraham Rosenberg), John Lithgow (Smith Keen), Anthony Heald, Nicholas Woodeson, Stanley Anderson, Matthew Barr, Cynthia Nixon, Jake Weber, Casey Biggs, Edwin Newman, Magee Hickey.

Dir and Screenplay: Alan J. Pakula. Pro: Pakula and Pieter Jan Brugge. Ph: Stephen Goldblatt. Ed: Tom Rolf and Trudy Ship. Pro Des: Philip Rosenberg. M: James Horner; numbers performed by Clarence Hollimon, Lynn August, Aretha Franklin, Irene and The Mikes, etc. Costumes: Albert Wolsky. Sound: Ron Bochar. (Warner.) Rel: 25 February 1994. 141 mins. Cert 12.

## A Perfect World

1963; Texas. Imprisoned for armed robbery, hardened criminal Butch Haynes escapes Huntsville jail and takes an 8-year-old boy hostage. As it happens, the kid – Phillip – is a Jehovah's Witness and has never had an exciting day out in his life. Well, Butch Haynes is about to change all that . . . Clint Eastwood, fresh from his Oscar-winning success with *Unforgiven*, turns in another masterpiece with this tough, tender, funny and moving drama that tackles a whole bunch of issues with surprising conviction and complexity. Clint himself plays the bull-headed Texas Ranger on the scent of Butch, saddled with a female criminologist (Laura Dern) on her first field trip. However, it is Costner who steals the acting honours with his most charismatic, multi-levelled performance to date, essaying a righteous bastard we care for in spite of ourselves. That's great screen acting for you – and direction and writing. [JC-W]

Cast: Kevin Costner (Butch Haynes), Clint Eastwood (Red Garnett), Laura Dern (Sally Gerber), T. J. Lowther (Phillip Perry), Keith Szarabajka (Terry Pugh), Jennifer Griffin (Gladys Perry), Linda Hart (Eileen), Leo Burmester, Paul Hewitt, Bradley Whitford, Ray McKinnon, Darryl Cox, Bruce McGill, John M. Jackson, Connie Cooper, Wayne Dehart, Mary Alice, Woody Watson.

Dir: Clint Eastwood. Pro: Mark Johnson and David Valdes. Screenplay: John Lee Hancock. Ph: Jack N. Green. Ed: Joel Cox. Pro Des: Henry Bumstead. M: Lennie Niehaus; numbers performed by Bob Wills and His Texas Cowboys, George Hamilton IV, Don Gibson, Perry Como, Johnny Cash, Chris Isaak, Willie Nelson, Marty Robbins, etc. Costumes: Erica Edell Phillips. Sound: Alan Robert Murray. (Malpaso–Warner.) Rel: 26 December 1993. 138 mins. Cert 15.

### Pétain

1940–5; France. Henri Philippe Omer Pétain was 84 years old when he took control of the French government in the Second World War. With the Nazis descending on Paris, Pétain and his suitcase administration set up shop in the small town of Vichy, where the old man collaborated with the Germans at arm's length, believing that the rebirth of France lay in his country's suffering. Jacques Dufilho makes a creditable Pétain and is ably matched by Jean Yanne's gruff, chain-smoking Laval. While French history buffs are likely to stay awake, others might find the film episodic, wordy and very long . . . [JC-W]

Cast: Jacques Dufilho (Marshal Philippe Pétain), Jean Yanne (Pierre Laval), Denis Manuel (Reynaud), Julie Marboeuf (Colette), Clovis Cornillac (François), Antoinette Moya (Eugenie Pétain), Jean-Claude Dreyfus, Jean-Pierre Cassel, Christian Charmetant, André Penvern, Frédérique Tirmont, Jean-François Perrier, Vincent Gauthier.

Dir: Jean Marboeuf. Pro: Jacques Kirsner. Screenplay: Marboeuf, Jean-Pierre Marchand and Alain Riou; from Marc Ferro's biography. Ph: Dominique Bouilleret. Ed: Anne-France Lebrun. Pro Des: Jérome Clement. M: Georges Garvarentz. Costumes: Odile Sauton. Sound: Philippe Arbez. (Mod Films/France 2/Canal Plus/Sofica Creations–Gala.) Rel: 11 March 1994. 133 mins. Cert 12.

### Le Petit Prince a Dit – And the Little Prince Said

Switzerland/France/Italy; now. When a divorced father discovers that his 10-year-old daughter is seriously ill, he cannot face anything but the transience of their companionship. A subtly seductive film that steadfastly refuses to kowtow to melodrama or sentimentality, *Le Petit Prince* allows the viewer to cherish the simple, sensual humanity of its tale. While tears may not flow, the heart is profoundly touched. A 1991 French-Swiss co-production. [JC-W]

Cast: Richard Berry (Adam Leibovich), Anémone (Melanie), Marie Kleiber (Violette Leibovich), Lucie Phan (Lucie), Mista Prechac (Minerve), Claude Muret (Jean-Pierre).

Dir: Christine Pascal. Pro: Robert Boner. Assoc Pro: Emmanuel Schlumberger. Screenplay: Pascal and Boner. Ph: Pascal Marti. Ed: Jacques Comets. M: Bruno Coulais. Costumes: Catherine Meurisse. Sound: Dominique Vieillard and Jean-Pierre Laforce. (Ciné Manufacture SA/French Prods–City Screen.) Rel: 24 June 1994. 106 mins. Cert PG.

*Past imperfect: Escaped convict Kevin Costner 'adopts' Jehovah's Witness T. J. Lowther in the seminal year of 1963 – in Clint Eastwood's brilliant* A Perfect World *(from Warner)*

### Philadelphia

The first major Hollywood film to tackle AIDS and it looks like it. Wearing its political correctness like a

*A thunder of silence: Richard Berry and Marie Kleiber in Christine Pascal's affecting* Le Petit Prince a Dit *(from City Screen)*

*Red banner day: Tom Hanks and Denzel Washington in Jonathan Demme's politically precise* Philadelphia *(from Columbia TriStar)*

badge, *Philadelphia* boasts a story made in computer heaven. A dedicated young attorney is the star attraction of the law firm Wyant, Wheeler, Hellerman, Tetlow and Brown, and keeps his private life private. Hell, a lawyer's not meant to *have* a private life. But when Andrew Beckett contracts AIDS, his firm summarily fires him and so he hires a homophobic black attorney to fight his case. Jonathan Demme, fresh off his success with *The Silence of the Lambs*, directs with big, meaningful close-ups and a thick coat of gloss. Tom Hanks as Beckett is surprisingly good, and is given a Great Scene in which he explains the ferocious emotion of his favourite aria to a disbelieving Denzel Washington. However, the film refuses to end as Demme battles the tear ducts in a finale which feels increasingly manufactured. Actually, dying is never as tasteful. [JC-W]

Cast: Tom Hanks (Andrew Beckett), Denzel Washington (Joe Miller), Jason Robards (Charles Wheeler), Mary Steenburgen (Belinda Conine), Antonio Banderas (Miguel Alvarez), Ron Vawter (Bob Seidman), Joanne Woodward (Sarah Beckett), Rev. Robert Castle (Mr Beckett), Robert Ridgley, Lisa Summerour, Roberta Maxwell, Karen Finley, Daniel Chapman, Charles Glenn, Anna Deavere Smith, Lisa Talerico, Chandra Wilson, David Drake, Peter Jacobs, Paul Lazar, Bradley Whitford, Warren Miller, Lauren Roselli, Joey Perillo, Bill Rowe, Tracey Walter, Julius Erving, Ann Dowd, John Bedford Lloyd, Dan Olmstead, Daniel Von Bargen, Harry Northup, Kenneth Utt, Obba Babatunde, Charles Napier, Roger Corman, Mayor Edward Rendell, Kathryn Witt, André B. Blake, Q Lazzarus, Quentin Crisp, Roy Blount Jr, Everett Quinten, Enrique Oliver, Garrett Brown.

Dir: Jonathan Demme. Pro: Demme and Edward Saxon. Ex Pro: Gary Goetzman, Kenneth Utt and Ron Bozman. Screenplay: Ron Nyswaner. Ph: Tak Fujimoto. Ed: Craig McKay. Pro Des: Kristi Zea. M: Howard Shore; Mozart; numbers performed by Bruce Springsteen, Neil Young, Sade, Indigo Girls, The Neville Brothers, Pauletta Washington, RAM, Spin Doctors, Peter Gabriel, The Flirtations, Q Lazzarus, Maria Callas, etc. Costumes: Colleen Atwood. Sound: Ron Bochar. (Clinica Estetico–Columbia Tristar.) Rel: 25 February 1994. 125 mins. Cert 12.

## The Piano

The 1800s; New Zealand. For Ada McGrath, a mute Scottish woman, her voice is her piano. Any man who can hear her notes can win her love, but when her father marries her off to a New Zealand settler, the latter leaves the piano on the beach where it was unloaded. Later, he gives the musical instrument (in return for land) to an illiterate neighbour, George Baines, a man who has adopted the culture of the Maoris. Baines is fascinated by the piano and offers to trade it back to Ada – key by key – in return for 'piano lessons' which gradually take on extraordinarily sexual connotations. Dousing her film in the bleak atmosphere of the New Zealand hinterland, director Jane Campion artfully unveils a tale of enormous intelligence and power as metaphor clashes with tragedy. The photography, production design and music are all top-rate – not to mention Holly Hunter's unconditional performance – making this a worthy winner of the 1993 Palme d'Or at Cannes. [JC-W]

Cast: Holly Hunter (Ada McGrath), Harvey Keitel (George Baines), Sam Neill (Stewart), Anna Paquin (Flora), Kerry Walker (Aunt Morag), Genevieve Lemon (Nessie), Tungia Baker, Ian Mune, Peter Dennett.

Dir and Screenplay: Jane Campion. Pro: Jan Chapman. Ex Pro: Alain Depardieu. Ph: Stuart Dryburgh. Ed: Veronika Jenet. Pro Des: Andrew McAlpine. M: Michael Nyman. Costumes: Janet Patterson. Sound: Lee Smith. (Jan Chapman Prods/CIBY 2000–Entertainment.) Rel: 29 October 1993. 120 mins. Cert 15.

## A Place in the World – Un Lugar en el Mundo

Argentina; the 1980s. Returning to the dusty homeland of his youth, Ernesto, now a young man, reflects on the time he grew up in deprivation and political uncertainty. His teacher father and his doctor mother resisted the military dictatorship of the 1970s and moved to Spain, where Ernesto was born. Then, faced with the prospect of being 'tourists in Madrid or middle-class vegetables in Buenos Aires', they settled in the Argentine countryside to form a cooperative for local sheep farmers. Eschewing the cosy, rose-tinted nostalgia of certain European 'childhood fables', Adolfo Aristarian's tale is an articulate, touching and even funny look at hard times. Nominated for an Oscar as 'Best Foreign Film', *A Place in the World* was disqualified over a dispute about its nationality. Originally the picture was submitted as best Uruguayan film! [JC-W]

Cast: Jose Sacristan (Hans Mayer Plaza), Federico Luppi (Mario), Cecilia Roth (Ana), Leonor Benedetto (Nelda), Gaston Batyi (Ernesto), Rodolfo Ranni (Andrada), Hugo Arana (Zamora), Lorena del Rio (Luciana).

Dir and Pro: Adolfo Aristarian. Ex Pro: Isidro Miguel. Screenplay: Aristarian and Alberto Leechi; from a story by Aristarian and Kathy Saavedra. Ph: Ricardo de Angelis. Ed: Eduardo Lopez. Art: Abel Facello. M: Emilio Kauderer. Costumes: Kathy Saavedra. Sound: Jose Luis Diaz. (Co-operative–Metro Tartan.) Rel: 9 September 1993. 120 mins. Cert 12.

## Point of No Return

See *The Assassin.*

## Police Academy: Mission to Moscow

Seventh instalment in the embarrassing comedy series that began in 1984, this one following the cretinous crime-busters to Moscow where they wreak more damage than Chernobyl. Ho, ho – *retch.* Filmed on genuine Russian locations. [HP]

Cast: George Gaynes (Commandant Lassard), Michael Winslow (Sgt Jones), David Graf (Sgt Tackleberry), Leslie Easterbrook (Capt. Callahan), Claire Forlani (Katrina Sergetova), Ron Perlman (Konstantin Konali), Christopher Lee (Alexander Rakov), Charlie Schlatter (Kyle Connors), G. W. Bailey (Capt. Harris), Richard Israel (Adam).

Dir: Alan Metter. Pro: Paul Maslansky. Screenplay: Randolph Davis and Michele S. Chodos. Ph: Ian Jones. Ed: Dennis Hill. Pro Des: Frederic Weiler. M: Robert Folk. (Warner.) Rel: 17 June 1994. 83 mins. Cert PG.

*Keyboard cargo: Holly Hunter and Anna Paquin in Jane Campion's overwhelming* The Piano *(from Entertainment)*

*Finding their feet: Leonor Benedetto and Cecilia Roth struggling for a better life in Adolfo Aristarain's* A Place in the World *(from Metro Tartan)*

## Posse

1892; the Wild West. Spaghetti-plotted horse opera that attempts to redress the balance of the Afro-American as depicted by the Hollywood Western. Mario Van Peebles, director of *New Jack City,* contends that almost a million blacks crossed the Mississippi River between 1870 and 1900 and that one cowboy in three was black. However, his 'untold story of the Wild West' is as stereotyped and meretricious as any Western in the last thirty years, while its glorification (and justification) of violence undermines whatever good Clint's *Unforgiven* did for the genre. Here, the blacks wear the white hats, the white guys are the baddies and the title is a misnomer. A posse is a group of men called on by a marshal to maintain law and order, while this 'posse' is a gaggle of black deserters running from the army (and a corrupt colonel). Worse still, the plot is as clear as mud and the camera-work infuriatingly restless, while Van Peebles, as the ringleader, looks like he's constantly posing for a Wrangler ad. [JC-W]

Cast: Mario Van Peebles (Jessie Lee), Stephen Baldwin (Little J), Charles Lane

*Down Mexican Way: Valeria Golino brightens up Gabriele Salvatores' lethargic* Puerto Escondido *(from Mayfair Entertainment)*

(Weezie), Tiny Lister Jr (Obobo), Big Daddy Kane (Father Time), Billy Zane (Colonel Graham), Blair Underwood, Melvin Van Peebles (Papa Joe), Salli Richardson (Lana), Tone Loc, Pam Grier, Vesta Williams, Isaac Hayes, Richard Jordan (Sheriff Bates), Paul Bartel, Nipsey Russell, Reginald VelJohnson, Wood Strode, Reginald Hudlin, Warringto Hudlin, Richard Edson, Aaron Nevill Lawrence Cook, Richard Gant, Robe Hooks, Sy Richardson, Dario Scardapane

Dir: Mario Van Peebles. Pro: Presto Holmes and Jim Steele. Ex Pro: Tir Bevan, Eric Fellner, Paul Webster and Bi Fishman. Screenplay: Sy Richardson an Dario Scardapane. Ph: Peter Menzies. Ec Mark Conte. Pro Des: Catherine Hard wicke. M: Michel Colombier; number performed by Badd Boyz of the Industry Vesta, Melvin Van Peebles, The Nevill Brothers, Intelligent Hoodlum, Tone Loc etc. Costumes: Paul Simmons. Sound Bruce Stambler. (PolyGram/Gramercy Working Title–Rank.) Rel: 19 Novembe 1993. 111 mins. Cert 15.

## The Premonition – Svart Lucia

Ponderous thriller from Sweden i which the heated fantasies scribble in a schoolgirl's diary seem to be coming true. And when the girl's thoughts turn to murder . . . While the bodycount and gore may be less than usual (and the pace slower), this sterile shocker follows the same rules of its genre – complete with sinister close-ups, false alarms, misleading sound effects and sudden, unexpected appearances of the mundane. Yet, for all its high production values the picture fails to deliver – on any level. Filmed in 1992. [JC-W]

Cast: Tova Magnusson (Mikaela), Figge Norling (Joakim), Bjorn Kjellman (Max), Niklas Hjulstrom (Johan), Liv Alsterlund (Sandra), Malin Berghagen, Lars Green, Agneta Ekmanner, Marie Goranzon, Reine Brynolfsson.

Dir: Rumle Hammerich. Pro: Waldemar Bergendahl. Screenplay: Carina Rydberg. Ph: Jens Fischer. Ed: Camilla Skousen. Pro Des: Gert Wibe. M: Jacob Groth. Costumes: Malin Birch-Jensen and Kersti Vitali. (Svensk Filmindustri–Mainline.) Rel: 27 May 1994. 116 mins. Cert 18.

## Puerto Escondido

Milan/Mexico; 1993. After a promising start, this episodic morality tale soon loses steam as one escapade follows another with diminishing returns in audience patience. Mario (Diego Abatantuono), vice-director of a large Italian bank, leads an ordered life in which his shirts, suits and ties are hand-picked best to reveal his material wealth. However, after witnessing one police murder too many, he is forced to leave the country, settling in Puerto Escondido in Mexico. There he is reduced to pawning his jewellery when his credit card is confiscated, and is soon facing penury after his last peso is stolen. From then on he struggles from one mishap to the next, his moral fibre steadily enriched as he constantly becomes poorer. Unfortunately, the humour becomes increasingly forced as the film rambles on, making this something of a disappointment for those who savoured the director's last, Oscar-winning film, *Mediterraneo*. [JC-W]

Cast: Diego Abatantuono (Mario), Valeria Golino (Anita), Claudio Bisio (Alex), Renato Carpentieri (Commissario Viola), Antonio Catania (Di Gennaro).

Dir: Gabriele Salvatores. Pro: Mario and Vittorio Cecchi Gori and Maurizio Totti. Screenplay: Enzo Monteleone, Diego Abatantuono and Salvatores; from the novel by Pino Cacucci. Ph: Italo Petriccione. Ed: Nino Baragli. Pro Des: Marco Belluzzi and Alejandro Olmas. M: Mauro Pagani and Federico De Robertis. Costumes: Francesco Panni. Sound: Amedeo Casati. (Penta Films/Colorado Film–Mayfair Entertainment.) Rel: 6 August 1993. 110 mins. Cert 15.

*It never pours: Ricky Tomlinson and Bruce Jones cope with real life in Ken Loach's riveting* Raining Stones *(from First Independent)*

## Raining Stones

Drawing from real events that occurred on a Manchester council estate where he lived for some years, writer Jim Allen (*Hidden Agenda*) focuses his story on Bob Williams, an

unemployed man trying to support a wife and young daughter. Unable to meet his £50 MOT bill, Bob steals sheep and unblocks drains (to little profit) when his van is stolen. Yet in spite of these dire circumstances, Bob is determined to find the £150 needed to pay for his daughter's communion dress, veil, gloves and shoes. At first eliciting laughs from the day-to-day drudgery of their simple working-class heroes, Allen and director Ken Loach punch their message home with some power in the third act – but never lose sight of the story's humanity. Winner of the Jury Prize at the 1993 Cannes festival. [JC-W]

Cast: Bruce Jones (Bob), Julie Brown (Anne), Gemma Phoenix (Coleen), Ricky Tomlinson (Tommy), Tom Hickey (Father Barry), Jonathan James (Tansey), Mike Fallon, Ronnie Ravey, Derek Alleyn.

Dir: Ken Loach. Pro: Sally Hibbin. Screenplay: Jim Allen. Ph: Barry Ackroyd. Ed: Jonathan Morris. Pro Des: Martin Johnson. M: Stewart Copeland; numbers performed by Utah Saints, Sy-Kick, and Zero B. Sound: Ray Beckett. (Parallax Pictures/Film Four International–First Independent.) Rel: 8 October 1993. 90 mins. Cert 15.

*Heist society: Kim Basinger as an ace bank robber in Russell Mulcahy's leaden* The Real McCoy *(from Guild)*

### The Real McCoy

Having served six years inside Atlanta's Correctional Facility, legendary bank robber Karen McCoy is determined to go straight and get to know her young son. But McCoy is too good at her job to be ignored by the criminal fraternity of Georgia and is forced to mastermind the biggest break-in of her life – or lose her son forever. While casting Kim Basinger as the antihero is a nice twist, the rest of this po-faced caper borrows heavily from other films – although its leaden pace is entirely its own. [JC-W]

*Facing the future with bite: Winona Ryder and Ethan Hawke cross the grunge divide in Ben Stiller's trenchant, touching but ultimately old-fashioned* Reality Bites *(from UIP)*

Cast: Kim Basinger (Karen McCoy), Val Kilmer (J. T. Barker), Terence Stamp (Jack Schmidt), Zach English (Patrick), Gailard Sartain (Gary Buckner), Marc Macaulay (Karl), Raynor Scheine (Baker), Andy Stahl (Mr Kroll), Nick Searcy (Roy Sweeney), Deborah Hobart, Pamela Stubbart, Dean Rader-Duval.

Dir: Russell Mulcahy. Pro: Martin Bregman, Willi Baer and Michael S. Bregman. Ex Pro: Ortwin Freyermuth, William Davies, William Osborne and Gary Levinsohn. Screenplay: Davies and Osborne. Ph: Denis Crossan. Ed: Peter Honess. Pro Des: Kim Colefax. M: Brad Fiedel. Costumes: Donna O'Neal. Sound: Martin Maryska. (Capella International–Guild.) Rel: 5 November 1993. 106 mins. Cert 12.

### Reality Bites

Houston; 1994. Some arch dialogue, good speeches, a lively soundtrack and fine performances enliven this honest, canny look at twentysomething angst in the 1990s. Winona Ryder top-bills as a self-assured young woman from

*The hitman misses: Dennis Hopper on fine reptilian form in John Dahl's exquisite* Red Rock West *(from Rank)*

an affluent, broken home who has the right dreams but finds it increasingly hard to put them into practice. Ethan Hawke, even better, plays her sometime soul mate, an aspiring musician whose veneer of laid-back supercool disguises his real feelings. Whether or not one gels with these people (and their friends) probably depends less on the efficiency of the film's direction and writing, than on one's own point of view. Either way, this is a polished, if occasionally familiar slice-of-lifer brimming with wonderful moments. [JC-W]

Cast: Winona Ryder (Lelaina Pierce), Ethan Hawke (Troy Dyer), Ben Stiller (Michael Grates), Janeane Garofalo (Vickie Miner), Steve Zahn (Sammy Gray), Joe Don Baker (Tom Pierce), John Mahoney (Grant Gubler), Swoosie Kurtz, Harry O'Reilly, Susan Norfleet, Renee Zellweger, James Rothenberg, David Pirner, Andy Dick, Keith David, Anne Meara, Kevin Pollak, Amy Stiller, Karen Duffy, Evan Dando.

Dir: Ben Stiller. Pro: Danny DeVito and Michael Shamberg. Ex Pro: Stacey Sher and Wm Barclay Malcolm. Screenplay: Helen Childress. Ph: Emmanuel Lubezki. Ed: Lisa Churgin. Pro Des: Sharon Seymour. M: Karl Wallinger; numbers performed by World Party, Gary Glitter, Crowded House, Squeeze, KMC, Ethan Hawke, Dinosaur Jr, The Knack, Peter Frampton, The Trammps, New Order, Arrested Development, Lenny Kravitz, Alice Cooper, Salt-N-Pepa, Talking Heads, The Indians, U2, Winona Ryder, Lisa Loeb, Big Mountain, etc. Costumes: Eugenie Bafaloukos. (Jersey Films/ Universal–UIP.) Rel: 17 June 1994, 99 mins. Cert 12.

## Red Rock West

Red Rock West, Wyoming; 1992. Michael Williams is basically an honest, upstanding guy, but he's just spent his last five dollars on gas and has lost the job for which he's driven 1,200 miles from Texas to Wyoming. When a local barman mistakes him for a hitman and offers him $10,000 to bump off his wife, Michael takes the job. However, marriage is a sacred institution in Texas, so he would like to discuss things with the man's wife first. She offers him $20,000 to bump off her husband which, let's face it, is an offer Michael cannot refuse. Actually, Michael has no intention of killing anybody, he just wants enough money to get out of town. But the folk in Red Rock would like him to stay – indefinitely. A leisurely twisted tale of fate, *Red Rock West* keeps you guessing until the final satisfying minute, making this one of the most enjoyable entries in the 'cowboy noir' genre yet. Label it *Blood Simple* without the artistic pretensions. [JC-W]

Cast: Nicolas Cage (Michael Williams), Dennis Hopper (Lyle), Lara Flynn Boyle (Suzanne Brown), Timothy Carhart (Deputy Greytack), J. T. Walsh (Wayne Brown), Dale Gibson (Kurt), Dwight Yoakam (truck driver), Craig Reay, Robert Guajardo, Sarah Sullivan, Dan Shor, Michael Rudd, Barbara Glover.

Dir: John Dahl. Pro: Sigurjon Sighvatsson and Steve Golin. Ex Pro: Michael Kuhn and Jane McCann. Screenplay: John Dahl and Rick Dahl. Ph: Marc Reshovsky. Ed: Scott Chestnut. Pro Des: Rob Pearson. M: William Olvis; numbers performed by Jeff Chance, Johnny Cash, The Kentucky Headhunters, Dwight Yoakam, etc. Costumes: Terry Dresbach. Sound: Jay Boekelheide. (Red Rock–Rank.) Rel: 2 July 1993, 98 mins. Cert 15.

## Redheads

Brisbane, Australia; 1993. Nine months after its release on video, *Redheads* emerged at a West End cinema (the Plaza) and received a full complement of reviews in the national press. But why? A modest, melodramatic Australian thriller from first-time director Danny Vendramini, it seems an odd choice for resurrection. To be kind, Claudia Karvan is not bad as the delinquent girl who unwittingly finds herself a catalyst in the uncovering of police corruption. After seducing a lawyer on video, she – and the camera – witness the said barrister murdered by an intruder. An interesting premise, but well overcooked here. Inspired by the award-winning play *Say Thank You To the Lady* by Rosie Scott. [EB]

Cast: Claudia Karvan (Lucy), Catherine McClements (Diana), Alexander Petersons (Simon), Sally McKenzie (Warden Zelda), Anthony Phelan (Inspector Quigley), Iain Gardiner, Mark Hembrow, Jennifer Flowers, Malcolm Cork, Suzie McKenzie, Josie Vendramini, Bella Vendramini.

Dir, Ex Pro and Screenplay: Danny Vendramini. Pro: Richard Mason. Ph: Steve Mason. Ed: Marc Van Buuren. Pro Des: Ross Wallace. M: Felicity Foxx. Costumes: Ross Wallace. Sound: Max Bowring. (Roxy Films/Australian Film Finance/ Beyond Films–Inner Eye Films.) Rel: 1 April 1994. 106 mins. Cert 15.

## The Ref

See *Hostile Hostages*.

## The Remains of the Day

Based on Kazuo Ishiguro's Booker prize-winning novel, *The Remains of the Day* is an immaculately crafted, emotionally uncompromising study of a man and the times that shape him. Set predominantly between the wars, the film focuses on the unruffled surface that keeps things running smoothly at Darlington Hall. A sort of subtle *Upstairs Downstairs*, the film gradually peels away the layers of a stately Utopia to reveal that the lord of the manor is not the jolly decent chap he appears nor the efficient staff as untroubled. Although both Meryl Streep and Glenn Close vied for the role of the housekeeper, Miss Kenton (played here by Emma Thompson), it is Anthony Hopkins as the butler who dominates the film. And if this impeccable Merchant-Ivory production is not up to the continuous pleasures provided by *A Room With a View* and *Howards End*, it offers many delights – particularly the acting, a superb script and some exquisite production design. [JC-W]

Cast: Anthony Hopkins (Stevens), Emma Thompson (Miss Kenton), James Fox (Lord Darlington), Christopher Reeve (Mr Lewis), Peter Vaughan (Stevens Sr), Hugh Grant (Cardinal), Michael Lonsdale (Dupont D'Ivry), Tim Pigott-Smith (Ben), Ben Chaplin (Charlie, head footman), Lena Headey (Lizzie), Paula Jacobs, Abigail Harrison, Patrick Godfrey, Peter Cellier, Terence Bayler, Jeffry Wickham, Brigitte Kahn, John Savident, Tony Aitken, Paul Copley, Ian Redford, Jo Kendall, Pip Torrens, Peter Eyre, Wolf Kahler.

Dir: James Ivory. Pro: Mike Nichols, John Calley and Ismail Merchant. Ex Pro: Paul Bradley. Screenplay: Ruth Prawer Jhabvala. Ph: Tony Pierce-Roberts. Ed: Andrew Marcus. Pro Des: Luciana Arrighi. M: Richard Robbins. Costumes: Jenny Beavan and John Bright. Sound: Colin Miller. (Columbia TriStar.) Rel: 12 November 1993. 134 mins. Cert U.

*Wasted lives: Anthony Hopkins and Emma Thompson look back at what could've been, in James Ivory's marvellous* The Remains of the Day *(from Columbia TriStar)*

## Rising Sun

Sean Connery and Wesley Snipes bring enormous class and considerable chemistry to this stylish screen adaptation of Michael Crichton's mega-selling novel. The book caused a ruckus in America for its exposé of certain Japanese business practices, and such (Japanese-owned) Hollywood studios as Columbia TriStar and Universal gave the property a wide berth (however, the Japs themselves loved it and devoured the book in its millions). But while Twentieth Century-Fox has dared bring *Rising Sun* to the screen, it has turned the novel's alleged xenophobia around to produce a politically correct buddy-buddy action-comedy. The film's

*The Yellow, The White and The Black: Stan Egi, Harvey Keitel and Wesley Snipes collide in Philip Kaufman's carefully controversial* Rising Sun *(from Fox)*

*Making a point: Cary Elwes as a frightfully jolly Robin in Mel Brooks' overdone* Robin Hood: Men in Tights *(from Columbia TriStar)*

greatest joy is its observation of the cultural clash between East and West and, in particular, Connery's insights into Japanese behaviour. As a thriller, the film is less successful and is frequently downright predictable, while never gaining the momentum of, say, *The Firm* or *In the Line of Fire*. But its incidental pleasures are numerous and Connery has never been more appealing. [JC-W]

Cast: Sean Connery (John Connor), Wesley Snipes (Web Smith), Harvey Keitel (Tom Graham), Cary-Hiroyuki Tagawa (Eddie Sakamura), Kevin Anderson (Bob Richmond), Mako (Yoshida-san), Ray Wise (Senator John Morton), Tia Carrere (Jingo Asakuma), Tatjana Patitz (Cheryl Lynn Austin), Stan Egi, Stan Shaw, Steve Buscemi, Peter Crombie, Sam Lloyd, Alexandra Powers, Daniel Von Bargen, Lauren Robinson, Amy Hill, Tom Dahlgren, Clyde Kusatsu, Michael Chapman, Shelley Michelle.

Dir: Philip Kaufman. Pro: Peter Kaufman. Ex Pro: Sean Connery. Screenplay: Philip Kaufman, Michael Crichton and Michael Backes. Ph: Michael Chapman. Ed: Stephen A. Rotter and William S. Scharf. Pro Des: Dean Tavoularis. M: Toru Takemitsu; numbers performed by Seiichi Tanaka, Cypress Hill, the B-52's, and Pam Tillis. Costumes: Jacqueline West. Sound: Alan Splet. (Walrus & Associates–Fox.) Rel: 15 October 1993. 129 mins. Cert 18.

## Roadside Prophets

A wry, off-beat *Easy Rider* for the '90s, this is the 'story' of two mismatched bikers in search of their own personal El Dorado – as well as a gambling haven in Nevada called El Dorado. Basically nothing more than a series of off-the-wall cameos, the film is fun if you're willing to go with it. Music enthusiasts should relish the in-jokes. [JC-W]

Cast: John Doe (Joe Mosely), Adam Horovitz (Sam), Jennifer Balgobin (Prudence/ Ms Labia Mirage), John Cusack (Caspar), David Anthony Marshall (Dave Coleman), Sonna Chavez (Angie Abbott), J. D. Cullum (Mr Andrews/'Andy'), Barton Heyman (Sheriff Durango), David Carradine (Othello Jones), Judith Thurman, Biff Yeager, Aaron Lustig, Arlo Guthrie, Timothy Leary, Dick Rude, Flea, Stephen Tobolowsky, Bill Cobbs, Lin Shaye, Harry Caesar, Ellie Raab.

Dir and Screenplay: Abbe Wool. Pro: Peter McCarthy and David Swinson. Ex Pro: Nancy Israel. Ph: Tom Richmond. Ed: Nancy Richardson. Pro Des: J. Rae Fox. M: Pray for Rain; number performed by Joe Doe, The Beastie Boys, Exene Cervenka, Broken Homes, The Pop Tigers, Different World, Little Patrick, The Pogues, Gary 'US' Bonds, David Carradine, Harry Dean Stanton, Bug Lamp and Too Free Stooges. Costumes: Prudence Moriaty. (Electric.) Rel: 24 September 1993. 96 mins. Cert 15.

## Robin Hood: Men in Tights

Desperate, over-the-top spoof of *Robin Hood: Prince of Thieves*, crammed with gags, mugging and primordial jokes. It's sad to see Mel Brooks, who started the movie spoof epidemic with *Blazing Saddles*, still trying to recycle such threadbare material. Still, many of the sketches *do* work (the Sherwood Forest rap, Dom DeLuise as a medieval Godfather) but are invariably pushed too far. [JC-W]

Cast: Cary Elwes (Robin Hood), Richard Lewis (Prince John), Roger Rees (Mervyn, Sheriff of Rottingham), Amy Yasbeck (Marian), Mark Blankfield (Blinkin), Dave Chappelle (Ahchoo), Isaac Hayes (Asneeze), Megan Cavanagh (Broomhilde), Eric Allan Kramer (Little John), Tracey Ullman (Latrine), Patrick Stewart (King Richard), Dom DeLuise (Don Giovanni), Mel Brooks (Rabbi Tuckman), Matthew Porretta, Dick Van Patten, Robert Ridgely, Steve Tancora, Joe Dimmick, Avery Schreiber, Chuck McCann, Brian George, Clive Revill, Malcolm Danare, Rudy De Luca, Matthew Saks, James Van Patten, David DeLuise, Ronny Graham.

Dir and Pro: Mel Brooks. Ex Pro: Peter Schindler. Screenplay: Brooks, Evan Chandler and J. David Shapiro. Ph: Michael D. O'Shea. Ed: Stephen E. Rivkin. Pro Des: Roy Forge Smith. M: Hummie Mann. Costumes: Dodie Shepard. Sound: Harry E. Snodgrass. (Brooksfilms/Gaumont–Columbia TriStar.) Rel: 17 December 1993. 104 mins. Cert PG.

## RoboCop 3

Sometime in the future, the Japanese corporation Omni Consumer Products is getting ready to turn old Detroit into the glistening, all-new Delta City. But first a few thousand sitting tenants have to be thrown out of their homes – at whatever cost. With or without the consent of the police. While careening deeper into comic-book caricature and cutting back on the emetic violence, this *RoboCop* aims for a wider audience and will be seen by fewer people. But then sequels are naturally subject to the law of diminishing returns – both commercially and artistically. Having said that, this OTT lunacy is still good value for money, with plenty of choice moments, fabulous action and good reason to cheer the mechanical hero when the (English) villain enquires of him, 'How may I help you officer?' to which RoboCop answers: 'By resisting arrest.' [JC-W]

Cast: Robert Burke (Alex J. Murphy/ RoboCop), Nancy Allen (Officer Anne Lewis), Rip Torn (The Ceo), John Castle

*Machine-tooled humour: Robert Burke steps into Peter Weller's ironware – in Fred Dekker's passable* RoboCop 3 *(from Columbia TriStar)*

(Paul McDaggett), Jill Hennessy (Dr Marie Lazarus), CCH Pounder (Bertha), Mako (Kanemitsu), Robert Do'Qui (Sgt Reed), Remy Ryan (Nikko), Stephen Root (Coontz), Daniel Von Bargen (Moreno), Felton Perry (Johnson), Bruce Locke, Stanley Anderson, Bradley Whitford, Mario Machado, Jodi Long, John Posey, Lee Arenberg, Shane Black, Beth Burns.

Dir: Fred Dekker. Pro: Patrick Crowley. Co-Pro: Jane Bartelme. Screenplay: Dekker and Frank Miller; based on characters created by Edward Neumeier and Michael Miner. Ph: Gary B. Kibbe. Ed: Bert Lovitt. Pro Des: Hilda Stark. M: Basil Poledouris. Costumes: Ha Nguyen. (Orion–Columbia TriStar.) Rel: 24 June 1994. 104 mins. Cert 15.

### Romeo Is Bleeding

For Jack Grimaldi it's a good life. Besides his devoted wife, there's his eager-to-please teenage mistress, a blonde with love to spare. And by leaking details of informants in the Witness Protection Program to the Mob he pockets $65,000 a time. That gives Grimaldi plenty of spare change to lavish gifts on his wife, although she just may be getting a little suspicious. 'Either I've been very good,' she reasons, 'or you've been very bad.' Make that *very* bad. So bad, that when Grimaldi is set up by a black widow-cum-Russian gangstress, we feel little pity, even though Mark Isham's gelatin score piles on the sympathetic sax. Gary Oldman certainly has the edge and the accent to play a New York cop low enough to two-time his wife and his own department, but he's a hard character to spend the better part of two hours with. Also, the film never seems sure whether it's solid *film noir* or an outlandish black comedy. Still, the dialogue is priceless and Lena Olin as the villainess is to die for. [JC-W]

Cast: Gary Oldman (Jack Grimaldi), Lena Olin (Mona Demarkov), Annabella Sciorra (Natalie Grimaldi), Juliette Lewis (Sheri), Roy Scheider (Don Falcone), Michael Wincott (Sal), Dennis Farina (Nick Gazzara), David Proval, Will Patton, Larry Joshua, Paul Butler, James Cromwell, Gene Canfield, Ron Perlman, Tony Sirico.

*Villainess of the year: Lena Olin flaunts her stuff in Peter Medak's gritty* Romeo Is Bleeding *(from Rank)*

*The boy with a golden arm: Dan Hedaya* (centre) *shows the media his star player, Thomas Ian Nicholas, as Eddie Bracken looks on – in Daniel Stern's agreeable* Rookie of the Year *(from Fox)*

Dir: Peter Medak. Pro: Paul Webster and Hilary Henkin. Screenplay: Henkin. Co-Pro: Michael Flynn. Ex Pro: Tim Bevan and Eric Fellner. Ph: Dariusz Wolski. Ed: Walter Murch. Pro Des: Stuart Wurtzel. M: Mark Isham. Costumes: Aude Bronson-Howard. (Working Title/PolyGram–Rank.) Rel: 29 April 1994. 110 mins. Cert 18.

*Paradise loss: Ashley Judd and Todd Field in Victor Nunez's indelible* Ruby in Paradise *(from Mainline)*

### Rookie of the Year

Chicago; today. Henry Rowengartner, 12, loves baseball but cannot play to save his life. Then, following a freak accident, he finds himself endowed with a killer arm: that is, he can hurl a ball faster than 100 mph. Soon, the ailing Chicago Cubs get wind of his talent and sign him up in a last ditch attempt to save their season. *Rookie of the Year* is a predictable, goofy family film with buckets of old-fashioned morality, but thanks to Thomas Ian Nicholas's engaging central presence and some good supporting turns, is an entertaining diversion. Actor Daniel Stern (*Diner*, *Home Alone*, *City Slickers*) makes his directorial debut, and does an efficient job, although he should have fired the overacting idiot who plays the Cubs' coach. [JC-W]

Cast: Thomas Ian Nicholas (Henry Rowengartner), Gary Busey (Chet Steadman), Dan Hedaya (Larry 'Fish' Fisher), Daniel Stern (Coach Brickma), Albert Hall (Sal Martinella), Amy Morton (Mary Rowengartner), Bruce Altman (Jack Bradfield), Eddie Bracken (Bob Carson), Robert Gorman (Clark), Patrick LaBrecque (George), John Candy (Cliff, the radio commentator), Colombe Jacobsen-Derstine, Kristie Davies, Tyler Ann Carrol, Tom Milanovich, Ross Lehman, Andrew Mark Berman, Don Forston, Robert Harper.

Dir: Daniel Stern. Pro: Robert Harper. Ex Pro: Jack Brodsky and Irby Smith. Screenplay: Sam Harper. Ph: Jack Green. Ed: Donn Cambern and Raja Gosnell. Pro Des: Steven Jordan. M: Bill Conti; numbers performed by Tony Bennett, Mike & The Mechanics, Karen Young, Ray Charles, and N'Dea. Costumes: Jay Hurley. (Fox.) Rel: 27 May 1994. 103 mins. Cert PG.

### Roujin Z – Rojin Z

Japan; 2020. Hugely entertaining piece of Japanese sci-fi animation, in which a computerised bed designed to cater for the elderly runs amok. Fast-paced, satirical fun that should delight both sci-fi and animation devotees. [HP]

Voices: Allan Wenger (Terada), Toni Barry (Haruko), Barbara Barnes (Nobuko), Adam Henderson (Maeda), Jane Carpenter (Norie), Ian Thompson (Kijuro Takazawa).

Dir: Hiroyuki Kitakubo. Pro: Yasuhito Nomura, Yasuku Kazama and Yoshiaki Motoya. Ex Pro: Laurence Guinness. Screenplay: Katsuhiro Otomo. Ph: Hideo Okazaki. Ed: Eiko Nishiide. Art: Hiroshi Sasaki. M: Fumi Itakura and Michio Ogawa. Computer Graphics: Kenichi Abe. (Tokyo Theatres Co/TV Asahi/Sony Music Ent.–Manga Entertainment.) Rel: 24 June 1994. 80 mins. Cert 12.

### Ruby in Paradise

Contemplative character study of a young woman who flees rural Tennessee for the jaded glamour of Panama City Beach in Florida. There, she learns to stand on her own two feet and appreciate the security and simple pleasures of her life back home. Winner of the Grand Jury prize at the Sundance Film Festival, *Ruby in Paradise* casts its own unique spell but does tend to drag its feet. Low-budget filmmaking with integrity. [JC-W]

Cast: Ashley Judd (Ruby Lee Gissing), Todd Field (Mike McCaslin), Bentley Mitchum (Ricky Chambers), Allison Dean (Rochelle Bridges), Dorothy Lyman (Mildred Chambers), Betsy Douds (Debrah Ann), Felicia Hernandez, Divya Satia, Bobby Barnes.

Dir, Screenplay and Ed: Victor Nunez. Line Pro: Keith Crofford. Ex Pro: Sam Gowan. Ph: Alex Vlacos. Pro Des: John Iacovelli. M: Charles Engstrom; numbers performed by Sam Phillips, Divya Satia, Boy George, Todd Field, Slapstick, etc. Costumes: Marilyn Wall-Asse. Sound: Pete Winter. A Full Crew/Say Yea–Mainline.) Rel: 26 November 1993. 114 mins. Cert 15.

### The Scent of Green Papaya – Mui Du Du Xanh/L'Odeur de la Papaye Verte

Saigon; 1951–1961. When the papaya is still green it is cooked like a vegetable, but when it ripens it is eaten like a fruit. This film, a remarkably assured directorial debut from the Vietnamese-born, French-educated Tran Anh Hung is, like the papaya, part vegetable and part fruit. The first act, set in a middle-class household fallen on hard times, is suffused in greens: the green of garden vegetation, frogs, lizards, and the green of the papaya itself. The heroine, the 10-year-old servant girl Mui, is also green to the ways of the world. In the film's second part the colour scheme erupts into a plethora of reds, oranges and yellows as Mui ripens into a sexual being, now working in the house of an accomplished composer. Filmed entirely on a sound stage in Bry-sur-Marne, France, the film escapes the claustrophobia of the studio film by celebrating – in glorious close-up – the detail of everyday life in Vietnam: the preparation of food, the insect life, the ritual of music . . . A film of enormous flavour, nominated for an Oscar as best foreign language picture. [JC-W]

Cast: Tran Nu Yên-Khê (Miu, at 20), Lu Man San (Mui, at 10), Truong Thi Lôc (the mother), Nguyen Anh Hoa (Old Thi), Vuong Hoa Hôi (Khuyen), Tran Ngoc Trung (the father), Talisman Vantha (Thu), Souvannavong Kéo, Nguyen Van Oanh, Neth Gérard, Do Nhat.

Dir and Screenplay: Tran Anh Hung. Ex Pro: Christophe Rossignon. Ph: Benoît Delhomme. Ed: Nicole Dedieu and Jean-Pierre Roques. Pro Des: Alain Negre. M: Ton-That Tiêt. Costumes: Jean-Philippe Abril and Danièle Laffargue. Sound: Michel Guiffan. (Les Productions Lazannec/Canal Plus–Artificial Eye.) Rel: 1 April 1994. 100 mins. Cert U.

*Miss Saigon: Tran Nu Yen-Khe in Tran Anh Hung's picturesque first film,* The Scent of Green Papaya *(from Artificial Eye)*

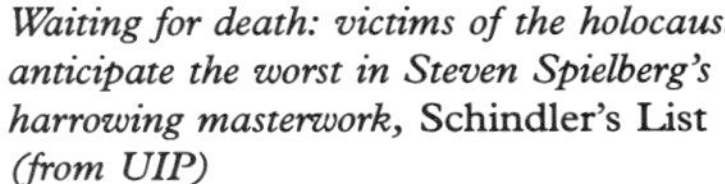

*Waiting for death: victims of the holocaust anticipate the worst in Steven Spielberg's harrowing masterwork,* Schindler's List *(from UIP)*

### Schindler's List

By bringing fresh detail to the subject and refraining from melodrama, Steven Spielberg has produced a totally convincing portrait of the Holocaust that is both moving and devastating. Based on Thomas Keneally's best-selling novel *Schindler's Ark*, the film chronicles the plight of the Polish Jews as they are turned out of their homes, confined to a ghetto in Krakow, sent to labour camps, transferred to Auschwitz and are – along the way – hunted down, enslaved, used as target practice, gassed and burned. The reality of the homicide of six million Jews has been well documented, but is given an all-too human face in this true story of a Nazy industrialist (Oskar Schindler) who exploits the Jews as cheap labour for his factories and then attempts to save them from certain death. Liam Neeson, as the self-possessed but haunted Schindler, gives the best performance of his career, and is well

*Estate-of-the-art: Kate Maberly and Andrew Knott transform* The Secret Garden *in Agnieszka Holland's sumptuous version of the Frances Hodgson Burnett novel (from Warner)*

matched by Ben Kingsley as his proud, doleful plant manager. Ralph Fiennes, too, has never been better than here as a sadistic Nazi commandant, a man who plays God with the lives of a people considered less than human. The stark, luminous black-and-white photography lends the story a persuasive documentary feel, and supplies the film with one of its most subtly horrifying moments. Looking up at the sky, Schindler perceives what appears to be gently falling snow. Then, brushing the white flakes from his car, he realises it is in fact a shower of human ash. [JC-W]

Cast: Liam Neeson (Oskar Schindler), Ben Kingsley (Itzhak Stern), Ralph Fiennes (Amon Goeth), Caroline Goodall (Emilie Schindler), Embeth Davidtz (Helen Hirsch), Adi Nitzan (Mila Pfefferberg), Jonathan Sagalle, Malgoscha Gebel, Shmulik Levy, Mark Ivanir, Beatrice Macola, Andrzej Seweryn, Rami Hauberger, Adam Siemion, Beata Rybotycka, Magdalena Komornicka, Martin Bergmann.

Dir: Steven Spielberg. Pro: Spielberg, Gerald R. Molen and Branko Lustig. Ex Pro: Kathleen Kennedy. Screenplay: Steven Zaillian. Ph: Janusz Kaminski. Ed: Michael Kahn. Pro Des: Alan Starski. M: John Williams; Elgar; violin solos by Itzhak Perlman. Costumes: Anna Biedrzycka-Sheppard. Sound: Ronald Judkins and Robert Jackson. (Amblin/Universal–UIP.) Rel: 18 February 1994. 195 mins. Cert 15.

## La Scorta

Credible, well-photographed drama about a judge's investigation into high-powered corruption in Sicily, in spite of the constant threat of assassination. Freely adapted from real events, the film concentrates in particular on the rapport that develops between the judge and his dedicated team of armed escorts, men prepared to lay down their lives for their job. Thanks to Ennio Morricone's urgent, pounding score, *La Scorta* exudes some dramatic momentum although, without it, the film could have been spectacularly dull. [JC-W]

Cast: Claudio Amendola (Angelo Mandolesi), Enrico Lo Verso (Andrea Corsale), Carlo Cecchi (Judge de Francesco), Ricky Memphis (Fabio Muzzi), Lorenza Indovina (Lia Corsale), Tony Sperandeo, Francesca D'Aloja, Giovanni Alamia, Giacinto Ferro, Nunzia Greco.

Dir: Ricky Tognazzi. Pro: Claudio Bonivento. Screenplay: Graziano Diana and Simona Izzo. Ph: Alessio Gelsini. Ed: Carla Simoncelli. Pro Des: Mariangela Capuano. M: Ennio Morricone. Costumes: Catia Dottori. Sound: Remo Ugolinelli. (Metro Tartan.) Rel: 6 May 1994. 95 mins. Cert 15.

*Intimate exchanges: Juliet Stevenson and Neil Pearson in David Hare's fascinating if unconvincing examination of English society – in* The Secret Rapture *(from Oasis)*

## Searching for Bobby Fischer

See *Innocent Moves.*

## The Secret Garden

Mary Lennox, a spoilt 10-year-old girl, is unceremoniously dumped in her uncle's Yorkshire mansion after her parents are killed in an earthquake in India. There, she meets her comeuppance in the form of the formidable, harsh Mrs Medlock, her uncle's housekeeper, and is railed against by her sickly cousin, Colin. To escape this unhappiness, Mary retreats into the overgrown garden of her late aunt and embarks on restoring it to its former glory, transforming her character and the lives of those around her in the process. Frances Hodgson Burnett's classic children's novel (first published in 1911) is brought to vivid life courtesy of executive producer Francis Ford Coppola. But although the film offers numerous visual pleasures (utilising matte backdrops and time-lapse photography), the acting of the juvenile protagonists is decidedly forced, while Maggie Smith's Medlock is an exercise in scene-stealing ham. A pinch more naturalism could have transformed this chocolate box tearjerker into a minor classic. [JC-W]

Cast: Kate Maberly (Mary Lennox), Heydon Prowse (Colin Craven), Andrew Knott (Dickon), Maggie Smith (Mrs Medlock), Laura Crossley (Martha), John Lynch (Lord Craven), Walter Sparrow (Ben Weatherstaff), Irene Jacob (Lilias Craven, Mary's mother), Frank Baker, Valerie Hill, Andrea Pickering.

Dir: Agnieszka Holland. Pro: Fred Fuchs, Fred Roos and Tom Luddy. Ex Pro: Francis Ford Coppola. Screenplay: Caroline Thompson. Ph: Roger Deakins. Ed: Isabelle Lorente. Pro Des: Stuart Craig. M: Zbigniew Preisner. Costumes: Marit Allen. Sound: Drew Kunin. (American Zoetrope–Warner.) Rel: 15 October 1993. 100 mins. Cert U.

## The Secret Rapture

When an elderly bookseller dies in the country, his daughters find themselves stuck with an extraordinary inheritance – his young alcoholic wife. It is she (gamely played by Joanne Whalley-Kilmer) who becomes a catalyst in their lives, threatening their personal and professional sanity. Adapted by David Hare from his own stage play, the dialogue reverberates with insight, but never seems to ring true. And, while Hare's characters are all painfully recognisable, they are never entirely real. Hence, in spite of our admiration for the author's intellect, we cannot give ourselves to his emotions. In short, *The Secret Rapture* is a fascinating, gripping exploration of the English psyche, but a detached one. Howard Davies, who directed the original play at Britain's National Theatre, here makes his screen debut with some confidence. [JC-W]

Cast: Juliet Stevenson (Isobel Coleridge), Joanne Whalley-Kilmer (Katherine Coleridge), Penelope Wilton (Marion French), Neil Pearson (Patrick Steadman), Alan Howard (Tom French), Robert Stephens (Max Lopert), Finty Williams (Greta), Saira Todd (Kiki), Hilton McRae, Robert Glenister, Richard Long, Julia Lane, Philip Voss, Diane Fletcher, Janet Steel.

Dir: Howard Davies. Pro: Simon Relph. Assoc Pro and Screenplay: David Hare. Ph: Ian Wilson. Ed: George Akers. Pro Des: Barbara Gosnold. M: Richard Hartley. Costumes: Consolata Boyle. (Greenpoint/British Screen/Channel Four–Oasis.) Rel: 3 June 1994. 95 mins. Cert 15.

## Serial Mom

Cheerfully tasteless comedy from sultan of smut John Waters, who casts Kathleen Turner in the homely role of Beverly Sutphin, a perfect mom and housewife with two teenage kids and some serious hang-ups. For instance, when an old dear returns a video of *Ghost Dad* unrewound, Beverly beats her brains out with a leg of lamb. She also has murderous designs on neighbours who don't recycle their garbage and filch parking spaces. Taking the scenario of *Blue Velvet* one step further, Waters paints his film with suburban idealism and then splatters it with offal. Broad, savagely entertaining, but not for all stomachs. N.B. No flies were killed or injured during the making of this motion picture – or so says a disclaimer during the closing credits. [JC-W]

Cast: Kathleen Turner (Beverly Sutphin), Sam Waterston (Eugene Sutphin), Ricki Lake (Misty Sutphin), Matthew Lillard (Chip Sutphin), Scott Wesley Morgan (Det. Pike), Walt MacPherson (Det. Gracey), Justin Whalin (Scotty), Mink Stole (Dottie Hinkle), Mary Jo Catlett (Rosemary Ackerman), Patricia Dunnock (Birdie), Lonnie Horsey, John Badila, Kathy Fannon, Doug Roberts, Traci Lords, Tim Caggiano, Jeff Mandon, Beau James, Stan Brandorff, Suzanne Somers, Patricia Hearst, Joan Rivers.

Dir and Screenplay: John Waters. Pro: John Fielder and Mark Tarlov. Ex Pro: Joseph Caracciolo, Jr. Ph: Robert M. Stevens. Ed: Janice Hampton and Erica Huggins. Pro Des: Vincent Peranio. M: Basil Poledouris; 'Daybreak' performed by

*Happily dysfunctional; or – Meet the Sutphins: Sam Waterston and Kathleen Turner in John Waters' outrageous* Serial Mom *(from Guild)*

*Stripping away the complacency: Debra Winger and Anthony Hopkins in Richard Attenborough's terribly moving* Shadowlands *(from UIP)*

Barry Manilow. Costumes: Van Smith. (Blizzard Film–Guild.) Rel: 10 June 1994. 89 mins. Cert 18.

## Shadowlands

Oxford; 1952. For C. S. Lewis, celebrated Oxford don and the author of *The Lion, The Witch and the Wardrobe*, life is just the way he would have it: comfortable and secure, with only the intellectual imponderables of Christianity to tax his mind. And even then he has all the answers. That is, until he meets the American poet Joy Gresham, an admirer prepared to challenge him. It is through Gresham that Lewis discovers he hasn't even started to live his emotional life. Sensitively adapted by William Nicholson from his own play and directed with remarkable restraint by Richard Attenborough, *Shadowlands* is an articulate, moving and thought-provoking film. And, thanks to the understated acting of Anthony Hopkins and Debra Winger, it never strikes a false note. Interestingly, Lewis and Gresham were previously played by Joss Ackland and Claire Bloom in the original 1985 BBC genesis of the play, which was released theatrically in the States. [JC-W]

Cast: Anthony Hopkins (Clive Staples 'Jack' Lewis), Debra Winger (Joy Gresham), Edward Hardwicke (Warnie Lewis), Michael Denison (Harry Harrington), John Wood (Christopher Riley), Joseph Mazzello (Douglas Gresham), Peter Firth (Dr Craig), James Frain (Peter Whistler), Pat Keen (Mrs Young), Julian Fellowes, Roddy Maude-Roxby, Andrew Seear, Tim McMullan, Andrew Hawkins, Peter Howell, Robert Flemyng, Toby Whithouse, Daniel Goode, Scott Handy, Charles Simon, Giles Oldershaw, Simon Cowell-Parker, Roger Ashton-Griffiths, Howard 'Lew' Lewis, John Quentin, Pauline Melville, Gerald Sim, Norman Bird, Abigail Harrison, Julian Firth.

Dir: Richard Attenborough. Pro: Attenborough and Brian Eastman. Ex Pro: Terence Clegg. Co-Pro: Diana Hawkins. Screenplay: William Nicholson. Ph: Roger Pratt. Ed: Lesley Walker. Pro Des: Stuart Craig. M: George Fenton. Costumes: Penny Rose. Sound: Simon Kaye, Jonathan Bates and Gerry Humphreys. (Spelling Films/Price Entertainment/Savoy Pictures–UIP.) Rel: 4 March 1994. 131 mins. Cert U.

## Shopping

Aggressive, dystopian view of Britain in the very near future when car-jack 'shopping' has become a routine form of transport. Opening with shots of belching industrial pollution set to a pounding heavy metal score, the tone is set for this jaundiced commercial for youth gone wrong. Not an easy film to like, although Tony Imi's cinematography is always arresting and Sadie Frost, transformed into an Irish *Nikita*, makes a feisty heroine. Yuppies, whose image is soundly thrashed here, will hate it. [JC-W]

Cast: Sadie Frost (Jo), Jude Law (Billy McKenzie), Sean Pertwee (Tommy), Marianne Faithfull (Bev), Sean Bean (Venning), Jonathan Pryce (Conway), Fraser James (Be Bop), Danny Newman, Lee Whitlock, Ralph Ineson, Eammon Walker, Jason Isaacs, Chris Constantinou, Tilly Vosburgh, Melanie Hill.

Dir and Screenplay: Paul Anderson. Pro: Jeremy Bolt. Line Pro: Laurie Borg. Ph: Tony Imi. Ed: David Stiven. Pro Des: Max Gottlieb. M: Barrington Pheloung; numbers performed by The Sabres of Paradise, One Dove, Elton John, Utah Saints, Perfecto, Wool, Jesus Jones, Orbital, Stereo MC's, Senser, Shakespear's Sister, EMF, Salt 'N' Pepa, etc. Costumes: Howard Burden. (Channel Four Films/PolyGram/Kuzui Enterprises/WMG/Impact Pictures–Rank.) Rel: 24 June 1994. 107 mins. Cert 18.

## Short Cuts

Twenty-two people living, loving and struggling in Los Angeles cross each other's paths in this multi-layered adaptation of eight short stories (and one poem) by the late American writer Raymond Carver. A TV commentator, housewife, painter, doctor, clown, unemployed salesman, phone-sex worker, swimming pool cleaner, make-up artist, policeman, waitress, chauffeur, helicopter pilot, jazz singer, cellist, baker and fisherman find their lives transformed over a short period of time in the LA basin. An enormous undertaking, this, but nobody could have pulled it off with such dramatic aplomb as Robert Altman, master of the multi-plotted narrative (cf. *Nashville, A Wedding, The Player*). At times funny, at others touching, and occasionally disturbing, *Short Cuts* is a masterpiece of modern American cinema, superbly played by a stellar cast. [JC-W]

Cast: Andie MacDowell (Anne Finnigan), Bruce Davison (Howard Finnigan), Julianne Moore (Marian Wyman), Matthew Modine (Dr Ralph Wyman), Anne Archer (Claire Kane), Fred Ward (Stuart Kane), Jennifer Jason Leigh (Lois Kaiser), Chris Penn (Jerry Kaiser), Lily Taylor (Honey Bush), Robert Downey Jr (Bill Bush), Madeleine Stowe (Sherri Shepard), Tim Robbins (Gene Shepard), Lily Tomlin (Doreen Piggott), Tom Waits (Earl Piggott), Frances McDormand (Betty Weathers), Peter Gallagher (Stormy Weathers), Annie Ross (Tess Trainer), Lori Singer (Zoe Trainer), Jack Lemmon (Paul Finnigan), Lyle Lovett (Andy Bitkower), Buck Henry (Gordon Johnson), Huey Lewis (Vern Miller), Zane Cassidy (Casey Finnigan), Jarrett Lennon (Chad Weathers), Margerie Bond, Robert Do'Qui, Michael Beach, Andi Chapman, Deborah Falconer, Susie Cusack, Charles Rocket, Christian Altman, Dirk Blocker, Natalie Strong.

Dir: Robert Altman. Pro: Cary Brokaw. Ex Pro: Scott Bushnell. Screenplay: Altman and Frank Barhydt. Ph: Walt Lloyd. Ed: Geraldine Peroni. Pro Des: Stephen Altman. M: Mark Isham; numbers performed by Annie Ross and the Low Note Quartet. Costumes: John Hay. Sound: John Pritchett. (Avenue Pictures/ Fine Line/Spelling Films-Artificial Eye.) Rel: 4 March 1994. 188 mins. Cert 18.

*Smiling through: Julianne Moore and Anne Archer take a break from Los Angeles angst in Robert Altman's simply brilliant* Short Cuts *(from Artificial Eye)*

## Sister Act 2: Back In the Habit

Faithfully recreating the formula of the first film, this spirited sequel may not be as funny but does, thankfully, dispense with idiotic subplots featuring Mafia goons and hit men. Again, Vegas lounge singer Deloris Van Cartier (Whoopi Goldberg) is coaxed into a wimple, this time at the behest of her old friends Mary Lazarus, Mary Robert and a rejuvenated Mother Superior (Maggie Smith all smiles and upraised eyes). Now ensconced at the rundown St Francis school in San Francisco, the sisters need Deloris to salvage their music class. But can she? Will she? While the film is predictable and derivative, director Bill Duke invests it with a gritty rap sensibility that is infectious. Also, the music is wonderful and the supporting players on scene-stealing good form (particularly Mary Wickes and Michael Jeter). For this one, Whoopi was paid $7 million, an all-time record for a female star (since surpassed by Julia Roberts in the forthcoming *Mary Reilly*). [JC-W]

Cast: Whoopi Goldberg (Deloris Van Cartier/Sister Mary Clarence), Kathy Najimy (Sister Mary Patrick), James Coburn (Mr Crisp), Maggie Smith (Mother Superior), Barnard Hughes (Father Maurice), Mary

*Sisterz N The Hood: Kathy Najimy, Whoopi Goldberg and Wendy Makkena in Bill Duke's buzzin'* Sister Act 2: Back in the Habit *(from Buena Vista)*

*An affair to anticipate: Tom Hanks spills his emotions in Nora Ephron's sublime* Sleepless in Seattle *(from Columbia TriStar). Ross Malinger looks on*

Wickes (Sister Mary Lazarus), Michael Jeter (Father Ignatius), Wendy Makkena (Sister Mary Robert), Sheryl Lee Ralph (Florence Watson), Lauryn Hill (Rita Watson), Robert Pastorelli, Thomas Gottschalk, Brad Sullivan, Alanna Ubach, Ryan Toby, Ron Johnson, Jennifer 'Love' Hewitt, Devin Kamin, Christian Fitzharris, Tanya Blount, Edith Diaz, Jenifer Lewis, Pamala Tyson, Sharon Brown, Robin Gammell, Yolanda Whitaker, Bill Duke, Sydney Lassick.

Dir: Bill Duke. Pro: Scott Rudin and Dawn Steel. Ex Pro: Laurence Mark and Mark Iscovich. Co-Ex Pro: Christopher Meledandri. Screenplay: James Orr, Jim Cruickshank and Judi Ann Mason. Ph: Oliver Wood. Ed: John Carter, Pem Herring and Stuart Pappé. Pro Des: John De Cuir Jr. M: Miles Goodman; numbers performed by Aretha Franklin, Whoopi Goldberg, Ron Johnson and Lauryn Hill, Ryan Toby, Hi-Five, etc. Costumes: Francine Jamison-Tanchuck. Sound: Jim Webb. (Touchstone Pictures–Buena Vista.) Rel: 25 March 1994. 107 mins. Cert PG.

## Sleepless in Seattle

Hopelessly romantic, frequently very funny love story in which the two protagonists fall in love long distance. Sam Baldwin is a regular guy who moves to Seattle and tries to start life afresh with his young son after his wife dies. However, for Sam, Maggie was the only one and he doesn't believe he can grow another heart. Annie Reed, a journalist for *The Baltimore Sun*, is engaged to Walter, a nice boring man who collects allergies for a hobby. Then, one night, Annie tunes in to a radio call-in show and finds herself anticipating the words of one Sam Baldwin, whose sentiments seem to mirror her own. Until writer-director Nora Ephron (*When Harry Met Sally . . .*) fine-tuned Jeff Arch's screenplay, *Sleepless in Seattle* was just a high-concept sniffler. Now it's a vibrant, ingenious comedy peppered with priceless cameos (Rob Reiner, Rosie O'Donnell, Barbara Garrick, Amanda Maher), the celluloid equivalent to a romantic weekend in Paris – with all expenses paid. [JC-W]

Cast: Tom Hanks (Sam Baldwin), Meg Ryan (Annie Reed), Bill Pullman (Walter Jackson), Rob Reiner (Jay), Ross Malinger (Jonah Baldwin), Rosie O'Donnell (Becky), Gaby Hoffmann (Jessica), Rita Wilson (Suzy), Barbara Garrick (Victoria), Carey Lowell (Maggie Baldwin), Le Clanché du Rand (Barbara Reed), Caroline Aaron (Dr Marcia Fieldstone), Amanda Maher (Clarise), Victor Garber, David Hyde Pierce, Dana Ivey, Kevin O'Morrison, Valerie Wright, Frances Conroy, Tom Tammi, Tom McGowan, Stephen Mellor, Brian McConnachie, Mary A. Kelly, Bruce Stevenson.

Dir: Nora Ephron. Pro: Gary Foster. Ex Pro: Lynda Obst and Patrick Crowley. Assoc Pro: Delia Ephron. Screenplay: Ephron, David S. Ward and Jeff Arch. Ph: Sven Kykvist. Ed: Robert Reitano. Pro Des: Jeffrey Townsend. M: Marc Shaiman; numbers performed by Celine Dion and Clive Griffin, Jimmy Durante, Roy Rogers and Dale Evans, Ray Charles, Guy Lombardo and His Royal Canadians, Nat King Cole, Dr John, Carly Simon, Gene Autry, Joe Cocker, Harry Connick Jr, Tammy Wynette and Louis Armstrong. Costumes: Judy Ruskin. Sound: Michael Kirchberger. (TriStar–Columbia Tri-Star.) Rel: 24 September 1993. 105 mins. Cert PG.

## Sliver

Joe Eszterhas, who scripted *Jagged Edge* and *Basic Instinct*, returns yet again to the territory of the psychological corkscrew thriller, this time updating the concept of Hitchcock's *Rear Window* to the electronic age. Somebody is killing a lot of people in an exclusive apartment high-rise in Manhattan and somebody is watching through an elaborate surveillance system. Voyeurism is the order of the day as embodied by video cameras, telescopes and door peepholes and book editor Carly Norris (Sharon Stone) is at the receiving end, although her own fascination with voyeurism is piqued. Stone, who was so compelling as the *femme fatale* in *Basic Instinct*, is less credible here as the damsel in distress, although William Baldwin is suitably (and ambivalently) seductive as her suitor. Unfortunately, the characters are unconvincing and the pace a tad too ponderous. [JC-W]

Cast: Sharon Stone (Carly Norris), William Baldwin (Zeke Hawkins), Tom Berenger (Jack Landsford), Martin Landau (Alex Parsons), Polly Walker (Vida Jordan), Colleen Camp (Judy), Amanda Foreman (Samantha), Nina Foch (Mrs McEvoy), CCH Pounder (Lt Victoria Hendrix), Keene Curtis (Gus Hale), Allison Mackie (Naomi Singer), Nicholas Pryor, Anne Betancourt, Tony Peck, Frantz Turner, Robin Groves, Matthew Faison.

Dir: Phillip Noyce. Pro: Robert Evans. Ex Pro: Howard W. Koch Jr and Joe Eszterhas. Co-Pro: William J. MacDonald. Screenplay: Eszterhas; from the novel by Ira Levin. Ph: Vilmos Zsigmond. Ed: Richard Francis-Bruce. Pro Des: Paul Sylbert. M: Howard Shore; numbers performed by Enigma, Aftershock, Shaggy, Neneh Cherry, UB40, Heaven 17, Fluke, Lords of Acid, Massive Attack, Verve, etc. Costumes: Deborah L. Scott. Sound: Tom Nelson. (Paramount–UIP.) Rel: 3 September 1993. 107 mins. Cert 18.

## The Snapper

Barrytown, Dublin; 1993. Superb adaptation of Roddy Doyle's second novel (his first, *The Commitments*, was filmed in 1991), vividly capturing the turbulent, funny, drab world of the over-crowded Curley family. Life – revolving around the TV, the pub and the kitchen – is chaotic, but nothing compared to what it becomes when Sharon, 20, announces that she's pregnant. Refusing to reveal the identity of the father, Sharon soon finds herself a local figure of scorn and – even worse – alienated from her father. Colm Meaney, as Dad, reprises his role from *The Commitments* (here re-named Dessie Curley because Twentieth Century-Fox holds the copyright to the original Rabbitte family name) and transforms his character from a hard-drinking, uneducated couch potato to a New Man as he struggles to reconcile himself to his daughter's dilemma. The acting, pacing and particularly Doyle's dialogue are all spot-on, producing a work of enormous warmth, wit and compassion. [JC-W]

*Doyle's Dublin: Tina Kellegher and the girls discuss the meaning of life at their Barrytown local – in Stephen Frears'* The Snapper *(from Electric)*

Cast: Colm Meaney (Dessie Curley), Tina Kellegher (Sharon Curley), Ruth McCabe (Kay Curley), Fionnula Murphy (Jackie), Deirdre O'Brien (Mary), Karen Woodley (Yvonne Burgess), Pat Laffan (George Burgess), Virginia Cole (Doris Burgess), Colm O'Byrne, Eanna MacLiam, Ciara Duffy, Joanne Gerrard, Peter Rowan, Brendon Gleeson, Stuart Duine, Ronan Wilmot.

Dir: Stephen Frears. Pro: Lynda Myles. Ex Pro: Mark Shivas. Assoc Pro: Ian Hopkins. Screenplay: Roddy Doyle. Ph: Oliver Stapleton. Ed: Mick Audsley. Pro Des: Mark Geraghty. M: 'Can't Help Falling in Love' sung by Kirsty MacColl. Costumes: Consolata Boyle. Sound: Kieran Horgan. (BBC–Electric.) Rel: 6 August 1993. 90 mins. Cert 15.

*Till death do us part: Mike Myers and Nancy Travis exchange vows in Thomas Schlamme's hilarious* So I Married an Axe Murderer *(from Columbia TriStar)*

## So I Married an Axe Murderer

Mike Myers's much-anticipated follow-up to *Wayne's World* was – at

*The losing hour: In the heat of* Stalingrad *(from Entertainment)*

one time or another – earmarked as a vehicle for Woody Allen, Chevy Chase, Billy Crystal, Steve Martin and Martin Short. Myers picked up the project and transformed the forty-something Jewish neurotic into a young, hip, personable beat poet called Charlie, with women trouble. Indeed. Sherri was a kleptomaniac who stole Charlie's cat. Jill was a member of the Mafia. And Pam smelled of beef vegetable soup. Then Charlie meets Harriet (in a butcher's shop), the ideal woman – sunny, intelligent and beautiful, and not against intercourse on a first date. And then Charlie discovers something he wished he hadn't . . . Although a flop in the States (maybe they thought it was a horror film), this is one of the funniest movies of the '90s, a charming, witty, broad, wicked, detailed comedy that never stops volleying the laughs. Myers is a most agreeable leading man and – as Charlie's rude Scottish father – is side-splitting. And yet the comedian never lets his personality overshadow the supporting cast, all of whom are excellent – from an unbilled Alan Arkin to the smallest bit-player. [JC-W]

Cast: Mike Myers (Charlie Mackenzie/ Stuart Mackenzie), Nancy Travis (Harriet Michaels), Anthony LaPaglia (Tony Giardino), Amanda Plummer (Rose Michaels), Brenda Fricker (May Mackenzie), Alan Arkin (police captain), Matt Doherty, Charles Grodin, Phil Hartman (Vickie), Debi Mazar, Steven Wright, Maureen O'Boyle, Michael Richards, Robert Nichols, Greg Germann, Cynthia Frost, Fred Ornstein.

Dir: Thomas Schlamme. Pro: Robert N. Fried and Cary Woods. Ex Pro: Bernie Williams. Co-Pro: Jana Sue Memel. Screenplay: Robbie Fox. Ph: Julio Macat. Ed: Richard Halsey and Colleen Halsey. Pro Des: John Graysmark. M: Bruce Broughton; numbers performed by The Boo Radleys, Suede, Chris Whitley, Sun–60, Soul Asylum, Mike Myers, etc. Costumes: Kimberly Tillman. Sound: Larry Mann. (Columbia TriStar.) Rel: 19 November 1993. 93 mins. Cert 12.

## Son-in-Law

Witless vehicle for MTV icon Pauly Shore, who plays an obnoxious LA student invited to stay with his new girlfriend's folks for Thanksgiving. He's a braindead whacked-out loon; they're simple, God-fearing farm people. After the obvious friction, the pat ending is inevitable. Crass, banal, predictable. They *released* this? [CB]

Cast: Pauly Shore (Crawl), Carla Gugino (Rebecca Warner), Lane Smith (Walter Warner), Cindy Pickett (Connie Warner), Mason Adams (Walter Warner Sr), Patrick Renna (Zack), Dennis Burkley, Tiffani-Amber Thiessen, Dan Gauthier, Ria Pavia, Lisa Lawrence, Graham Jarvis.

Dir: Steve Rash. Pro: Michael Rotenberg and Peter M. Lenkov. Ex Pro: Hilton Green. Screenplay: Fax Bahr, Adam Small and Shawn Schepps; from a story by Patrick J. Clifton, Susan McMartin and Peter M. Lenkov. Ph: Peter Deming. Ed: Dennis M. Hill. Pro Des: Joseph T. Garrity. M: Richard Gibbs. Costumes: Molly Maginnis. Sound: Bruce Bisenz. (Hollywood Pictures–Buena Vista.) Rel: 21 January 1994. 96 mins. Cert 12.

## Stalingrad

In September of 1942 an army of over half-a-million men (comprising Germans, Italians, Hungarians and Rumanians) descended on the small town of Stalingrad (now Volgograd) in Russia. Germany alone sent 350,000 soldiers, of whom only 6000 were to return. According to the film's publicity, a total of two million men lost their lives at Stalingrad. This epic, strikingly photographed film is the Germans' viewpoint of the bloodbath, told in horrifying detail and making no concessions to German sensibilities. Although the piece is often confusing in its delineation of character, a number of personalities emerge with whom we can sympathise, albeit reluctantly. While both good Germans and bad Germans are portrayed here, the atrocities that their army inflicted on the Russian people are hard to watch. So, as viewers, our loyalties are torn. Strong stuff, indeed, with some of the mutilations depicted bordering on the emetic. The on-the-spot amputations are particularly hard to stomach. [JC-W]

Cast: Thomas Kretschmann (Lt Hans Von Witzland), Dominique Horwitz (Fritz Reiser), Jochen Nickel (Rollo Rohleder), Sebastian Rudolph (Gege), Sylvester Groth (Otto), Dieter Okras (Haller), Karel Hermanek (Musk), Dana Vavrova (Irina).

Dir and Ph: Joseph Vilsmaier. Pro: Vilsmaier, Hanno Huth and Gunter Rohrbach. Ex Pro: Michael Krohne and Mark Damon. Screenplay: Vilsmaier, Johannes Heide and Jurgen Buscher. Ed: Hannes Nikel. Pro Des: Wolfgang Hundhammer. M: Norbert J. Schneider. Costumes: Ute Hofinger. Sound: Milan Bor. (Royal/Bavaria/B.A./Perathonm–Entertainment.) Rel: 15 April 1994. 137 mins. Cert 15.

*Street life: Enrico Lo Verso and Giuseppe Ieracitano in Gianni Amelio's delicate character study,* The Stolen Children *(from Mayfair Entertainment)*

### Stepping Razor – Red X

Fascinating, uncompromising and muddled portrait of radical reggae star Peter Tosh, combining interviews, concert footage and film of Tosh pondering the meaning of life. Tosh, who helped form The Wailers with Bob Marley and became one of the music industry's most outspoken Rastafarians, died as dramatically as he lived – at the hands of a burglar in 1987. Directed by the Canadian film actor Nicholas Campbell. [CB]

Dir and Screenplay: Nicholas Campbell. Pro and Ph: Edgar Egger. Ex Pro: Syd Cappe and Nicolas Stiliadis. Co-Ex Pro: Wayne Jobson. Ed: Trevor Ambrose. Art: Bora Bulajic. Sound: Paul Durand. (Bush Doctor Films–Feature Film Co.) Rel: 20 August 1993. 104 mins. Cert 15.

### The Stolen Children – Il Ladro di Bambini

Milan/Bologna/Sicily; 1992. A bleak, uncompromising (true) story of two children – an 11-year-old girl and her 9-year-old brother – who are left in the charge of two carabinieri when their mother is arrested for prostituting her daughter. After his partner deserts him without leave, cop Antonio finds that the allotted 'home' for his wards will not take the girl because of her circumstances. And so he is forced to escort his reluctant young companions down to an alternative institute in Sicily. On the way, he learns much about the two children and they discover a new life outside the brutality of their upbringing. Stripped of sentimentality and melodrama, *The Stolen Children* is an honest, understated and finely realised portrait of the underbelly of Italy. [JC-W]

Cast: Enrico Lo Verso (Antonio), Valentina Scalici (Rosetta), Giuseppe Ieracitano (Luciano), Florence Darel, Marina Golovine, Fabio Alessandrini, Vitalba Andrea, Antonino Vittorioso.

Dir: Gianni Amelio. Pro: Angelo Rizzoli. Ex Pro: Enzo Porcelli. Screenplay: Sandro Petraglia and Stefano Rulli. Ph: Tonino Nardi and Renato Tafuri. Ed: Simona Paggi. Pro Des: Andrea Crisanti. M: Franco Piersanti. Costumes: Gianna Gissi and Luciana Morosetti. Sound: Alessandro Zanon. (Erre/Alia/RAI Radiotelevisione Italiana RAIDUE/Arena/Vega–Mayfair Entertainment.) Rel: 19 November 1993. 112 mins. Cert 15.

### Storyville

Louisiana; 1991. It's rare to find a film that's convoluted, ludicrous *and* soporific, but *Storyville* manages to orchestrate all these attributes. James Spader is wantonly miscast as a former lawyer and congressional candidate from a rich New Orleans dynasty, who's embroiled in a clandestine plot beyond his control. Other characters pop up all over the place like second thoughts (can you imagine Joanne Whalley-Kilmer as a Southern lawyer?), while the story rumbles on like a disjointed dream. Mark Frost, co-creator of TV's *Twin Peaks*, makes his big-screen directorial debut. [JC-W]

Cast: James Spader (Cray Fowler), Joanne Whalley-Kilmer (Natalie Tate), Jason Robards (Clifford Fowler), Charlotte Lewis (Lee), Michael Warren (Nathan LeFleur), Justine Arlin (Melanie Fowler), Piper Laurie (Constance Fowler), Philip Carter (Avner Hollister), Michael Parks, Chuck McCann, Charles Haid, Chino Fats Williams, Woody Strode, Jeff Perry, George Kee Cheung, Steve Forrest, Lionel Ferbos.

Dir: Mark Frost. Pro: David Roe and Edward R. Pressman. Ex Pro: John Davis and John Flock. Co-Pro: Evzen Kolar. Screenplay: Frost and Lee Reynolds; based on the novel *Juryman* by Frank Galbally and Robert Macklin. Ph: Ron Garcia. Ed: B. J. Sears. Pro Des: Richard Hoover. M: Carter Burwell; numbers performed by New Leviathan Oriental Foxtrot Orchestra, Louis Armstrong and Zette. Costumes: Louise Frogley. Sound: Stephen Halbert.

*A test of faith: Mamata Shankar and Deepankar De in Satyajit Ray's last film,* The Stranger *(from Artificial Eye)*

(Davis Entertainment–Arrow.) Rel: 23 July 1993. 112 mins. Cert 15.

## The Stranger – Agantuk

Calcutta; 1991. Just four days before he arrives on her doorstep, Manmohan Mitra sends a letter to his niece Anila, whom he hasn't seen for 35 years. He wants to be a guest in her home for one week, before resuming his travels in Australasia. But is he who he says he is? This predicament arouses much interest and agitation for Anila and her husband, whose lives will be changed forever by this amicable stranger. Satyajit Ray's final film, completed when he was very ill, *Agantuk* not only glows with the master's trademark humanism and poetry, but is a gentle, dignified comedy which exemplifies filmmaking at its most subtle and elegant. [JC-W]

Cast: Deepankar De (Sudhindra Bose), Mamata Shankar (Anila Bose), Bikram Bhattacharya (Satyaki/Bablu), Utpal Dutt (Manmohan Mitra), Dhritiman Chatterji, Rabi Ghosh, Subrata Chatterji, Promode Ganguly, Ajit Bannerji.

Dir, Pro, Screenplay, M and Sound: Satyajit Ray. Ph: Barun Raha. Ed: Dulal Dutt. Pro Des: Ashoke Bose. Costumes: Lalita Ray. (National Film Development Corporation of India–Artificial Eye.) Rel: 19 November 1993. 120 mins. Cert U.

*Down the river: Bruce Willis tied to a corrupt police force in Rowdy Herrington's subtlety-free* Striking Distance *(from Columbia TriStar)*

## Striking Distance

Pittsburgh; 1991–3. His father (a cop) always told him, 'loyalty above all else – except honour'. But when homicide detective Tom Hardy rats on his cousin, a bad cop, the force turns on him and relegates him to the river rescue service. This is a shame as Hardy has the inside scoop on a serial killer who not only continues his killing spree after he's supposedly jailed, but is picking off Hardy's former girlfriends. A surprisingly dark action thriller, *Striking Distance* would have qualified as *film noir* if it had more atmosphere. Sadly, the testosterone slinging carries little conviction, while the characters are stock. Only Sarah Jessica Parker, as Hardy's partner, provides any human muscle. Previously known as *Three Rivers*. [JC-W]

Cast: Bruce Willis (Tom Hardy), Sarah Jessica Parker (Jo Christman), Dennis Farina (Nick Detillo), Tom Sizemore (Danny Detillo), Brion James (Det. Eddie Eiler), Robert Pastorelli (Jimmy Detillo), John Mahoney (Vince Hardy), Jodi Long (Kim Lee), Bob the cat (himself), Timothy Busfield, Andre Braugher, Tom Atkins, Mike Hodge, Roscoe Orman, Ed Hooks, Julianna McCarthy, Andrea Martin, Elva Branson.

Dir: Rowdy Herrington. Pro: Arnon Milchan, Tony Thomopoulos and Hunt Lowry. Ex Pro: Steven Reuther. Co-Pro: Carmine Zozznora. Screenplay: Herrington and Martin Kaplan. Ph: Mac Ahlberg. Ed: Pasquale Buba and Mark Helfrich. Pro Des: Gregg Fonseca. M: Brad Fiedel; numbers performed by Sam The Sham & The Pharoahs, 2 Die 4, Bob Seger & The Silver Bullet Band and Little Feat. Costumes: Betsy Cox. Sound: John Sutton III. (Sony Pictures–Columbia TriStar.) Rel: 15 April 1994. 101 mins. Cert 18.

## Super Mario Bros

Brooklyn/'Dinohattan'; 1993. The danger of basing a film on a video game is that the end product may well end up feeling like a video game. *Super Mario Bros* falls prey to the predicament with a very silly story about two Brooklyn plumbers (Mario and Luigi Mario), who are plunged into an alternative reality in pursuit of a comely palaeontologist. This dimension, which broke off from the real world when 'that' meteorite finished off the dinosaurs, is ruled by the reptilian King Koopa, himself evolved from a dino. Much derivative sci-fi nonsense ensues, involving odd creatures, omnipresent fungus and subterranean royalty. Nevertheless, the acting is above par for this sort of thing, with Bob Hoskins, Dennis Hopper and Samantha Mathis bringing a shred more conviction than called for. There is also much incidental humour, backed up by state-of-the-art special effects, courtesy of a $50m budget. [JC-W]

Cast: Bob Hoskins (Mario Mario), John Leguizamo (Luigi Mario), Dennis Hopper (King Koopa), Samantha Mathis (Daisy), Fisher Stevens (Iggy), Richard Edson (Spike), Fiona Shaw (Lena), Dana Kaminski (Daniella), Gianni Russo (Scapelli), Mojo Nixon, Francesca Roberts, Lance Henriksen, Sylvia Harman, Desiree Marie Velez, Andrea Powell, Heather Pendergast, Melanie Salvatore.

Dir: Rocky Morton and Annabel Jankel. Pro: Jake Eberts and Roland Joffé. Co-Pro: Fred Caruso. Screenplay: Parker Bennett, Terry Runté and Ed Solomon. Ph: Dean Semler. Ed: Mark Goldblatt. Pro Des: David L. Snyder. M: Alan Silvestri; numbers performed by Roxette, diVinyls, Charles & Eddie, Extreme, Megadeth, Queen, US3, etc. Costumes: Joseph Porro. Sound: Richard Van Dyke. (Lightmotive/Allied/Cinergi–Entertainment.) Rel: 9 July 1993. 104 mins. Cert PG.

*Plumbing for fantasy: John Leguizamo and Bob Hoskins cross the line of reality in Rocky Morton and Annabel Jankel's lively* Super Mario Bros. *(from Entertainment)*

## Tango

Patrice Leconte, having explored male adoration of women in *Monsieur Hire* and *The Hairdresser's Husband*, turns to full-blown misogyny with this energetic, cheerfully irreverent black comedy. Philippe Noiret stars as a powerful judge and confirmed bachelor, a man who doesn't consider wife-killing a crime. When his nephew (Thierry Lhermitte) is deserted by his wife (Miou-Miou), Noiret hires a hitman (Richard Bohringer) to dispose of her. Lhermitte explains that he can now only love her if she is dead, but Bohringer is getting decidedly cold feet . . . A perfect Gallic antidote to *Thelma & Louise* which is both cynical and ingenious and should promote considerable discussion. [JC-W]

Cast: Philippe Noiret (François L'Elegant), Richard Bohringer (Vincent), Thierry Lhermitte (Paul), Miou-Miou (Marie), Judith Godrèche (Madeleine), Carol Bouquet (female guest), Jean Rochefort (bellhop), Michele Laroque, Maxime Leroux, Laurent Gamelon.

Dir: Patrice Leconte. Pro: Henri Brichetti. Ex Pro: Philippe Carcassonne and René Cleitman. Screenplay: Leconte and Patrick Dewolf. Ph: Eduardo Serra. Ed: Genevieve Winding. Art: Ivan Maussion. M: Angelique Nachon and Jean-Claude Nachon. Costumes: Cecile Magnan. Sound: Pierre Lenoir. (Cinea/Hachette Premiere & Cie/Canal Plus–Artificial Eye.) Rel: 16 July 1993. 88 mins. Cert 15.

*Killing fields: Thierry Lhermitte, Philippe Noiret and Richard Bohringer in Patrice Leconte's delightfully abrasive* Tango *(from Artificial Eye)*

## Teenage Mutant Ninja Turtles III – The Turtles Are Back . . . In Time

Shameful excuse for a movie in which the four loveable reptiles are transported back in time to 17th-century Japan, where they find themselves in

*Love with complications: Juliette Lewis and C. Thomas Howell in Craig Bolotin's* That Night *(from Warner)*

the midst of a dynastic spat. Sluggish pacing, risible plotting, awful jokes and appalling production values all add to the misery. [CB]

Cast: Elias Koteas (Casey Jones/Whit Whitley), Paige Turco (April O'Neil), Stuart Wilson (Capt. Dirk Walker), Sab Shimono (Lord Norinaga), Vivian Wu (Princess Mitsu), Mark Caso (Leonardo), Matt Hill (Raphael), Jim Raposa (Donatello), David Fraser (Michaelangelo), James Murray (Splinter), Henry Hayashi, John Aylward; Voices: Robbie Rist (Michaelangelo), Brian Tochi (Leonardo), Tim Kelleher (Raphael), James Murray (Splinter), Corey Feldman (Donatello).

Dir and Screenplay: Stuart Gillard; based on characters created by Kevin Eastman and Peter Laird. Pro: Thomas K. Gray, Kim Dawson and David Chan. Ex Pro: Raymond Chow. Co-Pro: Terry Morse. Ph: David Gurfinkel. Ed: William D. Gordean and James R. Symons. Pro Des: Roy Forge Smith. M: John Du Prez; numbers performed by ZZ Top, The Barrio Boyzz, Baltimora and Technotronic. Costumes: Christine Heinz. Sound: Larry Kemp and Lon E. Bender. (Golden Harvest–Fox.) Rel: 23 July 1993. 95 mins. Cert PG.

## That Night

Long Island, New York; 1961. Yet another rites-of-passage dip into Sixties nostalgia, this time a look at rebellion and teenage love as seen through the eyes of an uncomprehending 10-year-old girl. With a perfect view of the bedroom of 17-year-old Sheryl O'Connor, the girl-next-door, young Alice models herself on her adopted heroine, playing her records, wearing her scent and cooing on the soundtrack, 'I wanted to laugh her laugh and dream her dreams . . .' Then, one night, Alice and Sheryl become inexorably involved in a romantic scenario that is destined to lead to tears. Sincere, slow-moving, banal. [JC-W]

Cast: C. Thomas Howell (Rick), Juliette Lewis (Sheryl O'Connor), Helen Shaver (Ann O'Connor), Eliza Dushku (Alice Bloom), John Dossett (Larry Bloom), J. Smith-Cameron (Carol Bloom), Katherine Heigl (Katherine), Benjamin Terzulli, Thomas Terzulli, Sarah Joy Stevenson, Michael Costello.

Dir and Screenplay: Craig Bolotin; from the novel by Alice McDermott. Pro: Arnon Milchan and Steven Reuther. Ex Pro: Julie Kirkham and Elliott Lewitt. Co-Pro: Llewellyn Wells. Ph: Bruce Surtees. Ed: Priscilla Nedd-Friendly. Pro Des: Maher Ahmad. M: David Newman; numbers performed by Aretha Franklin, Jackie Wilson, Jack Jones, Ritchie Valens, Dion, Frankie Valli and The Four Seasons, Nat King Cole, The Marvelettes, Elvis Presley, Roy Orbison, etc. Costumes: Carol Ramsey. Sound: Bruce Stambler. (Le Studio Canal Plus/Regency Enterprises/Alcor Films–Warner.) Rel: 15 April 1994. 89 mins. Cert 12.

## Thirty Two Short Films About Glenn Gould

Mirroring the structure of Bach's *Goldberg Variations*, the recording that made concert pianist Glenn Gould famous, this remarkably original film is a series of reflections of an extraordinary man. Gould, who turned the world of piano music on its head in the Fifties, insisted on his own, deeply personal interpretations of the classics, leading to his refusal to perform live. Francois Girard's film is an equally personal treatment, offering us 32 glimpses of a unique, private man, mixing interview footage with re-enacted events. [HP]

Cast: Colm Feore (Glenn Gould), Derek Keurvorst (Gould's father), Katya Ladan (Gould's mother), Devon Anderson (Gould aged 3), Joshua Greenblatt (Gould aged 8), Sean Ryan (Gould aged 12), Kate Hennig, Sean Doyle, Sharon Bernbaum, Don McKellar, Gerry Quigley, Ian D. Clark, David Clement, Yehudi Menuhin, Jessie Grieg.

Dir: Francois Girard. Pro: Niv Fichman. Ex Pro: Dennis Murphy. Line Pro: Screenplay: Girard and Don McKellar. Ph: Alain Dostie. Ed: Gaetan Huot. M: J. S. Bach, Richard Wagner, Beethoven, Richard Strauss, Sibelius, Prokofiev, etc. Costumes: Linda Muir. Animation: Norman McLaren. (Rhombus Media Inc/Telefilm Canada/CBC National Film Board of Canada, etc–Electric.) Rel: 17 June 1994. 90 mins. Cert U.

## This Boy's Life

The late 1950s; Washington State. A true story detailing the emotional rollercoaster life of a teenage boy, his mother and her string of boyfriends, this is one of those films that derails itself in its eagerness to capture the period. The same old songs haunt the soundtrack, while TV news bulletins constantly remind us where we are historically. The drama itself, as embodied by De Niro's brutish, exaggerated turn as the boy's stepfather, is one-dimensional, although Leonardo DiCaprio is exceptional as the bad kid with a heart of gold. [JC-W]

Cast: Robert De Niro (Dwight Hansen), Ellen Barkin (Caroline Wolff), Leonardo DiCaprio (Toby 'Jack' Wolff), Jonah Blechman (Arthur Gayle), Chris Cooper (Roy), Kathy Kinney (Marian), Eliza Dushku, Carla Gugino, Zack Ansley, Tracey Ellis, Bobby Zameroski, Tobey Maguire, Tristan Tait, Richard Liss, Gerrit Graham, Lee Wilkof, Bill Dow.

Dir: Michael Caton-Jones. Pro: Art Linson. Ex Pro: Peter Guber and Jon Peters. Screenplay: Robert Getchell; based on the book by Tobias Wolff. Ph: David Watkin. Ed: Jim Clark. Pro Des: Stephen J. Lineweaver. M: Carter Burwell. Costumes: Richard Hornung. Sound: Richard King. (Warner.) Rel: 3 September 1993. 115 mins. Cert 15.

## Three Colours Blue – Trois Couleurs Bleu

Paris; today. Lying in a hospital bed with her neck in traction, Julie is told that her husband and 5-year-old daughter have died in a car crash. Unable to carry out a suicide attempt, she decides that her only chance of emotional survival is to eliminate all traces of her past: the people, the places, the memories. But the past is a formidable animal . . . The first instalment of a trilogy surveying the three colours of the French Revolution – blue for liberty, white for equality and red for fraternity – *Blue* is bathed in its eponymous colour both literally and figuratively. But, more significantly, the film explores the ramifications of freedom today in a free society and how we are chained to our possessions, our feelings and, above all, our past. Krzysztof Kieslowski, who's also working on a series of films examining the Ten Commandments, has produced here his most visually seductive, intellectually complex work to date. Alive with ideas and threaded with a strong emotional core, the film haunts the soul while provoking the mind. A masterpiece. [JC-W]

Cast: Juliette Binoche (Julie), Benoit Regent (Olivier), Florence Pernel (Sandrine), Charlotte Very (Lucille), Helene Vincent (the journalist), Emmanuelle Riva (mother), Philippe Volter, Hughes Quester, Isabelle Sadoyan, Julie Delpy.

Dir: Krzysztof Kieslowski. Pro: Marin Karmitz. Screenplay: Kieslowski and Krzysztof Piesiewicz. Ph: Slawomir Idziak. Ed: Jacques Witta. Pro Des: Claude Lenoir. M: Zbigniew Preisner. Costumes: Virginie Vlard and Naima Lagrange. Sound: Jean-Claude Laureux. (MK2 Prods/'Tor'/Canal Plus–Artificial Eye.) Rel: 15 October 1993. 100 mins. Cert 15.

*Are you talking to me? Robert De Niro on the fast-forward button, with the excellent Leonardo DiCaprio, in Michael Caton-Jones' picturesque* This Boy's Life *(from Warner)*

## Three Colours White – Trois Couleurs Blanc

The second instalment of Krzysztof Kieslowski's trilogy based on the colours of the French flag (embodying liberty, equality and fraternity) represents a surprising shift in tone. The bitter-sweet tale of a schlemiel who adores his ex-wife the crueller she is to him, the film is more black in tone than white. However, Kieslowski is the first to admit that his trilogy's colour scheme is nothing more than a dramatic pretext. Here, he tells the story of two cities, Paris and Warsaw, and how the bureaucracy of the former and the corrupt capitalism of the other shapes the downfall and rise of a lovestruck Polish barber. The director's traditional attention to detail, human nuance and ironic symbolism constantly beguiles the mind, even if the film fails to recruit the emotions. Nevertheless, the final scene in which the little barber realises that both his love and his wealth have eluded him once more does prick the heart. [JC-W]

Cast: Zbigniew Zamachowski (Karol Karol), Julie Delpy (Dominique), Janusz Gajos (Mikolaj), Jerzy Stuhr (Jurek Karol), Jerzy Nowak, Jerzy Trela, Piotr Machalica, Marzena Trybala, Juliette Binoche, Florence Pernel.

Dir: Krzysztof Kieslowski. Pro: Marin Karmitz. Ex Pro: Yvon Crenn. Screenplay: Kieslowski and Krzysztof Piesiewicz. Ph: Edward Klosinski. Ed: Urzula Lesiak. Pro Des: Halina Dobrowolska and Claude

*The inequality of love: Julie Delpy and Zbigniew Zamachowski in Krzysztof Kieslowski's funny, touching* Three Colours White *(from Artificial Eye)*

*All for one and awful dumb: Kiefer Sutherland, Charlie Sheen, Chris O'Donnell and Oliver Platt cross swords in Stephen Herek's rambunctious* The Three Musketeers *(from Buena Vista)*

Lenoir. M: Zbigniew Preisner. Costumes: Elzbieta Radke, Teresa Wardzala, Jolanta Luczak and Virginie Viard. Sound: Jean-Claude Laureux. (MK2 Prods/France 3 Cinema/Cab Prods/TOR/Canal Plus–Artificial Eye.) Rel: 10 June 1994. 91 mins. Cert 15.

## Three of Hearts

Joe Casella is a male escort who claims he can win 'any woman – any time – any place – guaranteed.' When Ellen ditches her girlfriend Connie, Connie hires Joe to win Ellen back. The idea is that Joe will court Ellen, capture her heart and then dump her so that she will go running back to Connie. Simple, eh? But Joe is ready to fall in love himself. But to whom? The 'who loves who?' premise is neat, but can succeed only if the protagonists behave in character. Unfortunately, *Three of Hearts* betrays our trust by short-changing its own intelligence. And the stars' costumes are most unflattering. [JC-W]

Cast: William Baldwin (Joe Casella), Kelly Lynch (Connie), Sherilyn Fenn (Ellen), Joe Pantoliano (Mickey), Cec Verrell (Allison), Tony Amendola (Harvey), Gail Strickland, Claire Callaway, Marek Johnson, Monique Mannen, Timothy D. Stricknev, Frank Ray Perilli, Gloria Gifford, Tawny Kitaen.

Dir: Yurek Bogayevicz. Pro: Joel B. Michaels and Matthew Irmas. Ex Pro: David Permut. Co-Pro: Hannah Hempstead. Screenplay: Adam Greenman and Mitch Glazer. Ph: Andrzej Sekula. Ed: Dennis M. Hill. Pro Des: Nelson Coates. M: Richard Gibbs; numbers performed by Moe Z, Suzan Rivera, Sam Phillips, etc. Costumes: Barbara Tfank. (New Line Cinema–Guild.) Rel: 9 July 1993. 110 mins. Cert 18.

## The Three Musketeers

Energetic, rambunctious but ultimately bland Disneyfication of the classic Alexandre Dumas novel of romance, honour and betrayal in 17th-century France. While a sprinkling of visual and verbal gags punctuates the chaos with varying degrees of success, it is the acting of Oliver Platt, Tim Curry and Michael Wincott (and some impressive production design) that lends the film any distinction at all. In short, a classic of French literature has been reduced to an entertainment without suspense, credibility or an original bone in its body. Interestingly, this was one of four versions of *The Three Musketeers* in pre-production in Hollywood at the same time, with Oliver Platt already earmarked as Porthos in a TriStar edition starring Robert Downey Jr and William Baldwin. [JC-W]

Cast: Charlie Sheen (Aramis), Kiefer Sutherland (Athos), Chris O'Donnell (D'Artagnan), Oliver Platt (Porthos), Tim Curry (Cardinal Richelieu), Rebecca De Mornay (Milady Sabine), Gabrielle Anwar (Queen Anne d'Autriche), Michael Wincott (Rochefort), Paul McGann (Girard/ Jussac), Julie Delpy (Constance), Hugh O'Conor (King Louis XIII), Christopher Adamson, Philip Tan, Emma Moore.

Dir: Stephen Herek. Pro: Joe Roth and Roger Birnbaum. Ex Pro: Jordan Kerner and Jon Avnet. Screenplay: David Loughery. Ph: Dean Semler. Ed: John F. Link. Pro Des: Wolf Kroeger. M: Michael Kamen; 'All For Love' performed by Bryan Adams, Rod Stewart and Sting. Costumes: John Mollo. Sound: Colin Charles. (Walt

Disney/Caravan Pictures–Buena Vista.) Rel: 11 February 1994. 106 mins. Cert PG.

### Tom and Jerry The Movie

53 years after their inception by MGM (in 1940) – and their appearance in over 200 shorts – the forbidding feline and resourceful rodent arrive on the big screen in their first full-length feature. When their home is demolished by a wrecking ball, Jerry and Tom are forced to become friends, learn to speak and get to sing some forgettable songs by Leslie Bricusse and Henry Mancini. Although the animation is traditionally slick, the plot is so banal and the message so mawkish that the whole point of what made Tom and Jerry irresistible is lost. [CB]

Voices: Richard Kind (Tom), Dana Hill (Jerry), Anndi McAfee (Robyn), Henry Gibson (Applecheek), Charlotte Rae (Aunt Figg), Tony Jay, Rip Taylor, Michael Bell, Ed Gilbert, Sydney Lassick.

Dir and Pro: Phil Roman. Ex Pro: Roger Mayer, Jack Petrik, Hans Brockmann and Justin Ackerman. Screenplay: Dennis Marks; based on William Hanna and Joseph Barbera's cartoon characters. Ed: Sam Horta. M: Henry Mancini; lyrics: Leslie Bricusse. Art: Michael Peraza Jr and Michael Humphries. Sound: Gordon Hunt. Creative Consultant: Barbera. (Turner Entertainment/WMG/Film Roman–First Independent.) Rel: 2 July 1993. 84 mins. Cert U.

### Tom & Viv

Thomas Stearns Eliot – Tom to his friends, T. S. to his readers – is an American obsessed with the gentility of England. In Vivienne Haigh-Wood, an impulsive, beautiful and aristocratic young woman, he sees an attractive passport to high society. The couple fall in love and marry and Tom discovers that Viv is nothing like what he had imagined. According to her doctors, she is suffering from 'moral insanity'. In short, she is a threat to Tom's burgeoning career as a brilliant poet. A fascinating, terrible story, to be sure, but the characters as portrayed here are so unsympathetic that the film is a trial to sit through. Willem Dafoe, sporting a most extraordinary accent, is, frankly, as dull as bauxite, while Miranda Richardson's wild and neurotic showdowns are a test of the nerves. While the film is obviously on the side of Viv, it makes her out to be an impossible creature (albeit at the mercy of her 'medicines'), and one that we can't wait to see the back of. [JC-W]

*For better for verse: Willem Dafoe and Miranda Richardson as T. S. Eliot and wife in Brian Gilbert's torturous* Tom & Viv *(from Entertainment)*

*Dangerous when wet: Kurt Russell as Wyatt Earp and Val Kilmer as Doc Holliday are caught in the crossfire in George P. Cosmatos's gung-ho Western* Tombstone *(from Entertainment)*

Cast: Willem Dafoe (T. S. Eliot), Miranda Richardson (Vivienne Haigh-Wood), Rosemary Harris (Rose Haigh-Wood), Tim Dutton (Maurice Haigh-Wood), Nickolas Grace (Bertrand Russell), Clare Holman (Louise Purdon), Joanna McCallum (Virginia Woolf), Linda Spurrier (Edith Sitwell), Geoffrey Bayldon, Philip Locke, Joseph O'Connor, John Savident, Michael Attwell, Sharon Bower, Roberta Taylor, Christopher Baines.

Dir: Brian Gilbert. Pro: Marc Samuelson, Harvey Kass and Peter Samuelson. Ex Pro: Miles A. Copeland III and Paul Colichman. Line Pro: John Kay. Screenplay: Michael Hastings and Adrian Hodges; based on Hastings's play. Ph: Martin Fuhrer. Ed: Tony Lawson. Pro Des: Jamie Leonard. M: Debbie Wiseman. Costumes: Phoebe De Gaye. Sound: Peter Glossop. (Samuelson Prods/Harvey Kass/IRS Media Inc./British Screen–Entertainment.) Rel: 15 April 1994. 130 mins. Cert 15.

### Tombstone

Arizona; 1879–81. Wyatt Earp and Doc Holliday strap on their guns yet again in the legendary town of the title in which the local cowpokes are becoming a nuisance. In spite of a substantial budget and painstaking attempts at authenticity, this overblown shootout from the director of

*Modern love: Patricia Arquette and Christian Slater take on the Mob in Tony Scott's explosive* True Romance *(from Warner)*

*Rambo* is ludicrous and styleless. The film not only lacks atmosphere and a feel for the times, but is so poorly lit that it might vanish completely on video. Rushed through production to pre-empt the release of *Wyatt Earp*, *Tombstone* looks and feels like a cut-price epic. Still, there are some nice turns from the cast, with Val Kilmer memorable as a jaundiced, eccentric Holliday, and a wild-eyed Michael Biehn surpassing himself with an acrobatic display of gun juggling. [JC-W]

Cast: Kurt Russell (Wyatt Earp), Val Kilmer (Doc Holliday), Michael Biehn (Johnny Ringo), Powers Boothe (Curly Bill Brocius), Sam Elliott (Virgil Earp), Bill Paxton (Morgan Earp), Jason Priestley (Billy Breckenridge), Jon Tenney (John Behan), Stephen Lang (Ike Clanton), Dana Delany (Josephine Marcus), Paula Malcomson (Allie Earp), Lisa Collins (Louisa Earp), Dana Wheeler-Nicholson (Mattie Earp), Joanna Pacula (Kate), Charlton Heston, Thomas Haden Church, Michael Rooker, Harry Carey Jr, Billy Bob Thornton, Tomas Arana, Pat Brady, Paul Ben Victor, John Philbin, Robert Burke, Billy Zane, Wyatt Earp, John Corbett, Buck Taylor, Terry O'Quinn, Frank Stallone, Pedro Armendariz Jr, Cecil Hoffman, Chris Mitchum, Robert Mitchum (narrator).

Dir: George P. Cosmatos. Pro: James Jacks, Sean Daniel and Bob Misiorowski. Ex Pro: Buzz Feitshans and Andrew G. Vajna. Screenplay: Kevin Jarre. Ph: William A. Fraker, Ed: Frank J. Urioste, Roberto Silvi and Harvey Rosenstock. Pro Des: Catherine Hardwicke. M: Bruce Broughton. Costumes: Joseph Porro. Sound: Walt Martin. (Hollywood Pictures/Cinergi–Entertainment.) Rel: 21 January 1994. 116 mins. Cert 15.

### True Romance

Detroit/Los Angeles; 1993. Take the visually-driven, hard-hitting direction of Tony Scott (*Top Gun*, *The Last Boy Scout*), the pop-cultural, profane dialogue of Quentin Tarantino (*Reservoir Dogs*) and a cast that includes Dennis Hopper as a good guy, Gary Oldman as a Rastafarian and Val Kilmer as the ghost of Elvis Presley and you have a film that will grab you by the throat, take you to hell and back and entertain the living daylights out of you. Clarence Worley, a kung-fu and Elvis fanatic, falls in love with the call girl his boss furnishes him for his birthday. And, just to show how romantic he is, he kills her pimp and ends up with a stash of cocaine worth $500,000. Unfortunately, the snow belongs to the mob and so Worley and his girlfriend (now his wife) hightail it to LA to unload their booty on the movie community. Armed with a series of unforgettable scenes and a pace that never lets up, *True Romance* is shocking, hilarious and stimulating cinema. [JC-W]

Cast: Christian Slater (Clarence Worley), Patricia Arquette (Alabama Whitman), Dennis Hopper (Clifford Worley), Val Kilmer (Mentor), Gary Oldman (Drexl Spivey), Brad Pitt (Floyd, Dick's roommate), Christopher Walken (Vincenzo Coccotti), Bronson Pinchot (Elliot Blitzer), Michael Rapaport (Dick Ritchie), Saul Rubinek (Lee Donowitz), Samuel L. Jackson, Conchata Ferrell, James Gandolfini, Anna Thomson, Victor Argo, Paul Bates, Chris Penn, Tom Sizemore, Kevin Corrigan, Michael Beach, Eric Allan Kramer, Patrick John Hurley, Ed Lauter.

Dir: Tony Scott. Pro: Bill Unger, Steve Perry and Samuel Hadida. Ex Pro: James G. Robinson, Gary Barber, Bob Weinstein, Harvey Weinstein and Stanley Margolis. Screenplay: Quentin Tarantino. Ph: Jeffrey L. Kimball. Ed: Michael Tronick and Christian Wagner. Pro Des: Benjamin Fernandez. M: Hans Zimmer; numbers performed by Charlie Sexton, John Waite, Charles & Eddie, Billy Idol, Val Kilmer, Nymphomania, Shelby Lynne, Big Bopper, Aerosmith, The Shirelles, Robert Palmer, Soundgarden, Jerry Delmonico, etc. Costumes: Susan Becker. Sound: Robert G. Henderson. (Morgan Creek/Davis Film–Warner.) Rel: 15 October 1993. 119 mins. Cert 18.

### U.F.O.

The film they dared not screen to the national press corps. And it's easy to understand why. Chaotic, artless, gross and downright infantile, this vehicle for the popular, scatological stand-up comic Roy 'Chubby' Brown *might* succeed on video as a curio for his fans, but should be avoided by all others. For the record, Chubby plays himself, and is carted off to a distant galaxy by a futuristic cartel of feminists who charge him with male chauvinism. Found guilty, his punishment includes giving birth via his anal canal. You get the drift. [CB]

Cast: Roy 'Chubby' Brown (himself), Sara Stockbridge (Zoe), Amanda Symonds (Ava), Roger Lloyd Pack (the hermaphrodite Solo), Shirley Anne Field (supreme commander), Sue Lloyd (judge), Kiran Shah (Genghis Khan), Kenny Baker (Casanova), Rusty Goffe (Henry VIII), Anthony Georghiou (Dracula), James Culshaw, Sheila Gill, Paul Sarony, Ben Aris, Walter Sparrow, Shaun Curry.

Dir: Tony Dow. Pro: Simon Wright. Ex Pro: Peter Smith. Line Pro: Paul Sarony. Screenplay: Wright, Roy 'Chubby' Brown and Richard Hall. Ph: Paul Wheeler. Ed: Geoff Hogg. Pro Des: David McHenry. M: Clever Music; numbers performed by Gloria Gaynor, Yes No People, and Kool and the Gang. Costumes: Liz Da Costa. Sound: John Rodda. (PolyGram/George Forster–Feature Film Co.) Rel: 10 December 1993. 79 mins. Cert 18.

## Undercover Blues

Kathleen Turner and Dennis Quaid are married espionage agents on extended maternity leave in exotic New Orleans. They now have a baby – but can't make up their mind what to call her – and want to put all that James Bond stuff behind them. But the cops, the Feds, the CIA, an international crime syndicate and even a petty mugger just won't leave these good-humoured folks alone. This is a farce as broad as the Mississippi itself, complemented by funny speech impediments, lots of falling in mud and ferociously hammy performances from Fiona Shaw, Stanley Tucci and Larry Miller. Incomprehensibly, the dependable Herbert Ross directed this garbage. Formerly boasted the much wittier title *Cloak and Diaper*. [JC-W]

Cast: Kathleen Turner (Jane Blue), Dennis Quaid (Jeff Blue), Fiona Shaw (Novacek), Stanley Tucci (Muerte/'Morty'), Larry Miller (Halsey), Obba Babatunde (Sawyer), Tom Arnold, Park Overall, Ralph Brown, Jan Triska, Marshall Bell, Richard Jenkins, Dennis Lipscomb, Saul Rubinek, Dakin Matthews, Michael Greene, Olek Krupa, Jenifer Lewis, David Chappelle, Katherine Gaskin.

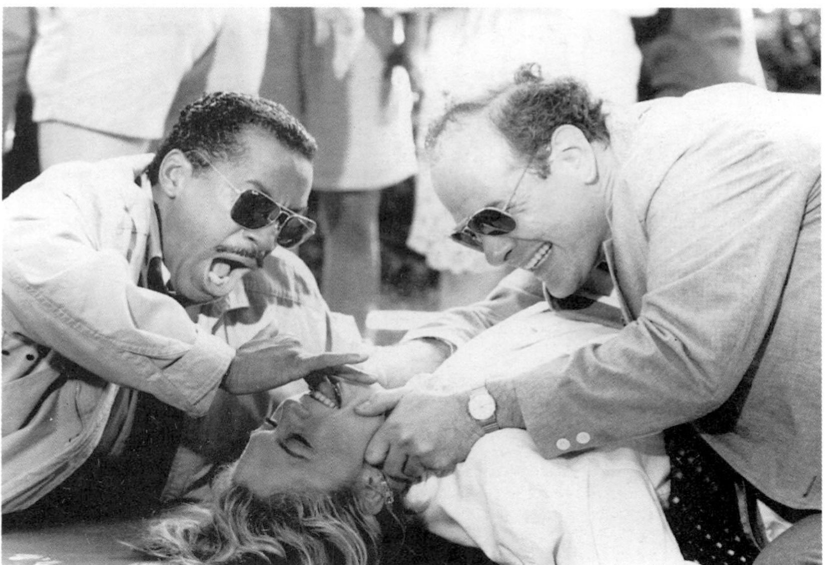

*Cloak and diaper: Kathleen Turner detains undercover cops Obba Babatunde and Larry Miller with a faked epileptic fit in Herbert Ross's enthusiastic farce* Undercover Blues *(from UIP)*

Dir: Herbert Ross. Pro: Mike Lobell. Ex Pro: Ross and Andrew Bergman. Screenplay: Ian Abrams. Ph: Donald E. Thorin. Ed: Priscilla Nedd-Friendly. Pro Des: Ken Adam. M: David Newman; numbers performed by Muddy Waters and numerous jazz ensembles. Costumes: Wayne Finkelman. Sound: Dennis L. Maitland. (Lobell/Bergman/Hera/MGM–UIP.) Rel: 14 January 1994. 90 mins. Cert 12.

*Perverted justice: Takeshi Kitano makes the mistake of his life as he tortures hit man Haku Ryu – in the ICA's* Violent Cop

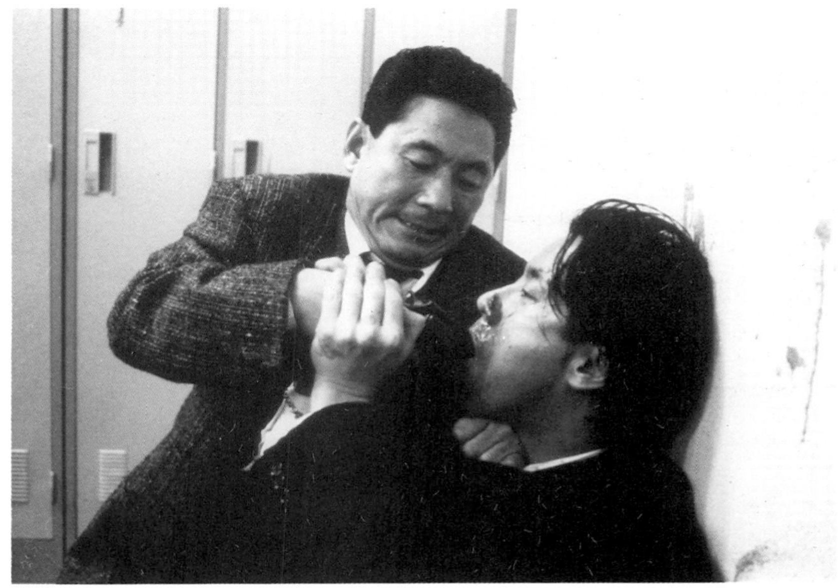

## Violent Cop – Sono Otoko Kyobo Ni Tsuki

Dressed in the nerdy apparel of cardigan, tie and suit and brandishing an emotionless stare, Det. Azuma is an unlikely screen cop. As a gang of teenagers beat a vagrant senseless, he looks on from the shadows but fails to intervene. Later, he beats up the ringleader in the security of the boy's own bedroom. Azuma's system of justice is arbitrary and unpredictable, and he displays the same contempt for his superiors as for the criminals on the street. This is a fascinating character study of a man and the society that shapes him, but at times the film is so styleless and rambling that it's hard to get fired up by it. [JC-W]

*Staying afloat: Walter Quiroz struggles to survive the political floodwaters of South America in Fernando Solanas's distinctive* The Voyage *(from Metro Tartan)*

Cast: 'Beat' Takeshi, aka Takeshi Kitano (Det. Azuma), Maiko Kawakami (Akari), Makoto Ashigawa (Kikuchi, the rookie), Shiro Sano (police chief Yoshinari), Shigeru Hiraizumi (Det. Iwaki), Haku Ryu (Kiyohiro, the hit man), Mikiko Otonashi, Ittoku Kishibe, Ken Yoshizawa.

Dir: Takeshi Kitano. Pro: Hisao Nabeshima, Takio Yoshida and Shozo Ichiyama. Ex Pro: Kazuyoshi Okuyama. Screenplay: Hisashi Nozawa. Ph: Yasushi Sakakibara. Ed: Nobutake Kamiya. Art: Masuteru Mochizuki. M: Daisaku Kume and Eric Satie. Sound: Senji Horiuchi. (Bandai Company Media Division/Shochiku/Fuji Co–ICA.) Rel: 19 November 1993. 103 mins. No cert.

### Visions of Light

Crammed with fascinating anecdotes and illuminated by some of the greatest images that the fusion of technology and art have ever offered, this documentary on the history of cinematography is a gift to film buffs. Excerpts from 125 films include *Birth of a Nation*, *Citizen Kane*, *Lawrence of Arabia*, *In Cold Blood*, *The Godfather*, *Days of Heaven* and *Apocalypse Now*. Made in 1992. [JC-W]

Cinematographers interviewed: Nestor Almendros, John A. Alonzo, John Bailey, Michael Ballhaus, Stephen H. Burum, Bill Butler, Michael Chapman, Allen Daviau, Caleb Deschanel, Ernest Dickerson, Frederick Elmes, William Fraker, Conrad Hall, James Wong Howe, Victor Kemper, Lazslo Kovacs, Charles Lang, Sven Nykvist, Lisa Rinzler, Owen Roizman, Charles Rosher Jr, Sandi Sissel, Vittorio Storaro, Haskell Wexler, Gordon Willis, Vilmos Zsigmond.

Dir: Arnold Glassman, Todd McCarthy and Stuart Samuels. Pro: Samuels. Co-Pro and Ed: Glassman. Ex Pro: Terry Lawler and Yoshiki Nishimuri. Screenplay: McCarthy. Ph: Nancy Schreiber. (American Film Institute/NHK/Japan Broadcasting Corporation–City Screen.) Rel: 15 April 1994. 90 mins. No cert.

### Les Visiteurs

The most popular French film ever made, *Les Visiteurs* is a rollicking farce in which a 12th-century nobleman and his disgusting vassal are accidentally transported forward in time to contemporary France. There, they wreak no end of havoc while working out the finer points of modern amenities and attempt to make their way back to the primitive world they understand. Opportunities for shrewd satire are wasted, while the wholesale destruction of everything in the time-travellers' path seems a poor substitute for wit. [JC-W]

Cast: Christian Clavier (Jacquouille/Jacquart/Jacquasse/Mr Crass), Jean Reno (Godefroy), Valerie Lemercier (Frenegonde/Beatrice), Gerard Sety (Edgar Bernay), Marie-Anne Chazel, Christian Bujeau, Isabelle Nanty, Didier Pain, Michel Peyrelon, Pierre Vial, Frederic Baptiste.

Dir: Jean-Marie Poire. Pro: Alain Terzian. Screenplay: Poire and Christian Clavier. Ph: Jean-Yves Le Mener. Ed: Catherine Kelber. Pro Des: Hugues Tissandier. M: Eric Levi. Costumes: Catherine Leterrier. Sound: Jean Goudier. (Gaumont/France 3 Cinema/Alpilles Prods/Amigo Prods/Canal Plus–Arrow.) Rel: 4 February 1994. 105 mins. Cert 15.

### The Voyage

Combining elements of the magic-realism of Gabriel Garcia Marquez with Pythonesque slapstick, this Argentine epic is a genuine original, both a giddy geography lesson and a surreal journey into the metaphorical. Following a 17-year-old boy's quest to find his father (and, indeed, himself), the film takes a sweeping, subversive look at the cultural, political and ecological climate of Latin America as young Martin cycles from the southern tip of Argentina to Mexico. Following the film's completion in May 1991, Fernando Solanas was shot outside his Buenos Aires home by a masked gunman, confining the director to a wheelchair for five months and delaying post-production by eight months. Filmed in five countries over sixteen weeks, the picture's locations include the snowy wastes of Tierra del Fuego, Patagonia, Peru, the biggest gold mine in Brazil, Venezuela and the Maya ruins in Yucatan. [JC-W]

Cast: Walter Quiroz (Martin), Soledad Alfaro (Vidala), Ricardo Bartis (Celador Salas), Cristina Becerra (Violeta), Dominique Sanda (Helena), Marc Berman, Chiquinho Brandao, Carlos Carella.

Dir, Screenplay and Art: Fernando Solanas. Pro: Solanas and Envar El Kadri. Ex Pro: Assuncao Hernandes, Djamila Olivesi,

Luis Figueroa and Grazi Rade. Ph: Felix Monti. Ed: Alberto Borella and Jacqueline Meppiel. M: Solanas, Egberto Gismonti and Astor Piazzolia. Sound: Anibal Libenson. (Cinesur/Les Films du Sud/Channel Four/Canal Plus/Films A2–Metro Tartan.) Rel: 3 September 1993. 133 mins. Cert 12.

### Wayne's World 2

The nerdy party animals are back with a bigger budget, more babes and Aerosmith in person. Although this critic found the first film unbearable, he's warming to the innocent charm of these lunatics. There *are* plenty of good gags (the DJ who doesn't listen to his guests, the telegraphed plate of glass routine, the *Graduate* sketch), plus a jumble of in-jokes and star cameos (Kim Basinger, Drew Barrymore, Charlton Heston, Ed O'Neill). But to appreciate fully this extraordinary phenomenon you have to have a fair knowledge of the music world (and a loathing for Kenny G), plus a screw or two loose. Join the queue. [JC-W]

Cast: Mike Myers (Wayne Campbell), Dana Carvey (Garth Algar), Christopher Walken (Bobby G. Cahn), Tia Carrere (Cassandra), Ralph Brown (Del), Larry Sellers (naked Indian), Michael Nickles (Jim Morrison), Frank DiLeo (Mr Big), Olivia d'Abo (Betty Jo), Kim Basinger (Honey Hornée), Drew Barrymore (Bjergen Kjergen), Tim Meadows (Sammy Davis Jr), Lee Tergesen, Dan Bell, Gavin Grazer, Googy Gress, Heather Locklear, Rip Taylor, Kevin Pollak, James Hong, Chris Farley, Harry Shearer, Ted McGinley, Scott Coffey, Lance Edwards, Jay Leno, Charlton Heston, Ed O'Neill, Aerosmith.

Dir: Stephen Surjik. Pro: Lorne Michaels. Ex Pro: Howard W. Koch Jr. Co-Pro: Dinah Minot and Barnaby Thompson. Screenplay: Mike Myers, Bonnie Turner and Terry Turner. Ph: Francis Kenny. Ed: Malcolm Campbell. Pro Des: Gregg Fonseca. M: Carter Burwell; numbers performed by Aerosmith, Robert Plant, Gin Blossoms, Superfan, Joan Jett and the Blackhearts, Norman Greenbaum, Dinosaur Jr, 4 Non Blondes, Golden Earring, Bad Company, Edgar Winter, Village People, etc. Costumes: Melina Root. Sound: Keith A. Wester. (Paramount–UIP.) Rel: 4 February 1994. 95 mins. Cert PG.

*Partying on: Dana Carvey, Mike Myers, Tia Carrere and Christopher Walken talk music in Stephen Surjik's* Wayne's World 2 *(from UIP)*

### The Wedding Banquet

Manhattan; 1992. Wai-Tung is rich, handsome and successful. He is also Taiwanese and far, far away from the conservative parents that irritate him and constantly pressurise him to marry. But they don't know that he's gay. A solution to everybody's problems would seem to be a quick, unfussy wedding to Wei-Wei, a struggling Chinese painter who needs a green card to stay in New York. But then Wai-Tung's parents arrive to celebrate the big event . . . Simply one of the freshest, most delightful and touching comedies of the year that manages to engender genuine laughs from real people in believably impossible situations. Mitchell Lichtenstein as Wai-Tung's sympathetic lover is a stand-out, while the registry office marriage itself is a *coup de cinéma*. A Taiwanese–American co-production. [JC-W]

Cast: Sihung Lung (Mr Gao), Ah-Leh Gua (Mrs Gao), Winston Chao (Gao Wai-

*Rising son: Winston Chao (*centre*) finds himself in no end of trouble when he agrees to a marriage of 'convenience' – in Ang Lee's delightful* The Wedding Banquet. *May Chin and Mitchell Lichtenstein flank him*

*Simply the best: Angela Bassett as Tina Turner with Laurence Fishburne as Ike Turner – in Brian Gibson's* What's Love Got To Do With It *(from Buena Vista)*

Tung), Mitchell Lichtenstein (Simon), May Chin (Wei-Wei), Dion Birney (Andrew), Jeanne Kuo Chang, Chung-Wei Chou, Ang Lee.

Dir: Ang Lee. Pro: Ang Lee, Ted Hope and James Schamus. Ex Pro: Jiang Feng-Chyi. Line Pro: Dolly Hall. Screenplay: Ang Lee, Schamus and Neil Peng. Ph: Jong Lin. Ed: Tim Squyres. Pro Des: Steve Rosenzweig. M: Mader. Costumes: Michael Clancy. Sound: Pamela Martin. (Central Motion Picture Corp/Good Machine–Mainline.) Rel: 24 September 1993. 108 mins. Cert 15.

### What's Eating Gilbert Grape?

Gilbert Grape is a product of the ultimate dysfunctional family. His younger brother is mentally retarded, his mother weighs in at 36 stone and his father is dead. And, stranded in a nowhere town in Iowa, Gilbert works in a grocery store that's lost most of its customers to the local megamart. If Gilbert is going to make sense of his life, he better do something about it. Maybe Becky, the new girl in town, could help him out . . . For all its quirkiness, gentle charm and fine performances, *Gilbert Grape* goes absolutely nowhere and ultimately fails to captivate. Incidentally, the role of Gilbert's agoraphobic, overweight mother is played by newcomer Darlene Cates, a former agoraphobic (and still astonishingly fat). [JC-W]

Cast: Johnny Depp (Gilbert Grape), Juliette Lewis (Becky), Mary Steenburgen (Betty Carver), Leonardo DiCaprio (Arnie Grape), John C. Reilly (Tucker), Darlene Cates (Bonnie Grape), Laura Harrington (Amy Grape), Mary Kate Schellhardt (Ellen Grape), Crispin Glover (Bobby McBurney), Kevin Tighe (Mr Carver), Penelope Branning, Tim Green, Susan Loughran, Robert B. Hedges, Brady Coleman.

Dir: Lasse Hallstrom. Pro: David Matalon, Meir Teper and Bertil Ohlsson. Ex Pro: Hallstrom and Alan Blomquist. Screenplay: Peter Hedges; based on his novel. Ph: Sven Nykvist. Ed: Andrew Mondshein. Pro Des: Bernt Capra. M: Alan Parker and Bjorn Isfalt. Costumes: Renee Ehrlich Kalfus. (J&M Entertainment/Paramount–Entertainment.) Rel: 6 May 1994. 117 mins. Cert 12.

### What's Love Got To Do With It

Before Tina Turner became the rock 'n' roll legend she is today, she was the second half of Ike & Tina Turner, a successful, enduring soul act engineered by her husband. Indeed, Ike wrote most of the songs, fronted the band, played guitar and keyboards, choreographed the stage shows and handled the money. But Tina had to pay a terrible price for this success, as she revealed in her searing autobiography, *I, Tina*. Angela Bassett, who played Betty Shabazz (Malcolm's wife) in *Malcolm X*, is simply sensational as the shy girl from rural Tennessee who clings on to the man who beats and humiliates her, sticking with him and his band for an incredible 17 years. Laurence Fishburne is less successful as Ike, as he has to play a man who is unremittingly (and monotonously) evil. A little light in his character would have made the scenes of domestic violence even more unbearable. TT herself supplies the inspiring numbers. [JC-W]

Cast: Angela Bassett (Anna Mae 'Tina' Bullock Turner), Laurence Fishburne (Ike Turner), Vanessa Bell Calloway (Jackie), Jenifer Lewis (Zelma Bullock), Phyllis Yvonne Stickney (Alline Bullock), Khandi Alexander (Darlene), Penny Johnson (Lorraine), Rob LaBelle (Phil Spector), Rae'ven Kelly, Virginia Capers, Chi, Jennifer Leigh Warren, Pamala Tyson, Damon Hines, Wynonna Smith, Rosemarie Jackson, O'Neal Compton, James Reyne.

Dir: Brian Gibson. Pro: Doug Chapin and Barry Krost. Ex Pro: Roger Davies and Mario Iscovich. Screenplay: Kate Lanier. Ph: Jamie Anderson. Ed: Stuart Pappé. Pro Des: Stephen Altman. M: Stanley Clarke; numbers performed by Tina Turner, Laurence Fishburne, Big Joe Turner, Dusty Springfield, Manfred Mann, Ike & Tina Turner, Edgar Winter, etc. Costumes: Ruth Carter. Sound: John Stacy. (Touchstone–Buena Vista.) Rel: 17 September 1993. 118 mins. Cert 18.

### Where Sleeping Dogs Lie

Long overdue release of this 1991 thriller, in which a struggling 'serious' novelist is forced to write a gory book to meet his mounting debts. Evicted from his apartment, Bruce Simmons moves into an old mansion, from which he draws inspiration for his new story. As it happens, the crumbling building is the site of a gruesome, unsolved murder. And Simmons is reluctantly drawn into its nefarious secret . . . Far-fetched, to be sure, but the acting is above par for this sort of thing, with Sharon Stone (pre-*Basic Instinct*) contributing a nifty cameo. Directed by Charles Finch, son of Peter Finch, and scripted by Finch and his mother, Yolanda Turner. [EB]

Cast: Dylan McDermott (Bruce Simmons), Tom Sizemore (Eddie Hale), Sharon Stone (Serena Black), Mary Woronov, David Combs, Shawne Rowe, Jillian McWhirter, Brett Cullen, Richard Zavaglia, Ron Karabatsos.

Dir: Charles Finch. Pro: Finch and Mario Sotela. Ex Pro: Paul Mason. Screenplay: Finch and Yolanda Turner. Ph: Monty Rowan. Ed: B. J. Sears and Gene M. Gemaine. Pro Des: Eve Cauley. M: Hans Zimmer and Mark Mancina. Costumes: Lynn Pickwell. Sound: Virgil Clemintine. (Sotela Pictures–Columbia TriStar.) Rel: 3 June 1994. 91 mins. Cert 15.

### White

See *Three Colours White*.

### White Angel

Leslie Steckler, a mild-mannered dentist, likes to dress up in frocks and murder women in white – hence his nickname, 'the white angel'. Ellen Carter is a crime writer who kills her abusive husband in a fit of rage. She is also Steckler's landlady. When Steckler discovers the body of Ellen's husband he makes her a deal: he won't go to the police if she writes his life story (without bias). Not only has writer-director Chris Jones, aged 24, come up with an intriguing premise for his first film, but he has directed it with a commendable lack of melodrama, soliciting naturalistic performances from his two leads. The result is a chillingly real drama that is not above keeping its audience in uncomfortable apprehension. [JC-W]

Cast: Peter Firth (Leslie Steckler), Harriet Robinson (Ellen Carter), Don Henderson (Inspector Taylor), Anne Catherine Arton (Mik), Harry Miller (Alan Smith), Joe Collins (Graham), Caroline Staunton, Mark Stevens, Inez Thorn, Ken Sharrock, Samantha Norman, John Bennett.

Dir: Chris Jones. Pro: Genevieve Jolliffe. Screenplay: Jones and Jolliffe. Ph: Jon Walker. Ed: John Holland. Pro Des: Mark Sutherland. M: Harry Gregson-Williams. Costumes: Sheena Gunn. Sound: Wyndham Vincent. (Living Spirit–Pilgrim Entertainment.) Rel: 15 April 1994. 92 mins. Cert 15.

### Widows Peak

The late 1920s; County Wicklow, Ireland. Exceedingly witty, deliciously acted comedy-mystery set in the snug village community of Kilshannon, where women come into their own on the coattails of widowhood. Head dowager and meddlesome snob is Mrs Doyle Counihan, the community's richest member and mother of the eligible bachelor Godfrey Counihan. But is she any match for the beautiful, terribly rich Edwina Broome, the latest addition to the elitist widowhood and – wait for it – an *Englishwoman*? It is rare to find such a superb piece of writing concocted solely for the screen (what? no play adaptation, or *at least* a modification of a novella?), but this is a true original in every sense of the word. A perfect jewel, to be sure. P.S. The part of Miss O'Hare, played by Mia Farrow, was originally written for Ms Farrow's mother Maureen O'Sullivan, while Edwina Broome was intended for Farrow! [JC-W]

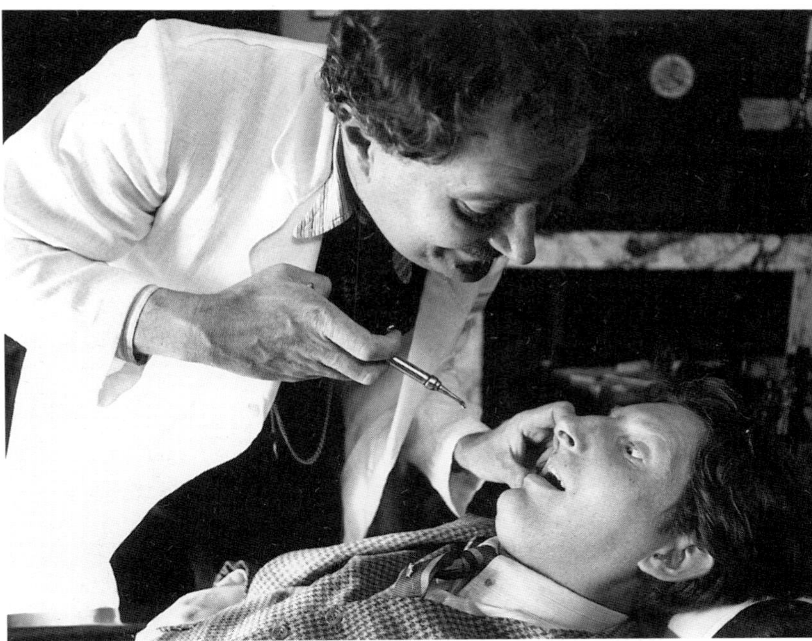

*Cor Blarney! Another screen dentist: Jim Broadbent follows in the cavities of Laurence Olivier, Walter Matthau, Steve Martin, Joe Mantegna, Sam Waterston, Peter Firth, etc, in John Irvin's pleasing piece of Irish whimsy,* Widows Peak *(from Rank). Adrian Dunbar is the victim*

Cast: Mia Farrow (Miss O'Hare), Joan Plowright (Mrs DC 'Doyle' Counihan), Natasha Richardson (Edwina Broome), Adrian Dunbar (Godfrey Counihan), Jim Broadbent (Clancy), Anne Kent (Miss Grubb), John Kavanagh (Canon), Rynagh O'Grady (Maddie), Gerard McSorley (Mr Gaffney), Michael James Ford (Rokesby), Doreen Keogh, Oliver Maguire, Tina Kellegher, Rachel Dowling.

Dir: John Irvin. Pro: Jo Manuel. Ex Pro: Michael White. Co-Pro: Tracey Seaward. Screenplay: Hugh Leonard. Ph: Ashley Rowe. Ed: Peter Tanner. Pro Des: Leo Austin. M: Carl Davis. Costumes: Consolata Boyle. Sound: Peter Lindsay. (Fine Line/British Screen–Rank.) Rel: 15 April 1994. 101 mins. Cert PG.

### The Young Americans

An LA DEA official is called to the UK to advise on a series of inexplicable killings in London's drug underworld. What could be more exciting than a contemporary hard-nosed thriller set in London's seedy back streets à la *Mona Lisa* and *The Long Good Friday*? Throw in Harvey Keitel, fresh from his cult success in *Reservoir Dogs* and *Bad Lieutenant*, and surely you have the makings of an instant classic. Even without sympathetic or interesting characters, sparkling dialogue, a decent plot, wit, sex, action or a central love theme of any conviction, this could still've been a film to admire had it been remotely credible or at least original. Nothing doing. [JC-W]

Cast: Harvey Keitel (John Harris), Iain Glen (Edward Foster), John Wood (Richard Donnelly), Terence Rigby (Sidney Callow), Keith Allen (Jack Doyle), Craig Kelly (Christian O'Neill), Thandie Newton (Rachael Stevens), Viggo Mortensen (Fraser), Dave Duffy, Geoffrey McGivern, Nigel Clauzel, Huggy Leaver, Chris Adamson, Anna Keaveney, David Doyle, Norman Roberts, Toni Palmer.

Dir: Danny Cannon. Pro: Paul Trijbits and Alison Owen. Ex Pro: Richard N. Gladstein, Ronna B. Wallace and Philippe Maigret. Screenplay: Cannon and David Hilton. Ph: Vernon Layton. Ed: Alex Mackie. Pro Des: Laurence Dorman. M: David Arnold. Costumes: Howard Burden. Sound: Clive Winter. (PolyGram/LIVE Entertainment/British Screen/Working Title/Trijbits Worrell Associates–Rank.) Rel: 8 October 1993. 104 mins. Cert 18.

# Letter from Hollywood

## Anthony Slide

What next? Locusts? Los Angeles has suffered through riots, floods and mudslides. Firestorms swept the Southern California coast for an entire week in November 1993, threatening the Malibu homes of Burgess Meredith, Tony Danza, Charles Bronson, Mark Hamill and others. Surprisingly, there was only one fatality, and that was a British director-screenwriter named Duncan Gibbons, who died from burns he suffered while trying to save his pet cat from the flames. There was a curious irony in that Gibbons's last three films were titled *Eve of Destruction*, *Fire with Fire* and *Third Degree Burn*.

While the damage from the fires was placed only in the tens of millions of dollars, the damage from the 6.8 earthquake that struck at 4.31 a.m. on Monday, 17 January 1994 was placed in the hundreds of millions. Apartment buildings collapsed, the plate glass in store windows smashed, banks fell off their foundations, the roofs of department stores subsided, and just about every other houseowner (including this writer) watched as his or her chimney came down.

The earthquake itself caused little damage to the studios, but sprinkler systems went crazy, flooding much of the office space at Walt Disney. There was severe water damage at the Academy of Motion Picture Arts and Sciences, although its library was, happily, untouched, with only a few books falling from the shelves. The UCLA Film and Television Archive was also relatively untouched but films fell from the shelves making it impossible to open the doors of a number of the nitrate storage vaults. Some stars suffered damage to their homes, with the biggest loser being Walter Matthau. Property loss sustained by the actor amounted to more than $5 million, and, ironically, only a couple of months earlier he had cancelled his earthquake insurance, considering the premiums too high.

Of more concern to the Hollywood community than harm to buildings was damage to their awards. There were urgent pleas for replacements for destroyed People's Choice and Emmy trophies. Power cuts made it impossible to open electronically-operated garage doors, and studio stars and executives were faced with the terrifying prospect of perhaps having to use public transport! An added torment was that most of the film community's popular restaurants were closed for a few days, with every bottle in their wine cellars smashed.

Only one major film production was shooting at the time of the earthquake – and that at its epicentre in Northridge. The leading man was a British actor noted for his 'vicious' roles; his first response was catatonic shock followed by a demand to be put on the next plane back to London.

Of course, the earthquake affected us all personally in different ways. Silent screen star Esther Ralston had died the previous Friday, and her colleague Mary Brian and I had planned

*The Academy of Motion Picture Arts and Sciences doesn't just present awards. Two 1993 events organised by the Academy were the Marvin Borowsky Memorial Lecture in Screenwriting, given by Lowell Ganz* (centre) *and Babaloo Mandel* (right) *and hosted by Academy president Arthur Hiller; and the Don Nicholl Screenwriting Awards, attended by Felicia Farr* (left), *husband Jack Lemmon and Nora Ephron*

to drive up to Ventura, north of Los Angeles, for the funeral. The funeral went ahead, but we were unable to attend. Andre de Toth, director of such well-known films as *Ramrod*, *House of Wax* and *Play Dirty*, told me that damage to the contents of his apartment included a cookie jar that fell to the floor, dispersing its contents. His two dogs quickly found and consumed the cookies. Thereafter, following each aftershock, the two dogs would immediately rush to the location of the cookie jar in anticipation of further treats. (Andre recently completed his autobiography, *Fragments*, which will be published in the UK by Faber and Faber just as this edition of *Film Review* appears.)

During the past year, Hollywood lost more than it gained. The addition was a piece of artwork titled the La Brea Gateway, placed at the junction of Al Brea Avenue and Hollywood Boulevard. Looking something like a 30-foot tall gazebo, overly decorated with the name Hollywood – it appears eight times, four in neon – the structure is held aloft by stylised statues of Mae West, Dolores Del Rio, Anna May Wong, and Dorothy Dandridge. Note the political correctness here! The statues are all female and representative of the Caucasian, Hispanic, Chinese and Afro-American communities. At one point, there was talk of placing a statue of D. W. Griffith at this intersection, and that would have been a far more appropriate monument to Hollywood than what has rightly been described by *Los Angeles Times* art critic Christopher Knight as 'the most depressingly awful work of public art in recent memory'.

Not yet a reality but definitely in the planning stage is a museum devoted to the work of Bob Hope, which will also include a theatre presenting his films and television programmes on a regular basis. 'There's an interest in the man's career and life, so there is demand for a museum,' said a spokesperson for Bob Hope Enterprises. Perhaps. . . .

There is probably equal interest in Hopalong Cassidy. Yet a museum devoted to the career of his real life persona, William Boyd, closed in January 1994. It was located just outside Los Angeles, in the city of Downey.

The closure of the Hopalong Cassidy Museum is a relatively minor loss in comparison to the demolition on 24 January 1994 of the Brown Derby Restaurant on Vine Street in Hollywood. Opened in 1929 in a building owned by Cecil B. DeMille, the Brown Derby was the favourite eating place of Hollywood stars for more than three decades; in booth 5, Clark Gable proposed to Carole Lombard in 1939. The restaurant closed in 1985 and was damaged by squatters and by fires. The earthquake further damaged the building and the owners claimed there was no alternative but to demolish it.

A portion of the Hollywood Walk of Fame is located outside the Brown Derby, and more stars continue to be added to the sidewalk (often dubbed the Hollywood Walk of Shame because of the mediocrity or lack of fame of many of those honoured thereon). A ceremony adding the Pointer Sisters to the tourist attractions was postponed because of the earthquake. There was no postponing or cancellation of Mel Gibson's putting his hand and footprints in the cement forecourt of Grauman's Chinese Theatre on 23 August 1993, despite vocal protests from gay and lesbian groups angered at his reported anti-gay remarks in a Spanish magazine.

Another star (or perhaps that is an overstatement) who is a constant source of controversy and a favourite with this column is Zsa Zsa Gabor. She didn't manage to grab any headlines during the earthquake, but the fires did provide her with the opportunity to display the humanitarian side of her character as she offered to take in horses, made homeless by the fire, at her Simi Valley ranch.

A less altruistic element in Miss Gabor's makeup came public in December 1993, when fellow actress Elke Sommer was awarded a $3.3 million judgment against Gabor. It seems that back in 1990, Zsa Zsa gave interviews to a couple of German magazines in which she claimed that Elke Sommer was a penniless 68-year-old who looked far worse. The 51-year-old Sommer denied Gabor's accusations and claimed that the indeterminately-aged actress had a big behind.

Zsa Zsa Gabor and her husband, Frederick von Anhalt, were far from pleased with the verdict. The latter announced, 'I'm a German citizen. I won't have to pay a cent.' Miss Gabor was even less restrained: 'I'd rather see her starve to death than give her one single dollar.'

Zsa Zsa was unable to attend court on the day of judgment. She was busy appearing in a British pantomime, *Cinderella*, being presented at, of all places, the Freud Playhouse at UCLA. Unfortunately, Los Angeles audiences would seem to have no great fondness for either Miss Gabor or British pantomime, for the production, which the *Los Angeles Times* claimed rivalled that of *Springtime for Hitler*, closed after the first week of a projected three-week run.

Somewhat more successful has been Andrew Lloyd Webber's *Sunset Blvd.*, starring Glenn Close, and doing phenomenal business at the Shubert Theatre in Century City. Although he apparently earns no royalties from the stageplay, the author of the original film, Billy Wilder, is full of praise for the production.

Wilder's unique sense of humour is evidenced by an art exhibition, 'Billy Wilder's Marché aux Puces', at the Louis Stern Galleries in Beverly Hills during January 1994. The exhibition included far-from-serious pieces by David Hockney, Pablo Picasso, Alexander Calder and others. Its highspot was a series of busts of Nefertete, designed by Bruce Houston in the personae of everyone from Albert Einstein to Groucho Marx. Billy Wilder has had a lifelong interest in art; in 1989, he sold his collection of 85 Impressionist, modern and contemporary pieces of artwork for more than $32 million. As he states, 'It has really enriched my life to dabble, to have art, to hang it and rehang it – and to have fun with it'.

Humour was very much on the mind of producer George Schlatter when he created the Comedy Hall of Fame. The first inductees – George Burns, Carol Burnett, Milton Berle, Walter Matthau and Jonathan Winters – were introduced at an awards ceremony, shown on NBC on 24 November 1993. George Burns showed up in company with Sharon Stone, but the biggest attention was given to alleged Hollywood madam Heidi Fleiss. 'It's nice to see Heidi get out of the house,' quipped one guest.

Milton Berle celebrated his 85th birthday by receiving an award from a group called the Poetry Academy. Poets and celebrities intermingled at the Beverly Hills Hotel and listened as Berle explained that he wrote his first poem at the age of fourteen; it began, 'There was a young man from Nantucket'.

Western fans mourned the loss of the standing Western Street set at the Warner Bros ranch in June 1993. The street was used in such films as *High Noon*, *Cat Ballou* and *3.10 to Yuma*. It was demolished to make way for a parking lot. Warner Bros is filming its new Western, *Wyatt Earp*, starring Kevin Costner, on location in New Mexico.

The fans lost a street but they still have a Western film festival in the Los Angeles area. The Lone Pine Film Festival takes place in an area noted for Western location shooting from the 1920s through to the present.

In June 1993, it honoured the Lone Ranger, noting that here in the shadow of Mount Whitney, the 1938 Republic serial of the *Lone Ranger* was filmed. On hand was television's Lone Ranger, Clayton Moore, who paid tribute to his partner Jay Silverheels, reminded his audience of the Lone Ranger creed, 'I believe in order to have a friend, a man must be one,' and noted that guns are dangerous. The highspot of the festival was an open-air evening concert of music from the Lone Ranger films and radio and television shows, performed by the 28-piece CinemaSound orchestra, consisting of studio musicians. The concert took place in a canyon in the Alabama Hills, but the evening turned cold and many in the audience left, including a number of old-time cowboy stars who should have been made of sturdier stuff.

Celebrities making news in the past year included the Fonda (Jane, Peter, Bridget, etc) and the Bergen (Candice, Frances, etc) families who were honoured in November 1993 with the fifth annual Hollywood Legacy Awards. Gregory Peck spoke of Henry Fonda, while Robert Stack paid tribute to Edgar Bergen. Louis Malle, Karl Malden and James Garner were among the celebrities on hand for the event which helped to raise money for the proposed Hollywood Entertainment Museum.

'How do I look? Considering I've been dead forty-three years, I think I look pretty good,' said Al Jolson lookalike Ira Green at the International Al Jolson Society's Festival in July 1993. (Political correctness was in evidence here with Jolson's lookalike no longer wearing blackface.) On hand for the event were two child performers who had worked with Jolson in the 1930s: Davey Lee from *The Singing Fool* (1928) and Sybil Jason from *The Singing Kid* (1936). There was also a posthumous lifetime achievement award for Ruby Keeler. Had she been alive, it is doubtful she would have accepted the honour. When asked by an overenthusiastic fan once as to whether she was aware she had been married to a living legend, Miss Keeler responded, 'Yes, he told me so himself every morning.'

It is very obvious that the American Film Institute Life Achievement Award will in future go to those celebrities who will garner a major television audience for the show rather than those who are worthy of the tribute. In view of Jack Nicholson's age and future career potential, he was an unworthy choice to receive the award in the International Ballroom of the Beverly Hills Hotel on 3 March 1994. On hand for the event were Sean Penn, Cher, Kathleen Turner, Candice Bergen, Shirley MacLaine, Faye Dunaway, Shelley Duvall, Ellen Burstyn, Warren Beatty, Michael Keaton, Dennis Hopper and many others. In accepting the award, Nicholson said, 'I'm touched and I'm fortunate. And I'm lucky to be at large.' That remark and the laughter from the audience is demonstrative of the arrogance of so many of today's film personalities. On 8 February in Studio City, Nicholson allegedly took a golf club and smashed the windshield of a motorist who he believed had cut him up in traffic. Nicholson later settled with the motorist but was the subject of a criminal complaint. Obviously, his behaviour did not disquiet the American Film Institute, nor did it bother the Los Angeles Police Department who had invited him to host its 23rd celebrity golf (of all sports) tournament.

Aside from the AFI Lifetime Achievement Award, the biggest social event of the year in Hollywood is the Academy Awards presentation – or to be more precise, the parties that follow it. The party which everyone traditionally wanted to attend was that hosted by agent Irving 'Swifty' Lazar, which took place at the West Hollywood restaurant, Spago. With Lazar's death last year, the owners of Spago decided to keep the restaurant closed as a memorial to the man. Academy Award attendees had the option of four other major parties. The biggest was hosted at Morton's Restaurant by producer Steve Tisch and Graydon Carter, editor-in-chief of *Vanity Fair*. Seen here were Candice Bergen, Gore Vidal, Anjelica Huston, Nancy Reagan, Liam Neeson, Tom Cruise, Debra Winger, Whitney Houston, Anthony Hopkins, Goldie Hawn and Nancy Kerrigan.

Elton John gave a party to raise funds for his AIDS Foundation at the Maple Drive Restaurant in Beverly Hills. On hand here were Whoopi Goldberg (albeit briefly), Tom Hanks, Ralph Fiennes, George Michael, Rod Stewart and Bonnie Raitt. The third annual Women in Film's Academy Awards viewing party took place at the Beverly Hills Hotel. Spotted here were Bruce Davison, Stockard Channing, Diane Ladd, Michael Learned, Shelley Winters and (surprise, surprise) Lita Grey Chaplin. Finally, El Rescate's seventh annual Academy Awards benefit was held at the Mondrian Hotel. The group concerns itself with immigration from Central America, and the biggest star it was able to induce to appear was Cheech Marin.

My favourite event of the year was the second annual Screen Actors Guild Foundation Jack Oakie Award for Comedy in Motion Pictures. The honoree was the brilliant John Cleese, and on hand to pay tribute to him were Jamie Lee Curtis, Eric Idle, Lawrence Kasden, Dudley Moore, Frank Oz and Michael Palin. The humour was Pythonesque in quality, sometimes reduced to a rather earthy level, as when, for example, Ms Curtis pointed out that the microphone was set low so that she had to bend down and thus give the audience a good look at her breasts. I don't know exactly what the audience at the Beverly Wilshire Hotel on 11 January 1994 made of the evening. There was some nervous laughter as Cleese denounced the speakers for their inability to pay adequate tribute to his many talents, not to mention his 'fucking humanity'. He then proceeded to point out his numerous attributes, ending with a note from his former writing partner Graham Chapman, who, despite being dead, had sent a positive tribute to Cleese via a ouija board.

Shortly after witnessing the brilliance of John Cleese, I took time out to speak with Anna Lee, a British star from an earlier age, who represents the last remnant of the British colony in Hollywood. With her then-husband director Robert Stevenson, she came to Los Angeles in 1939. Her first evening in the city was spent in David O. Selznick's screening room, watching a rough cut of *Gone With the Wind* in company with Clark Gable and Carole Lombard. It was a glamorous introduction to an industry that Miss Lee has seen rapidly decline over the fifty years since *Film Review* was first published.

She comments, 'It's a different world, entirely different. There are no father figures. There is no Louis B. Mayer or David Selznick or Harry Cohn. They had their faults, but it was wonderful for an actor because you were with a studio and everything was done for you. Today, you go for interviews and the producers and casting people are just young kids. They wear dirty jeans and are bare footed. And they say, "What have you done?" And my reply is, "When I was doing it, you were in diapers." People like Louis B. Mayer and Harry Cohn were filmmakers. They knew how to handle actors. And in those days there was discipline. There is no discipline today. There is no glamour. There is no elegance.'

For the past nine years, Anna Lee has been confined to a wheelchair, but that has not stopped her acting. Prior to spinal surgery, she had played the

*John Cleese* (centre) *receives the Screen Actors Guild Foundation Jack Oakie Award for Comedy in Motion Pictures, with* (from left to right) *master of ceremonies Robert Klein, Jamie Lee Curtis, Michael Palin, Eric Idle and Frank Oz*

matriarchal character on the popular daytime soap opera, *General Hospital*. So popular is she with television audiences throughout the United States that the producers wrote into the storyline that she had suffered a severe accident and was coming back on the show in a wheelchair.

Anna Lee still keeps up with the new films; she found *The Age of Innocence* pretentious and thought *The Remains of the Day* a better film. She remains resolutely English. Despite being a close friend and a favourite actress of John Ford, who she insists had the greatest admiration for the English, Anna Lee is at her angriest and most formidable when discussing the IRA. She was outraged by *In the Name of the Father*, and cannot condone Daniel Day-Lewis's appearance in the film, even though, when a Gaumont-British actress in the 1930s, she used to bathe his mother, Jill Balcon.

The actress has experienced some trouble in her outspoken criticism of the IRA. At an English event in Los Angeles, picketed by IRA sympathisers, Miss Lee took a hammer to the signs of the protesters. A few days later, the pickets arrived at her home, smeared blood on the Union Jack on her front door, and wrote 'Death' in red paint. She was not so much concerned for herself as for her ageing husband, poet and novelist Robert Nathan.

Anna Lee remembers the British colony headed by Sir C. Aubrey Smith and regrets its passing, noting that British actors in Hollywood today have become Americanised. Every day of her life, she says, she has regretted leaving England. But England's loss is also England's gain. For Anna Lee has steadfastly remained an English rose in the thorny Hollywood garden. There may not be an English bowling team as there was fifty years ago, or even a corner of a Hollywood field that is forever England. But there is a cottage in West Hollywood with a Union Jack on the door, with Royal Staffordshire pottery on the mantelpiece, where tea is still served promptly at four, complete with cucumber sandwiches, and the last of the English colony carries on its Hollywood version of English tradition.

# Movie Quotations of the Year

: new nanny, admiring Morticia's
band: 'Isn't he a lady-killer!'
mez, reassuringly: 'Acquitted!'

Joan Cusack and Raul Julia in *Addams Family Values*

Nanny: 'Children, where's the baby?' Wednesday Addams (Christina Ricci): 'Which part?'

From *Addams Family Values*

omez, encouraging brother Fester
: his romantic future: 'You'll meet
omeone. Someone special. Someone
who won't press charges.'

From *Addams Family Values*

'I want you to know I used to be a virgin.'

Lucinda Jenney to Jeff Bridges in *American Heart*

ind man to Dana Carvey: 'Why do
ind people skydive?' Carvey: 'Why?'
lind man: 'To scare the shit out of
eir dogs.'

From *Clean Slate*

We're going to be bigger than
Hamburg. Bigger than Liverpool.
igger than for our own good.'

Ian Hart as a young John Lennon in *Backbeat*

*Ian Hart, in* Backbeat

*Michael J. Fox, in* The Concierge

'Nothing's impossible. Impossible just means an extra two phone calls.'

Can-do achiever Michael J. Fox as *The Concierge*

Jodie, defensively: 'Ted and I are platonic.' Prying (and ignorant) mother: 'What's *that*?' Jodie: 'Platonic. It's Greek for having lunch occasionally.'

Jane Horrocks and Brenda Fricker in *Deadly Advice*

Sandra Bullock, turning down Sylvester Stallone's offer of physical intimacy. 'Sex? Do you know what sex leads to?' Stallone: 'Yeah. Kids. Smoking. Raiding the fridge.'

From *Demolition Man*

'A woman is like a tree. You must judge it not by its flowers, but by its fruit.'

Bushman Sarel Bok in *A Far Off Place*

Michael Madsen – concluding his administration of a biker marriage ceremony – to groom: 'Alright, give the broad some tongue.'

In *Fixing the Shadow*

*Hugh Grant, in* Four Weddings & a Funeral

'In the words of David Cassidy – while he was still with *The Partridge Family* – I think I love you.'

Hugh Grant to Andie MacDowell in *Four Weddings & a Funeral*

Doctor on the run, cornered by a cop with a gun. 'I didn't kill my wife!' Cop: 'I don't care.'

Harrison Ford and Tommy Lee Jones in *The Fugitive*

A defensive Wilma: 'Mother, Fred is a loving husband and a good provider.' Mother: 'Oh, really? What has he ever provided you besides shade?'

Elizabeth Perkins and Elizabeth Taylor in *The Flintstones*

Irate woman: 'Kiss my ass!' Furious man: 'That would take all night!'

Arguing couple heard through the wall of Michael J. Fox and Nancy Travis's hotel bedroom in *Greedy*

Mom: 'No more jokes about Jean-Pierre's cologne.' Josh: 'It's not cologne. It's a fire hazard.'

Joan Allen and Jacob Tierney in *Josh and S.A.M.*

Joan Plowright (as an English teacher) explaining to her class who the 1948 screen Hamlet, Laurence Olivier, is: 'You may have seen him in the Polaroid commercials.'

From *Last Action Hero*

Austin O'Brien to his fictitious hero Jack Slater (Schwarzenegger): 'You can't die – until the grosses go down.'

From *Last Action Hero*

Ian McKellen as Ingmar Bergman's 'Death' from *The Seventh Seal* – answering Austin O'Brien's plea to help Schwarzenegger's dying Jack Slater: 'I don't do fiction.'

From *Last Action Hero*

'Winston's idea of foreplay was, "Effie, brace yourself!" '

Robin Williams as gentle widow *Mrs Doubtfire*

'Life shuffles the deck and there you are with the Joker again.'

Bad loser Matt Dillon in Anthony Minghella's *Mr Wonderful*

'I like my sex like I like my basketball: one on one and with as little dribbling as possible.'

Leslie Nielsen as Frank Drebin in *Naked Gun 33⅓: The Final Insult*

' "You might end up dead" is my middle name.'

Leslie Nielsen as Frank Drebin in *Naked Gun 33⅓: The Final Insult*

*Leslie Nielsen, in* Naked Gun 33⅓: The Final Insult

*Max Von Sydow, in* Needful Things

'I'm not The Father, The Son and The Holy Ghost. I'm just one lonely guy.'

Max Von Sydow as an apologetic Satan in *Needful Things*

Night watch security guard to vagrant (David Thewlis) in his doorway: 'Have you got anywhere to go?' Thewlis: 'I've got an infinite number of places to go. The question is "do I have anywhere to stay?".'

From Mike Leigh's *Naked*

Scatty aunt to nephew: 'So, where's your mother now?' Nephew: 'She's dead.' Aunt (flustered): 'Yeh, but where's she buried?'

Mercedes Ruehl and Brad Stoll in Neil Simon's *Lost in Yonkers*

Editor Bernie White to his managing editor Alicia Clark: 'If everybody loved you, you'd be doing something wrong.'

Robert Duvall and Glenn Close in *The Paper*

'I don't know nothin'. Not one damn thing.'

Texas ranger Clint Eastwood near the end of *A Perfect World*

'The choices we make dictate the life we lead.'

Danny DeVito in *Renaissance Man*

The villainous commander of OCP's Rehabilitation forces – to RoboCop: 'How may I help you, officer?' RoboCop: 'By resisting arrest.'

John Castle and Robert Burke in *RoboCop 3*

'You know right from wrong. You just don't care. It's the most natural thing in the world.'

Roy Scheider (to Gary Oldman) in *Romeo Is Bleeding*

'Do you know what makes love so frightening? You don't own it. It owns you.'

Gary Oldman in *Romeo Is Bleeding*

'Somewhere I heard, "Hell is where all your dreams come true." '

Ashley Judd in *Ruby in Paradise*

'The homeless can't afford to be embarrassed.'

Vagrant Danny Glover in *The Saint of Fort Washington*

'This is your world – we just live in it.'

Windscreen cleaner Matt Dillon, trying to butter up a client – in *The Saint of Fort Washington*

'I'm a Jew. I'm divorced. I'm broke. And I'm dying of cancer. Do you think I'll get a discount?'

Debra Winger in *Shadowlands*

'Experience is a brutal teacher. But you learn. By god, you learn.'

Anthony Hopkins in *Shadowlands*

'The pain now is part of the happiness then. That is the deal.'

Anthony Hopkins as C. S. Lewis, finally understanding the importance of emotional commitment – in *Shadowlands*

'Give your mother a kiss – or I'll kick your teeth in.'

Mike Myers Sr encouraging filial affection from his son – in *So I Married an Axe Murderer*

Girlfriend: 'Charlie, what do you look for in a woman?' Charlie: 'I know most people say a sense of humour, but I have to go for breast size.'

Nancy Travis and Mike Myers in *So I Married an Axe Murderer*

'That's the way it goes – but once in a while it goes the other way too.'

Patricia Arquette's dreamy voice-over at the beginning of *True Romance*

*Patricia Arquette, in* True Romance

Milady, holding her dagger up against Cardinal Richelieu's crotch: 'With a flick of my wrist I could change your religion.'

Rebecca De Mornay in *The Three Musketeers*

'Here I am – you lucky people!'

Robert De Niro's catchphrase in *This Boy's Life*

'I know a thing or two about a thing or two.'

De Niro's other catchphrase in *This Boy's Life*

'He's not so much a good guy as a bad motherfucker.'

Christian Slater describing the character Sonny Chiba plays in *The Streetfighter* – from *True Romance*

Wayne Campbell, on the sex appeal of his girlfriend, Cassandra: 'She'd give a *dog* a bone.'

Mike Myers, in *Wayne's World 2*

Blonde babe, seductively: 'Would you like to have dinner one night?' Garth Algar, coyly: 'I like to have dinner *every* night.'

Kim Basinger and Dana Carvey in *Wayne's World 2*

**The year's most moving marriage proposal**:
C. S. Lewis, to a cancer-wracked Joy Gresham in her hospital bed: 'Will you marry this foolish, frightened old man who needs you more than he can bear to say, and loves you even though he hardly knows how?' Gresham: 'Just this once.'
Anthony Hopkins and Debra Winger in *Shadowlands*

**Sound familiar?**
Ted Danson in *Getting Even With Dad*: 'You've been watching way too much Oprah!'

Aida Turturro in *Angie*: 'You're gonna end up on Oprah!'

Denis Leary in *Hostile Hostages*: 'Let's go on Oprah and get it over with!'

# TV Feature Films of the Year

F. Maurice Speed

In this section you will find listed all the made-for-television movies shown for the first time in the UK during the year 1 July 1993 to 30 June 1994. Films shown during the year which have been previously televised in the UK are not listed, but can be found in the edition of *Film Review* for the year when they were first shown. The date given in brackets after each title is the year when the movie was made or originally shown (often in the US).

In a few cases, despite being first shown on television, these films may have been made originally for the cinema.

When a film made for American TV receives its first UK showing in a cinema, it is of course reviewed in the 'Releases of the Year' section.

**After the Promise** (1987). Based on a factual case, this is the thoughtful story of a father's struggle to gain custody of his four sons. With Mark Harrison, Diana Scarwid. ITV, 23 February 1994.

**And Then You Die** (1987). Tough Canadian thriller, with Hell's Angels, the Mafia and drugs making a punchy mixture. With Kenneth Welsh, R. H. Thomson. Dir: Francis Mankiewicz. ITV, 20 March 1994.

**Another Woman's Child** (1983). Superficial sob-stuff about a childless couple whose lives are disrupted by the arrival of the husband's child by another woman. With Linda Lavin, Tony LoBianco. Dir: John Erman. ITV, 22 August 1993.

**Anything to Survive** (1990). Superior telefilm about a father (Robert Conrad) and his three children wrecked on the desolate Alaskan coast and having to trek across ice and snow to safety. Dir: Zala Dalen. BBC2, 2 August 1993.

**Apology for Murder** (1986). Familiar story of a Manhattan artist (Lesley Ann Warren) being stalked by a psycho killer, in turn being stalked by a cop. Dir: Robert Bierman. BBC1, 28 November 1993.

**ASIS** (1986). Writer Robert Carradine trying to come to terms with AIDS. Dir: Michael Lindsay-Hogg. BBC2, 28 May 1994.

**Assassin** (1986). Routine, minor SF story about a mechanical man programmed to kill a list of people, and retired tec William Conrad doing his best to thwart villain Richard Young's nasty plans. ITV, 15 September 1993.

**Babies** (1990). Intelligent piece about three mature women and their doubts about having the babies they all want. Problems, problems: but very real ones and carefully presented. With Lindsay Wagner, Dinah Manoff, Marly Walker. Dir: Michael Rhodes. Channel 4, 21 September 1993.

**The Bait** (1973). Female cop taking chances in order to trap a rapist killer. With Donna Mills. Dir: Leonard Horn. ITV, 8 August 1993.

**The Barbary Coast** (1975). Mildly amusing and entertaining pilot feature for a brief TV series of the 1970s. A good cast headed by William ('Star Trek') Shatner. Dir: Bill Bixby. ITV, 7 September 1993.

**Baywatch: Nightmare Bay** (1991). The eventful life of the Los Angeles coastguards. Routine watching. With David Hassellhoff, Monte Markham. ITV, 30 January 1994.

**Bellamy: Massage Girls Murders** (1980). Bellamy (John Stanton) up against a psychopath murderer: Australian and highly unpleasant. Dir: Gary Colway. ITV, 22 March 1994.

**Bermuda Grace** (1993). Murder most foul against lovely backgrounds. The puzzle faced by the charmless cop – did she fall or was she pushed? With William Sadler. Dir: Mark Sobell. ITV, 2 April 1994.

**Between Love and Hate** (1993). Conventional story about a passionate love affair between a young student and a mature married woman. With Patrick Van Horn, Susan Lucci. Dir: Rod Hardy. ITV, 9 September 1993.

**Billy the Kid** (1989). Writer Gore Vidal's second effort to whiten blackhearted villain Billy. Not a bad Western but an unremarkable one. With Val Kilmer. Dir: W. A. Graham. BBC1, 6 August 1993.

**Blind Vengeance** (1990). A father whose son has been killed by racists seeks personal vengeance when the killers are released because of lack of evidence. With Gerald McRaney. Dir: Lee Philips. ITV, 18 March 1994.

**Buried Alive** (1990). Superior but grim thriller with Jennifer Jason-Leigh (terrific) planning to murder hubbie Tim Matheson. Dir: Frank Darabont. ITV, 11 March 1994; also BBC2, 3 June 1994.

**Burning Bridges** (1990). Highly unlikely story of a faithless wife who tells hubby all! Meredith Baxter Birney tries hard and commendably to save a sinking ship. Dir: Sheldon Larry. ITV, 23 February 1994.

**Call to Glory** (1983). Routine family drama: a USAF colonel (Craig T. Nelson) is faced with a difficult career problem: whichever choice he makes, his wife and family will suffer. Also with Cindy Pickett. Dir: Peter Wemev and Arthur Allan. ITV, 24 November 1993.

**Champion** (1989). An endearing New Zealand film about the friendship that develops between a young boy and a black American soldier billeted on his family during the war. Moving, memorable and superbly acted. With Milan Borich, Michael James. Dir: Peter Sharp. Channel 4, 28 June 1994.

**A Child in the Night** (1990). An original whodunnit. An 8-year-old boy (Elijah Wood – very good) was the only witness to his dad's dreadful murder and the psychiatrists try to get him to reveal who was the killer. Also with JoBeth Williams, Tom Skerritt. Dir: Mike Robe. ITV, 6 December 1993.

**The China Lake Murders** (1990). Sheriff Tom Skerritt doggedly tracking down an odd sort of serial killer. An unusual whodunnit. Also with Michael Parks. Dir: Alan Metzger. ITV, 14 January 1994.

**The Christmas Stallion** (1992). Pleasant, sentimental but entertaining family film about a young Welsh orphan fighting a nasty land developer in order to keep her granddad's farm and horses. Very well made. With Daniel J. Travanti, Sian Maclean, Lynette Davies. Dir: Peter Edwards. Channel 4, 22 December 1993.

**Closing Numbers** (1993). Shocked wife (Jane Asher) finds out hubbie is homosexual and his lover is dying from AIDS. No director's credit. Channel 4, 2 December 1993.

**Cold Comfort** (1989). Not very thrilling thriller about a motorist who crashes in the snow, to be taken home as a present to his very odd rescuer's nubile daughter. Canadian TV feature. With Maury Chaykin, Paul Gross, Margaret Landrick. Dir: Vic Sarin. Channel 4, 18 June 1994.

**Columbo: Murder in Malibu** (1990). A new Columbo case: the sleuth in the dirty raincoat is called in to solve the murder of a novelist. Routine. With Peter Falk. ITV, 15 August 1993.

**Columbo: Uneasy Lies the Crown** (1990). Another new case for the scruffy little tec to solve: and he takes feature-length time to put his finger on the killer. With Peter Falk. Dir: Alan Levi. ITV, 22 August 1993.

**The Concrete Cowboys** (1979). A couple of saddle pals turn detectives when two Western singers vanish. With Jerry Reed, Tom Selleck. Dir: Burt Kennedy. ITV, 13 March 1994.

**The Confessions of Pastor Burg** (1992). Swiss TV film about a dour pastor's revenge on his sinning flock. So-so. With Frederic Van Den Driessche. Dir: Jean-Jacques Lalrange. Channel 4, 9 June 1994.

**The Cops and Robin** (1978). Cop Ernest Borgnine just about keeps this flimsy film afloat: it's a wry sort of buddy-buddy story. Dir: Allen Reisner. ITV, 21 September 1993.

**The Cops Are Robbers** (1991). Edward Asner as the top cop determined to root out corruption in the force. Based on a true story. Also with Ray Sharkey. Dir: Paul Wendkos. BBC1, 21 January 1994.

**Crash: the Mystery of Flight 1501** (1990). Cheryl Ladd as the pilot's wife valiantly determined to clear her husband's name after a terrible crash. Also with Doug Sheehan. Dir: Philip Saville. BBC1, 9 September 1993.

**Danielle Steel's Palomino** (1991). Newly divorced Lindsay Frost finds consolation at her pal's (Eva Marie Saint) horse ranch. And it all works out entertainingly. Dir: Michael Miller. ITV, 3 September 1993.

**Day of the Wolves** (1973). Made-for-TV movie that won a general release. Richard Egan ridding an American small town of the criminal element that has taken it over. Also with Marsha Hyer. Dir: Ferde Grofe. ITV, 18 September 1993.

**The Day the Loving Stopped** (1981). Sob stuff about a family thrown into misery by a divorce. With Dennis Weaver, Valerie Harper. Dir: Daniel Mann. ITV, 8 April 1994.

**Dead Liquor** (1992). Unsatisfactory Greek TV movie based on a popular novel. Dir: George Karypidas. Channel 4, 12 May 1994.

**Dead Reckoning** (1990). Pretty dull romantic tangle with a young lover coming between a doctor and his wife. With Rick Springfield, Cliff Robertson, Susan Blakely. Dir: Robert Lewis. ITV, 28 January 1994.

**Dead Run** (1991). A pursuit thriller: tails off a bit after brilliant opening, but always watchable. A Texas wife flees from the danger of knowing hubbie is a killer and meets up with another lot of fugitives. With Markie Post, Robert Urich. Dir: Vincent McEveety. ITV, 8 January 1994.

**Deadly Innocents** (1988). Thriller with some exciting scenes but, alas, very little else. An escaped psycho patient goes on a man-killing spree. With Mary Crosby. Dir: John Patterson. BBC1, 14 June 1994.

**The Death of Me Yet** (1971). Doug McClure as former US agent in Russia suddenly finds his happy retirement threatened by his past. Dir: J. Llewellyn Moxey. ITV, 15 August 1993.

**Destination America** (1987). A man returns to his aristocratic family and becomes a prime suspect for his father's murder. With Bruce Greenwood, Rip Torn. Dir: Carey Allen. ITV, 26 June 1994.

**Donor** (1990). Consistently fast-moving, gripping and generally superior thriller set in a hospital where surreptitious experiments have been carried out on the patients and where doctor Melissa Gilbert-Brinkman begins to suspect the truth. A don't-miss movie. Dir: Larry Shaw. ITV, 15 January 1994.

**Dying Room Only** (1973). Excellent mystery thriller about a husband (Dabney Coleman) who vanishes when he and his wife (Cloris Leachman) stop to eat at an isolated wayside diner in the desert. A 'don't miss' movie. Dir: Philip Leacock. BBC1, 31 July 1993.

**83 Hours Till Dawn** (1990). Tense and exciting though somewhat unpleasant thriller about a kidnapper who keeps his young girl victim in a coffin while he waits for the ransom money. Echoes of some true-life events here. With Peter Strauss, Robert Urich. Dir: Donald Wrye. BBC1, 26 February 1994.

**Elvis and Me** (1988). Thin to skinny adaptation of Mrs E's autobiography: what it was like to be married to the mega-star. With Dale Midkiff. Dir: Larry Peerce. ITV, 29 August 1993.

**The Empty Beach** (1985). Tough Australian thriller with Bryan Brown as the private eye feverishly searching for a corrupt businessman. Gripping. And the Sydney settings are fascinating. Dir: Chris Thomson. BBC1, 13 February 1994.

**An Evening with Gary Lineker** (1994). An adaptation of the popular play. Should please more than football fans. With Paul Merton, Lizzie McInnerney, etc. Dir: Andy Wilson. ITV, 14 June 1994.

**Face to Face** (1990). Neatly packaged romantic comedy with real-life husband and wife Robert Foxworth and Elizabeth Montgomery playing wedded rival diggers – he for pipe clay, she for prehistoric remains – in Africa. Stunning settings. BBC2, 2 November 1993.

**The Father Clements Story** (1987). Tolerably interesting true story about a black priest who fights his church to adopt a teenager. With Louis Gossett Jr, Malcolm Jamal-Warner. Dir: Ed Sherrin. Channel 4, 13 July 1993.

**A Father's Revenge** (1987). Incredible story about a defiant dad who persuades a gang of hoodlums to help him rescue his daughter from a gang of German terrorists! Brian Dennehy is the best thing about it. Dir: John Herzfeld. ITV, 28 August 1993.

**Favourite Son – The Movie** (1978). Veteran FBI agent (Robert Loggia) is called in to clear up a nasty political mess, including murder. Fast, value-for-money political thriller. Also with Harry Hamlin. Dir: Dan Baker. (A condensed 3-part mini-series.) ITV, 1 January 1994.

**The Final Heist** (1991). Thriller about an art thief who plans the final 'big one' before going out of business. With Jan-Michael Vincent. Dir: George Mihalka. ITV, 21 August 1993.

**Fire: Trapped on the 37th Floor** (1991). Mediocre TV feature based on the true story of the 1988 Los Angeles fire which trapped two men on the upper part of LA's tallest building. With Lee Majors, Lisa Hartman. Dir: Robert Day. ITV, 12 September 1993.

**Fountain of Youth** (1991). Unusual and fascinating Spanish TV film about a group of artists searching for the mythical fountain that regenerates those who bathe in it. Dir: Julio Sanchez Valdes. Channel 4, 1 June 1994.

**Fragments of War: The Story of Damien Parer** (1988). Well-made Australian small-screen bio-pic about the first Aussie war photographer, who after some magnificent work was killed in World War 2. Absorbing. With Nicholas Eadie. Dir: John Duigan. BBC1, 25 August 1993.

**Framed** (1990). Light comedy with Jeff Goldblum as the expert art forger duped by his attractive girlfriend, Kristin Scott Thomas. Frothy fun. Dir: Dean Parisot. BBC1, 13 May 1994.

**Frankenstein – The College Years** (1983). Teenage-aimed comedy with William Ragsdale and Christopher Daniel Barnes as the medical students who raise the long-dead body and call it Frank N. Stein. Dir: Tom Shadyac. BBC2, 10 February 1994.

**Freeze Frame** (1989). Routine thriller about a high school kid who investigates a local politician and finds far more exciting stuff than she had anticipated. With Shannen Doherty. Dir: William Bindley. ITV, 28 August 1993.

**Fulfillment** (1989). Miserable soapy drama; Cheryl Ladd in a dilemma, torn between her impotent husband and his virile brother. Also with Ted Levine, Lewis Smith. Dir: Piers Haggard. ITV, 5 April 1994.

**Full Exposure: The Sex Tapes Scandal** (1989). Routine, uninvolving thriller about an assistant DA trying, with cop sidekick, to track down a call-girl killer. With Lisa Hartman. Dir: Noel Nosseck. ITV, 11 February 1994.

**A Ghost in Monte Carlo** (1990). Adaptation of a typical Barbara Cartland novel about a convent girl husband-hunting in Monte Carlo. In the right frame of mind you might even enjoy it. With Lysette Anthony, Christopher Plummer, Oliver Reed, Sarah Miles. Dir: John Hough. BBC1, 5 December 1993.

**Gideon Oliver: The Last Plane from Coramaya** (1989). Thrills, action and mystery in South America, where a professor gets into plenty of trouble when he tries to find his missing friend. Well-made hokum. With Louis Gossett Jr. ITV, 22 January 1994.

**Gideon Oliver: Tongs** (1988). Louis Gossett Jr as a crime-busting professor. The projected series was dropped after four episodes. Here, the professor gets mixed up with two opposing gangs in New York's Chinatown. ITV, 29 January 1994.

**God on the Rocks** (1992). Gripping domestic drama about a small-town bank manager who finds release in religious fervour, watched with interest by his 9-year-old daughter. With Bill Paterson, Sinead Cussack. Dir: Ross Cramer. Channel 4, 1 June 1994.

**Grand Slam** (1990). Nicely tongue-in-cheek thriller about a couple of modern bounty hunters trailing a dangerous criminal. With John Schneider, Dave Rodriguez. Dir: Bill Norton. BBC2, 7 March 1994.

**Gunsmoke: Return to Dodge** (1989). Excellent feature follow-up to the very popular Western TV series of the 1950s and 60s. Marshal Matt Dillon dragged out of retirement to face an old adversary. Also with James Arness. Dir: Vincent McEveety. ITV, 12 June 1994.

**The Hard Way** (1979). Tired hitman Patrick McGoohan persuaded unwillingly to carry out one last assignment by his ex-boss Lee Van Cleef. Lots of tough action stuff. (And note the cameo contributed by novelist Edna O'Brien.) Dir: Michael Dryhurst. ITV, 12 February 1994.

**Hell Hath No Fury** (1990). Typical, machine-made thriller about a housewife framed – by a jealous mistress – for her husband's murder. With Barbara Eden. Dir: Thomas J. Wright. ITV, 14 June 1994.

**Hollow Point** (1987). Familiar story about a woman witness to a killing who is terrorised by the killer when he is freed by the courts. With Linda Purl, Yaphet Kotto. Dir: Bruce Seth Green. ITV, 8 November 1993.

**Home for Christmas** (1990). Mickey Rooney very professionally ladling out the syrup in a story about a small-time thief who becomes the answer to a small girl's wish for Christmas. Dir: Peter McCubbin. ITV, 26 December 1993.

**Homefront** (1991). Excellent, thoughtful feature introduction to a new 24-part series about the problems of a bunch of GI's returning home from World War 2. Channel 4, 10 January 1994.

**Hot Paint** (1988). Mediocre comedy thriller about a couple of bumbling crooks trying to sell a stolen priceless painting and pursued by both the Mafia and the cops. With Gregory Harrison, John Larroquette. Dir: Larry Sheldon. ITV, 10 November 1993.

**I Want Him Back** (1990). Perfectly lightly played – by Elliott Gould and Valerie Harper – romantic comedy about a husband who gets the middle-aged itch. Dir: Catlin Adams. Channel 4, 14 September 1993.

**The Incident** (1990). 1941: Walter Matthau at his best as he defends a German officer on a murder charge. Polished and gripping court-room drama: above-average film fare in all departments. Also with Peter Firth. Dir: Joseph Sargent. BBC2, 11 April 1994.

**Into the Homeland** (1987). Exciting, fast-paced thriller with careless credibility holes about a father's search for his daughter which leads him into a morass of trouble. With Powers Boothe. Dir: Lesli Linka Glatter. BBC1, 17 May 1994.

**Into Thin Air** (1989). Altogether superior, consistently tense thriller about a mother's desperate search for her teenage son who vanishes on his way to summer camp holiday. Again it's all based on fact. Ellen Burstyn heads a fine cast. Dir: Roger Young. ITV, 4 March 1994.

**Kojak: The Price of Justice** (1987). Telly Savalas, now promoted with his own office, investigates the case of a mother suspected of killing her own sons. Reliably entertaining. Also with Kate Nelligan. Dir: Alan Metzger. ITV, 11 July 1993.

**Lassie – A New Beginning** (1978). Pilot feature for a new series of canine capers that never got started. As usual, the dog gives the best performance. BBC1, 17 July 1993.

**Lassie: Peace Is Our Profession** (1971). The cute canine wanders around an army camp. Fun for the youngsters. Dir: Ezra Stone. BBC2, 12 August 1993.

**Last Stop Harem Bar** (1991). German TV feature about a young man on the run from the cops who revisits the scenes of his youth. Dir:

Rainer Wolffhardt. Channel 4, 16 June 1994.

**The Last To Go** (1991). Good family drama thanks largely to the warm and expert playing of Tyne Daly (of *Cagney and Lacey* fame) as the cast-off housewife trying to cope. Dir: John Erman. BBC2, 9 May 1994.

**Leap of Faith** (1988). True story about a woman cancer patient (Anne Archer) who elects to fight the disease with alternative medicine. Sincere but a little hard to take. Dir: Stephen Gyllenhaal. Channel 4, 7 September 1993.

**The Long Journey Home** (1977). Story of a Vietnam vet and his wife which goes along so fast that you hardly notice the holes in the script. With Meredith Baxter Birney, David Birney. Dir: Rod Holcomb. BBC2, 13 June 1994.

**Long Road Home** (1991). A family tries to find a better life in California in the Great Depression era. Not bad – but *The Grapes of Wrath* did it much better. With Mark Harmon, Lee Purcell. Dir: John Korty. BBC2, 8 November 1993.

**The Lost Capone** (1990). Gangster movie with Al Capone's US marshal younger brother sucked into the strife. Tough stuff. With Adrian Pasda, Eric Roberts. Dir: John Cray. BBC1, 19 February 1994.

**Lucky Village** (1993). In this modest Anglo-Georgian production, Tim Pigott-Smith plays a British diplomat admitted to a mental hospital in Tbilisi while something like a civil war rages outside the walls. Interesting. Dir: Georg Levashov-Tumanishvili. Channel 4, 3 July 1993.

**Lucy and Desi** (1991). Bio-pic about the famous radio and TV comedy team which, though good enough, naturally lacks the sparkle of the originals. With Frances Fisher, Maurice Bernard. Dir: Charles Jarrott. BBC1, 4 January 1994.

**Making the Case for Murder: The Howard Beach Story** (1989). True 1986 story about racial tensions in New York after the death of a white youth, one of the gang that set upon three blacks when their car broke down. With Daniel J. Travanti, William Daniels. Dir: Dick Lowry. BBC1, 7 September 1993.

**The Man Who Broke 1000 Chains** (1987). TV re-make of *I Was a Fugitive from a Chain Gang*; true story about the reform of the brutal US prison regime. With Val Kilmer. Dir: Daniel Mann. BBC1, 28 & 29 June 1994.

**Margaret Bourke-White** (1989). Bio-pic about the sensational photo-reporter for *Life* magazine in the 1930s and 40s. With Farrah Fawcett and Frederic Forrest (as her lover). Dir: Lawrence Schiller. ITV, 21 July 1993.

**Marilyn and Me** (1991). Bio-pic about Marilyn Monroe's earlier years as she struggled towards a screen career. With Susan Griffiths. Dir: John Patterson. ITV, 21 August 1993.

**A Matter of Wife . . . and Death** (1978). Remake of the 1973 Burt Reynolds film *Shamus*; unfortunately Rod Taylor hasn't the same amusing personality. So why did they do it? Dir: Marvin J. Chomsky. ITV, 1 December 1993.

**McCloud: The Barefoot Stewardess Caper** (1972). Mac chases across the world trying to smash a crime ring of air stewardess criminals. With Dennis Weaver. ITV, 22 August 1993.

**McCloud: The Solid Gold Swingers** (1973). Well-acted cop thriller with Dennis Weaver trying to trap a serial killer, and jealous fellow cop Neville Brand trying to thwart him. Dir: Lou Antonio. ITV, 24 July 1993.

**A Message from Holly** (1992). Sobby routine drama about a dying woman and her friend (Lindsay Wagner and Shelley Long). Missable. Dir: Rod Holcomb. ITV, 6 July 1993.

**Mistress** (1989). Reviewed in the 'Releases of the Year' section of *Film Review 1993–4* after a 14 May 1993 release. ITV, 4 February 1994.

**Mom's Army** (1989). Entirely predictable derivative comedy about an unlikely mother who joins the army to get her son out of it. With Barbara Eden. Dir: Anson Williams. BBC2, 4 October 1993.

**Moon of the Wolf** (1972). Werewolves in Louisiana! David Janssen as the miserable-looking sheriff investigating a macabre murder way down South. Also with Barbara Rush, Bradford Dillman. Dir: Daniel Petrie. ITV, 12 September 1993.

**Murder by Night** (1989). Routine thriller about a murder witness suffering from amnesia. With Robert Urich. Dir: Paul Lynch. ITV, 7 January 1994.

**Murder in New Hampshire** (1991). Unpleasant story about a high-school teacher who seduces a schoolboy and gets him to further her plan to murder her husband. Nasty but gripping. With Helen Hunt, Chad Allen, Michael Learned. Dir: Joyce Chopra. BBC1, 28 January 1994.

**Murder or Mercy** (1974). Courtroom drama about a medical man who helps his patient to die but as a result is accused of murder: the old but ever topical theme of the rights and wrongs of 'mercy killing'. With Melvyn Douglas, Bradford Dillman, Denver Pyle. ITV, 12 January 1994.

**The Murder that Wouldn't Die** (1980). William ('Conrad') Cannon in a quite original detection thriller; using all sorts of means to try to solve two murders twenty years apart. Very watchable. ITV, 1 July 1993.

**Naked Lie** (1989). Corruption in high places. Empty but watchable courtroom drama. With Victoria Principal, James Farentino. Dir: Richard Colla. ITV, 15 March 1994.

**Nasty Hero** (1987). Low-interest thriller about a loner's search for the kidnappers of his best friend's niece. With Scott Feraco, Robert Sedgwick. Dir: Nick Barwood. ITV, 25 September 1993.

**The New Adventures of Superman** (1993). The introduction to a new series of Superman adventures. With Dean Cain. BBC1, 8 January 1994.

**Night Games** (1974). The original pilot feature for the subsequent series *Petrocelli.* Lawyer Barry Newman defending socialite client Stefanie Powers on a murder charge. Routine stuff. Dir: Don Taylor. ITV, 8 August 1993.

**Nightmare at Bitter Creek** (1988). Four holidaying city gals find travail and terror during their trek in the wild mountain-and-lake countryside. Tense at times but could have been tenser. With Lindsay Wagner, Joanna Cassidy, Tom Skerritt. Dir: Tim Burstall.

**Oceans of Fire** (1986). Routine drama about an oil rig and the drillers' struggle against the elements. With Gregory Harrison. Dir: Steve Carver. ITV, 20 October 1993.

**One in a Million: The Ron Le Fore Story** (1978). True story of an American convict who struggles his way up to baseball star. Quite entertaining, too. With LeVar Burton. Dir: William A. Graham. ITV, 30 November 1993.

**One Police Plaza** (1986). Good if routine thriller about a cop who investigates a killing and uncovers some nasty dirt under the carpet. With Robert Conrad. Dir: Jerry Jameson. ITV, 5 August 1993.

**The Outside Woman** (1989). Sharon Gless (half the *Cagney and Lacey* team) as the glamorous mill girl charmed by convict Scott Glenn into helping him escape from jail. Entertainingly worked out and so very watchable – and apparently true. Dir: Lou Antonio. ITV, 2 September 1993.

**Panache** (1976). In 17th-century France Cardinal Richelieu weaves his evil plan finally to remove the Queen's most loyal Musketeer. Rompish history. With René Auberjonois, David Healey. Dir: Gary Nelson. ITV, 25 December 1993.

**Panic in Echo Park** (1997). Missable story of a doctor tracking down a mysterious illness affecting the occupants of a run-down block of Los Angeles flats. With Dorian Harwood. Dir: John Llewellyn Moxey. ITV, 26 March 1994.

**Parent Trap 3** (1989). *PT3* sees the routine wearing a bit thin. Hayley Mills once again playing twin sisters, this time as rivals for Barry Bostwick. Dir: Mollie Miller. ITV, 18 December 1993.

**Parent Trap 4: Hawaiian Honeymoon** (1990). The *PT* formula was already exhausted by *PT3* so *PT4* hasn't got much left going for it. Hayley Mills once again playing twin sisters. Also with Barry Boswick. Dir: Mollie Miller. ITV, 9 January 1994.

**The Park Is Mine** (1985). Daft story about a Vietnam vet who takes over New York's Central Park with the obvious violent result. With Tommy Lee Jones, Helen Shaver, Yaphet Kotto. Dir: Steven Hilliard Stern. ITV, 28 March 1994.

**Perfect Witness** (1989). Uninvolving but adequate story of a gangland murder and the refusal of the only witness to testify, going to prison rather than talk. A reasonably credible story. With Brian Dennehy, Aidan Quinn, Stockard Channing. Dir: Robert Mandel. BBC1, 18 August 1993.

**Perry Mason: The Case of the Posthumous Painter** (1992). Perry (the late Raymond Burr) unmasks the killer of the painter cheat. BBC1, 19 June 1994.

**Planet Earth** (1974). A re-make of the 1973 TV movie about a scientist who wakes up after a 150-year-long sleep to find some changes have occurred in the interval. Light SF fun. With John Saxon. Dir: Marc Daniels. BBC2, 23 May 1994.

**The Plot to Kill Hitler** (1990). Occasionally exciting thriller based on the actual plot by some of Hitler's disillusioned followers to remove the failing dictator and sue for peace towards the end of World War 2. Spoilt by some faulty casting. With Brad Davis, Madolyn Smith. Dir: Lawrence Schiller. ITV, 13 May 1994.

**The President's Child** (1992). Boring though glossy story of US political chicanery. With Donna Mills. Dir: Sam Pillsbury. ITV, 30 June 1994.

**A Private Affair** (1992). An Italian TV movie about a partisan's passionate search for the truth about his girlfriend. With Rupert Graves. Dir: Alberto Negrim. Channel 4, 26 May 1994.

**The Rape of Richard Beck** (1985). Richard Crenna makes this grim and unpleasant story watchable: he's a New York cop who gets raped by a couple of thugs, an event which alters his character. Strictly adult stuff, well managed. Dir: Karen Arthur. ITV, 17 July 1993.

**Rock Hudson** (1990). Superficial bio-pic about the first homosexual star to admit he was dying from AIDS. Indifferently acted. With Thomas Ian Griffith. Dir: John Nicolella. ITV, 25 July 1993.

**Rockabye** (1986). Large handkerchiefs required! A mother hunting for her stolen child in New York. Totally incredible but well enough acted. With Valerie Bertinelli, Rachel Ticotin. Dir: Richard Michaels. ITV, 7 July 1993.

**The Room Upstairs** (1987). Romantic comedy-drama about teacher Stockard Channing falling in love with her cello-playing lodger Sam Waterston. Weak script almost outweighed by the charming performances. Dir: Stuart Margolin. BBC2, 11 October 1993.

**Runaway Father** (1991). True story about a mother who sues her absent hubbie for the seventeen years she should have been supported. With Donna Mills, Jack Scalia. Dir: Jack Nicolella. Channel 4, 20 July 1993.

**Ryan's Four** (1983). Back to the wards: Tom Skerritt as the new medic trying to make it an easier life for the young doctors. Dir: Jeff Bleckner. ITV, 24 December 1993.

**Sam and Me** (1991). Sincere but less than involving story about the unlikely friendship between an elderly Jew and his young Indian immigrant minder. With Ranjit Chowdhry, Peter Boretski. Dir: Deepa Mehta. Channel 4, 21 February 1994.

**The Scalp Merchants** (1977). Routine thriller with private eye John

Waters trying to recover the stolen gold. Also with Cameron Mitchell. Dir: Howard Rubie. ITV, 1 March 1994.

**The Secret Steak** (1992). Mediocre, dismally slow French film about a vegetarian dad who enjoys a juicy steak (and a pretty mistress) when the family are not around. Channel 4, 18 May 1994.

**Shadow of a Stranger** (1992). Don't help folk in distress seems to be the lesson here; it leads to terror for the well-intentioned couple in this case. An almost plotless thriller. With Emma Samms, Parker Stevenson. Dir: Richard Friedman. ITV, 3 March 1994.

**Shadows of the Past** (1991). French-Canadian movie about a photo-journalist with a car-crash-impaired memory who finds herself caught up in a criminal plot. Uninspired. With Erika Anderson. ITV, 20 May 1994.

**Sharing Richard** (1988). Sex comedy with very little of either. Ed Marinano as the handsome doctor with three glamorous girls vying for his favours. Dir: Peter Bonerz. ITV, 18 July 1993.

**She Said No** (1990). The victim of a rape takes her attacker – a lawyer – to court and finds attack turning to defence as the case proceeds. With Veronica Hamel, Judd Hirsch. Dir: John Patterson. ITV, 17 August 1993.

**She Was Marked for Murder** (1988). Tepid re-make of the Joan Crawford suspense drama *Sudden Fear* (1952). With Stefanie Powers. Dir: Charles Thomson. BBC1, 5 March 1994.

**Siege at Marion** (1991). Based-on-truth story about an armed religious sect who defy and are besieged by the authorities. Too leisurely to grip. With Ed Begley, Tess Harper. Dir: Charles Haid. BBC1, 23 March 1994.

**Skyhigh** (1985). Typical, pleasant Disney movie about two friends who buy an old barn with a veteran airplane in it, and agree to renovate it. With James Whitmore. ITV, 14, 21 and 28 August 1993.

**Ski Lift to Death** (1978). All too familiar story of a group of characters marooned in a broken-down ski lift. With Don Johnson, Veronica Hamel, Deborah Raffin. Dir: William Wiard. ITV, 6 July 1993.

**Smokey and the Good Times Outlaws** (1978). Routine road movie about a Country and Western singer's journey to Nashville. Good to see Slim Pickens as the sheriff. Dir: Alex Grasshoff. BBC2, 31 August 1993.

**Somebody Has to Shoot the Picture** (1990). Unpleasant story about a cop killer who pays a photographer to take pictures of his execution. With Roy Scheider. Dir: Frank Pierson. ITV, 25 March 1994.

**Spirit of the Eagle** (1993). A good, entertaining if leisurely Western with Don Haggerty tracking down the Indians who have bought his kidnapped son. Superb open-air backgrounds. Also with William Smith. Dir: Boon Collins. BBC1, 1 January 1994.

**Spooner** (1989). Disney film about a prisoner on the run who wangles himself a job as a teacher and teaches his class to stay on the straight and narrow. Mildly entertaining. With Robert Urich. Dir: George Miller. ITV, 22 May 1994.

**The Story of the Beach Boys: Summer Dreams** (1990). Just that. Bio-pic strictly for BB fans. With Bruce Greenwood, Greg Kean. Dir: Michael Switzer. ITV, 15 April 1994.

**Stranger in the Family** (1991). Routine loss-of-memory drama with student Neil Patrick trying to remember. Dir: Donald Wrye. Channel 4, 10 August 1993.

**Street War** (1992). Hoary old story about the partner of a murdered cop swearing to get revenge on the gang responsible. Fast-moving thriller set against seedy New York backgrounds. Watchable. With Ray Sharkey, Peter Boyle, Mario Van Peebles. Dir: Dick Lowry. BBC1, 4 February 1994.

**A Summer Without Boys** (1973). Take no notice of that misleading title – it's all about a mother and daughter competing for the favours of the same man. With Barbara Bain, Kay Lenz, Michael Moriarty. Dir: Jeanot Szwarc. BBC2, 4 April 1994.

**El Sur – The South** (1990). Spanish-speaking film based on a short story by Luis Borges about a man and his past. Leisurely. Dir: Carlos Saura. BBC2, 17 October 1993.

**Swimsuit** (1980). Almost story-less film about the search for the perfect swimsuit model, not even saved by the still delectable Cyd Charisse. Also with William Katt. Dir: Chris Thomson. ITV, 26 March 1994.

**Terror in the Sky** (1971). A has-been helicopter pilot is forced to take over the controls of a passenger plane when the crew go down with poisoning. Conventional but exciting. With Doug McClure, Lois Nettleton. Dir: Bernard Kowalski. ITV, 9 September 1993.

**Three O'Clock High** (1987). Teenager-aimed story of the new boy at school who is driven to a physical showdown with the local bully in the playground. With Casey Siemaszko. Dir: Phil Joanou. BBC1, 14 May 1994.

**Three on a Match** (1987). Utterly incredible story about three escaped convicts doing good turns to all and sundry while on the run. With Patrick Cassidy, David Hemmings, Bruce Young. Dir: Donald P. Bellisario. ITV, 8 July 1993.

**Tidy Endings** (1988). Romance in the shadow of AIDS. With Harvey Fierstein, Stockard Channing. Dir: Gavin Miller. ITV, 27 November 1993.

**Trouble in Paradise** (1988). Quite good fun: a rich, spoiled widow (Raquel Welch) is marooned on a desert island with rough, tough Aussie sailor Jack Thompson. And guess what! Dir: Robert Sherman. BBC2, 6 December 1993.

**True Betrayal** (1990). Wholly uninvolving and pretty incomprehensible: a shadowy story of a couple of detectives trying to solve an old murder. Based on a true story. With

Mare Winningham. Dir: Robert Young. BBC1, 14 September 1993.

**Turn Back the Clock** (1989). An actress kills her husband and then looks back on what did happen and what might have happened. A very reasonable re-make of the 1947 cinema film *Repeat Performance*. With Connie Sellecca, David Dukes. Dir: Larry Elikann. ITV, 11 May 1994.

**Vengeance: The Story of Tony Cimo** (1986). Tough, true, TV film about a son determined to speed up the law and bring rough justice to the killer of his parents. With Brad Davis. Dir: Marc Daniels. ITV, 4 June 1994.

**Vigilante Cop** (1991). Basically true story of a tough and very brutal Texas cop. With Alex McArthur. Dir: Mel Damski. BBC1, 27 July 1993.

**War of the Worlds** (1988). Pilot feature for a new TV series eventually called 'Resurrection'. With Jared Martin, Lynda Mason Green. ITV, 5 September 1993.

**Warm Hearts and Cold Feet** (1987). Familiar story freshly told: a female journalist is suddenly faced with motherhood. BBC2, 16 August 1993.

**The Watch Commander** (1988). Jack Warden wasted in the role of a New York cop facing routine official and private dilemmas. Dir: Nell T. Maffeo. BBC1, 23 July 1993.

**Weekend War** (1988). A company of US National Guards on an exercise is suddenly faced with the real thing. A mild anti-war film. With Daniel Stern, Stephen Collins. Dir: Steven Hilliard Stern. ITV, 10 June 1994.

**What Price Victory?** (1988). An American college football yarn about a star player and the coach wanting to play fairly, but everyone else being less scrupulous – all very predictable. With George Kennedy, Mac Davis, Robert Culp. Dir: Kevin Connor (oddly, a British director for such an all-American film). BBC2, 13 December 1993.

**When Angels Fly** (1983). Dud thriller about a nurse who takes a job at a clinic in order to find out some more about her sister's death there. With Jennifer Dale. Dir: Jack Nixon-Browne. ITV, 29 March 1994.

**Which Way Home** (1991). Agonisingly over-long and overblown Australian film about a nurse (Cybill Shepherd – who just about holds things together) who brings out a group of orphans from war-torn Cambodia in the 1970s. BBC1: Part 1, 26 May 1994; Part 2, 27 May 1994.

**The World's Oldest Living Bridesmaid** (1990). Reversal of convention. The boss is a mature and successful female solicitor who falls in love with her new and handsome male secretary. Entertainingly bubbly. With Donna Mills and Brian Wimmer. Dir: Joseph L. Scanlon. Channel 4, 3 August 1993.

**Yes, Virginia, There Is a Santa Claus** (1991). Far away from his usual vigilante role, Charles Bronson is a newspaper man (circa 1890) whose relationship with an 8-year-old reader brings him to a new awareness of himself. Charming. Also with Katharine Isobel. Dir: Charles Jarrot. BBC1, 23 December 1993.

# Video Releases

## James Cameron-Wilson

*(from July 1993 through to June 1994)*

**Acting on Impulse** See *Secret Lies.*

**The Adventures of the Flying Pickle** Real stinker about an arty, unsuccessful film director who sells out to make a real stinker. US title: *The Pickle.* With Danny Aiello, Dyan Cannon, Shelley Winters, Barry Miller, Jerry Stiller, Chris Penn, Stephen Tobolowsky, Ally Sheedy, Spalding Gray, Griffin Dunne, Isabella Rossellini, Dudley Moore. Dir & Screenplay: Paul Mazursky. 15. June 1994 (Columbia TriStar).

**Ambush in Waco: In the Line of Duty** Exploitative, hastily assembled TV movie about would-be Messiah David Koresh and his ill-fated commune. With Timothy Daly, Dan Lauria. Dir: Dick Lowry. 15. August 1993 (Odyssey).

**Amos and Andrew** Inept farce (parading as social satire) in which a black, Pulitzer Prize-winning author is mistaken for a burglar in his own house. With Nicolas Cage, Samuel L. Jackson, Dabney Coleman, Michael Lerner, Margaret Colin, Brad Dourif, Giancarlo Esposito, Bob Balaban. Dir and Screenplay: E. Max Frye. 15. June 1994 (PolyGram).

**Aspen Extreme** Banal, romantic snow opera set at the famous Colorado resort where two bland dudes look for love and adventure. Incredibly, this received a theatrical release in the States. With Paul Gross, Peter Berg, Finola Hughes, Teri Polo, William Russ, Trevor Eve, Martin Kemp, William McNamara, Nicolette Scorsese. Dir and Screenplay: Patrick Hasburgh. 15. November 1993 (Buena Vista).

**Barbarians at the Gate** Compulsively entertaining look at big business, in which James Garner's brash, coarse F. Ross Johnson attempts to buy out Nabisco. An intriguing, witty and suspenseful TV movie with Garner at the top of his form. With Jonathan Pryce, Peter Riegert, Joanna Cassidy, Fred Dalton Thompson, Rita Wilson. Dir: Glenn Jordan. Teleplay: Larry Gelbart. 15. November 1993 (Warner).

**Betrayed by Love** 'Inspired by actual events,' this is the emotional drama of the first FBI agent to be convicted of murder. With Mare Winningham, Steven Weber, Patricia Arquette, Perry Lang. Dir: John Power. 15. January 1994 (Odyssey).

**Blind Side** Gripping thriller about a couple blackmailed by a stranger following a fatal hit-and-run accident in Mexico. With Rutger Hauer, Rebecca De Mornay, Ron Silver, Jonathan Banks. Dir: Geoff Murphy. 18. August 1993 (EV).

**Blindsided** Awful 'erotic' thriller about a corrupt cop who becomes involved with a femme fatale while convalescing at an upscale resort. With Jeff Fahey, Mia Sara, Ben Gazzara,

Jack Kehler. Dir: Tom Donnelly. 15. November 1993 (Universal/CIC).

**Bloodstream** Provocative futuristic drama in which diseased Americans are herded up and incarcerated in dingy 'units'. Enter resistance fighter Cuba Gooding Jr and his beautiful ally Moira Kelly . . . Will AIDS victims of the future be subjected to a new Holocaust? Also with Omar Epps, Jon Cedar. Dir: Stephen Tolkin. 18. January 1994 (Columbia TriStar/New Age Entertainment).

**Body Snatchers** Third (and least successful) screen incarnation of Jack Finney's novel, the story of an alien race taking over earthlings via some intricate transmogrification. However, the atmospheric photography and action sequences hit home. With Gabrielle Anwar, Terry Kinney, Billy Wirth, Meg Tilly, Forest Whitaker, R. Lee Ermey. Dir: Abel Ferrara. 18. January 1994 (Warner).

**Bopha!** The son of a senior South African policeman becomes involved in anti-apartheid reprisals when an officer from Special Branch incites violence in a small, tranquil township. A highly-charged, convincing, astute and impeccably crafted drama marking actor Morgan Freeman's directorial debut. With Danny Glover, Malcolm McDowell, Alfre Woodard, Marius Weyers, Maynard Eziashi. 15. May 1994 (Paramount/CIC).

**Born Too Soon** Another true-life tearjerker from Odyssey about a couple struggling to keep their sanity as their premature baby fights for its life. With Pamela Reed, Michael Moriarty, Terry O'Quinn, Joanna Gleason. Dir: Noel Nossek. 15. July 1993 (Odyssey).

**Captain Ron** Broad, erratic comedy in which a Chicago businessman clashes with a dipsomaniac sailor on a cruise from hell. With Kurt Russell, Martin Short, Mary Kay Place. Dir: Thom Eberhardt. PG. July 1993 (Touchstone).

**The Cemetery Club** Unfocused, fractured and over-the-top comedy-drama about three close friends and how they cope with widowhood. With Olympia Dukakis, Ellen Burstyn, Diane Ladd, Danny Aiello, Lainie Kazan, Christina Ricci, Bernie Casey, Wallace Shawn. Dir: Bill Duke. 15. December 1993 (Touchstone).

**Cold Sweat** Inventive and snappy erotic thriller in which a hitman is haunted by his last fatality. With Ben Cross, Adam Baldwin, Dave Thomas, Shannon Tweed. Dir: Gail Harvey. 18. April 1994 (First Independent).

**Coneheads** Agreeable, amusing big-screen reincarnation of the recurring *Saturday Night Live* sketch, in which Dan Aykroyd and Jane Curtin repeat their original roles as the highbrow aliens attempting to blend into American suburbia when their spaceship is grounded. However, the film bombed in the States and ends up on video here. With Michael McKean, Jason Alexander, Lisa Jane Persky, Chris Farley, Phil Hartman, Dave Thomas, Sinbad. Dir: Steve Barron. PG. February 1994 (Paramount/CIC).

**Crossfire** After a pair of killers kidnap an accountant they find themselves pursued not only by the police but by a gang of crooks. When it's not unintelligible, this mundane thriller manages to be surprisingly obvious. With Jeff Fahey, Robert Davi, Tia Carrere, Teri Polo, Martin Donovan. Aka *Quick*. Dir: Rick King. 18. March 1994 (High Fliers).

**Curacao** Two men, one a former sea captain, the other a disillusioned ex-CIA agent, find their pasts catching up with them during carnival time on the Caribbean island of the title. Suitably exotic, suspenseful action-thriller with a crackerjack cast. With George C. Scott, William Petersen, Julie Carmen, Alexei Sayle, Trish Van Devere, Philip Anglim. Dir: Carl Schultz. 18. February 1994 (Warner).

**Cyborg Agent** When a female cop is murdered she's mechanically and electronically rebuilt to track down her killers. Mrs RoboCop lives! With Kim Cattrall, Billy Zane. October 1993 (Columbia TriStar/Medusa).

**Danielle Steel's Heartbeat** Familiar frothy soap opera in which a pregnant TV producer is jilted by her husband and finds true happiness with a divorced father who writes soap operas. With John Ritter, Polly Draper, Kevin Kilner. Dir: Michael Miller. PG. July 1993 (Imperial Entertainment).

**The Dark Backward** See *The Man With Three Arms*.

**Day of Atonement** Bumbling French-Italian co-production about a mob boss whose attempts to go straight are sabotaged by his son's involvement with a drug lord. Degrading for all concerned. With Roger Hanin, Richard Berry, Gerard Darmon, Christopher Walken, Jill Clayburgh, Jennifer Beals. Dir. Alexandre Arcady. 18. January 1994 (Guild).

**Death Wish 5: The Face of Death** Sadistic, tired and flabby retread of the old vigilante theme with Charles Bronson (now 72) still at it after his fiancée is murdered. With Lesley-Anne Down, Michael Parks, Saul Rubinek, Kenneth Welsh. Dir: Allan A. Goldstein. 18. February 1994 (Guild).

**December** See *An Innocent War*.

**Diary of a Hitman** Belated release of this atmospheric, well-acted thriller about a hitman who develops a conscience before his final kill. With Forest Whitaker, James Belushi, Lois Chiles, Sharon Stone, Sherilyn Fenn, Seymour Cassel. Dir: Roy London. 18. October 1993 (FoxVideo).

**Dr Giggles** Decidedly gory, satirical slice of blood 'n' guts about a loony seeking revenge for the death of his father, a psychotic doctor. Okay acting and splendid special effects cannot make up for the corn. With Larry Drake, Holly Marie Combs, Cliff DeYoung, Richard Bradford, Michelle Johnson. Dir: Manny Coto. 18. October 1993 (CIC Video).

**Ed and His Dead Mother** See *Motherhood*.

**Extreme Justice** See *SIS*.

**A Family Divided** Heartfelt, well-acted drama about how the breakdown of a marriage affects a couple's young son. Sadly, pedestrian direction and gormless writing lends little distinction to the proceedings. With Joe Mantegna, Anne Archer, Tzvi Ratner-Stauber, Patti LuPone, Allen Garfield, Paul Reiser, Conchata Ferrell. Dir: Scott Rosenfelt. PG. February 1994 (Columbia TriStar).

**Family Pictures** The perfect marriage is pushed to breaking point when David and Lainy Eberlin spawn an autistic child. Engrossing drama well played, adapted from the novel by Sue Miller. With Anjelica Huston, Sam Neill, Kyra Sedgwick, Dermot Mulroney. Dir: Philip Saville. 15. July 1993 (Odyssey).

**Family Prayers** See *A Family Divided.*

**Fatal Proposal** Routine affair about a female TV reporter stalked by the killer she's covered. With Richard Thomas, Brooke Shields, Viveka Davis. Dir: Michael Switzer. 18. August 1993 (20.20 Vision).

**Father Hood** A ne'er-do-well dad yanks his two brats out of foster care and heads for the road. He should have left his kids behind. With Patrick Swayze, Halle Berry, Brian Bonsall, Michael Ironside, Diane Ladd. Dir: Darrell James Roodt. Screenplay: Scott Spencer. PG. June 1994 (Buena Vista).

**Final Appeal** Murder mystery inspired by a true story in which the wife of a wealthy, much-loved doctor is accused of her husband's murder. With Brian Dennehy, JoBeth Williams, Tom Mason, Betsy Brantley, Lindsay Crouse. Dir: Eric Till. 15. February 1994 (Odyssey).

**For Their Own Good** Well-acted and (amazingly) true story about a woman who takes up legal arms against the McCabe chemical corporation for insisting on the sterilisation of its staff. With Elizabeth Perkins, Laura San Giacomo, Charles Haid, C. C. H. Pounder. Dir: Ed Kaplan. PG. September 1993 (Odyssey).

**Freefall** Resourceful, sexy, fast-paced thriller in which a wildlife photographer is chased from South Africa to London to the US for unknowingly carrying a top-secret list of undercover Interpol assassins. Great stunts, great locations, great fun. A South African-Venezuelan-British co-production. With Eric Roberts, Jeff Fahey, Pamela Gidley. Dir: John Irvin. 18. April 1994 (Medusa).

**The Gamble** Hackneyed medieval romp in which young cad Matthew Modine bets himself in a wager with wicked noblewoman Faye Dunaway, loses, and then spends the rest of the picture being hunted by the latter and her evil henchmen. Filmed in Italy. With Jennifer Beals, Corinne Clery, Vernon Wells, Ian Bannen. Dir: Carlo Vanzina. 15. October 1993 (Columbia TriStar).

**Ghost in the Machine** The soul of a serial killer gets into the electrical appliances and creates no end of havoc. Some electric visuals disguise a somewhat wiry story line, while a sense of gruesome fun makes up for the conventional plotting. With Karen Allen, Chris Mulkey, Ted Marcoux, Jessica Walter. Dir: Rachel Talahay. 18. June 1994 (FoxVideo).

**Give Me a Break** A former child star runs an agency for juvenile talent, discovers a 10-year-old natural-cum-kleptomaniac and learns a few life lessons from her. Cute, likeable and obvious. US title: *Life With Mikey.* With Michael J. Fox, Nathan Lane, Cyndi Lauper, Christina Vidal, David Huddleston. Dir: James Lapine. Music: Alan Menken. PG. June 1994 (Touchstone).

*Can I see your licence please? C. J. Graham as the policeman from purgatory – in Ate De Jong's* Highway to Hell *(from 20.20 Vision)*

**The Good Fight** See *To Win Alone.*

**Gross Misconduct** True story about a married philosophy professor trying to clear his name after being accused of raping a student. Top quality, credible Australian drama, exceptionally well acted by all. With Jimmy Smits, Naomi Watts, Sarah Chadwick. Dir: George Miller. 18. August 1993 (PolyGram).

**Guilty as Charged** Rod Steiger is on fine form here as a meatpacking tycoon who takes it on himself to cremate murderers on his very own homemade electric chair. Good, dark fun, well-crafted by first-time director Sam Irvin, former production associate of Brian De Palma (and it shows). With Lauren Hutton, Isaac Hayes, Michael Beach, Lyman Ward, Heather Graham. Dir: Sam Irvin. 15. July 1993 (Columbia TriStar).

**Hard Promises** The character of William Petersen is so unremittingly unpleasant that it's hard to find the humour in this 'black comedy' in which Petersen attempts to wreck his ex-wife's new marriage. With Sissy Spacek, Brian Kerwin, Mare Winningham, Olivia Burnette, Peter MacNicol, Ann Wedgeworth, Rip Torn. Dir: Martin Davidson. PG. November 1993 (FoxVideo).

**Highway to Hell** On their way to elope in Vegas, teen lovers Charlie and Rachel (Chad Lowe, Kristy Swanson) take a back road to avoid detection and find themselves chased by a cop from hell. Soon all hell is let loose when the cop kidnaps Rachel and Charlie follows – into the depths of Hades. A jokey thriller which never misses a cheap pun ('let's give 'em hell', Pluto's Donuts Store), this is an entertaining romp that looks good but fails to thrill. With Patrick Bergin, Adam Storke, Pamela Gidley, Richard Farnsworth. Dir: Ate De Jong. 15. August 1993 (20.20 Vision).

**Hostage** Dated, mechanical and rather dull drama in which MI6 operative Sam Neill decides to quit his job after a crisis of conscience and runs off to Buenos Aires. With Talisa Soto, James Fox, Art Malik, Michael Kitchen. Dir: Robert Young. 18. February 1994 (20.20 Vision).

**Hostage for a Day** Off-beat action-comedy about a loser with wife trouble and life trouble. Marking John Candy's directorial debut, this is like many of the late comic's own star vehicles, and teeters into mawkishness and farce. However, George Wendt as the loser is surprisingly moving. With John Vernon, Robin Duke, John Candy. PG. June 1994 (Guild).

**House of Cards** Powerful, articulate story of a mother's endeavour to 'reach' her autistic daughter. With Kathleen Turner, Tommy Lee Jones, Esther Rolle, Park Overall, Michael Horse. Dir: Michael Lessaic. 15. August 1993 (First Independent).

**In the Company of Darkness** When a female cop goes undercover to trap a serial killer, she finds herself caught in a psychological game of cat-and-mouse. Remarkably, inspired by true events. With Helen Hunt, Steven Weber, Jeff Fahey. Dir: David Anspaugh. Ex Pro: Don Johnson. 15. September 1993 (Universal/CIC).

**An Innocent War** Stagy, melodramatic drama in which five senior students debate whether or not they should join the war after the bombing of Pearl Harbor. Aka *December*. With Balthazar Getty, Jason London, Brian Krause, Wil Wheaton, Chris Young. Dir: Gabe Torres. PG. January 1994 (Columbia TriStar).

**Jack Reed: Badge of Courage** Another true story: acceptable follow-up to the Odyssey video *Shattered Promises*, with Brian Dennehy repeating his turn as the tough Chicago detective fighting undercover corruption, international arms dealing and, yes, murder. With Susan Ruttan, Alice Krige, William Sadler. Dir: Kevin Connor. 15. April 1994 (Odyssey).

**Jennifer 8** Sgt John Berlin is a conscientious, neurotic cop sick of Los Angeles and his broken private life. No sooner has he arrived in the quiet backwater of Eureka, Northern California, than he becomes obsessed with an old, unsolved murder case that the local police have long given up on. Berlin believes the killer is still in the area . . . and active. A well-made, thinking man's thriller layered with clues and soaked in atmosphere, but terribly slow to get started. *Too* slow for most tastes. With Andy Garcia, Uma Thurman, Lance Henriksen, Kathy Baker, Kevin Conway, John Malkovich. Dir: Bruce Robinson. 15. August 1993 (Paramount/CIC).

*John Malkovich taunts Andy Garcia in Bruce Robinson's atmospheric* Jennifer 8 *(from Paramount Pictures/CIC UK)*

**Judith Krantz's Torch Song** TV adaptation of Judith Krantz's bestseller about a faded Hollywood actress and a fireman who combine forces to fight their alcoholism. With Raquel Welch, Jack Scalia, Alicia Silverstone, George Newbern, Laurie Innes. Dir: Michael Miller. 15. December 1993 (Guild).

**Keeper of the City** Well-acted, forcible thriller about a psychotic vigilante's battle against the Mafia. With Louis Gossett Jr, Anthony LaPaglia, Peter Coyote, Rene Soutendijk, Barbara Williams. Dir: Bobby Roth. 15. August 1993 (FoxVideo).

**Last Light** Supercharged, insightful drama about a hopeless serial killer on death row and the sympathetic guard who tries to understand him. Kiefer Sutherland, who makes an impressive directorial debut, also gives one of his best performances as the killer. With Forest Whitaker, Amanda Plummer, Kathleen Quinlan, Lynne Moody, Clancy Brown. June 1994 (High Fliers).

**The Lemon Sisters** Self-described as 'a tangy comedy', this sentimental farce might have benefited from a shot of lemon juice. Three life-long friends dream of opening their own Atlantic City nightclub and performing there as the 'Lemon Sisters'. Unfortunately, reality is a constant and often tragic intrusion into their dreams of celebrity. Canny direction and some good performances buoy this ragbag of anecdotage, which is always engaging, sometimes very funny but seldom very good. With Diane Keaton, Carol Kane, Kathryn Grody, Elliott Gould, Ruben Blades, Aidan Quinn, Estelle

Parsons. Dir: Joyce Chopra. Pro: Keaton. 15. April 1994 (Entertainment).

**Life with Mikey** See *Give Me a Break*.

**Linda** Engrossing if unconvincing TV movie in which an absolute bitch frames her loving husband for the murder of her lover's wife. With Virginia Madsen, Richard Thomas, Ted McGinley, Laura Harrington. Dir: Nathaniel Gutman. 15. May 1994 (Paramount/CIC).

**Love Field** Thanks to copyright haggling this little gem of a movie failed to secure a theatrical release in Britain, even though Michelle Pfeiffer was nominated for an Oscar. Pfeiffer plays a Dallas beautician who's enraptured with the Kennedys and goes on a pilgrimage to Washington, falling for a black man and his daughter on the way. With Dennis Haysbert (replacing Denzel Washington), Stephanie McFadden, Brian Kerwin, Louise Latham, Peggy Rea. Dir: Jonathan Kaplan. 15. November 1993 (Columbia TriStar).

**Love Potion No. 9** A biochemist and animal psychologist offer themselves up as guinea pigs for a new love drug in this slow-moving, rather silly comedy starring real-life lovebirds Tate Donovan and Sandra Bullock (so the potion worked!). With Dale Midkiff, Dylan Baker, Anne Bancroft. Dir: Dale Launer. 15. February 1994 (First Independent).

**The Man with Three Arms** Ludicrous, unendurable and self-conscious black comedy about a lousy stand-up comic who wins a professional reprieve when he sprouts a third arm. Aka *The Dark Backward*. With Judd Nelson, Bill Paxton, Wayne Newton, Lara Flynn Boyle, James Caan, Rob Lowe, Claudia Christian. Dir: Adam Rifkin. 15. March 1994 (20.20 Vision).

**The Man with Three Wives** Yet another true story, this one about a polygamist who looks back on his ten years of marital subterfuge after the strain of it all threatens his health. An entertaining human drama. With Beau Bridges, Kathleen Lloyd, Pam Dawber. PG. February 1994 (Fox).

**Married to It** Three Manhattan couples become the best of friends and combine forces to cope with life. Sentimental and prosaic. With Beau Bridges, Stockard Channing, Robert Sean Leonard, Mary Stuart Masterson, Cybill Shepherd, Ron Silver. Dir: Arthur Hiller. 15. November 1993 (20.20 Vision).

**Mom and Dad Save the World** Preposterous comic fantasy in which a suburban couple are kidnapped by an extraterrestrial cretin. With Teri Garr, Jeffrey Jones, Jon Lovitz, Wallace Shawn, Kathy Ireland. Dir: Greg Beeman. PG. July 1993 (First Independent).

**The Mommy Market** Occasionally engaging if somewhat unremarkable family film in which three children are magically given the chance to experience three new mothers, all played by Sissy Spacek. Aka *Trading Mom*. With Anna Chlumsky, Maureen Stapleton. Dir: Tia Brelis. PG. March 1994 (FoxVideo).

**Mortal Sins** When a serial killer confesses to a priest, the cleric takes the law into his own hands. With Christopher Reeve, Roxanne Biggs. Dir: Bradford May. 15. July 1993 (Braveworld).

**Motherhood** Surprisingly tame but lively and occasionally amusing black comedy in which a mourning hardware store manager has to contend with his cryogenically resurrected mother. Aka *Ed and His Dead Mother*. With Steve Buscemi, Ned Beatty, Miriam Margolyes, John Glover, Gary Farmer. Dir: Jonathan Wacks. 15. April 1994 (ITC).

**A Mother's Right: The Elizabeth Morgan Story** See *Shattered Silence*.

**Motorama** Kitsch, sluggish, but occasionally amusing road movie in which a 10-year-old steals a car and takes off to make his fortune. With Jordan Christopher Michael, John Diehl, Mary Woronov, Garrett Morris, Drew Barrymore, Meat Loaf, Flea, Michael J. Pollard, Susan Tyrell. Dir: Barry Shils. M: Andy Summers. 15. June 1994 (20.20 Vision).

**Mr Baseball** Agreeable if pedestrian comedy about a baseball legend fallen on hard times who's sold to Japan. With Tom Selleck, Ken Takakura, Dennis Haysbert. Dir: Fred Schepisi. 15. November 1993 (Universal/CIC).

**Murder in the Heartland** Riveting and horrific look at the killing spree of Charlie Starkweather (the inspiration for the 1973 film *Badlands*), the 19-year-old who murdered 11 people in Nebraska in 1957–8. London-born Tim Roth is frightening and brilliant in the central role. With Brian Dennehy, Randy Quaid, Milo O'Shea, Fairuza Balk, Kate Reid, Bob Gunton. Dir: Robert Markowitz. 18. November 1993 (High Fliers).

**A Murderous Affair: The Carolyn Warmus Story** Another true story from Odyssey, this one about a man suspected of killing his wife. With Virginia Madsen, Chris Sarandon. Dir: Martin Davidson. 15. August 1993 (Odyssey).

**Nurses on the Line** When four distinguished doctors survive a plane crash in the Mexican jungle, they are nurtured against impossible odds (not least a local drugs war) by four student nurses. An extremely well-made, absorbing drama 'inspired' by true events. With Lindsay Wagner, Robert Loggia, David Clennon, Gary Frank. Dir: Larry Shaw. PG. March 1994 (Odyssey).

**Only You** A dollhouse furniture designer with a bias for bimbos changes his outlook when he meets a real woman on holiday. An obvious but agreeably performed romantic comedy. With Andrew McCarthy, Kelly Preston, Helen Hunt, Daniel Roebuck, Reni Santoni. Dir: Betty Thomas. 15. July 1993 (Columbia TriStar).

**Other Women's Children** Arresting drama in which a successful paediatrician faces a professional crisis when her own son falls ill. With Melanie Mayron, Geraint Wynn Davies, Ja'net Du Bois. Dir: Anne Wheeler. 15. February 1994 (Odyssey).

**Out on a Limb** Appalling, brain-dead farce about a yuppie stockbroker attempting to close a $140m deal without his trousers, BMW or wallet. With Matthew Broderick, Jeffrey Jones, Heidi King, John C. Reilly. Dir: Francis Veber. PG. October 1993 (CIC Video).

**The Palermo Connection** Plodding political thriller (co-scripted by Gore Vidal) about a New York politician who crosses wires with the Mafia while on honeymoon in Sicily. Aka *To Forget Palermo*. With James Belushi, Mimi Rogers, Joss Ackland, Philippe Noiret, Vittorio Gassman. Dir: Francesco Rosi. 15. October 1993 (20.20 Vision).

**A Passion for Murder** Enjoyable, well-acted thriller in which a Detroit cabbie drives femme fatale Joanna Pacula to Seattle – to his detriment. With Michael Nouri, Michael Ironside. Dir: Neill Fearnley. 18. September 1993 (Columbia TriStar).

**Pet Sematary Two** Nasty, pointless sequel (to the Stephen King original) in which a teenage outcast discovers the dreaded Indian burial ground. Thankfully, this one was buried before a theatrical release in Britain. With Edward Furlong, Anthony Edwards, Clancy Brown, Jared Rushton, Darlanne Fluegel, Sarah Trigger. Dir: Mary Lambert. 18. August 1993 (Paramount/CIC).

**The Pickle** See *The Adventures of the Flying Pickle*.

**Prophet of Evil** Brian Dennehy lends his considerable bulk to the role of Ervil LeBaron, the real-life cult leader who turned children into assassins and ordered the death of his own daughter. Engrossing, if a tad corny. With William Devane, Tracey Needham, Dee Wallace Stone. Dir: Jud Taylor. 15. December 1993 (Odyssey).

**Pure Country** A big-time country singer opts out of the fast lane to smell the roses. An amiable (if occasionally banal) vehicle for real-life big-time country singer George Strait, who increased his workload to make this well-intentioned amble. With Lesley Ann Warren, Isabel Glasser, Kyle Chandler, John Doe, Rory Calhoun. Dir: Christopher Cain. M: Steve Dorff. PG. May 1994 (Warner).

*Another true story: Brian Dennehy as cult leader Ervil LeBaron in Jud Taylor's* Prophet of Evil

**Radio Flyer** To escape the brutality of their stepfather two young brothers invent a dream world in which their toy wagon becomes a flying machine. This expensive, troubled production provides some pat answers to child abuse, but is an imaginative tale sensitively played. With Lorraine Bracco, John Heard, Elijah Wood, Joseph Mazzello, Adam Baldwin, Ben Johnson, Tom Hanks (as narrator). Dir: Richard Donner. PG. August 1993 (Columbia TriStar).

**Sad Inheritance** True story about a cocaine addict struggling to gain custody of her prematurely-born child. With Susan Dey, Lorraine Toussaint, D. W. Moffett, Kathleen York. Dir: Rod Hardy. 15. July 1993 (Odyssey).

**Salt on Our Skin** More spiced-up bonking between the classes, this one a sensitive adaptation of Benoite Groult's 1988 best-seller. Greta Scacchi is the Scotswoman of privilege who falls for Vincent D'Onofrio's lowly fisherman. A Franco-German-Canadian co-production. Dir: Andrew Birkin. 18. October 1993 (Warner).

**School Ties** 1955; Massachusetts. Jewish David Greene is a promising student whose skill as a football quarterback is the answer to the prayers of elite St Matthew's school. But first David has to come to terms with his classmates, a regiment of the privileged who take their position in society for granted. After a choppy beginning, *School Ties* settles down into an absorbing, powerful drama about American classism and anti-Semitism, two subjects seldom touched on by Hollywood. The overall acting of the young cast is very good indeed, particularly Brendan Fraser as David. With Chris O'Donnell, Matt Damon, Randall Batinkoff, Amy

*Brendan Fraser* (centre) *defends his ethnic roots in Robert Mandel's superb* School Ties *(from Paramount Pictures/CIC UK). Unbelievably, the film was denied a theatrical release in Britain*

Locane, Peter Donat, Ed Lauter. Dir: Robert Mandel. PG. November 1993 (Universal/CIC).

**The Sea Wolf** Drab retelling of Jack London's classic tale about the battle of wills between an aristocratic passenger and his brutal captain. With Charles Bronson, Christopher Reeve, Catherine Mary Stewart, Marc Singer, Len Cariou, Clive Revill. Dir: Michael Anderson. PG. August 1993 (First Independent).

**Secret Lies** Constantly surprising and original satire of the strip-'em-and-slice-'em genre, with Linda Fiorentino as a scream queen suspected of murder. Funny, credible and sexy. Aka *Acting on Impulse*. With C. Thomas Howell, Nancy Allen, Judith Hoag, Adam Ant, Patrick Bachau, Isaac Hayes, Paul Bartel, Miles O'Keeffe, Charles Lane, Mary Woronov, Zelda Rubinstein. Dir: Sam Irvin. 18. January 1994 (High Fliers).

**Shadow of the Wolf** Good-looking Canadian-French epic based on the best-selling novel *Agaguk*, a melodramatic tale of murder and survival in the frozen Arctic. The most expensive Canadian picture ever made. With Lou Diamond Phillips, Toshiro Mifune, Jennifer Tilly, Donald Sutherland. Dir: Jacques Dorfman. 15. December 1993 (EV).

**Shattered Silence** Touching, potent true story with Bonnie Bedelia on splendid form as a mother who attempts to protect her daughter from the sexual advances of her ex-husband. US title: *A Mother's Right: The Elizabeth Morgan Story*. With Terence Knox, Kenneth Welsh, Pam Grier, Patricia Neal, Rip Torn. Dir: Linda Otto. 15. August 1993 (Imperial).

**Shooting Elizabeth** Genuinely amusing black comedy in which Jeff Goldblum decides to terminate his wife to solve his mid-life crisis. Scripted by Robbie Fox, who wrote that other spouse-killing comedy *So I Married an Axe Murderer*. With Mimi Rogers, Burt Kwouk. Dir: Baz Taylor. 15. July 1993 (Medusa).

**Sidekicks** *The Karate Kid* meets *Last Action Hero* in this juvenile fantasy in which a daydreaming asthmatic kid takes up karate to emulate his hero Chuck Norris. With Chuck Norris (as Chuck Norris), Jonathan Brandis, Beau Bridges, Mako, Julia Nickson-Soul, Joe Piscopo, Richard Moll. Dir: Aaron Norris. 15. September 1993 (EV).

**Silent Victim** Yet another woman-in-jeopardy thriller, but thanks to Courtney Cox's estimable performance this one holds us by the throat. Previously known as *Blue Desert*. With D. B. Sweeney, Craig Sheffer. Dir: Bradley Battersby. 18. August 1993 (High Fliers).

**SIS** Fact-based, brutal and tense crime thriller about the LAPD's 'Special Investigation Section' with Lou Diamond Phillips as a rookie at loggerheads with his certifiable boss, played with quiet strength by Scott Glenn. Aka *Extreme Justice*. With Chelsea Field, Yaphet Kotto, Ed Lauter. Dir: Mark L. Lester. 18. March 1994 (Reflective).

**Sketch Artist** Atmospheric, suspenseful and sharply scripted thriller about a police artist (Jeff Fahey on excellent form) who realises that his wife fits the picture he draws of a murder suspect. With Sean Young, Drew Barrymore, Frank McRae, Tcheky Karyo, Charlotte Lewis. Dir: Phedon Papamichael. 18. October 1993 (Warner).

**Stolen Babies** Fascinating true story (set in the 1940s) given the TV movie treatment with Lea Thompson the social worker exposing an illegal adoption ring. With Mary Tyler Moore, Kathleen Quinlan. Dir: Eric Laneuville. PG. September 1993 (Odyssey).

**The Substitute** Schlocky, vaguely entertaining thriller with Amanda Donohoe as a substitute teacher from hell. With Dalton James, Marky Mark. Dir: Martin Donovan. 15. April 1994 (Paramount/CIC).

**Surf Ninjas** Infantile, impotent action-comedy in which a pair of surfer dudes find that they are the rightful heirs to an obscure monarchy now ruled over by a ruthless dictator. With Ernie Reyes Jr, Rob Schneider, Nicolas Cowan, Leslie Nielsen, Tone Loc, Kelly Hu. Dir: Neal Israel. PG. March 1994 (EV).

**Tattle Tale** Ally Sheedy is on top form here as a writer who slanders her ex-husband, an out-of-work actor (C. Thomas Howell), in a best-selling book. Otherwise the laughs are few. Aka *Kiss and Tell*. Dir: Baz Taylor. PG. July 1993 (Medusa).

**T Bone N Weasel** Very funny road movie in which two petty criminals just cannot make crime pay. With Gregory Hines, Christopher Lloyd, Ned Beatty, Rip Torn, Wayne Knight. Dir: Lewis Teague. 15. November 1993 (ITC).

**The Temp** As the secretary from hell, the always reliable Lara Flynn Boyle lifts this absurd, predictable thriller out of the bargain bin. There *are* some nice twists, but silliness ruins the day. With Timothy Hutton, Faye Dunaway, Dwight Schultz, Oliver Platt, Steven Weber. Dir: Tom Holland. 15. December 1993 (Paramount/CIC).

**The Thing Called Love** Astute, credible (if ultimately predictable) romantic drama chronicling the lives of four young musicians looking for their big break in Nashville. With River Phoenix, Samantha Mathis, Dermot Mulroney, Sandra Bullock. Dir: Peter Bogdanovich. 15. March 1994 (Paramount/CIC).

**To Be the Best** Sequel to *A Woman of Substance* and *Hold the Dream*, this soap operatic epic concludes the Barbara Taylor Bradford saga of the Harte dynasty. With Lindsay Wagner, Anthony Hopkins, Stephanie Beacham, Christopher Cazenove, Stuart Wilson, Fiona Fullerton. Dir: Tony Wharmby. 15. February 1994 (Odyssey).

**To Forget Palermo** See *The Palermo Connection*.

**To Win Alone** Accomplished courtroom/hospital drama about a female law professor who sets about uncovering corruption in a powerful tobacco corporation. US title: *The Good Fight*. With Christine Lahti, Terry O'Quinn, Kenneth Welsh, Lawrence Dane. Dir: John David Coles. PG. July 1993 (Columbia TriStar/New Age Entertainment).

**The Tommyknockers** When an unseen force engulfs the small town of Haven in Maine, the local populace start taking on supernatural powers. Adapted from the Stephen King best seller, this should have been a real corker in the sci-fi horror genre, but a lame script and predictable characters let the show down. With Jimmy Smits, Joanna Cassidy, John Ashton, E. G. Marshall, Traci Lords, Robert Carradine, Cliff DeYoung. Dir: John Power. 15. August 1993 (Warner).

**Torch Song** See *Judith Krantz's Torch Song*.

**Trading Mom** See *The Mommy Market*.

**Trauma** Formulaic, visually self-conscious shocker from Italian horror king Dario Argento, in which the daughter of a medium and a TV employee fall in love as they resolve the mystery surrounding a series of hideous decapitations. With Christopher Rydell, Asia Argento (Dario's daughter), Piper Laurie, Frederic Forrest, James Russo, Brad Dourif. Dir: Dario Argento. M: Pino Donaggio. 18. April 1994 (High Fliers).

**12:01** A man's life is turned upside down when his worst day keeps repeating itself. *Groundhog Day* without the laughs. With Jonathan Silverman, Helen Slater, Jeremy Piven, Martin Landau. Dir: Jack Sholder. 15. December 1993 (Guild).

**29th Street** Involving, redolent look at Italian-Americans in New York, in particular father and son Danny Aiello and Anthony LaPaglia. Well acted. With Lainie Kazan, Frank Pesce, Robert Forster. Dir: George Gallo. 15. January 1994 (First Independent).

**Under Threat** Father and daughter, both cops, team up to track down a killer and rapist terrorising LA's convent community. With Charles Bronson, Dana Delany, Xander Berkeley. Dir: Roy Holcomb. 15. August 1993 (Columbia TriStar).

*Soap in a lather: Anthony Hopkins and Lindsay Wagner add lustre to Barbara Taylor Bradford's* To Be the Best *(from Odyssey)*

**Voyage** An architect and his wife find that their dream cruise is threatened by the sudden appearance of an unsavoury couple from their past. With Rutger Hauer, Eric Roberts, Karen Allen, Connie Nielsen. Dir: John MacKenzie. 15. January 1994 (Entertainment).

**The War for Baby Jessica** Instant, predictable and sugar-coated TV movie based on the 1991–3 headlines about the fight for parenthood of the titular infant (still too young to comprehend the movie). Amanda Plummer abducts the acting honours as the biological mother struggling for custody. Aka *Whose Child Is This?* With Susan Dey, Michael Ontkean, David Keith. Dir: John Kent Harrison. PG. January 1994 (Odyssey).

**Warlock: The Armageddon** Satan's right hand man pops up in contemporary Northern California to requisition six 17th-century Druidic rune stones that have the power to quash the devil's power. Familiar hokum blessed by a splendidly evil turn from Julian Sands as the time-travelling fiend. With Chris Young, Paula Marshall, R. G. Armstrong, Zach Galligan, Joanna Pacula. Dir: Anthony Hickox. 18. May 1994 (Reflective).

**Watch It** Diverting if somewhat gossamer look at a group of posturing blokes who like to play humiliating tricks on each other. While some of the dialogue scores, the film's uneven pace and predictable set-ups undermine the misogynistic high jinks. The French *Tango* had much more style. With Peter Gallagher, Suzy Amis, John C. McGinley, Jon Tenney, Cynthia Stevenson, Lili Taylor, Tom Sizemore. Dir and Screenplay: Tom Flynn. 15. May 1994 (EV).

**Whose Child Is This?** See *The War for Baby Jessica*.

**Wilder Napalm** Odd tale about sparring brothers who happen to be pyrokinetic. A romantic comedy with this theme should ignite the screen, but the result is a sluggish, incomprehensible shambles. With Debra Winger, Dennis Quaid, Arliss Howard, M. Emmet Walsh, Jim Varney. Dir: Glenn Gordon Caron. 15. June 1994 (Columbia TriStar).

**With Hostile Intent** Uneven but well-acted true-life drama in which two female police officers bring a sexual harassment case against the Long Beach Police Department. With Melissa Gilbert, Mel Harris, Cotter Smith, Holland Taylor. Dir: Paul Schneider. 15. January 1994 (FoxVideo).

**Witness to the Execution** Intelligent, gripping and inspired futuristic thriller in which a TV channel decides to broadcast a live execution to boost its ratings. But is the charismatic 'star' of the show guilty of his crimes? With Sean Young, Tim Daly, Len Cariou, George Newbern, Dee Wallace Stone. Dir: Tommy Lee Wallace. 15. April 1994 (PolyGram).

**Year of the Comet** Extra-lite romantic fantasy in which a comely wine merchant discovers a priceless bottle of vino, leading to international intrigue. An undistinguished outing for veteran scriptwriter William Goldman. With Penelope Ann Miller, Timothy Daly, Louis Jourdan, Art Malik, Ian Richardson, Ian McNeice. Dir: Peter Yates. 15. September 1993 (First Independent).

## Other Video Releases:

*Adrift*. 15. March 1994 (Reflective).

*Aladdin*. Non-Disney cartoon. U. August 1993 (Columbia TriStar).

*All Shook Up*. With Ayre Gross, Claudia Christian, Adrienne Shelly. 15. October 1993 (20.20 Vision).

*All Tied Up*. With Zach Galligan, Teri Hatcher, Lara Harris, Tracy Griffith. 15. February 1994 (Medusa).

*American Cyborg*. With Joe Lara, John Ryan. 18. August 1993 (Warner).

*American Shaolin*. With Reese Madigan. 18. July 1993 (EV).

*American Yakuza*. With Viggo Mortensen, Michael Nouri. 18. June 1994 (Medusa).

*Amityville: A New Generation*. With Terry O'Quinn, David Naughton, Richard Roundtree. 18. September 1993 (Medusa).

*A.P.E.X.* With Richard Keats. 15. May 1994 (20.20 Vision/New Age Entertainment).

*Appointment for Killing*. With Corbin Bernsen, Markie Post. 18. February 1994 (New Age Entertainment/ 20.20 Vision).

*Arcade*. March 1994 (EV).

*Back in Action*. With Billy Blanks, Roddy Piper. 18. March 1994 (Guild).

*Bad Attitude*. With Gina Lim. 18. July 1993 (Guild).

*Bad Boys 2*. With Steve Lieberman. 18. July 1993 (Columbia TriStar).

*The Barefoot Kid*. With Maggie Cheung. 15. June 1994 (Made in Hong Kong).

*Based on a True Story*. With Dyan Cannon, Morgan Fairchild. 15. March 1994 (FoxVideo).

*A Bear Named Arthur*. With George Segal, Carol Alt. December 1993 (Columbia TriStar).

*Bikini Carwash II*. With Kristi Ducati. 18. November 1993 (20.20 Vision).

*Bird of Prey*. With Jennifer Beals. 18. March 1994 (20.20 Vision/New Age Entertainment).

*Bitter Harvest*. With Patsy Kensit, Stephen Baldwin, Jennifer Rubin, Adam Baldwin, M. Emmet Walsh. 18. April 1994 (Guild).

*Black Belt*. With Don 'The Dragon' Wilson. 18. February 1994 (Imperial Entertainment).

*Blood Fist 3 – Forced To Fight*. With Don 'The Dragon' Wilson, Richard Roundtree. 18. September 1993 (Universal/CIC).

*Bloodstone: Subspecies II*. With Anders Hove. 18. November 1993 (Full Moon Entertainment).

*Blood Warriors*. With David Bradley. 18. March 1994 (Columbia TriStar).

*Blue Flame*. With Brian Wimmer, Kerri Green. 15. January 1994 (Columbia TriStar).

*Body Melt*. With Gerard Kennedy, Ian Smith, Vince Gil. 18. March 1994 (First Independent).

*Bounty Tracker*. With Lorenzo Lamas. 18. February 1994 (Reflective).

*Brainsmasher . . . A Love Story*. With Andrew Dice Clay, Teri Hatcher. 15. November 1993 (Columbia TriStar).

*Broken Promises*. With Cheryl Ladd, Polly Draper. 15. May 1994 (First Independent).

*Carnosaur*. With Diane Ladd, Jennifer Runyon. 15. October 1993 (First Independent).

*A Case for Murder*. With Jennifer Grey,

Peter Berg. 15. January 1994 (Universal/CIC).

*Caught in the Act.* With Gregory Hines, Leslie Hope. PG. January 1994 (Universal/CIC).

*Chain of Command.* With Michael Dudikoff, R. Lee Ermey. June 1994 (Warner).

*Chained Heat II.* With Brigitte Nielsen, Paul Koslo. 18. August 1993 (Guild).

*A Child Lost Forever: The Jerry Sherwood Story.* With Beverly D'Angelo, Will Patton. 15. November 1993 (Odyssey).

*A Child Too Many.* With Michelle Greene. PG. October 1993 (High Fliers).

*Children of the Night.* With Karen Black, Ami Dolenz. 18. November 1993 (Columbia TriStar).

*The Church.* With Hugh Quarshie. 18. October 1993 (Reflective).

*CIA Codename Alexa.* With Lorenzo Lamas, Kathleen Kinmont, O. J. Simpson. 18. November 1993 (20.20 Vision).

*Circuitry Man.* With Jim Metzler, Dennis Christopher. 15. May 1994 (20.20 Vision).

*Class of '61.* With Clive Owen, Sophie Ward. PG. April 1994 (CIC).

*Complex of Fear.* With Hart Bochner, Joe Don Baker, Chelsea Field. 18. October 1993 (Odyssey).

*Confessions: Two Faces of Evil.* With Jason Bateman, James Wilder, Melinda Dillon, James Earl Jones. 15. March 1994 (Odyssey).

*Conflict of Interest.* With Christopher McDonald, Alyssa Milano, Judd Nelson. 18. November 1993 (First Independent).

*Conviction: The Kitty Dodds Story.* With Veronica Hamel, Kevin Dobson. 15. May 1994 (Odyssey).

*The Cool Surface.* With Robert Patrick, Teri Hatcher, Matt McCoy, Cyril O'Reilly. 18. June 1994 (Columbia TriStar).

*Corrupt Justice.* With Jacqueline Bisset. 15. May 1994 (Columbia TriStar).

*The Cover Girl Murders.* With Lee Majors, Jennifer O'Neill, Vanessa Angel. 15. April 1994 (CIC/Paramount).

*Criminal Mind.* With Lance Henriksen. 15. April 1994 (Columbia TriStar).

*Crisis in the Kremlin.* With Robert Rusler, Theodore Bikel. 15. October 1993 (Paramount/CIC).

*Cthulhu Mansion.* With Frank Finlay. 18. December 1993 (First Independent).

*Cyber Tracker.* With Don 'The Dragon' Wilson. 18. April 1994 (Guild).

*Cyborg II.* With Elias Koteas, Billy Drago, Jack Palance. October 1993 (PolyGram).

*Dangerous Desire.* With Richard Grieco, Maryam D'Abo. 18. January 1994 (20.20 Vision).

*Dangerous Heart.* With Tim Daly, Lauren Holly. 15. June 1994 (Universal/CIC).

*Dangerous Touch.* With Lou Diamond Phillips, Kate Vernon. 18. February 1994 (PolyGram).

*Danielle Steel's Star.* With Terry Farrel. 15. March 1994 (Imperial Entertainment).

*Dark Justice.* With Ramy Zada. 15. July 1993 (Warner).

*Dark Reflection.* With C. Thomas Howell, Lisa Zane. 18. April 1994 (Columbia TriStar).

*The Dark Universe.* 15. October 1993 (Columbia TriStar).

*Dead Before Dawn.* With Cheryl Ladd, Jameson Parker. 15. September 1993 (Odyssey).

*Deadly Exposure.* Aka *Lethal Exposure.* With Robby Benson, Laura Johnson, Andrew Prine, Isaac Hayes. 18. April 1994 (High Fliers).

*Deadly Recall.* With Veronica Hamel, Dennis Farina. 15. March 1994 (Imperial Entertainment).

*Deadly Rivals.* With Joseph Bologna, Andrew Stevens, Margaux Hemingway, Richard Roundtree. 18. February 1994 (20.20 Vision).

*Death in Small Doses.* With Richard Thomas, Tess Harper, Glynnis O'Connor. 15. December 1993 (Odyssey).

*Death Train.* With Pierce Brosnan, Patrick Stewart, Alexandra Paul, Christopher Lee. 15. November 1993 (EV).

*Deep Down.* With Tanya Roberts, George Segal. 18. March 1994 (20.20 Vision).

*Desperate Justice.* With Lesley Ann Warren, Bruce Davison, Annette O'Toole. 15. January 1994 (Odyssey).

*Desperate Motive.* With Mel Harris, David Keith, Mary Crosby. 18. November 1993 (Reflective).

*Die Watching.* With Christopher Atkins, Tim Thomerson. 18. August 1993 (High Fliers).

*The Disappearance of Christina.* With Robert Carradine, John Stamos, Kim Delaney. 15. June 1994 (Universal/CIC).

*Distant Justice.* With David Carradine, George Kennedy. 18. March 1994 (High Fliers).

*Dollman vs Demonic Toys.* With Tim Thomerson, Tracy Scoggins. May 1994 (Full Moon Entertainment/CIC).

*Doorways.* With George Newbern. 15. December 1993 (Columbia TriStar).

*Double Jeopardy.* With Bruce Boxleitner, Rachel Ward. 18. September 1993 (FoxVideo).

*Double Obsession.* Aka *Mirror Image.* With Margaux Hemingway, Frederic Forrest, Maryam d'Abo, Scott Valentine. 18. April 1994 (Columbia TriStar).

*Double Suspicion.* With Gary Busey, Kim Cattrall, Darlanne Fluegal. 18. March 1994 (Medusa).

*Double Trouble.* With Peter and David Paul (The Barbarian Brothers), Roddy McDowall, David Carradine. 18. July 1993 (Columbia TriStar).

*Dracula Rising.* With Christopher Atkins, Stacy Travis. July 1993 (Universal/CIC).

*Dragon Cop.* With Ron Marchini, David Carradine. 18. September 1993 (Columbia TriStar/New Age Entertainment).

*Dying to Remember.* With Melissa Gilbert, Christopher Stone, Jay Robinson. 15. May 1994 (Paramount/CIC).

*Emmanuelle Forever.* With Sylvia Kristel, George Lazenby. 18. January 1994 (Reflective).

*Emmanuelle's Love.* With Sylvia Kristel. 18. April 1994 (Reflective).

*Empty Cradle.* With Kate Jackson, Lori Loughlin. 15. June 1994 (Odyssey).

*Every Breath.* With Judd Nelson, Joanna Pacula. 18. May 1994 (Columbia TriStar).

*Eye of the Stranger.* 18. March 1994 (Columbia TriStar).

*Fade to Black.* With Timothy Busfield, Heather Locklear, Michael Beck. 15. November 1993 (Paramount/CIC).

*Falsely Accused.* With Lisa Hartman

Black, David Ogden Stiers. PG. August 1993 (20.20 Vision).

*Family of Strangers*. With Melissa Gilbert, Patty Duke, William Shatner. PG. September 1993 (Braveworld).

*Fatal Deception*. With Helena Bonham-Carter, Frank Whaley. 18. January 1994 (Warner).

*Fatal Temptation*. 18. January 1994 (Santa Monica Studios).

*Fearless Tiger*. With Jalal Merhi, Bolo Yeung. 18. May 1994 (Imperial Entertainment).

*Final Mission*. With Billy Wirth, Steve Railsback. 15. June 1994 (Guild).

*Final Round*. With Lorenzo Lamas, Kathleen Kinmont. 18. February 1994 (High Fliers).

*The Final Temptation*. With Paul McGann, Sophie Ward. 18. October 1993 (Columbia TriStar).

*Fist of Honor*. With Sam Jones, Bubba Smith. 18. June 1994 (Imperial).

*Fit to Kill*. With Dona Spier. 18. February 1994 (Columbia TriStar).

*For Love and Glory*. With Robert Foxworth, Kate Mulgrew, Olivia d'Abo. PG. May 1994 (FoxVideo).

*Frozen Assets*. With Shelley Long, Corbin Bernsen, Larry Miller, Dody Goodman, Matt Clark. 15. December 1993 (20.20 Vision).

*Full Contact*. With Jerry Trimble. 18. November 1993 (Columbia TriStar).

*Fuzz the Hero*. PG. March 1994 (Columbia TriStar/New Age Entertainment).

*Genuine Risk*. With Terence Stamp, Michelle Johnson, Peter Berg. 18. September 1993 (High Fliers).

*God of Gamblers*. With Chow Yun-Fat. 18. June 1994 (Made in Hong Kong).

*Good Cop, Bad Cop*. With Stacy Keach, Leo Rossi, Robert Hays. 18. February 1994 (Medusa).

*Hellborn*. With Karen Black. 18. April 1994 (New Age).

*The Hidden II*. With Kate Hodge. 18. January 1994 (PolyGram).

*Homewrecker*. With Robby Benson, Kate Jackson. PG. July 1993. (Paramount/CIC).

*Honor and Glory*. With Cynthia Rothrock. 15. March 1994 (Columbia TriStar).

*House of Secrets*. With Melissa Gilbert, Bruce Boxleitner, Cicely Tyson, Kate Vernon. 15. March 1994 (Odyssey).

*Hunted*. With Victoria Principal, Peter Onorati. PG. February 1994 (Imperial Entertainment).

*Illegal Entry: Formula for Fear*. 18. January 1994 (Imperial Entertainment).

*Incredible Kung Fu Mission*. 15. April 1994 (Imperial Entertainment).

*Indecent Behaviour*. With Shannon Tweed. 18. June 1994 (High Fliers).

*Inside Edge*. With Michael Madsen, Richard Lynch. 18. May 1994 (20.20 Vision).

*Intent to Kill*. With Traci Lords, Yaphet Kotto. 18. January 1994 (20.20 Vision).

*Interceptor*. With Andrew Divoff, Jurgen Prochnow. 15. December 1993 (CIC Video).

*In Too Deep*. With Michael Ironside, Barbara Carrera, Michael Pare. 18. January 1994 (Medusa).

*It's Nothing Personal*. With Amanda Donohoe, Bruce Dern, Yaphet Kotto. 15. August 1993 (Warner).

*Jason Goes to Hell: The Final Friday*. 18. January 1994 (Guild).

*Jericho Fever*. With Stephanie Zimbalist, Perry King. PG. June 1994 (Paramount/CIC).

*Jonathan: The Boy Nobody Wanted*. With JoBeth Williams, Jeffrey De Munn. PG. October 1993 (Odyssey).

*Joshua Tree*. With Dolph Lundgren, George Segal, Michelle Phillips. 18. October 1993 (EV).

*Judgement Day: The John List Story*. With Robert Blake, Beverly D'Angelo, Carroll Baker. 15. August 1993 (Odyssey).

*Jury of One*. With John Spencer, Rachel Ticotin. 15. October 1993 (20.20 Vision).

*Just One of the Girls*. With Corey Haim. 15. October 1993 (20.20 Vision).

*Killer Instinct*. With Scott Valentine, Charles Napier, Vanessa Angel, Talia Balsam. 18. July 1993 (20.20 Vision).

*Kiss and Be Killed*. With Jimmy Baio, Ken Norton, William Smith. 18. August 1993 (Universal/CIC).

*The Knife*. With Peter Coyote. April 1994 (Entertainment).

*Knife Edge*. With Brad Dourif, Sammi Davis, Max Perlich. 15. July 1993 (High Fliers).

*Labour of Love*. With Ann Jillian. PG. February 1994 (Fox).

*Last Dance*. With Cynthia Bassinet. 18. July 1993 (Columbia TriStar).

*The Last Mafia Marriage*. With Eric Roberts, Nancy McKeon, Ben Gazzara. 15. January 1994 (FoxVideo).

*Legacy of Rage*. Brandon Lee, Michael Wong. 18. August 1993 (Imperial).

*Leprechaun*. With Jennifer Aniston. 15. October 1993 (Reflective).

*Lethal Exposure*. See *Deadly Exposure*.

*Lethal White Female*. With Tim Matheson, Tracy Pollan, Christine Ebersole. 15. July 1993 (20.20 Vision).

*Lifepod*. With Robert Loggia, Ron Silver. 15. January 1994 (ITC).

*Little Devils: The Birth*. Marc Price, Russ Tamblyn. 15. October 1993 (High Fliers).

*The Little Ninja Dragon*. 15. Stephen Furst. July 1993 (Braveworld).

*Live by the Fist*. With Jerry Trimble, George Takei. 18. December 1993 (Imperial Entertainment).

*The Lost World*. With John Rhys-Davies, David Warner. PG. November 1993 (Ocean Pictures).

*Love Bites*. Adam Ant. 15. September 1993 (First Independent).

*Majority Rule*. PG. October 1993 (20.20 Vision).

*Mandroid*. With Brian Cousins. 15. December 1993 (Full Moon Entertainment).

*Marked for Murder*. With Powers Boothe, Billy Dee Williams. 15. October 1993 (Imperial Entertainment).

*Martial Outlaw*. With Jeff Wincott. 18. January 1994 (First Independent).

*Matt Miller: Party Dude*. With Matt Frewer. 15. June 1994 (Reflective).

*Message from Nam*. With Jenny Robertson, Rue McClanahan, Esther Rolle. PG. May 1994 (Imperial Entertainment).

*Millions*. With Billy Zane, Lauren Hutton, Carol Alt. 15. February 1994 (Columbia TriStar).

*Mindwarp*. With Bruce Campbell, Angus Scrimm. 18. January 1994 (20.20 Vision).

*Miracle on Interstate 880*. With Ruben Blades, David Morse. PG. November 1993 (Columbia TriStar).

*Mirror Image*. See *Double Obsession*.

*Mister Sister.* With Jonathan Silverman, Alyssa Milano. 15. May 1994 (Guild).

*Mood Indigo: Mind of a Killer.* With Tim Matheson. 15. February 1994 (Universal/CIC).

*The Mummy Lives.* With Tony Curtis. June 1994 (Warner).

*Munchie.* With Loni Anderson, Andrew Stevens. PG. August 1993 (Universal/CIC).

*Murder Between Friends.* With Timothy Busfield, Stephen Lang, Martin Kemp. 15. December 1993 (Odyssey).

*Murder So Sweet.* With Harry Hamlin, Helen Shaver. PG. August 1993. (20.20 Vision).

*Murder Without Motive.* With Georg Stanford Brown, Cuba Gooding Jr. PG. June 1994 (Odyssey).

*The Mutilator.* With Matt Miller. 18. September 1993 (VIPCO).

*My Grandad's a Vampire.* With Al Lewis. PG. July 1993 (Medusa).

*My Name is Kate.* With Donna Mills, Daniel J. Travanti. 15. May 1994 (Odyssey).

*My Samurai.* With Bubba Smith, Terry O'Quinn. 15. October 1993 (Columbia TriStar).

*Naked Robot $4^1/_2$.* With Hans Bachman. 15. August 1993 (20.20 Vision).

*The Neighbor.* With Rod Steiger, Linda Kozlowski. 18. June 1994 (First Independent).

*Nemesis.* With Olivier Gruner, Tim Thomerson, Brion James. 18. August 1993 (Columbia TriStar).

*Nervous Ticks.* With Bill Pullman, Julie Brown, Peter Boyle. 15. January 1994 (20.20 Vision).

*New York Cop.* With Chad McQueen, Mira Sorvino, Andreas Katsulas. 18. December 1993 (High Fliers).

*Night Eyes III.* March 1994 (EV).

*Night Trap.* With Robert Davi, Michael Ironside. 18. September 1993 (Guild).

*A Nightmare in Daylight.* With Jaclyn Smith, Christopher Reeve. 15. October 1993 (Columbia TriStar).

*No Escape No Return.* With Michael Nouri, John Saxon, Maxwell Caulfield. 18. April 1994 (Imperial Entertainment).

*The November Men.* With Robert Davi. 18. March 1994 (Guild).

*October 32nd.* With Peter Phelps, Richard Lynch, James Hong. 15. November 1993 (Columbia TriStar).

*Ordeal in the Arctic.* With Richard Chamberlain, Melanie Mayron. PG. February 1994 (20.20 Vision).

*Out for Blood.* With Don 'The Dragon' Wilson. 18. October 1993 (Imperial Entertainment).

*The Outfit.* With Martin Kove, Billy Drago, Lance Henriksen. 18. November 1993 (New Age Entertainment).

*Overexposed.* With Marcy Walker, Dan Lauria, Terence Knox. 15. April 1994 (Odyssey).

*Over the Line.* With Lesley-Anne Down, Michael Parks. 18. September 1993 (Warner).

*A Part of the Family.* With Elizabeth Arlen, Robert Carradine, Ronny Cox. 15. June 1994 (PolyGram).

*Perfect Family.* With Bruce Boxleitner, Jennifer O'Neill, Joanna Cassidy. 15. July 1993 (Paramount/CIC).

*Perfect Victim.* With Jacques Penot. 18. September 1993 (20.20 Vision).

*The Philadelphia Experiment 2.* With Brad Johnson. 15. November 1993 (PolyGram).

*Praying Mantis.* With Jane Seymour, Barry Bostwick, Frances Fisher. 15. February 1994 (Paramount/CIC).

*Prehysteria.* With Austin O'Brien. PG. August 1993 (Paramount/CIC).

*The Price of Vengeance: In the Line of Duty.* With Dean Stockwell, Michael Gross, Mary Kay Place. 15. February 1994 (Odyssey).

*Prison Heat.* With Rebecca Chambers. 18. September 1993 (Warner).

*The Prisoner.* With Jackie Chan. November 1993 (Imperial).

*Private Wars.* With Steve Railsback. 18. November 1993 (Imperial).

*Psycho Cop Returns.* With Bobby Ray Shafer. 18. August 1993 (Columbia TriStar).

*Puppet Master 4.* With Gordon Currie, Guy Rolfe. 15. June 1994 (Paramount/CIC).

*Quick.* See *Crossfire*.

*Rage Ring of Fire II.* With Don 'The Dragon' Wilson. 18. January 1994 (Imperial Entertainment).

*Redheads.* With Claudia Karvan. 15. July 1993 (High Fliers).

*Relentless III.* With Leo Rossi, William Forsythe. 18. September 1993 (Warner).

*Remember.* With Donna Mills, Stephen Collins, Derek De Lint, Claire Bloom, Cathy Tyson. 15. April 1994 (Odyssey).

*Remote.* U. January 1994 (Universal/CIC).

*Renegade.* With Lorenzo Lamas, Kathleen Kinmont. 18. January 1994 (Warner).

*Resort to Kill.* With Roddy Piper, Sonny Chiba, Meg Foster. 18. May 1994 (Medusa).

*Return of Ironside.* With Raymond Burr, Cliff Gorman. PG. February 1994 (Universal/CIC).

*Return of the Living Dead 3.* With Sarah Douglas, Anthony Hickox. 18. February 1994 (High Fliers).

*The Return to the Lost World.* With John Rhys-Davies, David Warner. PG. November 1993 (Ocean Pictures).

*Ring of Musketeers.* With David Hasselhoff, Cheech Marin, Alison Doody, John Rhys-Davies, Corbin Bernsen. 15. March 1994 (20.20 Vision).

*A Robot Called Golddigger.* With Joe Pantoliano, John Rhys-Davies, Amy Wright. PG. July 1993. (20.20 Vision/New Age Entertainment).

*Robot Wars.* With Barbara Crampton, Don Michael Paul. October 1993 (Paramount/CIC).

*Round Trip to Heaven.* With Corey Feldman, Zach Galligan. 15. September 1993 (20.20 Vision).

*Rubdown.* With Michelle Phillips, Jack Coleman, Catherine Oxenberg, William Devane. 15. February 1994 (Paramount/CIC).

*Running Cool.* With Paul Gleason, Dedee Pfeiffer. November 1993 (Paramount/CIC).

*Samurai Cowboy.* With Hiromi Go, Catherine Mary Stewart, Matt McCoy. PG. May 1994 (20.20 Vision).

*The Sands of Time.* With Deborah Raffin, Michael Nouri. July 1993 (Warner).

*Saviour of the Soul.* With Andy Lau. 15. June 1994 (Made in Hong Kong).

*Scandalous Liaisons.* With Tracey Kelly. 18. October 1993 (Rio).

*Scanner Cop.* With Daniel Quinn, Richard Lynch, Darlanne Fluegel. 18. April 1994 (Reflective).

*Scattered Dreams.* With Tyne Daly, Gerald McRaney. 15. June 1994 (Odyssey).

*A Scent of Midnight.* With Jack Palmer. 18. July 1993 (20.20 Vision).

*Secret Games: The Escort.* With Martin Hewitt. 18. November 1993 (Columbia TriStar).

*The Secret of Bruce Lee.* With Bruce Li. 18. May 1994 (Imperial Entertainment).

*Severed Ties.* With Oliver Reed, Elke Sommer. 18. October 1993 (Columbia TriStar).

*Shakes the Clown.* With Bobcat Goldthwait, Julie Brown. 18. August 1993 (20.20 Vision).

*Shattering the Silence.* With Joanna Kerns, Michael Brandon, Tony Roberts. 15. November 1993 (Odyssey).

*Sidney Sheldon's A Stranger in the Mirror.* With Perry King, Lori Loughlin, Christopher Plummer. 15. September 1993 (Imperial Entertainment).

*Sins of Desire.* With Tanya Roberts, Nick Cassavetes, Delia Sheppard, Jan-Michael Vincent. 18. February 1994 (Reflective).

*Slaughter of the Innocents.* With Scott Glenn. February 1994 (Entertainment).

*Snapdragon.* With Pamela Anderson, Steven Bauer, Chelsea Field. 18. May 1994 (Guild).

*Soldier of Fortune.* With Brandon Lee, Ernest Borgnine. 15. March 1994 (ITC).

*Spirit of '76.* With David Cassidy, Olivia d'Abo, Leif Garrett, Moon Zappa. 15. January 1994 (20.20 Vision).

*Split Images.* With Gregory Harrison, Nicholas Campbell, Rebecca Jenkins. 18. December 1993 (20.20 Vision)

*Stalking Back.* With Shanna Reed. 15. December 1993 (High Fliers).

*The Stepmother.* With Diane Ladd, Geraint Wyn Davies. 18. February 1994 (New Age/Columbia TriStar).

*Street Night.* With Jeff Speakman, Christopher Neame. 18. August 1993 (Warner).

*Sweet Justice.* With Marc Singer, Mickey Rooney, Finn Carter, Kathleen Kinmont. 15. March 1994 (Columbia TriStar).

*The Switch.* With Craig T. Nelson, Gary Cole, Beverly D'Angelo. PG. November 1993 (Odyssey).

*Sworn to Vengeance.* With Robert Conrad, William McNamara. 18. October 1993 (Odyssey).

*Tainted Blood.* With Raquel Welch, Joan Van Ark, Kerri Green. 15. November 1993 (Paramount/CIC).

*TC2000.* With Bolo Yeung, Jalal Merhi, Billy Blanks. 18. November 1993 (Guild).

*Tennessee Nights.* With Julian Sands, Rod Steiger, Stacey Dash, Ned Beatty. 15. March 1994 (20.20 Vision).

*Terror in the Night.* With Matt Mulhern, Joe Penny, Justine Bateman. 18. April 1994 (FoxVideo).

*Thicker Than Blood.* With Peter Strauss, Lynne Whitfield. PG. May 1994 (Odyssey).

*Through the Eyes of a Killer.* With David Marshall Grant, Tippi Hedren, Joe Pantoliano. 18. September 1993 (Paramount/CIC).

*Thunder in Paradise.* With Hulk Hogan, Chris Lemmon. 15. February 1994 (20.20 Vision).

*Ticks.* With Ami Dolenz, Seth Green. 18. May 1994 (Columbia TriStar).

*Time Runner.* With Mark Hamill, Brion James, Rae Dawn Chong. 15. August 1993 (Medusa).

*To Be the Best.* With Martin Kove, Alex Cord. 18. January 1994 (Columbia TriStar).

*To the Death.* With John Barrett. 18. July 1993 (Warner).

*Tobe Hooper's Night Terrors.* With Robert Englund. 18. June 1994 (Cannon).

*Tomohawk.* With Rodney Grant, Richard Tyson, Barbara Carrera. 15. March 1994 (Columbia TriStar).

*Trancers 4: Jack of Swords.* With Tim Thomerson, Stephen Macht. April 1994 (CIC/Paramount).

*Treacherous.* With Tia Carrere, Adam Baldwin, C. Thomas Howell. 18. March 1994 (Medusa).

*Trial and Error.* With Helen Shaver, Tim Matheson. 15. August 1993 (Braveworld).

*Tropical Nights.* With Lee Anne Beaman, Maryam d'Abo, Rick Rossovich. 18. September 1993 (Columbia TriStar).

*Troubleshooters: Trapped Beneath the Earth.* With Kris Kristofferson. PG. January 1994 (Universal/CIC).

*The Turning.* With Karen Allen, Raymond J. Barry, Tess Harper. 18. May 1994 (High Fliers).

*Twin Dragons.* With Jackie Chan. PG. September 1993 (Imperial Entertainment).

*Ulterior Motives.* With Thomas Ian Griffith, Ken Howard. 18. July 1993 (First Independent).

*Undefeatable.* With Cynthia Rothrock. 18. September 1993 (Medusa).

*Undercover Assassin.* With Robert Davi, Tony Curtis, Charles Napier. 18. November 1993 (New Age Entertainment).

*Vampire Cop.* With Michelle Owens. 18. May 1994 (High Fliers).

*Vice Academy: The Next Assignment.* With Ginger Lynn Allen. 18. October 1993 (Santa Monica Studios).

*Victim of Love.* With Dwight Schultz, Bonnie Bartlett. PG. April 1994 (Odyssey).

*Walker, Texas Ranger: One Riot, One Ranger.* With Chuck Norris, Marshall Teague. October 1993 (Warner).

*We're Talkin' Serious Money.* With Dennis Farina, Leo Rossi, Fran Drescher. 15. July 1993 (20.20 Vision).

*When a Stranger Calls Back.* With Carol Kane, Charles Durning. 15. March 1994 (Universal/CIC).

*When No One Would Listen.* With Michele Lee, James Farentino. 15. September 1993 (Warner).

*Why My Daughter?* With Linda Gray. 15. September 1993 (High Fliers).

*Wild Cactus.* With Robert D'Zar, India Allen. 18. October 1993 (20.20 Vision).

*Wild Orchid II: Shades of Blue.* With Nina Siemaszko, Tom Skerritt, Robert Davi. 18. July 1993 (20.20 Vision).

*Willing to Kill.* With Lesley Ann Warren, Tess Harper. PG. November 1993 (Warner).

*Witchboard: The Return.* With Ami Dolenz, Laraine Newman. 15. November 1993 (Medusa).

*With a Vengeance.* With Melissa Gilbert Brinkman, Jack Scalia, Michael Gross. 15. October 1993 (Braveworld).

*With Harmful Intent.* With Joan Van Ark, Daniel J. Travanti, Rick Springfield. 15. June 1994 (Columbia TriStar).

*Without Warning: Terror in the Towers.* With James Avery, Fran Drescher. 15. March 1994 (Paramount/CIC).

*Woman of Desire.* With Jeff Fahey, Bo Derek, Robert Mitchum. 18. February 1994 (Medusa).

# The Ten Most Promising Faces of 1994

## James Cameron-Wilson

### Angela Bassett

Like such fine Afro-American actresses as Cicely Tyson and Alfre Woodard, Angela Bassett is unlikely to secure a *major* toe-hold in Hollywood. But her dynamic performance as Tina Turner in *What's Love Got To Do With It*, not to mention the starring role in the big-budget sci-fi thriller *Strange Days* (scripted by James Cameron), are breakthroughs not to be dismissed lightly.

Like many 'newcomers', Angela Bassett, 36, has served her dues. Yet it wasn't until her star-making turn as Tina (and a Golden Globe award and Oscar nomination) that anybody seemed to know who she was. But listen up. She was the caring college professor Reesha Himes in John Sayles's outstanding *City of Hope*. She was Cuba Gooding Jr's mother in *Boyz N the Hood*. She was Betty Shabazz, wife of *Malcolm X*. And she was another mom – Michael Jackson & Co's – in the high-profile TV movie *The Jacksons – An American Dream*.

Of course, all these parts were essentially supporting ones, but more often than not Bassett provided strong girders for fancy brickwork. And like real girders – a support system which is generally invisible – Bassett's work went largely unheralded. That is until her turn as Tina, when she delivered a performance of astonishing range, depth and complexity, exposing both an enormous well of vulnerability and a superhuman drive. And if the emotional spectrum that the part demanded was not enough, Bassett had to duplicate a legend still very much alive. It's one thing to interpret a myth that has passed on, another entirely to mimic a larger-than-life figure such as Tina, who still dominates the media. But not only did Bassett capture the physical stance of the rock 'n' roll singer, she also made us

*Angela Bassett in the role that made her a star – Tina Turner in* What's Love Got To Do With It

*Jim Carrey as* Ace Ventura: Pet Detective

believe in her as a wife, mother and emotional casualty.

Reared by an aunt in Harlem, Angela Bassett moved south to St Petersburg, Florida, at the age of five. There, she was reunited with her mother who worked at a local dole office. Her first contact with acting arrived when she saw James Earl Jones in a production of *Of Mice and Men* and was reduced to tears. At Yale University she opted for Afro-American studies and drama, and graduated with a master's degree in the latter. Following a variety of roles in regional theatre and off-Broadway, she made her mark on Broadway in two productions, both by August Wilson: *Joe Turner's Come and Gone* and *Ma Rainey's Black Bottom*. Meanwhile, on television, she appeared in episodes of *thirtysomething*, *The Cosby Show* and *Equal Justice*. In the last-named, Joe Morton was a regular cast member and it was he who convinced John Sayles to sign Bassett up to play his wife in *City of Hope*. The actress's other film credits include *F/X*, *Kindergarten Cop*, *Critters 4*, *Innocent Blood* and Sayles's *Passion Fish*.

## Jim Carrey

Judged by salary alone, nobody in 1994 rose faster through the Hollywood ranks than Jim Carrey. Thanks to the success of one film – *Ace Ventura: Pet Detective* – Carrey was paid a startling $7m for the comedy *Dumb and Dumber*. He was also to get $7m for *The Best Man*, $5m for *Ace Ventura II* and another $7m for *The Mask II*. And these salaries were all negotiated in a matter of weeks. Look at it this way: in February of 1994 Carrey was an unknown quantity. By May he was looking at a future worth $26m. Eat your heart out Robin Williams.

But is Jim Carrey worth it? Reminiscent of a latter-day Jerry Lewis, Carrey is all facial contortions and rubber limbs. He *is* funny, but it's a moot point whether or not he can sustain a whole film. At any rate, audiences seemed happy, and *Ace Ventura* went on to gross over $72 million in the States alone. *Still*, that's hardly the stuff of *Jurassic Park* (which grossed over $880m worldwide). And you don't hear Sam Neill asking for $7m.

Anyhow, Carrey had served his dues. Born in Newmarket, Ontario, on 17 January 1962, Carrey was fine-tuning his outrageous comedy act at the age of 15 at Yuk Yuk's, a club in Toronto. By the time he was 19, he had appeared on the comedy circuit all over Canada, then packed his bags and headed for Los Angeles. In LA, he was spotted by Rodney Dangerfield at Mitzi Shore's Comedy Store, and opened for the latter on a national tour that seemed to seal his future. He also 'opened' for Andy Williams, but nevertheless continued to build his reputation.

On TV, he landed the leading role in the NBC sitcom *The Duck Factory*, playing Skip Tarkenton, employee of a floundering cartoon studio. Later, he starred in his own Showtime special, *Jim Carrey's Unnatural Act*, and in the TV movie *Doing Time on Maple Drive*. On film, he had a small part in Richard Lester's *Finders Keepers*; skewered the male lead (as a virgin at the mercy of vampire Lauren Hutton) in the perfectly awful black comedy *Once Bitten*; took a supporting turn in *Peggy Sue Got Married*; had an even smaller role (billed as James Carrey) in *The Dead Pool*; and played a furry alien opposite Geena Davis in *Earth Girls Are Easy*.

In 1990 he joined the comic ensemble on the TV series *In Living Color*, an Afro-American answer to *Saturday Night Live* created by Keenen Ivory Wayans. Although a platform for such black talents as Wayans, his brothers Damon and Shawn, and David Alan Grier, Carrey carved his own niche with such outlandish characters as the controversial Fire Marshal Bill and the steroid-enhanced bodybuilder Vera De Milo. The show was a hit and Carrey found himself in a position to star in his first major motion picture.

The film he chose to do was *Ace Ventura: Pet Detective*, a relatively low-budget comedy in which he played a manic private eye dedicated to locating lost animals. While Ventura behaved like a total idiot, he was actually smarter than such celluloid rivals as Inspector Clouseau and Frank Drebin. And that may be Ventura's allure. There's nothing more enjoyable than watching a smart-ass constantly receive his comeuppance, and Carrey milked the formula until the cows came home. It will be interesting to see if Ventura can maintain his appeal in what looks like a burgeoning series.

The actor then starred in *The Mask*, a special effects-laden comedy about a put-upon fellow with a magic mask that helps him beat the bad guys. 'It's *Falling Down* with a little Jekyll and Hyde twist,' the star promises us. It had better make a *lot* of money. After that Carrey was signed up to play the Riddler in *Batman Forever*, a role long earmarked for Robin Williams.

*David Caruso holds a gun to Christopher Walken in the 1990 film* King of New York

**David Caruso**

There is a scene in *Mad Dog and Glory* in which Robert De Niro, as a meek cop, is intimidated by a large, bald man played by Tom Towles. Not one to take any crap from anybody, De Niro's colleague, Mike – played by David Caruso – takes the man on in a staring contest. Although he is considerably smaller than Towles, Caruso adopts a threatening demeanour that frightens the bully off. Later, he takes on an even beefier actor – Mike Starr – in a spectacular, bloody brawl that leaves one in no doubt that Caruso is cast from reinforced steel.

To look at him – he is small, freckled and topped with a mop of red hair – Caruso hardly fills the bill as tough guy. But such is his intensity and acting smarts, he makes you believe that he could go the distance with Mike Tyson – and live to tell the tale.

The 38-year-old actor has actually been going the distance for a while now, clocking up conspicuous turns in such movies as *Hudson Hawk*, *Thief of Hearts*, *China Girl*, *Blue City* and *Twins*.

Born in Queens, New York, in 1955, Caruso made his film debut in *An Officer and a Gentleman* as the frail Naval cadet Topper Daniels, was Brian Dennehy's outspoken deputy in *First Blood* and played the hard-nosed cop on Christopher Walken's back in *King of New York*. But it was the role of the battle-scarred cop John Kelly in ABC TV's *NYPD Blue* that turned Caruso into an overnight sensation and won him a 1994 Golden Globe award as best actor.

Although as hard as they come, Kelly also has his sensitive side, a prerequisite in an era steeped in political correctness. 'Kelly knows that to survive, you have to be a compassionate person,' Caruso says of his character, a victim of personal disappointment and considerable emotional pain.

*NYPD Blue*, which also snared a Golden Globe as best TV series, has shot Caruso's career into high gear. He landed his first movie lead with *Kiss of Death*, in which he plays an ex-con trying to go straight – based on the 1947 classic that starred Victor Mature. Directed by Barbet Schroeder from a script by Richard Price (*The Color of Money, Sea of Love*, *Mad Dog and Glory*), the update co-stars Nicolas Cage as the villain. For his part, Caruso will receive no less than one million dollars, a sure sign that he has arrived. Besides, he's already turned down roles in three major movies.

**Embeth Davidtz**

To all intents and purposes, *Deadly Matrimony* was just another 'inspired by real events' TV miniseries. The story of a cop trying to prove that a prominent Chicago lawyer had murdered his wife, the film was blessed with two good turns from its male leads – Brian Dennehy and Treat Williams – but otherwise was a standard affair. That is, except for the performance of an unknown actress called Embeth Davidtz. Playing the charming, naive wife of the lawyer (Williams), Embeth stoked the proceedings with an emotional fire that kept the film alive long after she was dead. Luckily for Embeth, Steven Spielberg caught her act and signed her up for the female lead in his next picture, *Schindler's List*. According to the actress, 'Steven saw me in *Deadly Matrimony* and said, "Who's that?" He said he *knew* I had to play the part.'

The part concerned was that of Helen Hirsch, the Jewish woman adopted by Ralph Fiennes's SS commandant (Amon Goeth) as his personal maid. Losing ten pounds from her already frail frame, Embeth had her head shaved daily to play the emaciated victim of Goeth's physical

*Embeth Davidtz as Helen Hirsch in Steven Spielberg's remarkable* Schindler's List

and emotional cruelty. Who can forget the scene in which Goeth, madly attracted to the woman he houses in his basement, embarks on his seduction with the words: 'I realise you're not a person in the strictest sense of the word . . .' before beating her to a pulp. In spite of being the only non-Jewish actress playing a Jew in the film, Embeth's impression of the proud, tortured Hirsch was one hundred per cent credible – and unforgettable.

Born in Trenton, New Jersey, 28 years ago, Embeth moved with her family to Cape Town at the age of nine. There, she earned top honours at Rhodes University and embarked on a successful acting career, chalking up film roles in such local features as *A Private Life*, *Time of the Beast*, *Sweet Murder* and *Night of the Nineteenth.* When, suddenly, she decided 'it was time to go', she left for Los Angeles and abruptly landed a good role in the TV film *Till Death Do Us Part*, again as an ill-fated wife, this time of a homicidal Treat Williams. After that she landed the female lead in Sam Raimi's jokey horror film *Army of Darkness*, as a 13th-century English maiden at romantic loggerheads with a 20th-century time traveller.

More recently, she teamed up with Christian Slater, Kevin Bacon and Gary Oldman in the legal drama *Murder in the First* – based on a true story.

## Leonardo DiCaprio

Good as he was as the abused stepson of Robert De Niro in Michael Caton-Jones's *This Boy's Life*, nobody expected Leonardo DiCaprio to become a star. The film that turned the actor around was the quirky, humane *What's Eating Gilbert Grape?* in which DiCaprio played the retarded 18-year-old Arnie, brother of Johnny Depp. Giving a performance of astonishing innocence and spontaneity, DiCaprio brought a touching credibility to a very difficult part.

'I had to really research and get into the mind of somebody with a disability like that,' the actor says. 'So I spent a few days at a home for mentally retarded teens. We just talked and I watched their mannerisms. People have these expectations that mentally retarded children are really crazy, but it's not so. It's refreshing to see them because everything's so new to them.'

*Leonardo DiCaprio as Arnie in Lasse Hallstrom's* What's Eating Gilbert Grape?

DiCaprio was nominated for an Oscar for his performance, and was suddenly the hottest teenage comer in town. The long-awaited screen biography of James Dean had landed in the lap of director Michael Mann, and the search for JD was approaching the legendary status of an *Evita* casting call. Brad Pitt, Brendan Fraser and even Gary Oldman were serious contenders for the coveted role, when Mann set his sights on DiCaprio. The filmmaker was so impressed with the 19-year-old that he abandoned the film for two years so that DiCaprio could grow into the part. Meanwhile, the frenzy over who would play Robin in *Batman Forever* was approaching a similar crisis point. Finally, Chris O'Donnell seemed to have the Boy Wonder sewn up when DiCaprio's name came up again. For a while it was touch and go, but this time O'Donnell managed to hang on to his cape.

Born in 1974 in Los Angeles, Leonardo DiCaprio was signed up by an agent at the age of 14 and was soon appearing regularly in commercials. He made his TV debut in two episodes of *Lassie*, and went on to appear in such regular fare as *Santa Barbara*, *Roseanne* and *The Outsiders* – before landing the recurring role of the 13-year-old Gary in *Parenthood.* In 1991

he appeared as a homeless boy, Luke, in the family sitcom *Growing Pains*, and went on to make his 'official' film debut in *Critters 3*, in the OK role of Leonard. The same year he also had a small part in the Drew Barrymore melodrama *Poison Ivy*.

DiCaprio won the central role of Tobias Wolff in *This Boy's Life*, he says, through 'ignorant confidence. I went into the audition, looked De Niro in the eye and got the part. I was confident, even though I'd never done anything like it before. I had no idea.'

*What's Eating Gilbert Grape?* followed, and he was then chosen by Sharon Stone to star opposite her in the Western *The Quick and the Dead*. In fact, Ms Stone was so eager to have him on board that she paid his salary out of her own pocket. 'I wanted him bad,' the actress relayed, 'and we'd topped out financially.' But will her investment pay off? 'It better, or I'm going to beat the living shit out of him. "You little punk, I want my money back!" '

DiCaprio then landed the starring role in *The Basketball Diaries*, a film based on the early years of Jim Carroll growing up on the 'mean streets' of New York.

*Erika Eleniak as Elly May in* The Beverly Hillbillies

## Erika Eleniak

Nobody accused Erika Eleniak of being able to act. But when she popped out of an outsize cake in *Under Siege* and promptly embarked on a striptease, we all knew we'd be hearing more of her. This we did when she illustrated a talent to amuse in the celluloid version of the hit Sixties' TV sitcom *The Beverly Hillbillies*. The film itself was excruciating, but whenever Erika was on screen her cod innocence and natural physical attributes temporarily alleviated the nausea. As Elly May, the strong-as-an-ox, tobacco-chewing beauty afraid of being thought a sissy, she was about the only thing worth watching.

Erika Eleniak hasn't always been well endowed. Born 25 years ago in California, Erika first showed off her body modelling children's underwear. At ten, she made her film debut in the most popular movie of all time, playing a classmate of Henry Thomas (and stealing a kiss off him) in *E.T. The Extra-Terrestrial*. She then went through a difficult patch, devouring heavy metal and hard liquor and ending up in Alcoholics Anonymous – at the sweet age of 17. But she pulled herself together, landed a small part in the 1988 remake of *The Blob* and then popped up in such TV fodder as *Full House*, *Charles in Charge* and *Still the Beaver*. She appeared on the cover of the April '89 *Playboy*, and then disrobed three months later as the magazine's Miss July. The exposure won her the role of rookie lifeguard Shauni McClain in the pilot movie of *Baywatch*, which led to two years as a regular on the subsequent (and very successful) series. She also appeared in the TV movies *Daughters of Darkness*, *Best Intentions* and *Shattered Angel*, before turning heads in *Under Siege*, Steven Seagal's biggest hit to date. As Jordan Tate, the stripper-for-hire and ex-Playmate who ends up in the middle of a terrorist war, she was a welcome distraction from the big guns.

Next, she adopted a drawl and denims for *The Beverly Hillbillies*, and then landed the lead in the Dennis Hopper-directed *Chasers*, a comedy about a sexy Naval prisoner (EE) escorted by sailor boys Tom Berenger and William McNamara to the clink. Next, she teamed up with William Baldwin, John Leguizamo and Sadie Frost for Disney's *A Pyromaniac's Love Story*.

## Ralph Fiennes

It's amazing what can happen in the space of one year. At the beginning of 1993 Ralph Fiennes was a little-known actor who had appeared in two negligible British films. Twelve months later he was a front-runner for an Oscar and Paramount was offering him a million dollars to play *The Saint*.

A *distant* relative of the explorer Sir Ranulph Fiennes, the actor is the son of an English photographer, and abandoned his aspirations to become a painter to enrol at RADA. Not long afterwards he cut his acting canines at the Royal Shakespeare Company and, over a period of three years, appeared with some distinction in *King Lear*, *Love's Labour's Lost* and *Troilus and Cressida*. He also made a brief but telling appearance – as the bitter boyfriend of a murder victim – in the hit TV drama *Prime Suspect*. David Puttnam, who periodically tips off Warner Brothers to British stars of the future, took note. 'In the past ten years I have let Warners know about four

*Ralph Fiennes*
*Sadie Frost*

people,' the producer swore two years ago: 'They were Jeremy Irons, Daniel Day-Lewis, Kenneth Branagh – and Ralph Fiennes.'

True to his word, Puttnam cast Fiennes as T. E. Lawrence in the prestigious TV film *A Dangerous Man*, which led to the role of Heathcliff in the American-financed *Emily Brontë's Wuthering Heights*. Then came the male lead in Peter Greenaway's 1993 film *The Baby of Macon*, in which the actor played the ill-fated son of a 17th-century French bishop.

Following all the hype surrounding Lawrence, the Brontë and the Greenaway, Fiennes refused to get carried away. 'I'm quite prepared for nothing to happen as a result of it all. I know I'll want to get back to the theatre before too long.' Yeh, right.

True, *Emily Brontë's Wuthering Heights* was a monumental flop. True, *The Baby of Macon* was savaged by the critics. True, Julia Roberts turned him down as her leading man in *Shakespeare in Love* (after which the film folded). But Steven Spielberg caught Fiennes's performance as Heathcliff, and decided he was perfect for the role of the sadistic SS officer Amon Goeth in *Schindler's List*. Fiennes attempted to live up to the challenge. Not only did he interview survivors of the Holocaust but put on 26 pounds to give his character a puffy, fleshy look. The ordeal paid off. With his hair shaved up the neck and his face set in a mask of permanent contempt, Fiennes was simply chilling. The performance won him an Oscar nomination, and he was a strong favourite for the award, but ultimately lost to Tommy Lee Jones.

Next, he was cast as the real-life 1950s quiz-show contestant Charles Van Doren in Robert Redford's *Quiz Show*, opposite John Turturro, and went on to star in Kathryn Bigelow's sci-fi thriller *Strange Days* (from a script by James Cameron), with Angela Bassett and Juliette Lewis in support. He was also announced to star opposite Holly Hunter in *Old Friends* for director Mike Newell.

### Sadie Frost

Besides running around half naked and biting people, Sadie Frost had little to do in *Bram Stoker's Dracula*. Nevertheless, she was voted best newcomer in a 1993 readers' poll conducted by the pre-eminent American film magazine *Premiere*. And that in the face of such competition as Whitney Houston and Brad Pitt. But it wasn't until her performance in the British *Shopping* that the actress revealed her true colours. Playing an Ulster-born rebel who's into stealing cars and assaulting the collective ego of yuppies, Frost created a credible, attractive femme fatale whose humanity glowed through the shock effect of her physical persona. While the film itself was a noisy, brash exercise in post-punk exhibitionism, the actress provided it with an emotional centre that it barely deserved.

But Sadie Frost is no newcomer. Born in London on 19 June 1967, and raised in Manchester, she enrolled at the Italia Conti Stage School aged 11, subsequently starring as a 12-year-old girl in the David Puttnam-produced short *Vardo*. As an adult, she had a small part in *The Krays* and married the film's star, Gary Kemp, by whom she now has a 4-year-old son, Finlay. She was with Kemp again in the Anglo-Polish romance *Paper Marriage*, and yet again in the Hungarian-French-Swiss co-production *Freischutz*, which won the Camera d'Or prize at the 1989 Cannes festival. But it was as Gabriel Byrne's rebellious sister in the British thriller *Diamond*

*Skulls* that she was spotted by Francis Ford Coppola. According to the actress, the filmmaker thought her sex appeal perfect for the role of Lucy Westenra in *Dracula*. Sadie reveals, 'Lucy was a 19-year-old virgin, an aristocrat who's used to these little English boys. Dracula represents the dark side. When Lucy gets aroused, she *wants* Dracula to come and suck her blood. She's so turned on, she sort of has an orgasm, then passes out.'

*Dracula* was a hit and Sadie's turn as the innocent-turned-vampire who emerges from a coffin with fangs bared was one of the film's most touted moments. Since then she's been seen in the awful Eric Idle comedy *Splitting Heirs*, and returned to Hollywood to play the love interest in the Tex-Mex Western *The Cisco Kid*, with Jimmy Smits and Cheech Marin.

Next, she teamed up with William Baldwin and John Leguizamo in Disney's *A Pyromaniac's Love Story*.

### Rosie Perez

Rosie Perez really made her mark as the peppery, fast-talking girlfriend of Woody Harrelson in Ron Shelton's superbly entertaining *White Men Can't Jump*. She then repeated the performance in Jim Jarmusch's equally wonderful *Night on Earth*. But it was her role in Peter Weir's stunning *Fearless* – as the Latino mother who loses her baby in a plane crash – that attracted the serious accolades.

Ironically, the part of Carla in Rafael Yglesias's novel was Italian-American, but Weir was so keen to have Perez in his film that he doctored the nationality. 'This was her part,' the director declared. 'She had something to give. She was looking for a change of direction and *Fearless* was it.' Perez adds: 'Peter told me that when I delivered the first line, he knew I was right. I asked him if it bothered him that I speak this way. He said, "What way?" I just hugged him.'

Although nobody can deny that Perez's fiery, expletive-driven screen persona is never less than compelling, the actress has been extremely lucky with her choice of films. From the introductory frames of Spike Lee's *Do the Right Thing* – in which she shadow danced in boxing gloves over the opening credits – to the wise-cracking waitress friend of Marisa Tomei in *Untamed Heart*, Perez has yet to find herself in a dud movie.

*Rosie Perez in her Oscar-nominated performance as Carla – in Peter Weir's thought-provoking* Fearless

Yet her start in life was inauspicious. The daughter of a merchant marine, Perez was the sixth of eleven children crammed into a small apartment in the unfashionable district of Bushwick in Brooklyn. She dreamed of being a dancer, but when she turned up for a programme for inner-city kids she was told she had no rhythm. She cursed the teacher and was ordered never to return. Later, when she attended school in Queens she landed a place in the cheerleading squad, but struggled in school. 'It was very hard for me,' she recalls now. 'I never had a bad attitude, but I was shy, and I had a bad mouth. For a while no one accepted me – because I was Puerto Rican.'

Nevertheless, she graduated with an A average and moved to Los Angeles to study biochemistry. But it was at a night club that her future changed course. Spotted on the floor in action by a 'dance coordinator', she was offered a job dancing on the TV show *Soul Train*, a gig she kept going for eight months. This in turn led her to choreographing a video for Bobby Brown, followed in quick succession by similar chores for Diana Ross, LL Cool J, El Debarge and Heavy D. She was still at school when Spike Lee spotted her at another club and approached her to play Tina, his girlfriend in *Do the Right Thing*. Perez accepted his offer reluctantly – 'I didn't want my grade-point average to drop' – but was hooked by the experience.

In quick succession she appeared in an episode of *21 Jump Street*, played an assaulted prostitute in the superior TV movie *Criminal Justice* (with Forest Whitaker as her alleged attacker), and then auditioned for the role of Gloria Clemente in *White Men Can't Jump* – the neurotic nymphomaniac who dreams of being a TV game show contestant. The part was a major one, and both Holly Hunter and Rosanna Arquette were up for it.

'I knew that getting the part was going to be a long shot,' the actress recalls. 'But when I saw Rosanna sitting there, I started bugging out. I said a prayer. I thought, "I survived the social welfare system of New York City. Surely I can survive one audition." '

Not only did Perez win the role, but she was funny and spontaneous in it and the film was a colossal hit. This, in turn, led to *Untamed Heart* and, for *Fearless*, an Oscar nomination as best supporting actress of 1993.

Perez was also kept busy choreographing 'The Fly Girls' on the hit TV show *In Loving Color*, and hosted and produced her own three-part special on HBO: *Rosie Perez Presents Society's Ride*. More recently she played Nicolas Cage's wife in *It Could Happen To You*, a money-grabbing woman forced to share her husband's lottery winnings with a waitress. She then landed the lead role in Alexandre Rockwell's *Somebody To Love*, co-starring Harvey Keitel and Anthony Quinn.

Yet for all the praise heaped on Perez's young shoulders (she refuses to divulge her age), the star insists, 'I'm not a deep actress. I do what the director tells me to and I find truth in what he wants me to deliver.'

### David Thewlis

From his surly, introspective turn in the little-seen English film *Resurrected*, it was hard to imagine that David Thewlis would ever star in another picture. Let alone a picture of such extraordinary power. Yet, thanks to Thewlis's blistering central performance, Mike Leigh's *Naked* was one of the most daring, articulate challenges

*David Thewlis*

to the Laura Ashley school of British filmmaking in aeons. And Thewlis was well honoured for his work. He was voted best actor at the 1993 Cannes film festival, as well as by the London Film Critics' Circle, the New York Film Critics' Circle and at the Evening Standard awards.

Born in Blackpool in 1964, where his parents ran a wallpaper and paint shop, Thewlis started out professionally as the lead guitarist of a punk group. When two of his band members left to study drama at the Guildhall school in London, he joined them, and graduated in 1984. Barely a year out of college, he won a good role in the stage production *Buddy Holly at the Regal* and toured with it for five months. He then landed a TV sitcom, *Valentine Park*, followed by a starring role in Beeban Kidron's first film, *Vroom*, as a spiky-haired nutcase who takes to the road. He also appeared in a Mike Leigh short, *The Short and Curlies*, before landing the lead in *Resurrected*.

The last-named was a dour slice-of-life piece (based on a true story), with Thewlis cast as a Falklands war hero who returns from the grave to bring disappointment to his Lancashire village, where many would have preferred him dead. Only in retrospect does one realise how good Thewlis actually was, in light of the roles he has played since.

The film's scenarist, Martin Allen, was impressed. 'I didn't have any official say in the casting, and the decision to have David Thewlis was the only one where I made a special point. David has a rare quality – presence, while looking a bit like a victim. This strange ambivalence would be difficult to act if you didn't have it.'

Modestly, Thewlis himself thought (at the time) that the part 'was great. The main thing was the challenge of a straight piece of acting. Generally, I tend to get character or comedy parts.'

He returned to comedy with a regular role (as an unappetising boyfriend) in the TV series *A Bit of a Do*, with David Jason. Numerous TV credits followed and supporting roles in films, including bits in *Afraid of the Dark*, *Damage* and *The Trial*. He had a good part in Mike Leigh's *Life Is Sweet*, as Jane Horrocks's obnoxious boyfriend, which paved the way to his star-making turn in *Naked*.

When he embarked on *Naked* he knew nothing of the character he was to play. Only by sifting through profiles of 150 different men he knew or had met, did he and Leigh finally settle on Johnny, a rough approximation of a real-life character. Thewlis then spent the better part of a year getting to grips with this man, reading the books he would have read, thinking his thoughts, living his life. And through improvisation with other cast members the story of *Naked* evolved. This is the way Leigh works, but it was the actor's commitment and intelligence that brought Johnny to such vigorous life, producing a rounded character of savage wit, emotional brutality and unexpected insight. Johnny is, without doubt, one of the most fascinating, compelling protagonists to emerge from a British film in the '90s. The subsequent kudos afforded Thewlis was well deserved.

After that, he took a supporting role in the new screen version of *Black Beauty*, and then co-starred alongside Robert Downey Jr, Hugh Grant and Meg Ryan in the American-backed *Restoration*. Next, he signed on to play the title role in the big-budget 10th-century fantasy *Dragonheart*, as an evil tyrant with, literally, the heart of a dragon. Dennis Quaid co-starred as the good guy.

The actor's motto, incidentally, is 'to wake up and dream'.

# Film World Diary

## James Cameron-Wilson

### July 1993

**Geena Davis** and **Renny Harlin** announce their engagement. Previously, Ms Davis was married to **Jeff Goldblum**, who's now going out with **Laura Dern**, who used to date Renny Harlin ⋆ **Fred Gwynne**, 66, dies of pancreatic cancer. Famous as the gargantuan Herman Munster in *The Munsters* TV series (1964–6), the actor most recently appeared in the films *Shadows and Fog* and *My Cousin Vinny* ⋆ *Jurassic Park* grosses $200 million in its first 23 days in the US ⋆ *Sommersby* grosses $130 million worldwide ⋆ *Jurassic Park* breaks box-office records in Britain and Ireland, grossing £9.2 million in its first week ⋆ Elstree Studios in Borehamwood, Hertfordshire, closes after 66 years. Britain's largest four-wall studio, Elstree was the home of such blockbuster productions as *Star Wars* and *Raiders of the Lost Ark* ⋆ **Jean Negulesco**, 93, the Romanian-born director of *Johnny Belinda, The Mudlark* and *Three Coins in the Fountain*, dies of heart failure in Marbella, Spain ⋆ *The Bodyguard* grosses $411m worldwide ⋆ *Jurassic Park* grosses $300m worldwide in under six weeks ⋆ Universal Pictures pays **John Grisham** a record $3.75 million for the film rights to his next (unwritten) novel ⋆ *The Firm* grosses $100 million in its first three weeks in the US ⋆ **Geena Davis** and fiancé **Renny Harlin** drop out of the swashbuckling epic *Mistress of the Seas.* **Paul Verhoeven** takes over as director (for the second time), while **Michelle Pfeiffer** is mooted as the new female lead ⋆ *Jurassic Park*, in its second week in Britain, smashes the box-office record it broke seven days earlier ⋆ **Woody Allen** and TriStar Pictures part company after two films. Woody's next project – *Bullets Over Broadway* – will be made for Sweetland Films and will star **John Cusack** and **Mary-Louise Parker** ⋆ *Star* magazine leaks the news that **Daryl Hannah** and **John Kennedy Jr** have taken out a secret marriage licence. But does anybody believe it? ⋆ **Tim Robbins** signs a three-year contract with PolyGram Filmed Entertainment to develop, produce and direct at least two films for the company. Whether or not he will star in either or any of them will be left up to the gods ⋆ Proud parents: **Steven Seagal** and **Kelly LeBrock** announce the birth of daughter Arissa, their third child ⋆ **Anthony Quinn**, 78 – already the father of ten children – becomes the proud dad of a baby girl, Patricia. However, Quinn's wife, Iolanda, is furious – as the baby's mother is none other than the personal secretary of her husband ⋆ **Walter Koenig**, Ensign Pavel Chekhov in the original *Star Trek* TV series and its six spin-off films, suffers a heart attack in Chicago.

### August 1993

After nearly three weeks on release, *Jurassic Park* becomes the highest-grossing film in Britain – ever. The

previous title holder was *Ghost* ⋆ In under eight weeks *Jurassic Park* grosses $400 million worldwide ⋆ Following an accident on his motorcycle in Hollywood, **Wesley Snipes** is arrested for carrying a concealed 9mm semi-automatic pistol ⋆ **Federico Fellini** suffers a stroke in Rimini, Italy ⋆ **Clint Eastwood**, 63, and the actress **Frances Fisher**, 41, become the proud parents of Francesca Ruth, named after Clint's mother ⋆ **Heidi Lynne Fleiss**, 27, nicknamed 'Madam to the Stars', pleads not guilty to charges of living off the immoral earnings of prostitutes. However, Hollywood is braced for a major scandal as Fleiss reportedly sells her 'little black book' of famous clients to a generous publisher. According to inside sources, her book poses a threat to 20 well-known marriages and contains the names of four major Hollywood stars. Tried in Los Angeles Municipal Court, Fleiss faces 11 years' imprisonment if found guilty ⋆ Doctors in Rimini report that **Federico Fellini** is no longer on the critical list after his stroke ⋆ **Burt Reynolds** owns up to his two-year extramarital affair with cocktail waitress Pam Seals ⋆ **Sean Penn** and **Robin Wright** are the proud parents of a baby boy, Hopper Jack. Obviously the birth was an Easy Ride ⋆ Actress **Christine Lahti** and husband **Thomas Schlamme** (director of *So I Married an Axe Murderer*) are the proud parents of twins – a boy and girl ⋆ *Sleeplesss in Seattle* grosses $100 million in the US ⋆ **Kim Basinger** and **Alec Baldwin** finally tie the knot in a private ceremony on the beach at East Hampton, Long Island. **Paul Newman, Billy Joel** and **Christie Brinkley** were among the guests ⋆ **James Donald**, 76, dies of stomach cancer in Wiltshire. He will be best remembered for his role as Major Clipton in *The Bridge on the River Kwai*, and for such films as *In Which We Serve, Lust for Life, The Great Escape* and *King Rat* ⋆ **Stewart Granger**, 80, dies of cancer in Santa Monica, California ⋆ *Jurassic Park* grosses $500m worldwide after 71 days on release ⋆ *The Fugitive* grosses $100m in the US after only 22 days on release ⋆ **Kenneth Branagh**, in England to work on pre-production of *Mary Shelley's Frankenstein* and to attend the London premiere of *Much Ado About Nothing*, is appointed to the board of the British Film Institute ⋆ **Loni Anderson** demands that **Burt Reynolds** pay her $75,000 a month and give her custody of their adopted son, Quinton, now four ⋆ **Anthony Quinn**'s wife, Iolanda, leaves him ⋆ **Kelsey Grammer**, Dr Frasier Crane in TV's *Cheers*, sues his estranged wife for breaking her promise to sign a pre-nuptial agreement and for menacing him with 'kitchen utensils' ⋆ Thanks to his father's inability to settle on 'the right director', **Macaulay Culkin** is kicked off the movie *Richie Rich*, in which he was to have starred opposite **John Cleese** for a cool $8 million. Warner Brothers are now looking for a cheaper 13-year-old ⋆ **Burt Reynolds** offers his estranged wife **Loni Anderson** his entire fortune if she agrees to take a truth serum with him. If, however, she confesses to all the extramarital affairs that Reynolds thinks she's had, he wins the stake and gets sole custody of their adopted son. Will she; won't she? ⋆ **Jennifer O'Neill**, 44, wraps up her seventh marriage (to actor Neil Bonin) after less than a year ⋆ **Burt Reynolds**' annual $500,000 contract with the Florida Citrus Commission (to advertise their orange juice) is terminated, as he 'no longer conveys the image of a happy family man' ⋆ **Richard Jordan**, 56, dies of a brain tumour in Los Angeles. The star of such TV films as *Les Miserables* and *The Biggest Bank Robbery*, Jordan was a commendable heavy in *The Secret of My Success* and was most recently seen in *Primary Motive, Posse* and *Gettysburg* ⋆ The Quaker State Corporation terminate their advertising contract with **Burt Reynolds**, who has plugged their automotive products for the last 18 months ⋆ **Marlee Matlin**, 28, marries police officer Kevin Grandalski, also 28, in Los Angeles.

## September 1993

**Juliette Binoche** becomes the proud mother of a bouncing boy – but refuses to name the father ⋆ *Jurassic Park* grosses $600m worldwide ⋆ **Raymond Burr**, 76, dies of metastatic cancer of the liver in Sonoma County, California ⋆ *The Firm* grosses $150m in the US ⋆ **Geena Davis** and **Renny Harlin** officially tie the knot ⋆ *In the Line of Fire* grosses $100m in the US ⋆ **Vincent Lindon**, 33, the Gallic star of the French hit *La Crise*, announces his intentions to marry **Princess Caroline** of Monaco, 36. Lindon, a Jew, is reportedly converting to Catholicism over Christmas ⋆ **Clint Eastwood, Bob Geldof, Billy Idol, Gary Glitter** and **Neil Kinnock** add star power to the opening of the new nine-screen Warner cinema in London's Leicester Square ⋆ **Arnold Schwarzenegger** and **Maria Shriver** become the proud parents of their first son (and third child) ⋆ **Loretta Young**, 80, marries costume designer **Jean Louis**, 85, in Beverly Hills ⋆ **William Hurt** is to divorce Heidi Henderson, his wife of four and a half years. Next month the star and the French actress **Sandrine Bonnaire** expect the birth of their first baby ⋆ **Steve Martin** and **Victoria Tennant** separate (amicably) after nearly seven years of marriage ⋆ **Roseanne** and **Tom Arnold** agree to pay $20,000 to photographer Gary Aloian, who sued the couple for assault. However, Mr Arnold claims he just smashed up the cameraman's equipment ⋆ **James Caan** is held by police for ten hours after a dead man is found outside the apartment where the actor was staying. Later, police called the death an accident, saying the man fell to his death from a fire escape ⋆ A prostitute formerly employed by **Heidi Fleiss** names names on the *Geraldo* chat show. She claims that both **Robert De Niro** and

**Michael Douglas** were 'clients' of Ms Fleiss ⋆ **Sherilyn Fenn** is expecting, courtesy of the grip (Toulouse Holliday) who worked on her last film, *Fatal Instinct* ⋆ **Shannen Doherty**, 22, marries actor **Ashley Hamilton**, 19, son of **George Hamilton** ⋆ **Whoopi Goldberg** is sued for $20 million for breaking an agreement to star in the movie *T. Rex*. On second thoughts, she accepts the part ⋆ **Sylvester Stallone** poses nude for the cover of *Vanity Fair* ⋆ *Indecent Proposal* grosses $250 million worldwide ⋆ **Daniel Day-Lewis** is fined a three-figure sum for speeding and is banned from driving for a week.

## October 1993

Time Warner Entertainment fails to stop 12 minutes, 30 seconds' worth of clips from **Stanley Kubrick**'s *A Clockwork Orange* being shown on a Channel 4 documentary. Kubrick withdrew the film in 1973 after it had been blamed for a spree of copycat violence. Time Warner subsequently takes legal action against the TV channel ⋆ *Aladdin* breaks records in America as the video shifts 10.6 million units in just three days ⋆ *Jurassic Park* becomes the highest-grossing film of all time, besting the world record previously set by *E.T. – The Extra-Terrestrial* ⋆ **Cyril Cusack**, aged 82, dies of motor neurone disease in London. His last films numbered *Far and Away* and *As You Like It* ⋆ *Aladdin* grosses $300m worldwide ⋆ **Gwen Welles**, 42, who played the would-be country singer Sueleen Gay in *Nashville* (and who also gave memorable turns in *California Split* and *Between the Lines*), dies of cancer. She was married to actor **Harris Yulin** ⋆ *The Fugitive* grosses $100m *outside* the States ⋆ **Sean Connery** reveals he is being treated for throat cancer ⋆ **Vincent Price**, 82, dies of lung cancer in Los Angeles ⋆ Residents of Malibu, Los Angeles, flee to safety as fires sweep through southern California, destroying up to 600 homes and cremating 90,000 acres. **Dwight Yoakam**'s house is badly burned while the homes of **Marlon Brando, Jack Nicholson** and **Tom Selleck** are also threatened ⋆ Tabloid special: **Jenny Seagrove** leaves **Michael Winner** ⋆ On *The Oprah Winfrey Show* **Diana Ross** reveals that the father of her oldest daughter (Rhonda Suzanne) is Motown founder **Berry Gordy** and *not* her first husband Bob Silberstein ⋆ When **Jan-Michael Vincent** bends down to pet a Rottweiler, the bitch bites off a thumb-sized chunk of his lip. Not surprisingly, the actor is in hospital ⋆ **Federico Fellini**, 73, dies in Rome ⋆ The same day, **River Phoenix**, 23, collapses and dies outside **Johnny Depp**'s Viper Club in LA – from a suspected cocaine reaction.

## November 1993

The bush fires in southern California spread and now threaten the homes of **Barbra Streisand, Sylvester Stallone, Sean Penn** and **Rod Steiger**. The British director **Duncan Gibbins**, 41, is critically burned after trying to rescue his cat. His films number *Fire with Fire, Eve of Destruction* and *Third Degree Burn* ⋆ **Tony Curtis**, 68, and his new bride, Hollywood lawyer Lisa Deutsch, are expecting ⋆ **Julia Roberts** is reportedly to be paid $10m for the title role in TriStar Pictures' *Mary Reilly*, to be directed by **Stephen Frears**. The sum would make her the highest-paid actress of all time ⋆ **Dennis Hopper, Peter Fonda** and **Dwight Yoakam** open their own restaurant, The Thunder Roadhouse, in West Hollywood ⋆ The homes of **George C. Scott, Charles Bronson, Sean Penn** and **Dick Van Dyke** are destroyed in the Malibu fires. As Van Dyke stays over at **Anthony Hopkins**' place, **Ali MacGraw, Larry Hagman, Burgess Meredith** and **Bob Newhart** flee their homes. Now the estates of **Robert Redford, Dustin Hoffman, Walter Matthau** and **Lynn Redgrave** are also threatened ⋆ **Roger Moore** is operated on in Los Angeles following diagnosis of a cancerous prostate ⋆ **Duncan Gibbins** dies from burns sustained in the Malibu fires ⋆ *Jurassic Park* grosses over $800m worldwide ⋆ After years of speculation and an international search, the next Scarlett O'Hara is finally announced. And the winner is . . . Manchester-born **Joanne Whalley-Kilmer**. She will play the title role in the £33m epic TV miniseries *Scarlet*, based on Alexandra Ripley's best-selling sequel to *Gone With the Wind* ⋆ **Whoopi Goldberg** and **Ted Danson** issue an official statement announcing their romantic separation. Danson is now looking for a reconciliation with his wife of 16 years, Casey, and Whoopi is dating her orthodontist ⋆ **Michelle Pfeiffer** marries TV producer **David Kelley**, much to the consternation of the male universe ⋆ Three weeks before its release, *Aladdin* has already shattered box-office records at London's Odeon Leicester Square, where advance ticket sales have clocked up £100,000. The previous record-holder was *Who Framed Roger Rabbit*, which boasted an advance box-office of £65,000 ⋆ *Sliver* grosses $100m worldwide ⋆ After kicking **Macaulay Culkin** off *Richie Rich*, Warner Bros approaches **Elijah Wood** for the title role. Wood, incidentally, played the Little Mac's nemesis in *The Good Son* ⋆ **Francis Ford Coppola** is appointed to the board of directors of MGM ⋆ **Michael Winner** undergoes a triple heart by-pass operation ⋆ The British film composer **Stanley Myers**, 63, dies of cancer. His most notable scores include *Moonlighting, My Beautiful Laundrette, Prick Up Your Ears, The Witches* and the 'Cavatina' theme tune to *The Deer Hunter* ⋆ **Ruben Blades**, 45, the film star and salsa musician, campaigns for the presidency of Panama ⋆ *Cliffhanger* grosses $200m worldwide ⋆ **Bill Bixby**, 59, star of TV's *The Incredible Hulk*, dies of cancer ⋆ **Barbra Streisand** donates her 24-acre Malibu estate

*Julia Roberts: phenomenal pay cheque*

(worth £10 million) to a conservation group to be used as an environmental research centre ⋆ Husband and wife **Gabriel Byrne** and **Ellen Barkin** call it quits after five years and two sons ⋆ **Barbara Hershey** separates from her husband, Stephen Douglas, after one year ⋆ **Emile Ardolino**, 50, director of *Dirty Dancing, Chances Are, Three Men and a Little Lady* and *Sister Act*, dies of AIDS in Bel-Air, California ⋆ As a Christmas bonus, Disney presents **Robin Williams** with a Picasso painting worth $1m. However, Williams – who was paid $75,000 for voicing the Genie in *Aladdin* – announces that he will never act for Disney again as they used his voice to advertise merchandise connected with the film. Williams also reveals that he doesn't like the painting.

## December 1993

**Don Ameche**, 85, dies of prostate cancer in Arizona ⋆ **Ally Sheedy** and her husband, actor **David Lansbury**, are expecting their first child in March ⋆ **Tupac Shakur**, rap singer and star of the films *Juice* and *Above the Rim*, pleads not guilty to charges of shooting and wounding two off-duty policemen in Atlanta ⋆ *Aladdin* breaks box-office records in Britain, grossing £1,615,179 in its first weekend ⋆ **Oliver Reed** is sued for damages by his stand-in and friend for 20 years, Reg Prince, for allegedly throwing Prince off a restaurant balcony. The incident occurred in 1986 in the Seychelles (during filming of *Castaway*) and, Prince says, he hasn't been able to work since because of a back injury ⋆ *Schindler's List* is voted best film by the New York Film Critics' Circle, the Los Angeles Film Critics' Association and the National Board of Review, but **Steven Spielberg** is ignored as best director. **Holly Hunter**, however, is voted best actress for her performance in *The Piano* by all three bodies ⋆ **Oliver Reed** is cleared of assault charges against Reg Prince ⋆ The acclaimed Lebanese director **Maroun Baghdadi** (*Hors la Vie, La Fille de l'Air*), 43, is killed falling down a lift shaft in Beirut ⋆ *The Firm* grosses $250 million worldwide ⋆ **Jean-Claude Van Damme** is sued by a woman who alleges that he forced her to participate in a sexual 'foursome' ⋆ **Tupac Shakur** is arraigned on a nine-count indictment for threatening the life of a woman who accused him of sexual assault ⋆ **Adam Horovitz**, sometime Beastie Boy and sometime movie star (*The Road Home, Roadside Prophets*), is sued for battery and grand theft after attacking a cameraman and stealing his videotape at last month's memorial service for **River Phoenix** (held at Horovitz's home) ⋆ **Myrna Loy**, 88, dies in New York ⋆ **Michael Douglas** is said to be looking for a divorce lawyer to end his marriage to Diandra ⋆ **Janet Margolin**, 50, whose films include *David and Lisa, Take the Money and Run, Annie Hall, Last Embrace* and, most recently, *Ghostbusters II*, dies of ovarian cancer in Los Angeles. She is survived by her husband, the actor **Ted Wass** ⋆ **Rosanna Arquette** marries for the third time, to restaurateur Johnny Sidel ⋆ **Sherilyn Fenn** gives birth to a baby boy, Myles Maximilian Holliday. The father is Fenn's boyfriend, musician Toulouse Holliday ⋆ **Alexander Mackendrick**, 81, the American-born, Scottish-raised director of such Ealing classics as *The Ladykillers, Whisky Galore!* and *The Man in the White Suit*, dies of pneumonia in Los Angeles ⋆ **Rodney Dangerfield**, 72, ties the knot with Joan Child, 42, a Malibu florist.

## January 1994

**Derek Jacobi**, 55, is knighted in the New Year's Honours ⋆ *Mrs Doubtfire* grosses $100m in the States ⋆ **Drew Barrymore** and **Billy Idol** are dating ⋆ **Mickey Rourke** is arrested for resisting a police officer during a skirmish at the actor's Miami Beach night club. Reportedly, 75 people were involved in the brawl ⋆ The Italian film star **Vittorio Mezzogiorno**, 52, dies of heart failure in Milan. His better-known films include *Three Brothers* and *The Moon in the Gutter* ⋆ Elstree Studios wins a reprieve from oblivion when the High Court reconsiders a plan to turn half the site into a superstore ⋆ The French magazine *Voici* claims that **Cindy Crawford** is having an extramarital affair and that her marriage to **Richard Gere** is on the rocks ⋆ The London-born actress **Heather Sears**, 57, dies. She will be best remembered for her role as Susan Brown in *Room at the Top* ⋆ *Mrs Doubtfire* grosses $150m Stateside ⋆ **Holly Hunter** wins the best actress award at the Golden Globes Awards, as does *Schindler's List* for best film. Other predictable winners include **Tom Hanks** (for *Philadelphia*) and **Tommy Lee Jones** (for best supporting actor in *The Fugitive*). Their Oscars are assured, as is **Steven Spielberg**'s, who wins as best director ⋆ **Natasha Richardson** announces plans to marry **Liam Neeson** in July ⋆ **Ted Danson** is reportedly dating actress **Mary Steenburgen**, former wife of **Malcolm McDowell**. The couple starred together in *Pontiac Moon* ⋆ **Telly Savalas**, 70, dies of prostate cancer in his sleep in California ⋆ **Holly Hunter** is voted best actress in the London Film Critics' awards ⋆ French police provide **Brigitte Bardot** with 24-hour protection following death threats after the animal activist urged television viewers to boycott horse meat ⋆ **Edward James Olmos** and **Lorraine Bracco** tie the knot.

## February 1994

**Liza Minnelli** and **Desi Arnaz Jr** are going steady ⋆ **Joseph Cotten**, 88, dies of pneumonia in Westwood, California ⋆ **Harrison Ford** is voted the top box-office star of the century by American cinema owners ⋆ **William Shatner** and his wife Marcy Lafferty are divorcing after 20 years of marriage ⋆ Two local councils in England – Scunthorpe in Humberside and Taunton Deane in Somerset – overrule the British Board of Film Classification by giving *Mrs Doubtfire* a PG certificate. The British censor rated the comedy (based on a children's book) '12' because of sexual innuendo ⋆ **Demi Moore** and **Bruce Willis** are the proud parents of a baby girl, Tallulah Belle, their third child ⋆ **Anna Nicole Smith**, Guess? supermodel and co-star of *Naked Gun 33⅓: The Final Insult*, is admitted to Cedar Sinai hospital after overdosing on drugs and a bottle of tequila ⋆ Model-photographer **Janice Dickinson** is the proud mother of a baby girl – and **Sylvester Stallone** is reportedly the father. The agent of **Jennifer Flavin**, Sly's girlfriend for five and a half years, breaks the news to her ⋆ **William Conrad**, 73, dies of cardiac arrest in North Hollywood ⋆ **Michelle Pfeiffer**

is pregnant ⋆ **James Ferman**, 63, director of the British Board of Film and Video Classification, dismisses his 13-strong 'part-time' advisory committee to much outrage. Ferman is now looking for a smaller body of permanent advisers, he says ⋆ **Sally Field** separates from her husband of nine years, movie executive **Alan Greisman** ⋆ Viacom, the American cable company, and the Blockbuster Video chain merge to buy Paramount Pictures for $10 billion ⋆ Derek Jarman, 52, dies of AIDS in London.

## March 1994

**John Candy**, 43, dies of a heart attack in Durango, Mexico, where he was filming the comedy Western *Wagons East*, with **Richard Lewis** and **Ellen Greene** ⋆ **Melina Mercouri**, 68, dies of cancer in New York ⋆ *Mrs Doubtfire* grosses $200 million in the US ⋆ **Fernando Rey**, 76, dies of cancer in Madrid. The Spanish actor will be best remembered for the films *The French Connection* and *The Discreet Charm of the Bourgeoisie* ⋆ **Jon Peters**, who produced the megahits *A Star Is Born* and *Batman* for Warner Brothers, is wooed back to the old studio. With his former colleague **Peter Guber**, Peters was bought by Sony in 1989 for a cool $700 million (divided between Guber, Peters and Warner). However, Peters failed to make a single picture for the Japanese-owned corporation ⋆ *Demolition Man* grosses $150 million worldwide ⋆ **Melanie Griffith** files for divorce from **Don Johnson** ⋆ *The Three Musketeers* grosses $100 million worldwide ⋆ **Mai Zetterling**, 68, dies of cancer in London. As an actress, her films numbered *Frieda, Only Two Can Play, The Witches* and *Hidden Agenda*. In 1982 she directed the hard-hitting British film *Scrubbers*, set in a girls' borstal ⋆ **Anna Paquin**, 11, stuns the media and the star-studded audience at the Dorothy Chandler Pavilion when she wins the Oscar for best supporting actress for her role in *The Piano*, beating out her competitors **Holly Hunter, Rosie Perez, Winona Ryder** and **Emma Thompson**. She is left speechless at the podium ⋆ **James Caan** is arrested for reportedly brandishing a loaded .38 pistol during an argument with a total stranger in North Hollywood ⋆ **Don**

*Michelle Pfeiffer: pregnancy and singing lessons*

**Johnson** enters the Betty Ford Center for alcohol and prescription drug rehab ⋆ **Dudley Moore**, 5ft 2in, is arrested for 'cohabitational abuse' after attacking his girlfriend, Nicole Rothschild, 5ft 10in, while watching the Oscar ceremony on television. Later, the actor-pianist is released on $50,000 bail ⋆ **Drew Barrymore**, 19, marries her boyfriend – British club owner Jeremy Thomas, 31 – on a whim and a prayer ⋆ **Giulietta Masina**, 74, dies from a tumour in Rome. She was admitted to hospital in October of '93, the month her husband, **Federico Fellini**, died. Her films included *La Strada, Juliet of the Spirits* and *Ginger and Fred*, all directed by Fellini ⋆ *Cool Runnings* grosses $100 million worldwide ⋆ **Burt Reynolds** collapses on the set of his TV sitcom *Evening Shade*. Earlier, the actor had complained of chest pains.

## April 1994

*The Pelican Brief* grosses $100 million in the US ⋆ **Dudley Moore** marries his girlfriend, Nicole Rothschild, one month after she reported him to the police for 'cohabitational abuse'. Ms Rothschild is the actor's fourth wife ⋆ A 17-year-old extra on the movie *Little Big League* sues star **Timothy Busfield** for sexual assault and 'fondling' ⋆ **Timothy Busfield**, star of *Little Big League*, sues a 17-year-old film extra for false accusations of sexual assault and 'fondling' ⋆ **Wesley Snipes** is charged with reckless driving after a 31-mile, 120-mph chase with police ⋆ The Czech actor **Rudolf Hrusinsky**, 73, dies after a protracted illness. He will be best remembered for the films *The Good Soldier Schweik, Capricious Summer* and *Lark on a String* ⋆ **Michael Howard**, British Home Secretary, succumbs to pressure from **David Alton**, Liberal Democratic MP for Liverpool Mossley Hill, and passes tough new legislation to protect children from unsuitable role models and psychologically harmful acts of violence as depicted by films on video. The new act – backed by 250 MPs – means that fewer adult films will be available on video, that the British Board of Film Classification will have to be even stricter when handing out certificates and that retailers and distributors can face high fines – or even imprisonment – if certain videos are rented out to juveniles. Britain, in which video censorship is *already* tougher than in most civilised countries, now faces yet another blow to its film and video industry ⋆ **Timothy Dalton**, who played James Bond in *The Living Daylights* and *Licence to Kill*, announces his retirement from the series ⋆ **Sylvester Stallone** and **Janice Dickinson** plan to marry – as soon as they can sort out a prenuptial agreement ⋆ **Rosanne** and **Tom Arnold** split after four years of marriage ⋆ **Nick Nolte** and his wife of ten years, Rebecca Linger, also call it a day. *Officially* ⋆ *Beyond Bedlam* is denied a British video release under the new government strictures ⋆ *Four Weddings & a Funeral* climbs to No. 1 in the US box-office charts, the first British film to do so since *A Fish Called Wanda* – six years ago ⋆ The French actor **Jean Carmet**, 73, dies in Sèvres, near Paris. He made indelible impressions in such films as *Violette Nozière, Buffet Froid, Les Fugitifs, My Father's Glory, Merci la Vie* and had the lead in the Oscar-winning *Black and White in Color* (1977). Most recently he played the tragic, embittered Bonnemort in *Germinal* ⋆ *Cliffhanger* grosses $260 million worldwide ⋆ **Lynne Frederick**, 39, former child star, widow of **Peter Sellers** and ex-wife of **David Frost**, dies, reportedly of drug and alcohol abuse.

## May 1994

For his next film, the futuristic action-adventure *Waterworld*, **Kevin Costner** will reportedly receive a record $22 million for his twin chores as star and producer ⋆ **Richard Gere** and **Cindy Crawford** take a full-page advertise-

*O. J. Simpson: happier days as Nordberg in* Naked Gun 33⅓: The Final Insult *– before the murder rap*

ment in *The Times* to defend their marriage, revealing, 'We are heterosexual and monogamous and take our commitment to each other very seriously . . . We remain very married. We both look forward to having a family' ⋆ Warner Bros' *Richie Rich* starts production with **Macaulay Culkin** after all. The director finally favoured by the Culkin clan is **Donald Petrie**. However, co-star **John Cleese** is replaced by **John Larroquette** ⋆ Following discussions with Twentieth Century Fox and the British Board of Film Classification, *Mrs Doubtfire* is finally given a PG certificate – after a small cut. However, the film has already been on release in Britain for over three months ⋆ **Steven Keats**, 49, is found dead in his Manhattan apartment, apparently having killed himself. The actor starred in the critically acclaimed 1975 film *Hester Street* and also appeared in the original *Death Wish*. Most recently he had a small part in Woody Allen's *Shadows and Fog* ⋆ It's official: not **Meryl Streep**, not **Madonna**, but **Michelle Pfeiffer** will play the title role in the film version of *Evita*. A pregnant Ms Pfeiffer embarks on singing lessons in preparation for the role she will start filming next year – under the direction of **Oliver Stone** ⋆ **George Peppard**, 65, dies of pneumonia following a bout of lung cancer – at Los Angeles Medical Center ⋆ *Dirty Weekend*, *Menace II Society* and *True Romance* are all denied video release in Britain ⋆ *Mrs Doubtfire* grosses $400 million worldwide ⋆ After ten weeks of release in North America, *Four Weddings & a Funeral* regains the No. 1 spot in the US charts ⋆ **Lynn Redgrave** files for bankruptcy after failing to meet the £400,000 cost of legal bills following a 13-year court battle. Ms Redgrave sued Universal Television in 1981 when they fired her from their show *House Calls* – for breast-feeding her daughter on set ⋆ **Michael Howard** passes a new law in which anyone caught renting or selling an unclassified video can face two years in prison. The supply of a classified video to a minor can now result in six months' imprisonment ⋆ Lancôme, the French cosmetic and skincare company, terminate their multi-million dollar contract with **Isabella Rossellini**, who has promoted their products for twelve years. Now, they say, she is too old (she's 41) ⋆ *The Flintstones* grosses $37.5 million in the US over the Memorial Day weekend.

## June 1994

**Drew Thomas** reveals she's changing her name back to **Barrymore** after the break-up of her marriage to club owner Jeremy Thomas. The couple exchanged vows back in March of '94 ⋆ In protest over the local mayor's refusal to ban a hunting convention, **Brigitte Bardot** says she'll be leaving St Tropez, her home for 36 years ⋆ **Pierce Brosnan**, 41, is such a hot favourite to play James Bond in the next 007 outing that bookmakers are no longer taking bets ⋆ **Pierce Brosnan** is signed up as the next 007 in *Goldeneye*, the 17th official Bond extravaganza. Asked to play Bond eight years ago (but unable to because of contractual obligations to the TV series *Remington Steele*), Brosnan is the widower of actress **Cassandra Harris**, herself a Bond girl in the 1981 *For Your Eyes Only* ⋆ The Advertising Standards Authority of Britain condemns posters for *In the Name of the Father* that claim the film is 'a true story' as misleading. The wording is changed to 'based on a true story' ⋆ **Henry Mancini**, 70, dies from complications of liver and pancreatic cancer at his home in Beverly Hills. He was best known as the composer of such songs as 'Moon River' and 'Days of Wine and Roses' and for *The Pink Panther* theme tune ⋆ **Burt Reynolds** and **Loni Anderson** are divorced (at last) ⋆ Following a 60-mile car chase (screened live on American TV), **O. J. Simpson** is arrested for the murder of his ex-wife Nicole and her companion ⋆ **Diana Rigg**, former *Avengers* star and James Bond girl, is made a dame in the Queen's birthday honours list ⋆ **Sean Connery** is under investigation by Spanish authorities for tax evasion over the sale of a multi-million pound property on the Costa del Sol. Connery reportedly owes £700,000 in unpaid taxes on the deal ⋆ *Jurassic Park* grosses $900m worldwide ⋆ *The Flintstones* grosses $100m in the US – in 30 days ⋆ After a conflict with director **Joel Schumacher, Michael Keaton** walks off *Batman Forever*, leaving a potential pay check of $35m behind him. **Val Kilmer** picks up his cape ⋆ **Anna Nicole Smith** is sued by a former nanny for imprisonment, sexual harassment and assault. In the words of the nanny's lawyer, 'we allege our client was overwhelmed by Ms Smith – who is a large woman' ⋆ *Four Weddings & a Funeral* grosses $100 million worldwide ⋆ After only three weeks of release in the US, *The Lion King* becomes the highest grossing film of the year.

*Sean Connery: throat and tax problems*

# Film Soundtracks

James Cameron-Wilson

With film soundtracks dominating more and more of the market-place, it seemed about time that *Film Review* dedicated some column inches to the phenomenon. Once a mere keepsake for devout film buffs, the soundtrack has grown into a giant industry of its own, spawning specialist record shops, hefty advertising budgets and even its own record labels.

Indeed, such is the power of the soundtrack that a top-selling album can salvage a film at the box-office. Ask Kevin Costner. The success of the Bryan Adams song '(Everything I do) I Do It For You' from *Robin Hood: Prince of Thieves* kept the film squarely in the public domain, with album and film each feeding off the other in a state of perpetual motion. But even Adams's success failed to forecast the phenomenal sales of the soundtrack for *The Bodyguard*, yet another Costner vehicle. Fuelled by Whitney Houston's cover of the Dolly Parton-penned 'I Will Always Love You', *The Bodyguard* reached No. 1 in the charts and, after Meat Loaf, became the second-highest selling album of 1993. To date it has sold over eight million copies, while the film itself has grossed over $413m worldwide.

Perversely, perhaps, some movie soundtracks achieve even greater popularity than their celluloid counterparts. Two of last year's more celebrated bombs – *Last Action Hero* and *Sliver* – actually parented chart-climbing CDs.

Recently, such soundtracks as *Above the Rim, The Commitments, The Crow, Four Weddings & a Funeral, The Lion King, Menace II Society, Philadelphia, Pure Country, Reality Bites, Sister Act, Sliver* and *Sleepless in Seattle* have all enjoyed chart success, but what is even more surprising is that *serious* film music is finding a toe-hold. To underline the point, record companies took out newspaper ads for the likes of *The Piano, Schindler's List* and even the belated release of Vangelis's music for *Blade Runner.*

It is *The Piano*, however, that has made inroads into the history books. At the time of going to press, the soundtrack had shifted 60,000 units which, in the parlance of the record industry, makes it a 'silver' seller. This must hold some irony for the film's composer, **Michael Nyman**, whose mesmerising, intoxicating score was inexplicably denied an Oscar nomination.

In fact, British composers in general have had a good year. The former Brighton-based jingles composer **Hans Zimmer** is currently in enormous demand in Hollywood, where he has written the music for such films as *The Assassin, Cool Runnings, The House of the Spirits, True Romance, Renaissance Man* and *The Lion King.* **Rachel Portman**, too, whose beguiling score for *Benny & Joon* is still lingering in my ears, has been busy, writing the music for *Ethan Frome, Friends, The Joy Luck Club* and *Used People.* While **Patrick Doyle**, who made his name with Kenneth Branagh's *Henry V,*

*Composer of the year? Michael Nyman stands proudly by his* Piano

excelled himself on *Much Ado About Nothing* and journeyed to Hollywood to score *Carlito's Way* and *Needful Things*.

Also, **John Barry, Stewart Copeland, Carl Davis, Richard Hartley, Michael Kamen** and **Richard Robbins** have all been active.

The only sad note of the year is that sounded by the death of **Stanley Myers**, the composer whose lush, melodic scores enhanced so many British films.

But, sales figures aside, what were the best film soundtracks of the year? Here I catalogue my top ten which, I readily admit, is a subjective list.

## Top Ten Albums of the Year

**The Age of Innocence**. A sumptuous return to form for **Elmer Bernstein**, 71, who superbly captures the elegance and restrained passions of 1870s New York. Lots of good classical stuff, too.

**Aladdin**. Not only **Alan Menken**'s Oscar-winning score, but Menken, Howard Ashman and Sir Tim Rice's entertaining songs. As far as musicals went, *Aladdin* had *no* competition.

**Four Weddings & a Funeral**. The perfect souvenir, with old hits, new hits (Wet Wet Wet's 'Love Is All Around'), a taste of **Richard Rodney Bennett**'s mellifluous score and even snatches of dialogue including John Hannah's moving recital of W. H. Auden's 'Funeral Blues'.

**Heaven & Earth**. Winner of the Golden Globe for best score, **Kitaro**'s Eastern melodies are simply haunting and hypnotic.

**Much Ado About Nothing**. Starting with Emma Thompson's dulcet recital of Balthasar's ballad, this tuneful memoir from **Patrick Doyle** is a constant pleasure.

**Philadelphia**. Action-packed, top-selling pop soundtrack, highlighted by Bruce Springsteen's Oscar-winning 'Streets of Philadelphia' – and with good acts from Spin Doctors, Indigo Girls and Maria Callas.

**The Piano**. Mesmerising, intoxicating score from **Michael Nyman**, with additional magic courtesy of Mozart.

**Schindler's List**. The year's best soundtrack (a deserved Oscar-winner), a moving masterpiece of classical film music from Hollywood's finest, **John Williams**.

**Short Cuts**. A bluesy collection of numbers sung by Annie Ross (backed by the Low Note Quartet), with impromptu jamming from Iggy Popp and Michael Stipe – while Lori Singer plays Dvorak and Stravinsky on cello.

**Sleepless in Seattle**. Profoundly sentimental, magical collection of certified classics crooned by such stalwarts as Jimmy Durante, Louis Armstrong and, of course, Nat King Cole.

# In Memoriam

## F. Maurice Speed

**Don Ameche**, who died on 6 December 1993 at the age of 85, had two quite distinct careers: first as a young debonair hero (though he seldom got the girl) opposite players like Betty Grable and Alice Faye in a series of popular musicals and, later, as an outstanding character actor, whose performance in *Cocoon* brought him a supporting actor Oscar. Suffering from cancer, Ameche carried on working until the end, completing his role in *Corrine, Corrine* only a few weeks before his death. One of eight children, Dominic Felix Amici – to give him his real name – was the son of an Italian immigrant family. He began his acting career in repertory in Madison, Wisconsin, later achieving a minor role in the Broadway production of *Jerry for Short*, although it was 25 years before he again appeared on the Broadway stage. Turned down by MGM, Ameche was signed by Fox and made his screen debut in *Sins of Man* in 1936. Although he was impressive in several straight roles (particularly in *Alexander Graham Bell*) he was at his best in musical films. After a series of fairly mediocre roles he moved to New York to concentrate on television and radio, making his long delayed return to the Broadway stage in 1955 in the Cole Porter musical *Silk Stockings*. He continued to make movies and in 1983 had a hit with a character role in *Trading Places*, followed by *Cocoon*, gaining him an Oscar and a new career in films like *Folks*, *Harry and the Hendersons*, *Coming to America* and *Oscar*. His films include: *Ladies in Love* (1936), *Alexander's Ragtime Band* and *In Old Chicago* (1938), *Hollywood Cavalcade* and *The Story of Alexander Graham Bell* (1939), *Down Argentine Way* (1940), *The Feminine Touch* and *Kiss the Boys Goodbye* (1941), *The Magnificent Dope* (1942), *Heaven Can Wait* (1943), *Wing and a Prayer* (1944), *Guest Wife* (1945), *Sleep, My Love* (1948), *Slightly French* (1949), *Picture Mommy Dead* (1966), *The Boatniks* (1970), *Trading Places* (1983), *Cocoon* (1985), *Harry and the Hendersons* (1987), *Cocoon: The Return* (1988), *Coming to America* (1988) and *Oscar* (1991).

*Don Ameche*

*Leon Ames*

**Leon Ames** (born Leon Wycoff), who died at the age of 91 on 12 October 1993, was a much loved character actor who appeared in as many as four or five films a year. He made his debut as the romantic hero in Edgar Allan Poe's 1932 film *Murders in the Rue Morgue*. His great success as the harassed father in *Meet Me in St Louis* in 1944 led to his mastery of the paternal roles, in both film and TV. He also appeared in a number of stage productions. In 1933, he secretly founded the Screen Actors' Guild. Here are just a few of his films: *45 Fathers* (1937), *Island in the Sky* and *Mysterious Mr Moto* (1938), *I Was a Convict* (1939), *No Greater Sin* (1941), *The Thin Man Goes Home* and *Thirty Seconds Over Tokyo* (1944), *Son of Lassie* and *They Were Expendable* (1945), *The Postman Always Rings Twice* (1946), *Merton of the Movies* (1947), *The Velvet Touch* (1948), *Any Number Can Play* and *Little Women* (1949), *Peyton Place* (1957), *The Absent Minded Professor* (1960), *On a Clear Day You Can See Forever* and *Tora! Tora! Tora!* (1970) and *Jake Speed* (1986).

Now almost forgotten, **David Brian** (born Brian David) was an actor who played opposite the great stars, finding fame as Joan Crawford's leading man. Brian, who died in July 1993, aged 82, started out as a theatre doorman, later becoming a chorus boy and vaudeville act before being given his first film chance – by Joan Crawford – in the 1949 film *Flamingo Road*. Strikingly handsome, he played forceful heroes and, latterly, villains. His output was considerable and included *Intruder in the Dust* and *The Damned Don't Cry* (1950), *Fort Worth* (1951), *This Woman is Dangerous* and *Springfield Rifle* (1952), *The High and the Mighty* (1954), *Timberjack* (1955), *Fury at Gunsight Pass* (1956), *The Rabbit Trap* (1959), *A Pocketful of Miracles* (1961), *How the West was Won* (1962), *Castle of Evil* (1966), *The Destructors* (1968), *Childish Things* (1969) and his final film *The Seven Minutes* (1971).

Although he appeared in more than a hundred films over a period of twenty years (including Hitchcock's *Rear Window*) it was on the small screen that **Raymond** (William Stacy) **Burr**, who died on 12 September 1993, at the age of 76, gained international acclaim. The *Perry Mason* series brought him some 30 million devoted viewers and 3000 fan letters every week. When he temporarily stopped playing Mason after nine years (he recently played the role again in a series of full-length episodes) he reappeared in another series as *Ironside*, the wheelchair-bound legal sleuth who never failed to prove the innocence of his clients. British Columbian-born Burr spent his teenage years doing all manner of jobs while acting in amateur productions. It was director Anatole Litvak who gave him his big break with an engagement at the Toronto Summer Theatre, after which he won a role in the London production of *Night Must Fall*, going on tour with the company around Australia. For a while Burr made a living singing in a Paris restaurant; he then joined the cast of the American musical *Crazy With the Heat*. During World War II, Burr took a break from acting to serve in the US Navy, resuming his career to take over the role of Perry Mason in the TV series from William Holden, a part which he played for nine years. Some of his rare free time he spent on the 3000-acre Pacific island he owned, where he raised

*Raymond Burr*

*Macdonald Carey*

cattle, exported timber and grew orchids. Incidentally, it was ironic that to complete his last Perry Mason feature, Burr had to play the role from a wheelchair suffering from the cancer which eventually killed him. Married three times, Burr was always reluctant to talk about his personal life, and he died an intensely private man.

Though he made some 50 feature films, **Macdonald Carey** was best known in America for his appearance in the TV series *Days of Our Lives*, which ran from its debut in 1965 until his death on 21 March 1994, at the age of 81, winning him the 1974 and 1975 Emmy awards along the way. His best-known film was Hitchcock's *Shadow of a Doubt* in 1943. His other films included: *Suddenly It's Spring* (1947), *Streets of Laredo* and *The Great Gatsby* (1949), *Dream Girl* (1948), *The Great Missouri Raid* (1952), *Fire Over America* (1954), *The Damned* (1962) and *End of the World* (1977). He published three volumes of poetry, and his autobiography, *The Days of My Life*, which appeared in 1991. In a tribute, his TV co-star Deidre Hall said of him: 'He was as gentle, nurturing and charming a man you could ever want to meet.'

Although he made some 75 films in all, the name of **Joseph Cotten** – who died on 6 February 1994 at the age of 88 – will be best remembered for his performances in Orson Welles's *Citizen Kane* (1941), *The Magnificent Ambersons* (1942), *Journey Into Fear* (1942) and Carol Reed's *The Third Man* (1949). Although he had studied acting, Cotten worked as a paint salesman, newspaper advertisement representative and drama critic before becoming understudy on a Broadway production. He appeared in several of Welles's Mercury Theatre productions, and when Welles went to Hollywood to shoot *Citizen Kane*, he took Cotten with him. In 1942 Cotten signed a long-term contract with David O. Selznick, who immediately loaned him out to Alfred Hitchcock for *Shadow of a Doubt* (1943), thus establishing him as a star. For his performance in *Portrait of Jennie* in 1948 he was awarded the Best Actor prize at the prestigious Venice Film Festival. This marked the height of his career and although he was to make many more movies, none of them gave him the same chance to assert himself. Cotten's films also included *Gaslight* (1944), *Duel in the Sun* (1947), *Under Capricorn* (1949), *Two Flags West* (1950), *Peking Express* (1951), *A Blueprint for Murder* (1953), *Touch of Evil* (1958), *Hush . . . Hush Sweet Charlotte* (1964), *The Oscar* (1966), *Jack of Diamonds* (1967), *Tora! Tora! Tora!* (1970), *Soylent Green* (1973), *F for Fake* (1973), *Airport 77* (1977), *Heaven's Gate* (1980) and *The Survivor* (1981).

*Joseph Cotten*

**Cyril Cusack**, known as the Irish Elf, who died on 7 October 1993, at the age of 82, was born of Anglo-Irish parents in Durban, South Africa. Whilst he was still a child, his family moved to Ireland, and he completed his education at Dublin University. Small it stature, he brought an impish sense of fun to most of his characters and, indeed, to everything he did – and he did plenty! Having quickly established himself as one of Ireland's foremost players, he found himself equally at home in the theatre, on film and TV, though his greatest triumphs

*Cyril Cusack*

were on stage. He made his screen debut in 1917 in *Knocknagow* but his full potential was not revealed until his memorable performance in Carol Reed's *Odd Man Out* (1947). His versatility was demonstrated by his work in *The Spy Who Came in From the Cold* (1965), *Fahrenheit 451* (1966) and *My Left Foot* (1989). His many other films included *The Small Back Room* (1948), *The Blue Lagoon* (1949), *The Man Who Never Was* (1955), *The Spanish Gardener* (1956), *Ill Met By Moonlight* (1957), *Gideon's Day* (1958), *A Terrible Beauty* (1960), *Waltz of the Toreadors* (1962), *The Taming of the Shrew* (1967), *David Copperfield* (1970), *King Lear* and *Harold and Maude* (1971), *The Day of the Jackal* (1973), *The Italian Connection* (1972), *Little Dorrit* (1988) and *The Fool* (1990). He performed in more than 100 plays, including *The Three Sisters* in 1990 at Dublin's Gate Theatre, with three of his four actress daughters, Sinead, Niamh and Sorcha (the fourth is Catherine).

**James** (Robert MacGeorge) **Donald**, who died aged 76 in August 1993, will be best recalled by moviegoers for his role as the doubting doctor in *The Bridge on the River Kwai*, who could not come to terms with Alec Guinness's determination to make such a fine bridge for their Japanese captors. The son of a Presbyterian minister – who was horrified when he learned of his son's decision to make acting his career – Donald made his stage debut at the Edinburgh Lyceum in *The Admirable Crichton*. He subsequently went to London to enrol with the London Theatre Studio, from where he joined the Old Vic, and enjoyed a steady stream of successes. Although devoted to the theatre, Donald managed to fit in a lively screen career, his more noteworthy films including *The Missing Million* (1941, his debut), *In Which We Serve* (1942), *The Way Ahead* (1944), *Edward My Son* (1949), *Trottie True* (1949), *Brandy for the Parson* and *The Gift Horse* (1952), *The Pickwick Papers* (1953), *Beau Brummel* (1954), *Lust for Life* (1956), *The Bridge on the River Kwai* (1957), *The Great Escape* (1963), *King Rat* (1965), *Cast a Giant Shadow* (1966), *The Jokers* (1967), *Hannibal Brooks* and *The Royal Hunt of the Sun* (1969), *Conduct Unbecoming* (1975) and *The Big Sleep* (1978). Donald was plagued with asthma all his life and finally retired to cultivate a vineyard in Wiltshire.

**Federico Fellini**, who died on 31 October 1993 at the age of 73, was one of the great masters of post-war cinema. His memorial is a succession of unique movies, all touched with magic, all rich in wit and imagination, the majority autobiographical in one way or another. Fellini was unique: he refused to conform to the usual cinematic conventions and went his own personal way. Born in Rimini – a favourite location for his films – Fellini began as a newspaper crime reporter and artist, specialising in caricatures. He later became a gag writer for films. His first big break came when Roberto Rossellini invited him to collaborate on the latter's script of the neo-realist masterpiece *Open City*. Fellini's first chance at directing came when Alberto Lattuada asked him to co-direct *Variety Lights* with him in 1950. Fellini jumped at the chance, and throughout his life, he never tired of the magic of vaudeville and the circus, a recurring theme in many of his later movies. Fellini's first big international success came in 1959 with *La Dolce Vita*, a searing commentary on the decadence of modern Rome which drew criticism from both the Church and the politicians. And so began a succession of personal, idiosyncratic movies, all touched with Fellini's wit and originality. Many of his films were noteworthy for their supporting cast – Fellini was particularly fascinated with faces, often selecting his supporting actors on the strength of their physical features. Latterly, his standards slipped a little with films like *Ginger et Fred* (1986), but his vision always remained fascinatingly original. Fellini's favourite actor was Marcello Mastroianni, but the greatest influence on his film-making remained his wife, Giulietta Masina, who appeared in several of his movies. Most typical of Fellini's attitude to the cinema was his *8½*; unable to settle on a subject he made the film about a film director searching for a subject for his next film. A masterpiece, it remains one of the most intimately personal films ever made. Other Fellini films include: *The White Sheik* (1952), *I Vitelloni* (1953), *La Strada* (1954), *Il Bidone* (1955), *Juliet of the Spirits* (1965), *Satyricon* (1969), *The Clowns* (1970), *Fellini's Roma* (1972), *Fellini's Amarcord* (1973), *Fellini's Casanova* (1976), *Orchestra Rehearsal* (1978), *And the Ship Sails On* (1983), *Voices of the Moon* (1990).

*James Donald*

From the day I first met him at the old Lime Grove studios at Shepherd's Bush until the day he died, on 16 August 1993, aged 80, **Stewart Granger** (real name James Lablanche Stewart) remained dismissive of his films and, more particularly, of his own roles. But the films were all of their time and Granger's performances were quite as good in my opinion as many of those of the much lauded, hyped and highly paid 'action' stars of today. Granger began his career in the routine way, with stage revues and plays, repertory seasons and the odd bit part in films, and it was only in 1939 that he made his real screen debut in *So This is London.* With foreign productions, he must have appeared in some fifty films in all, including *Convoy* (1940), *Secret Mission* (1942), *The Man in Grey* (1943), *Fanny By Gaslight*, *Love Story* and *Madonna of the Seven Moons* (1944), *Waterloo Road* and *Caesar and Cleopatra* (1945), *Caravan* and *The Magic Bow* (1946), *Captain Boycott* (1947) and *Saraband for Dead Lovers* (1949). In 1950 Granger was signed by Hollywood to star as Allan Quartermaine in *King Solomon's Mines* and stayed on to make a series of action films including *Soldiers Three* (1951), *Scaramouche* and *The Prisoner of Zenda* (1952), *All the Brothers Were Valiant* and *Salome* (1953), *Beau Brummel* (1954) *Bhowani Junction* (1956) and *Gun Glory* (1957). There followed numerous German, French and Italian films and a few more British movies including *The Trygon Factor* (1966), *The Last Safari* (1957) and *The Wild Geese* (1978). Granger became an American citizen in 1956. He also appeared on TV as Sherlock Holmes in 1972's *The Hound of the Baskervilles* and in the serial *The Virginian* (1970–71). A forthright, honest character, Stewart Granger was one of the few film stars who consistently undersold himself.

Lord Graves, better known as **Peter Graves**, the debonair, handsome actor who made his name in the thirties, died on 8 June 1994 at the age of 82. He never used his title after he rose to stardom in Ivor Novello's musicals, for which his pleasant singing voice was ideally suited. He made his debut with a small part in *Glamorous Night* in 1935 and reached stardom in *Arc de Triomph* (1943). His 25 films included *Kipps* (1941), his screen debut, *Give Us the Moon* (1944), *Waltz Time* (1945), *Gaiety George* (1946), *Mrs Fitzherbert* (1947), *Spring in Park Lane* (1948), *Maytime in Mayfair* (1949), *Derby Day* (1952), *Lilacs in the Spring* (1954), *Alfie* (1966) and *The Slipper and the Rose* (1976).

*Stewart Granger*

**Derek Jarman**, the controversial, gay, avant-garde British moviemaker, died from an AIDS-related illness at the age of 52 on 19 February 1994. Jarman, with his erotic, experimental and often difficult films, became something of a cult figure, his work dividing the critics – and the public – into two opposing camps. Although acclaimed for their artistry, few of Jarman's films were a commercial or popular success; the most accessible was probably his film about the artist *Caravaggio* (1986) though his production about the martyr *Sebastiane* (1976) also met with widespread critical acclaim, as did *The Last of England* (1987), a savage portrait of the Britain of the future. He made use of various media: *War Requiem* launched an attack on the horrors of war built around the Benjamin Britten oratorio *War Requiem* whilst *Edward II* (another of his more commercial productions) was an interpretation of the Marlowe play. Trained as an artist, Jarman also worked with the Royal and Festival Ballet companies and the London Contemporary Dance Company. His final film was the experimental, non-commercial, *Blue*. Jarman's other features include *Jubilee* (1978), *The Tempest* (1979), *In the Shadow of the Sun* (1981), *Aria* (1987), *The Garden* (1990) and *Wittgenstein* (1993).

Mention the name of **Myrna Loy** – who died on 14 December 1993 at the age of 88 – to any mature moviegoer and they will immediately think of the *Thin Man* series of slick, sophisticated detective movies, in which she co-starred with William Powell, and 'Asta' the terrier. These movies made Myrna Williams (her real name) a major star. She and her family had moved to California when her father died (she was 13), where she was lucky enough to be picked for Grauman's Chinese Theatre as soon as she left school. She was then cast in a small part in the old silent *Ben Hur, A Tale of the Christ*, and played a chorus girl in *Pretty Ladies* – the film which marked the screen debut of Joan Crawford. A five-year contract with Warner followed at the end of which she won an important role in Sam Goldwyn's *Arrowsmith.*

*Myrna Loy*

Then came the *Thin Man* films and a complete switch from the role of oriental-looking vamp to that of the slick, sophisticated wife of Nick Charles (Powell) in thirteen films. These led her to achieve pride of place in the *Motion Picture Herald*'s poll of the top box-office stars. During World War II Loy did very little acting, devoting herself to working with the Red Cross, and afterwards she became the first Hollywood star to work for the United Nations. Unlike many of the stars of the period, Miss Loy spoke out against Senator McCarthy's persecution of left-wing players in the so-called witch-hunts. Apart from her films, Myrna Loy appeared on the stage (making her Broadway debut in a revival of *The Women*) and worked in television. In spite of all her outstanding performances, she failed to win an Oscar, though she was awarded a 'special' Oscar in 1991 for 'Career Achievement'. She was the author of a book entitled *Being and Becoming*. One recalls with pleasure that little pert nose and the dry way in which she delivered her lines, as well as the hundred other little things which added up to her unique and winning personality. Her films include: *Ben Hur* (1925), *Across the Pacific* (1926), *Bitter Apples* and *The Jazz Singer* (1927), *Beware of Married Men* (1928), *The Desert Song* (1929), *Bride of the Regiment* (1930), *Arrowsmith* and *Body and Soul* (1931), *The Animal Kingdom*, *The Mask of Fu Manchu* and *Vanity Fair* (1932), *Night Flight* and *Topaze* (1933), *Evelyn Prentice*, *Stamboul Quest* and *The Thin Man* (1934), *Whipsaw* (1935), *After the Thin Man*, *The Great Ziegfeld*, *Libelled Lady* and *Wife vs. Secretary* (1936), *Parnell* (1937), *Test Pilot* and *Too Hot to Handle* (1938), *Another Thin Man* and *The Rains Came* (1939), *Third Finger, Left Hand* (1940), *The Thin Man Goes Home* (1944), *The Best Years of Our Lives* (1946), *The Bachelor and the Bobby Soxer* and *The Song of the Thin Man* (1947), *Mr Blandings Builds His Dream House* (1948), *The Red Pony* (1949), *Cheaper By the Dozen* (1956), *The Ambassador's Daughter* (1956), *Midnight Lace* (1960), *The April Fools* (1969), *Airport* (1975), *It's Showtime* (1976), *The End* (1978) and *Just Tell Me What You Want* (1980).

It is amusing that it was an American, **Alexander Mackendrick** – he died on 22 December 1993 at the age of 81 – who should have directed those most British of films, *Whisky Galore* (1949) (entitled *Tight Little Island* in the US), *The Man in the White Suit* (1951), and *The Lady Killers* (1955) for Ealing Studios. But in fact Mackendrick was raised in Scotland and began his working career in advertising. During World War II he made some propaganda shorts, but it was not until 1946 that he joined Ealing Studios under Sir Michael Balcon, for whom he also made *Mandy* (1952), which was released in the US as *The Crash of Silence*. Three years later Ealing was sold to the BBC and Mackendrick left for America, where he made *The Sweet Smell of Success* (1957). He also directed *The Devil's Disciple* (1959), *The Guns of Navarone* (1961), *Sammy Going South* (*A Boy Ten Feet Tall* in the US) (1963), *A High Wind in Jamaica* (1965) and *Don't Make Waves* (1967). This latter was his last film and in 1969 he was appointed Dean of the Film School at the California Institute of Arts.

**Giulietta Masina**, wife, favourite actress and guiding star of husband Federico Fellini (who died in October 1993), died on 23 March 1994 at the age of 74. Those who saw her in Fellini's *La Strada*, as the waif and companion of circus strong man Anthony Quinn, will never forget her wonderful performance in the film, which won an Oscar. Masina made her debut in

*Giulietta Masina*

1942 in a radio play written by fellow-student Fellini. They were married the following year and from then on were inseparable. Her films include: *Paisan* (1946), *Il Bidone* (1955), *Le Notti di Cabiria* – which won her the Best Actress award at the Cannes Film Festival (1956), *Fortunella* (1958), *La Grande Vie* (1960), *Juliet of the Spirits* (1965), *The Madwoman of Chaillot* (1969) and, after nearly a decade of retirement, *Ginger et Fred* (1986).

Internationally famous – and fiery – Greek actress and political activist **Melina Mercouri**, who died, aged 68, on 6 March 1994, will be best remembered in this country for her performance in *Never On Sunday* (1960) which made her an international star and brought her an Oscar nomination. Equally comfortable in comedy and dramatic roles, her *Phaedra* (1962) – again directed by husband Jules Dassin – brought her further acclaim. Both before and after the reign of the infamous *junta* known as the Colonels, Miss Mercouri was a socialist member of the Greek parliament. She became notorious for her struggle – still ongoing at the time of her death – to persuade the British Museum to return the Elgin Marbles to Greece, from whence they had been taken (stolen in Mercouri's words). Apart from her Oscar nomination, Miss Mercouri won the Best Actress award at the Cannes Film Festival. Apart from those mentioned above, her films – around 70 in total – included *Topkapi* (1964), *Once Is Not Enough* (1975) and *Dream of Passion* (1978).

*Melina Mercouri*

A versatile and gifted artiste, Romanian-born **Jean Negulesco** died, aged 93, on 18 July 1993. A painter, stage director, writer and film director in his time, it is as this latter that he will be best remembered, his films including *Johnny Belinda* (1948), *The Mask of Dimitrios* (1944), *The Mudlark* (1950), *Titanic* (1953), *Three Coins in the Fountain* (1954), *Boy on a Dolphin* (1957), and *The Rains of Ranchipur* (1957). His first film in 1941 was *Singapore Woman*, his last in 1970 *The Invisible Six*, though he did subsequently write the screenplay for the 1973 French film *Un Officier de Police sans Importance*. Other films include *The Conspirators* (1944), *Three Strangers* (1946), *Humoresque* (1946), *Daddy Long Legs* (1955), *A Certain Smile* (1958) and *Hello-Goodbye* (1970).

Canadian-born **Cecilia Parker**, who died in July 1993 at the age of 88, was the daughter of a British Army officer. She studied opera at the Toronto Academy of Music but was easily sidetracked into films. She was best known for her role as Mickey Rooney's elder sister in the famous *Andy Hardy* series, which she tried to revive in 1958 in what was to be her final film, *Andy Hardy Comes Home*. She had a tiny debut role in *Women of all Nations* in 1931, but more important roles came in the following year with the Westerns *Rainbow Trail* and *Mystery Ranch*. Other films include *Unknown Valley* (1933), *The Painted Veil* (1934), *Naughty Marietta* and *Ah, Wilderness!* (1935), *Old Hutch* and *Three Live Ghosts* (1936), *A Family Affair* (the first of the Andy Hardy films, 1937), *Grand Central Murder* and *Seven Sweethearts* (1942).

*Cecilia Parker*

**George Peppard**, who died on 8 May 1994 at the age of 65, found fame with important roles in *Breakfast at Tiffany's* (1961) and *The Carpetbaggers* (1964). He found his career tailing off until he gained a new popularity on the small screen in series like *The A-Team*. His original career was to have been in civil engineering (he became a BA) but after graduation he became

*George Peppard*

a disc jockey, turning to acting in the Oregon Shakespeare Festival. He made his Broadway debut in *Girls of Summer*, followed by his screen debut in 1957 in *The Strange One*. In 1978 Peppard directed his only film, *Five Days from Home*. Apart from those mentioned, Peppard's films include: *Pork Chop Hill* (1959), *How the West Was Won* (1962), *Operation Crossbow* (1965), *The Blue Max* (1966), *Tobruk* (1967), *What's So Bad About Feeling Good?* (1968), *The Executioner* (1970), *Newman's Law* (1974), *Damnation Alley* (1977), *Battle Beyond the Stars* (1980), *Target Eagle* (1982) and his last film *Night of the Fox* (1990).

**River Phoenix**, who died sensationally on the sidewalk outside an LA night club on 31 October 1993, aged 23, was one of tinseltown's most promising and versatile young actors. He made his screen debut in *Explorers* in 1985. But it was in his next film, the sensitive and unforgettable *Stand By Me* (1986), the story of four teenagers camping by a mysterious pool, that he showed his full promise, which was later confirmed by his performance in Peter Weir's *The Mosquito Coast* that same year. His other films were *Little Nikita, A Night in the Life of Jimmy Reardon* and *Running On Empty* (all 1988), *Indiana Jones and the Last Crusade* (1989), *I Love You To Death* (1990) and *Dogfight* (1991). For his role in *Running On Empty* he was nominated for the Best Supporting Actor award in the 1989 Oscars. At the time of his death he was still working on what was to be his last film, *Dark Blood.*

**Vincent Price**, who died, aged 82, on 25 October 1993, must have led a pretty hectic life. Apart from the 130 films in which he appeared, there were his numerous stage roles (including musicals and a one-man show about Oscar Wilde), more than 2000 TV shows, and some 1000 radio programmes. He was an authority on art, a subject on which, along with cookery, he gave public lectures and wrote books – in all, a formidable list. Born into a successful business family, the young Price studied art at the Universities of Yale, London and Nuremberg. He bought his first original etching when he was only 12 and from then on amassed a considerable art collection. His original intention was to become a painter, but he gave up the idea when he came to the conclusion he was not good enough to earn his living. So he turned to the acting profession, making his first professional appearance in London's West End in a play entitled *Chicago* (which, incidentally, starred John Gielgud). He had a personal triumph playing Prince Albert in *Victoria Regina*, a role he repeated in the Broadway production. For the next decade he divided his time between films and stage productions (including Orson Welles's Mercury Theater plays). It was his performance in the 1953 horror classic *House of Wax* that was to typecast him, reinforced by his appearance in Roger Corman's Edgar Allan Poe tinglers *The House of Usher* and *The Raven*. Price's final screen role was in a horror thriller, entitled *Edward Scissorhands*. One of the secrets of his success in this kind of movie was undoubtedly that while scaring the pants off his audience Price was obviously not taking it too seriously; there was always an element of self parody in his performance. Price served on the boards of the Los Angeles Museum of Art and the Museum of Latin Arts and Crafts. In

*River Phoenix*

*Rene Ray*

1962 he joined the famous firm of Sears and Roebuck, to select and buy paintings for them. His many films included *Service de Luxe* (1938) (his Hollywood debut), *Tower of London* (1939), *Hudson's Bay* and *The Invisible Man Returns* (1940), *The Song of Bernadette* (1943), *Laura* (1944), *Dragonwyck* (1946), *The Three Musketeers* (1948), *House of Wax* (1953), *The Ten Commandments* (1956), *The Fly* (1958), *The Bat* (1959), *The Tingler* (1959), *House of Usher* (1960), *The Pit and the Pendulum* (1961), *Tales of Terror* (1962), *The Masque of the Red Death* (1964), *The Abominable Doctor Phibes* (1971), *Theatre of Blood* (1973), *Journey Into Fear* (1976), *The Monster Club* (1981), *The Whales of August* (1987) and *Edward Scissorhands* (1990).

*Vincent Price*

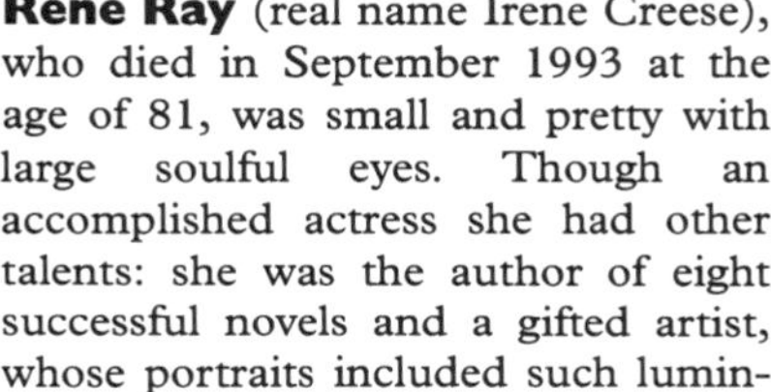

**Rene Ray** (real name Irene Creese), who died in September 1993 at the age of 81, was small and pretty with large soulful eyes. Though an accomplished actress she had other talents: she was the author of eight successful novels and a gifted artist, whose portraits included such luminaries as Albert Einstein. She was devoted to the theatre however, and at an early age was starring on Broadway and in London's West End. In the 1930s she went to live in Hollywood but at the outbreak of World War II returned to Britain to join ENSA, to entertain the troops. After the war she remained in this country concentrating increasingly on writing. Her films include *The Rat* (with Anton Walbrook, 1937), *The Green Cockatoo* (with John Mills, 1937), *If Winter Comes* (1947) and *The Good Die Young* (1953). In 1963 she retired to Jersey, where she died.

*Gilbert Roland*

Although he made around 70 films during his long career (which began in the silent era with *The Plastic Age* in 1925) handsome hero **Gilbert Roland** (real name Luis Antonio Damaso de Alonso), who died on 15 May 1994 at the age of 88, will be best remembered for his *Cisco Kid* films, of which he made eleven. Two of his most critically acclaimed movies were *Camille* in 1927, with Norma Talmadge, and 1951's *The Bullfighter and the Lady.* It is interesting to note, by the way, that Roland's father was actually a bullfighter and his son was initially trained for the same profession. Amongst his later films were John Ford's *Cheyenne Autumn* in 1964, *Captain Kidd* with Charles Laughton in 1945 and *The Sea Hawk* with Errol Flynn in 1940. His final film was *Barbarosa* in 1982.

*Cesar Romero*

The self-styled 'Latin from Manhattan' **Cesar Romero** died on 1 January 1994 at the age of 86. Romero was born of Cuban émigré parents in New York, and although untrained, he began his career as a dancer in night clubs, dance halls and stage musicals. He made his screen debut in 1933 in *The Shadow Laughs*. His early successes were in the *Cisco Kid* movies, first in supporting roles and then in the title role. He also appeared in *The Thin Man*. Romero never became a star (one theory was that there was always a degree of self-mockery in his playing) although at one time he was hailed as the new Valentino. He seldom – if indeed ever – won the girl in his films, though he did inject a certain romance into them, and in real life he never married. His films include: *Clive of India* (1935), *Love Before Breakfast* (1936), *Dangerously Yours* (1937), *Five of a Kind* (1938), *The Cisco Kid and the Lady* (the first time he played the title role, 1939), *He Married His Wife* (1940), *Tall, Dark and Handsome* and *Weekend in Havana* (1941), *Tales of Manhattan* (1942), *Coney Island* (1943), *Captain from Castille* (1948), *The Beautiful Blonde from Bashful Bend* (1949), *Vera Cruz* (1954), *Around the World in 80 ays* (1956), *Donovan's Reef* (1963), *Batman* (1966), *The Spectre of Edgar Allan Poe* (1973) and *The Strongest Man in the World* (1975). Romero made a few British films including *Scotland Yard Inspector* (1952), *Shadow Man* (1953) and *Crooks and Coronets* (1969).

**Telly Savalas** (whose real forename was Aristotle), who died on 22 January 1994 at the age of 70, will always be remembered as Kojak, the tough but sometimes tender-hearted, lollipop-sucking New York cop in the popular TV series of that name. Of Greek extraction, Savalas was a GI in World War II after university, and won a Purple Heart for being injured in action. His first post-war job was with the US State Department's Information Office; later he joined ABC TV as a director of news and special

*Telly Savalas*

*Barry Sullivan*

events. He left following a policy dispute, and tried his hand at theatrical direction and drama teaching before settling down as an actor, being cast mainly in 'heavy' roles. His first feature opportunity came in Burt Lancaster's *Birdman of Alcatraz*, for which he won a Supporting Actor Oscar nomination, in 1962. Other of his films include *Cape Fear* (1962), *Johnny Cool* (1963, one of three films he made that year), *The Greatest Story Ever Told* – in which, as Pontius Pilate, he first shaved his head – *Genghis Khan* and *The Battle of the Bulge* (1965), *Beau Geste* (1966), *The Dirty Dozen* (1967), *Sol Madrid* (1968), *Buona Sera Mrs Campbell* and *Mackenna's Gold* (1969) and *The Border* (1979). Savalas also appeared in a number of Spanish, Italian and other European movies including four made in Britain – *Sophie's Place* and *On Her Majesty's Secret Service* in 1969, *Land Raiders* in 1970 and *Escape to Athens* in 1979. He first appeared as Kojak in the TV feature *The Marcus Nelson Murders* and made such an impression that it was decided to follow up with an hour-long episode about the same character. He appeared regularly as Kojak from 1972 onwards, and his trademarks of a shaven pate, lollipop on a stick and the expression 'Who loves ya baby?' became famous and helped him create an unforgettable character. TV and the cinema will be the less entertaining without him.

**Barry Sullivan** (real name Patrick Barry), who died in mid-June 1994 at the age of 81, was a tough-guy actor who was equally at home in the role of hero or villain. He was a cinema attendant and a buyer for a general store before making his acting debut on Broadway in 1936 in *The Caine Mutiny*. In the early 1940s he moved to Hollywood where he made his film debut in *Woman of the Town* in 1943. He had a starring role in *The Great Gatsby* (1949). Among his other films were *Skirts Ahoy!* (1952), *The Bad and the Beautiful* (1952), *Queen Bee* (1955), *A Gathering of Eagles* (1963), *An American Dream* (1966), *The Savage Land* (1969), *Tell Them Willie Boy is Here* (1970), *Earthquake* (1974), *The Human Factor* (1975), and *Caravans* (1978). In all, Sullivan made around 50 feature films as well as a great deal of TV.

It is particularly sad that actor-director **Sam Wanamaker** – who died on 18 December 1993 at the age of 74 after a 5-year fight against cancer – should have lost his fight for life before his long campaign to build a replica of an Elizabethan playhouse on the South Bank of the Thames, could be finished. An American-born but resident in London for many years, Wanamaker came to Britain to escape Senator McCarthy's ill-famed persecution of suspected left-wing actors and directors in the US. He found it difficult, however, to get film work here for quite some time and turned to the theatre, where he achieved considerable success. Eventually the political climate changed and Wanamaker found film work again, achieving some notable performances, though his efforts at direction were generally less successful. Meanwhile he had become interested in the Globe Theatre project, and though he never saw it completed, he did have the satisfaction of seeing the first stage accomplished, marked by an unveiling ceremony by Prince Edward in 1993. Wanamaker was awarded the honour of being made a member of the Order of the British Empire. Of his three daughters, one, Zoe, has become a successful actress. His films include: *My Girl Tisa* (1948), *Give Us This Day* (1949), *The Spy Who Came in from the Cold* (1965), *The File of the Golden Goose* (which he also directed, 1969), *The Executioner* (also directed, 1970), *The Sell Out* and *Voyage of the Damned* (1976), *Private Benjamin* (1980), *Raw Deal* (1986), *Baby Boom* and *Superman IV* (1987), *Judgment in Berlin* (1988), *Cognac* (1990) and *Guilty By Suspicion* (1991). Wanamaker also acted in and produced a considerable number of TV features and directed operas at Covent Garden Opera House, as well as in San Francisco, Chicago and Sydney.

*Sam Wanamaker*

The last time I met **Mai Zetterling** – who died aged 68 on 25 March 1994 – was in a rain-misted Kensington High Street; with neither hat nor umbrella, and wearing an old raincoat, she looked anything but the lovely seductive film star that she was. But there were always two Zetterlings: the one, a glamorous film and stage star, the other a serious, dedicated and highly intelligent writer and director whose work sometimes bore traces of Bergman-like intensity. She was in fact a highly talented lady. Born in Vasteras in Sweden, she made her first stage appearance in Stockholm when she was sixteen, and quickly became a contract artist with the Swedish Royal Theatre. In 1943 she appeared in the film *Frenzy*, directed by Alf Sjöberg from a script by the then unknown Ingmar Bergman. She followed this in 1947 with the title role in *Frieda*, beating several German stars anxious for the part. This brought her the Best Actress of the Year award and a seven-year contract from Rank, who often used her in wholly unsuitable roles, though she shone in a few like Somerset Maugham's *Quartet*. She appeared, with great success, in as many stage productions as Rank would allow, gathering critical acclaim in plays such as *The Wild Duck*, *The Seagull*, *A Doll's House* and Strindberg's *Creditors*. In Hollywood, which she hated, she made *Knock on Wood* (1954) with Danny Kaye and *Seven Waves Away* (1957) with Tyrone Power, who became her lover. When she married her second husband, Welsh writer David Hughes, they planned her future as a director and together they made a series of BBC documentaries. Her first feature, *Loving Couples*, won a prize in Vienna and a ban for its supposed obscenity. *Night Games*, based on her own novel, was banned from the Cannes Film Festival for similar reasons. These and later films suggest that she was influenced by Bergman, Sartre and the Feminist movement. Her films include: *Giftas* (1955), *The Truth About Women* (1958), *The Main Attraction* (1962), *The Girls* (direction and screenplay, 1968), *Visions of Eight* (direction, 1973), *We Have Many Faces* (direction and screenplay, 1975), *Of Seals and Man* (direction, 1978), *Love* (direction and screenplay, 1981), *Scrubbers* (direction and screenplay, 1982), *Amarosa* (direction, story, screenplay and editing, 1986), *Hidden Agenda* (1990) and *The Witches* (1990).

*Mai Zetterling*

## Others who have died during the year include:

**Michael Aldrich**, who died in early 1994, was essentially a man of the theatre but made a considerable number of films including *Murder in the Cathedral* (1952), *The Public Eye* (1971) and *Clockwise* (1986).

**Jean-Louis Barrault**, the last of the great actor-managers, who died towards the end of January 1994 at the age of 83, will be most vividly remembered by moviegoers for his outstanding mime performance in the classic *Les Enfants du Paradis* (1945). He gave some notable performances in more than sixty films, including *Drôle de Drame* (1937) and *Mademoiselle Docteur* (1938). He also appeared in *The Longest Day* in 1962.

**Roy Budd**, self-taught pianist, the son of a Surrey grocer, who died late July 1983, at the age of 46, found international fame as a composer of film music. He scored more than fifty films, including the British *Get Carter*, *The Wild Geese* and *Who Dares Wins*. For Hollywood he composed the music for a number of movies including *Catlow*, *Stone Killer*, and *Marseilles Killer*. In addition he wrote the music for many TV series.

**Pat Buttram**, actor and comedian, who in the 50s was Western star Gene Autry's saddle-pal and sidekick, died on 8 January 1994 at the age of 78. He appeared in some 40 Autry features as well as in Autry's stage shows. He was also a popular TV performer in his own right.

**Jean Carmet**, very popular French actor-comedian who made more than two hundred films, won two Césars (for Hossein's *Les Misérables* and *Merci la Vie*) and became internationally famous. He was 73 when he died on 12 April 1994. He made his screen debut in *Les Enfants du Paradis* in 1944.

**Janet Chandler**, who died 6 April 1994 at the age of 78, starred in Douglas Fairbanks Senior's *The Three Musketeers* and was leading lady in George O'Brien's *The Golden West*. She bowed out of the movies in the mid-1930s.

**Kenneth Connor**, the comic actor who made his theatrical debut at the Old Vic and ended up as one of the stalwarts of the famed British 'Carry On' films, died on 28 November 1993, at the age of 77. Connor appeared in the first 'Carry On' film *Carry on Sergeant* in 1958 and thereafter was a regular in the series of farces. He also appeared in many other British comedies, including Ealing's *The Lady Killers*, and did a lot of television work. He was awarded the MBE in 1991 for his services to show business.

**William Conrad**, best known in Britain as the fat and food-loving detective Cannon in the TV series, died on 11 February 1994 at the age of 73. A United States Army fighter pilot during World War II, he became a popular radio, TV and film star. He was the original Marshal Dillon in the TV series

*Gunsmoke* for eleven years. Later he became a film and TV actor, director and producer. As an actor, his movies include *Sorry, Wrong Number* and *Joan of Arc* (1948), *East Side, West Side* (1949), *Cry Danger* (1951), *The Desert Song* (1953), and *Johnny Concho* (1956) as director, *My Blood Runs Cold* (1965), *An American Dream* (1966) and *An Assignment to Kill* (1969).

**Lili Damita** (real name Liliane Marie Madeleine Carre) began as a French music hall actress at the age of sixteen and became the star of the Casino de Paris. She started making films in 1921, in France, Austria and Germany and was brought to Hollywood by Samuel Goldwyn. She made headlines as the tempestuous wife of Errol Flynn. Her American films include *The Bridge of San Luis Rey* (1929), *Friends and Lovers* (1931), *This Is the Night* (1932), *Brewster's Millions* (1935) and *The Devil on Horseback* (1936).

**Royal Dano**, the veteran character actor, died 15 May 1994 at the age of 71. His first appearance before the camera was in 1950 in *Undercover Girl*, his last in *The Right Stuff* in 1983. He was in *The Red Badge of Courage* (1951), *Moby Dick* (1956), *King of Kings* (1961) and *The Outlaw Josey Wales* (1976), among many outstanding movies.

**Don Defore**, who died 22 December 1993 at the age of 80, was best known in America for his considerable TV work, but he made more than a score of movies starring actors like John Wayne and Spencer Tracy.

**Curly-Joe De Rita**, who died in July 1993, at the age of 83, was the last surviving member of the Three Stooges comedy team. Originally a stage act, they went on to make some 200 short films, as well as several features, including *The Three Stooges Meet Hercules* in 1961 and *The Three Stooges in Orbit* the following year. Presenters of crude slapstick, the Stooges have become cult figures.

A former comedy writer for Hal Roach, **Gordon Douglas**, who died, aged 85, on 30 September 1993, directed 30 of the *Our Gang* comedy shorts (one of which won him an Oscar) before graduating to feature films, which included *Yellowstone Kelly* (1959), *Rio Conchos* (1964), *I Was a Communist for the FBI* and *In Like Flint* (1967).

**Lynne Frederick**, actress, former wife of Peter Sellers, who died on 27 April 1994 at the age of 39. Her films include *No Blade of Grass* (1970), *Vampire Circus* (1971), *The Voyage of the Damned* (1976) and the 1979 remake of *The Prisoner of Zenda* (with Sellers).

**Betty Furness**, who died 11 April 1994 at the age of 78, made 36 Hollywood movies in her six-year career before becoming President Johnson's Special Assistant for Consumer Affairs and a fund-raiser for the US Democratic Party. Films include *Magnificent Obsession* (1935), *Swing Time* (1936) with Fred Astaire and Ginger Rogers and *North of Shanghai* (1939).

**Frances Gifford** (real name Mary Frances Gifford), who died early in 1994, aged 73, first gained fame as the heroine of the *Jungle Girl* series in 1941. She subsequently made a number of films including *Mr Smith Goes to Washington* (1939), *Tarzan Triumphs* and *Cry Havoc* (1941), *The Glass Key* (1944) and *Luxury Liner* (1948), the year in which she was seriously injured in a car crash, causing her to spend a long time in hospital. She made only two more films after this; the last was *Sky Commando* in 1953.

Screenwriter, producer and director **Sidney Gilliat**, who died at the end of May 1994, aged 86, was the long-time associate of Frank Launder with whom he made a number of noteworthy British films. He met Launder in 1929 during the making of *Under the Greenwood Tree* and during the next 40 years made 26 movies with him, including *Millions Like Us* (1943), *Waterloo Road* (1944), *The Rake's Progress* (1945), *Captain Boycott* (1947), *The Blue Lagoon* (1949), *State Secret* (1950), *Lady Godiva Rides Again* (1951), *The Story of Gilbert and Sullivan* (1953), *Belles of St Trinians* (the first of the *St Trinians* series), *The Smallest Show on Earth* (1957) and *The Lady Vanishes* (1979).

**Fred** (Frederick Hubbard) **Gwynne**, on 2 July 1993, at the age of 66. Best known for his performance as the lovable ghoul in the TV series *The Munsters.* Made his screen debut in *On the Waterfront*, and his last film was *My Cousin Vinny.* A popular writer of children's books, which he generally illustrated; the last, *Easy To See Why*, was published in late 1993. Appeared in numerous films and stage plays.

**James Leo Herlihy**, who died in November 1993, was a playwright, author and occasional actor, best known to moviegoers for his performance in *Midnight Cowboy* (1965) which was based on his own novel.

Milan-born **Joseph Janni** came to Britain in 1939 and was promptly arrested, spending the best part of the next six years in an internment camp! Released in 1947, he formed Victoria Films and produced the classic *The Glass Mountain.* Deaf to the siren call of Hollywood, he stayed in Britain to produce a noteworthy series of British films, including *A Town Like Alice* (1956), *Robbery Under Arms* (1957), *A Kind of Loving* (1962), *Billy Liar* (1963), *Poor Cow* (1967), *Darling* (1965), *Sunday, Bloody Sunday* (1971), *Far From the Madding Crowd* (1967) and in 1979 his final film, *Yanks* at the end of which he suffered a stroke. He was 78 when he died on 2 June 1994.

**Elmer Klos**, the Czech director and scenarist, died late July 1993 in Prague at the age of 83. His output of a dozen films included his Oscar-winning *The Shop on Main Street* in 1966. Banned from film work by the Communist régime, he was restored to the Czech Film Faculty after two decades, in 1989. He worked in close collaboration for many years with the Slovak director Jan Kadar.

**Charles Lamont**, who died on 12 September 1993 at the age of 98, directed more than a hundred movies, including almost all of the Abbott and Costello comedies. He was also responsible for many of the Ma and Pa Kettle series. Actor, prop man and assistant director, he began his career in 1922, graduating to features from handling Mack Sennett comedy shorts.

**Fernand Ledoux**, well-known and prolific stage and screen actor, died on 31 September 1993 at the age of 96. He gained acclaim for his first starring role in Jean Renoir's 1938 film *La Bête Humaine.* Also appeared in *Mayerling* (1936), *La Fille du Diable* (1946), *Les Misérables*

(1958), *The Longest Day* (1962), *Peau d'Ane* (1971) and some forty other films.

**George** (Spanky) **McFarland**, died 30 June 1993 at the age of 64. Was one of the famous 'Our Gang', featuring in the early Hal Roach series of films. He retired from the screen while still a teenager.

Essentially a stage actor, **Jeff Morrow** died on 26 December 1993 at the age of 86. Tempted to Hollywood in the 1950s, he appeared in both star roles and supporting parts, beginning with *The Robe* in 1953. Other films included *Captain Lightfoot* (1955) and *The Story of Ruth* (1960). He was a familiar face in science-fiction movies and did a great deal of TV work.

**Esther Ralston**, the silent screen star, died in January 1994 at the age of 91. She started her career at the age of two, when she was added to the family's vaudeville act billed as 'Baby Esther'. She appeared in Chaplin's *The Kid* (1928) and many other films including *A Kiss for Cinderella* (1925) and some early talkies including the British-made *Rome Express* (1932). Though she retired in 1941 she continued to appear in radio soap operas. Later she became a talent scout in New York. She was known as 'The American Venus' after appearing in a film of that title, made in 1926.

Cinematographer **Claude Renoir**, who died in September 1993 at the age of 79, was the nephew of director Jean Renoir and grandson of the famous artist Auguste, from whom he inherited a wonderful sense of colour. His first colour film was his uncle's *The River*, made in India and generally thought to be his masterpiece. Claude Renoir worked for a number of the foremost directors and his photography was often the best part of the movie. To quote writer-director Bryan Forbes, he literally painted with light.

**Dorothy Revier** (real name Doris Velegra), who died in December 1993 at the age of 89, was a star of the silent screen and early talkies. A former cabaret dancer, she made her screen debut in 1922 in *The Broadway Madonna*. She usually played the blonde vamp, as her films *The Tigress* and *The Siren* (1927) suggest. Her roles declined in the 30s and she ended up playing in Buck Jones Westerns.

**Fernando Rey** (born Fernando Casado Arambillet), who died on 9 March 1994 at the age of 76, was Spain's most internationally famous actor. He was Luis Buñuel's favourite male performer and appeared in a number of his films. His films, in excess of a hundred, were made in Spain, France, Italy, Germany and America. They include *Viridiana* (1961), *The French Connection* (1971), *Antony and Cleopatra* (1972), *The Discreet Charm of the Bourgeoisie* (1972), *Voyage of the Damned* (1976), *That Obscure Object of Desire* (1977), *Angel of Death* (1987) and *Naked Tango* (1990). His final film, *At the Other End of the Tunnel*, was premiered in Spain a few weeks before his death.

**Heather Sears**, the British star who was called 'The Thinking Actress' and gained some high critical praise for her stage performances, made some dozen films before she died in mid-January 1994 at the age of 57. Her films include *The Story of Esther Costello* (1957) and *Room at the Top* (1957), *Sons and Lovers* (1960), *The Phantom of the Opera* (1962) and *Great Expectations* (1975).

**Anne Shirley** (real name Dawn Paris) was aged 74 when she died on 4 July 1993. Made a big success in *Anne of Green Gables* and *Stella Dallas*, winning an Oscar nomination in 1937 for the latter. Her last film was *Farewell My Lovely* after which she retired, in 1944.

**Anna Sten**, who died on 12 November 1993, aged 85, was the Russian actress whom Sam Goldwyn hoped to promote as another Greta Garbo. But somehow, in spite of some good performances, the public never took to her and finally Goldwyn had to admit he had made a mistake and terminated her contract. She won good reviews from the critics for her performance opposite Gary Cooper in *The Wedding* but the moviegoers remained unconvinced and she slipped into obscurity.

**Gerald Thomas**, who died at the beginning of November 1993, aged 72, was best known as the director of the famous British 'Carry On' movies which were premiered at the rate of about two a year between 1958 and 1978. Born in Hull, Thomas entered the world of film as an assistant editor, but in 1956 directed his first film *Circus Friends*. His first 'Carry On' was *Carry on Sergeant*, which was a great success, and so began the series of broad, farcical comedies. They seldom met with critical acclaim but they pleased the public and made a fortune for Thomas.

**Bill Travers**, the British feature player who died in late March 1994 at the age of 72, is best known for his performance with his wife Virginia McKenna in the famous 'lion' film *Born Free* (1966). In recent years he had devoted all his time to animal welfare. Films include *The Wooden Horse* (1950), *The Browning Version* (1951), *Romeo and Juliet* (1954), *Bhowani Junction* (1956), *The Barretts of Wimpole Street* (1957), *The Green Helmet* (1961), *Ring of Bright Water* (1969), *An Elephant Called Slowly* (1970), *The Belstone Fox* (1973) and *Christian the Lion* (1976).

Said to have been the model for the Lady with the Lamp, the Columbia Pictures trade mark, **Evelyn Venable** died in March 1994 at the age of 80. The voice of the Blue Fairy in Disney's *Pinocchio* (1940), her other films include *Cradle Song* (1933), *Alice Adams* (1935), *The Hollywood Stadium Mystery* (1938), *Heritage of the Desert* (1939), *Lucky Cisco Kid* (1940) and *He Hired the Boss* (1943). She subsequently retired and taught at the University of California.

Though known mostly as a stage and television actress, **Gwen Watford** did appear in a number of British films, including *The Very Edge* (1962), *Cleopatra* (1963) and *Cry Freedom* (1987). She died, aged 66, early in February 1994.

**Richard Wordsworth**, who died late November 1993, aged 78, was the great-great grandson of the poet, who bought the latter's Lake District house and founded the International Wordsworth Summer Conference, now in its 23rd year. An actor, he appeared in numerous films including *The Man Who Knew Too Much* (1934) and *The Quatermass Experiment* (1955).

# Bookshelf

## Ivan Butler

Owing partly to the passage of the years, I have had reluctantly to give up my individual reviews of cinema books – though a list of titles, authors and publishers for the current year will be found at the end of this section. To mark *Film Review*'s fiftieth anniversary (and Bookshelf's twentieth), however, I have made a personal selection of books reviewed in past issues that for one reason or another I have found memorable. During the period 1973–93 I have covered some 1,700 titles, making the task of selecting around 150 a formidable as well as a heart-searching one.

My first contribution to *Film Review* was in the 1968–9 volume, on the 'Story of the Picture Palace' – this was followed by articles on various cinematic subjects, until the launching of 'Film Books of the Year' in 1973–4. The first one reviewed was Mary Astor's *A Life on Film* (an illustrated hardback, at £3). The top price of the year was £7 for Roger Manvell's large-scale and beautifully produced *The International Encyclopedia of Film*; and *Film Review* itself cost £3.50.

Some of the earlier publications, regrettably, will be out of print, but there is always the chance of discovering them in second-hand bookshops, the catalogues of specialist dealers, or in libraries, particularly that of the indispensable British Film Institute. Dates refer to the edition of *Film Review* in which the book was originally reviewed.

### Biography, Memoirs

**Being and Becoming**, Myrna Loy and James Kotsibas-Davis; 1988–9.
**Bette Davis**, Christopher Nickens; 1986–7.
**C. B. deMille**, Charles Higham; 1985–6.
**Celia Johnson**, Kate Fleming; 1992–3.
**Chaplin – His Life and Art**, Derek Robinson; 1985–6.
**Dark Star – The Meteoric Rise and Eclipse of John Gilbert**, Leatrice Gilbert Fountain; 1986–7.
**David Lean**, Stephen M. Silverman; 1990–1.
**The Divine Garbo**, Frederick Sands and Sven Broman; 1980–1.
**Dorothy and Lillian Gish**, Lillian Gish; 1974–5.
**D. W. Griffith and the Birth of Film**, Richard Schickel; 1984–5.
**Elizabeth Taylor**, Kitty Kelley; 1982–3.
**Emlyn Williams**, James Harding; 1993–4.
**Fatal Charm** (The Life of Rex

Harrison), Alexander Walker; 1993–4.
**Fritz Lang**, Lotte H. Eisner; 1977–8.
**George Sanders – An Exhausted Life**, Richard van der Beets; 1992–3.
**The Hustons**, Lawrence Grobel; 1990–1.
**Ingmar Bergman**, Peter Cowie; 1983–4.
**Jacques Tati – Frame by Frame**, James Harding; 1985–6.
**James Mason – Odd Man Out**, Sheridan Morley; 1988–9.
**James Whale**, James Curtis; 1983–4.
**Jessie Matthews**, Frank Thornton; 1975–6.
**J. Stuart Blackton**, Marian Blackton Trimble; 1986–7.
**Laurel and Hardy**, John McCabe, Al Kilgore, Richard W. Bann; 1976–7.
**The Life of Alfred Hitchcock**, Donald Spoto; 1984–5.
**Louise Brooks**, Barry Paris; 1990–1.
**The Man Between – Carol Reed**, Nicholas Wapshott; 1988–9.
**Marilyn Monroe**, Donald Spoto; 1993–4.
**Mary Pickford**, Scott Eyman; 1993–4.
**The Merchant of Dreams – L. B. Mayer**, Charles Higham; 1993–4.
**Noel Coward**, Clive Fisher; 1993–4.
**Norma Shearer**, Gavin Lambert; 1993–4.
**Olivier**, Anthony Holden; 1988–9.
**Orson Welles**, Barbara Leaming; 1985–6.
**Red – The Tempestuous Life of Susan Hayward**, Robert La Guardia and Gene Anceri; 1987–8.
**Rex Ingram**, Liam O'Leary; 1979–80.
**Tallulah**, Brendan Gill; 1974–5.
**Vivien**, Alexander Walker; 1988–9.
**William Desmond Taylor**, Bruce Long; 1992–3.
**The Zanucks of Hollywood**, Marlys J. Harris; 1990–1.

## History, Criticism, Analysis

**About John Ford**, Lindsay Anderson; 1972–3.
**Adventures with D. W. Griffith**, 1988–9.
**The Art of Alfred Hitchcock**, Donald Spoto; 1978–9.
**Beyond Ballyhoo – promotional excesses**, Mark Thomas McGee; 1990–1.
**The BFI Companion to the Western**, ed. Edward Buscombe; 1989–90.
**Big Bad Wolves**, Joan Mellen; 1978–9.
**The Big V**, Anthony Slide; 1988–9.
**Caligari's Children**, S. S. Prawer; 1980–1.
**City of Nets**, Otto Friedrich; 1988–9.
**The Clockwork Orange**, Stanley Kubrick; 1973–4.
**The Complete Films of Laurence Olivier**, 1993–4.
**The Day the Laughter Stopped – the Arbuckle Scandal**, David A. Yallop; 1975–6.
**Early Women Directors**, Anthony Slide 1978–9.
**Fifty Great American Silent Films – 1912–1920**, Anthony Slide and Edward Wagenknecht; 1981–2.
**Filming Literature – The Art of Screen Adaptation**, Neil Sinyard; 1987–8.
**The Films of Christopher Lee**, R. W. Rohle, Jr and J. C. Hart, with the participation of Christopher Lee; 1984–5.
**Forties Film Talk**, Doug McClelland; 1993–4.
**The Great British Films**, Jerry Vermilye; 1979–80.
**Hitchcock**, François Truffaut; 1986–7.
**Hollywood Destinies – European Directors in America 1922–1931**, Graham Petrie; 1986–7.
**Hollywood, England – The British Film Industry in the Sixties**, Alexander Walker; 1975–6.
**Hollywood Gothic**, David Skal; 1992–3.
**The Hollywood Musical**, Clive Hirschhorn; 1991–2.
**The Hollywood Studios**, Roy Pickard; 1979–80.
**Hollywood – The Pioneers**, Kevin Brownlow; 1980–81.
**Horror**, ed. Phil Hardy; 1987–8.
**Horror Film Directors 1931–1990**, Dennis Fisher; 1992–3.
**Inside Oscar**, Mason Wiley and Damien Bone; 1986–7.
**International Dictionary of Films and Filmmakers** (4 volumes + index); 1991–2, 1992–3, 1993–4, 1994–5.
**The International Encyclopedia of Film**, ed. Roger Manvell; 1973–4.
**International Film Guide**, *see* Variety International Film Guide.
**Karloff and Lugosi – The Story of a Haunting Collaboration**, Gregory William Mank; 1990–1.
**The MGM Story**, John Douglas Eames and Ronald Bergan; 1991–2.
**The Movies**, Richard Griffith, Arthur Mayer and Eileen Bowser; 1983–4.
**Movie Magic**, John Brosnan; 1975–6.
**The Oscars**, Anthony Holden; 1993–4.
**The Parade's Gone By**, Kevin Brownlow; 1990–1.
**The Paramount Story**, John Douglas Eames; 1986–7.
**A Pictorial History of the Silent Screen**, Daniel Blum; 1982–3.
**The Primal Scream**, John Brosnan; 1992–3.
**The Psychotronic Encyclopedia of Film**, M. Weldon; 1990–1.
**The RKO Story**, Richard B. Jewell and Vernon Harbin; 1983–4.
**Samuel Goldwyn Presents**, Alvin H. Marill; 1978–9.
**Scandinavian Cinema**, Peter Cowie; 1993–4.
**Shoot-Em-Ups**, Les Adams and Buck Rainey; 1980–1.
**The Shoot-Em-Ups Ride Again**, Buck Rainey; 1992–3.
**Silent Portraits**, Anthony Slide; 1992–3.
**The Spaghetti Westerns – The Good, the Bad and the Violent**; Thomas Weisser, 1993–4.
**The Story of Cinema**, David Shipman; Vol. 1: 1983–4, Vol. 2: 1985–6.
**That Was Hollywood – the 1930s**, Allen Eyles; 1988–9.
**Travels in Greeneland – The Cinema of Graham Greene**, Quentin Falk, 1985–6.
**The United Artists Story**, Ronald Bergan; 1987–8.
**The Universal Story**, Clive Hirschhorn; 1984–5.
**The Vampire Film**, Alain Silver and James Ursini; 1976–7.
**Visions of Yesterday**, Jeffrey Richards; 1974–5.
**The Warner Bros Story**, Clive Hirschhorn; 1980–1.

## Reference

**The American Film Industry – A Historical Dictionary**, Anthony Slide; 1987–8.
**The 'B' Directors – A Biographical Directory**; 1986–7.
**British Film Actors' Credits**, Scott Palmer; 1989–90.
**Cinema – A Critical Dictionary**, Richard Roud; 1980–1.
**Cinema Sequels and Remakes**, R. A. and G. W. Nowlan; 1989–90.
**The Columbia Checklist**, Leo D. Martin; 1992–3.
**Eighty Silent Film Stars**, George A. Katchmer; 1992–3.
**Encyclopedia of the Musical Film**, Stanley Green; 1982–3.
**Enser's Filmed Books and Plays**, revised and updated by Ellen Baskin and Mandy Hicken; 1993–4.
**Filmarama – The Flaming Years, 1920–1929**, John Stewart; 1978–9. (Note, a previous volume, **The Formidable Years, 1893–1919**, mentioned but not reviewed, was published in 1975)
**Film Directors and their Films**, Alison J. Filmer and Andre Golay; 1990–1.
**Film Directors Guide – Western Europe**, James Robert Parish; 1977–8.
**Foreign Film Guide**, Ronald Bergan and Robyn Karney; 1989–90.
**The Fox Girls**, James Robert Parish; 1973–4.
**The Great Movie Stars**, David Shipman; Vol. 1, 'The Golden Years' 1980–1, Vol. 2, 'The International Years' 1981–2.
**Illustrated Directory of Film Character Actors**, David Quinlan; 1986–7.
**Illustrated Directory of Film Comedy Stars**, David Quinlan; 1993–4.
**Illustrated Directory of Film Stars**, David Quinlan; 1992–3.
**Illustrated Guide to Film Directors**, David Quinlan; 1984–5.
**The Illustrated Who's Who of the Cinema**, Ann Lloyd and Graham Fuller; 1984–5.
**The Illustrated Who's Who in British Films**, Denis Gifford; 1979–80.
**The International Film Encyclopedia**, Ephraim Katz; 1981–2.
**International Film Prizes**, Tad Bentley Hammer; 1992–3.
**Masters of Lens and Light**, William Darby; 1992–3.
**The MGM Stock Company**, James Robert Parish; 1974–5.
**The Monogram Checklist**, Ted Okula; 1988–9.
**The Motion Picture Guide**, J. Robert Nash and Stanley Ralph Ross (12 volumes); 1987–8.
**The Motion Picture Guide Annual** – follow-up volumes to the above; 1991–2, 1992–3, 1993–4.
**Motion Picture Players' Credits**, Jeffrey Oliviero; 1991–2.
**The Paramount Pretties**, James Robert Parish; 1973–4.
**Science Fiction, Horror and Fantasy Films**, Harris M. Lentz; Vols. 1 & 2, 1984–5; Supplement, 1989–90.
**Screen World** (Annual), John Willis; reviewed throughout the period.
**Sound Films 1927–1939 – A US Filmography**, Alan J. Fetrow; 1993–4.
**Sports Films – A Complete Reference**, Harvey M. Zucker and L. J. Babich; 1988–9.
**Sweethearts of the Sage**, Buck Rainey; 1993–4.
**Those Fabulous Serial Heroines**, Buck Rainey; 1991–2.
**2000 Movies – the Forties**, Robin Cross; 1986–7.
**Variety International Film Guide Annual** (formerly **International Film Guide**), ed. Peter Cowie; reviewed throughout the period.
**Variety Movie Guide**, ed. Derek Elley; 1993–4.
**The Virgin Film Guide**, James Monaco and the editors of Baseline; 1993–4.
**The Virgin Encyclopedia of Film**, James Monaco and the editors of Baseline; 1992–3.
**Who Played Who on the Screen**, Roy Pickard; 1989–90.
**A Who's Who of Australian and New Zealand Film Actors**, Scott Palmer; 1989–90.
**A Who's Who of British Film Actors**, Scott Palmer; 1982–3.
**Who's Who of the Horrors and Other Fantasy Films**, David J. Hogan; 1983–4.
**Who's Who on the Screen**, John Walter Skinner; 1984–5.
**Who Was Who on Screen**, Evelyn Mack Truitt; 3rd edition 1983–4.
**World Filmography** (1) 1967 (2) 1968, ed. Peter Cowie; 1978–9. An exciting project which, sadly, proved over-ambitious; no further volumes were published.

*

In addition, four 'occasional' series must be listed:

1. Lorrimer Publishing's film scripts, each containing full text, many illustrations and notes; only rarely falling below a consistently high standard.
2. **The Great Movie Pictures** (Spy, Combat, Musicals, Cop, etc.), James Robert Parish and Michael R. Pitts.
3. The Classical Universal Filmscripts (MagicImage), Philip Riley. Complete shooting scripts, information and photographs.
4. The Virgin Film Library: basically a 'Films of . . .' series, though in fact it includes numerous other subjects, as varied as Black Hollywood, Sex in the Movies, Westerns, Character People, and films of various decades. Originally issued under the Citadel imprint, the series is now published in the UK by Virgin Publishing; it forms one of the most attractive and useful collections of large format, lavishly illustrated cinema books.

Finally a special mention for Denis Gifford's **The British Film Encyclopedia 1897–1970**. It arrived too late for more than a listed mention in *Film Review 1973–4*, but is the one essential reference book on the British cinema: it was revised and updated at a later date.

This purely personal selection is drawn only from the *Film Review* book sections. Film enthusiasts could undoubtedly draw up other equally full lists, and of course there are many other interesting, informative and entertaining books that could have been included.

# Film Books of the Year

**ABC – First Name in Entertainment**, Allen Eyles; BFI Publications
**Academy Awards Handbook**, John Harkness; Penguin/Pinnacle
**Academy Awards – The Complete Categorical and Chronological Record**, ed. Richard Shale; Greenwood Press, London
**Action and Image – Dramatic Structure in Cinema**, Roy Armes; Manchester University Press
**Actor and the Camera**, Malcolm Taylor; Black
**Adventures in the Skin Trade**, William Goldman; Warner
**Allied Artists Checklist – The Feature Films and Short Subjects of Allied Artists Pictures Corporation 1947–78**, Len D. Martin; McFarland/Shelwing
**American Film Institute Catalogue – Feature Films 1931–40**; University of California Press
**Anthony Hopkins**, Michael Feeney Callan; Sidgwick & Jackson
**Arnold Schwarzenegger – A Life on Film**, Adrian Wright; Robert Hale
**Atalante**, Marina Warner; BFI Film Classics
**Audrey Hepburn** (revised edition), Ian Woodward; Virgin
**Audrey Hepburn – a Celebration**, Sheridan Morley; Pavilion Books
**Australian Film 1978–1992**, ed. Murray Scott; OUP (Australia)
**Award Winning Films – A Viewer's Reference to 2,700 Acclaimed Motion Pictures**, Peter C. Mowrey; McFarland/Shelwing
**Behind the Mask – Secrets of Hollywood's Monster Makers**, Mark Salisbury and Alan Hedgcock; Titan Books
**Bette Davis – a Biography**, Barbara Leaming; Penguin
**Betty Grable – A Bio-Bibliography**, Larry Billman; Greenwood Press
**Biblical Epics – Sacred Narrative in the Hollywood Cinema**, Bruce Babington and Peter William Evans; Manchester University Press.
**Black American Cinema**, ed. Manthia Diawara; Routledge
**Book of 'Alien'**, Paul Scanlon and Michael Gross; Titan Books
**Border Crossing – Film in Ireland, Britain and Europe**, ed. John Hill, etc.; BFI Publications
**Boris Karloff – A Bio-Bibliography**, Beverley Bare Buehrer
**Brief Encounter**, Richard Dyer; BFI Film Classics
**Bruce Lee – a Fighting Spirit**, Thomas Bruce; Viking
**Calling the Shots – Interviews with Women Filmmakers**, Janis Cole & Holly Dale; Quarry Press, Canada/Bailey
**Cartoons – 100 Years of Cinema Animation**, Giannalberto Bendazzi; J. Libby
**Certain Realism – Making Use of Pasolini's Film Theory and Practice**, Maurizio Viano; University of California Press
**Chambers Film Facts**, ed. Allan Hunter; Chambers
**Cinema and Modernity**, John Orr; Polity Press
**Cinema of Eisenstein**, David Bordwell; Harvard University Press
**Classical Hollywood Comedy**, ed. Henry Jenkins & Kristine Brunovska; Routledge
**Clint Eastwood – Actor and Director**, Edward Gallafent; Studio Vista
**Comedy Quotes from the Movies**, Harry Langman & Paul Gold; McFarland/Shelwing
**Complete Films of Buster Keaton**, Jim Kline; Citadel
**The Complete 'Gone With The Wind' Source Book**, Pauline Bartel; Taylor Publishing, dist. Gazelle Services
**Contemporary Film Theory**, ed. Antony Easthope; Longman Critical Readers
**Cronenberg on Cronenberg**, ed. Chris Rodley; Faber & Faber
**Cross and the Cinema – Legion of Decency and the National Catholic Office for Motion Pictures 1939–1970**, James M. Skinner; Praeger
**Devil's Candy – 'Bonfire of the Vanities' Goes to Hollywood**, Julie Salamon; Picador
**Dirty Looks – Women, Pornography, Power**, ed. Pam Church-Gibson and Roma Gibson; BFI Publications
**Down and Dirty – Hollywood's Exploitation Filmmakers and Their Movies**, Mike Quarles; McFarland/Shelwing
**Ealing Studios** – revised edition, Charles Barr; Studio Vista
**Ernst Lubitsch – Laughter in Paradise – A Biography**, Scott Eyman; Simon & Schuster
**Famous Hollywood Locations – Films and TV Series**, Leon Smith; McFarland/Shelwing
**Fellini**, John Baxter; Fourth Estate
**Film – An International History of the Medium**, Robert Sklar, Thames & Hudson
**Film Quotations – 1,100 Lines Spoken on Screen**, Robert A. Nowlan and Gwendolyn Wright
**The Films of Agatha Christie**, Scott Palmer; Batsford
**The Films of Almos Gitai**, Paul Willemen; BFI Publications
**The Films of Arnold Schwarzenegger**, John L. Flynn; Virgin
**The Films of Brigitte Bardot**, Tony Crawley; Virgin
**The Films of D. W. Griffith**, Scott Simon; Cambridge University Press
**The Films of John Cassavetes – Embracing the World**, Raymond Carney; Cambridge Film Classics
**The Films of John Garfield**, Patrick J. McGrath; McFarland/Shelwing
**The Films of Joseph Losey**, James Palmer and Michael Riley; Cambridge University Press
**The Films of Paul Morrissey**, Maurice Yacowar; Cambridge University Press
**The Films of Robert de Niro**, Douglas Brode; Virgin
**The Films of Rodgers and Hammerstein**, Ethan Mordden; Virgin
**The Films of Stephen King**, Ann Lloyd; Brown Books: Biblios
**The Films of Vincente Minnelli**, James Naremore; Cambridge University Press
**Fire Over England – British Cinema comes under Friendly Fire**, Ken Russell; Hutchinson
**The First Hundred Years**, David Shipman; Weidenfeld & Nicolson
**François Truffaut**, David Nicholls; Batsford

**French Film Noir**, Robin Buss; M. Boyars

**French National Cinema**, Susan Hayward; Routledge

**Future Visions – New Technologies of the Screen**, ed. Tana Wollen and Philip Hayward; BFI Publications

**Gay Hollywood – Over Seventy-five Years of Male Homosexuality in the Movies**, Steve Stewart

**Gays and Lesbians in Mainstream Cinema**, James Robert Parish; McFarland/Shelwing

**Ginger Rogers – A Bio-Bibliography**, ed. Jocelyn Faris; Greenwood Press

**The Golden Age of Movie Stills Photography**, Joel Finler; Batsford

**Graham Greene Film Reader – Mornings in the Dark**, Graham Greene, ed. David Parkinson

**Great Scot – A Life of Sean Connery**, John Hunter; Bloomsbury

**The Guinness Book of Classic British TV**, Paul Cornell, etc.; Guinness Publishing

**Halliwell's Film Companion – Tenth Edition**, ed. J. Walker; Grafton

**Halliwell's Guide to the Best Children's Films**, ed. John Walker; HarperCollins

**Halliwell's Guide to the Best Comedy Films**, ed. John Walker; HarperCollins

**Helen Hayes – A Bio-Bibliography**, Donn B. Murphy and Stephen Moore; Greenwood Press

**Hollywood as Mirror – Changing Views of Outsiders and Enemies in American Movies**, ed. Robert Brent Toplin; Greenwood Press, London

**Hollywood Cauldron – Thirteen Horror Films from the Genre's Golden Age**, Gregory William Mank; McFarland/Shelwing

**Hollywood Rock – A Guide to Rock 'n' Roll in the Movies**, Marshall Crenshaw; Plexus Publishing

**Holocaust in French Film**, Andre Pierre Colombat; Scarecrow, dist. Shelwing

**House of Dracula** – original shooting script, ed. Philip J. Riley; MagicImage Filmbooks/Gazelle

**How to Make It in Hollywood**, Linda Buzell; HarperCollins

**100 Best Films of the Century**, Barry Norman; Chapman's

**I Was Interrupted**, Nicholas Ray, ed. Ray Susan; University of California

**The Illustrated Dinosaur Movie Guide**, Stephen Jones; Titan Books

**The Incredibly Strange Film Book**, Jonathan Ross; Simon & Schuster

**Indecent Exposures – Buñuel to Almodovar**, Gwynne Edwards; M. Boyars

**Ingmar Bergman – Film and Stage**, Robert Emmet Long; Abrams

**The International Dictionary of Films and Filmmakers. Vol. 4 – Writers and Production Artists**. Updated and greatly enlarged edition, fully illustrated. Ed. Samantha Cook; St James Press

**International Dictionary of Films and Filmmakers – Vol. 5 (Index)**, ed. Samantha Cook; St. James Press

**James Dean, Little Boy Lost – An Intimate Biography**, Joe Hyams & Jay Hyams; Arrow Books

**Joseph Losey – A Revenge on Life**, David Caute; Faber & Faber

**Just Tell Me When to Cry – Encounters with the Greats, the Near Greats and the Ingrates of Hollywood**, Richard Fleischer; Souvenir Press

**Katharine Hepburn**, Sarah Parker Danielson; Magna Books

**Keepers of the Frame – Film Archives**, Penelope Houston; BFI Publishing

**Kenneth Williams – Diaries**, ed. Russell Davies; HarperCollins

**Laurel and Hardy**, Annie McGarry; Magna Books

**Life after Sixty**, Lauren Bacall; Century

**The Life and Death of Peter Sellers**, Roger Lewis; Century

**Life Before and After Monty Python – The Solo Flights of the Flying Circus**, Kim Johnson; Plexus Publishing

**Life in Hollywood 1936–1952**, Peter Stackpole; Mainstream

**Like a Film – Ideological Fantasy on Screen, Camera and Canvas**, Timothy Murray; Routledge

**Lon Chaney – the Man Behind the Thousand Faces**, Michael F. Blake

**Looks and Frictions – Essays in Cultural Studies and Film Theory**, Paul Willemen; BFI Publications

**'Lost World' of Willis O'Brien** – The Original Shooting Script of the Landmark Special Dinosaur Film with Photographs, ed. Roy Kinnard; McFarland/Shelwing

**Lullabies of Hollywood – Movie Music and the Movie Musical 1915–1992**, Richard Fehr and Frederick G. Vogel; McFarland/Shelwing

**The Magnificent Ambersons – A Reconstruction**, Robert I. Carringer; University of California Press

**Making Movies Black – Hollywood Message Movies from World War II to the Civil Rights Era**, Thomas Cripps; OUP (New York)

**The Making of Jurassic Park**, Bob Shed; Boxtree

**Marilyn – The Ultimate Look at the Legend**, James Haspiel; Smith Gryphon

**Martin Scorsese** – An Analysis of His Feature Films with a Filmography of His Entire Directorial Career, Mary Katheryn Connelly; McFarland/Shelwing

**Marx Brothers – Three Films**, S. J. Perelman; Faber & Faber

**Mediating Two Worlds – Cinematic Encounters in the Americas**, ed. John King, etc.; BFI Publications

**Miracle on 34th Street**, Sarah Parker Danielson; Magna Books

**Monsters and Aliens from George Lucas**, Bob Carrau; Abrams

**Motion Picture Guide – 1993 Annual**, Baseline, US; Bowker-Saur

**'Movie Watch' Film Quiz and Trivia Book**, Will Adams; Signet

**Nicolas Roeg Film by Film**, Scott Salwolke; McFarland/Shelwing

**The Piano**, Jane Campion; Bloomsbury

**Poetry of Cinema**, John Madden; Crescent Moon

**Polanski**, John Parker; Gollancz

**Projections – A Year in Film**, ed. J. Boorman & W. Donohue; Faber & Faber

**Psychos and Madmen – Definitive Book on Film Psychopaths from Jekyll and Hyde to Hannibal Lecter**, John McCarty; Virgin

**Robert, My Father**, Sheridan Morley; Weidenfeld & Nicolson

**Robert Shaw – The Price of Success**, John French; Nick Hern Books

**Ronald Reagan in Hollywood – Movies and Politics**, Stephen Vaughan; Cambridge University Press

**Screening the Novel**, Gabriel Miller; Roundhouse Publishing

**The Secret Life of Bob Hope – An Unauthorised Biography**, Arthur Marx; Robson Books

**Sergei Eisenstein – Selected Writings – Towards a Theory of Montage**, tr. M. Glenny, ed. R. Taylor; BFI Publications

**Shepperton Studios – An Independent View**, Derek Threadgall; BFI Publications

**'Shoot the Piano Player' – François Truffaut, Director**, ed. Peter Brunette; Roundhouse Publishing

**Showstoppers – Busby Berkeley and the Tradition of Spectacle**, Martin Ruby; Columbia University Press

**A Siegel Film – An Autobiography**, Don Siegel; Faber & Faber

**Sight and Sound Film Reviews** – Jan.-Dec. 1993; BFI Publications

**Silent Comedians**, Richard Dyer MacCann; Scarecrow, dist. Shelwing

**Soul in Suspense – Hitchcock's Fright and Delight**, Neil P. Hurley; Scarecrow/Shelwing

**Spectacular Bodies – Gender, Genre and the Action Cinema**; Routledge

**A Star Danced – The Life of Audrey Hepburn**, Robyn Karney; Bloomsbury Publishing

**Star Gazing – Hollywood Cinema and Female Spectatorship**, Jackie Stacey; Routledge

**Starring Roles**, Ron Base; Little, Brown

**Taxi Driver**, Amy Taubin; BFI Film Classics

**They Also Wrote for the Fan Magazines** – Film Articles by Literary Giants from e. e. cummings to Eleanor Roosevelt 1920–1939, ed. Anthony Slide; McFarland, dist. Shelwing

**Three Screenplays**, Richard Price; Studio Vista

**Tony Curtis** – An Autobiography, ed. Barry Paris; Heinemann

**TV Times Film and Video Guide**, ed. David Quinlan; Mandarin

**Variety Book of Movie Lists**, ed. Fred Lombardi; Hamlyn

**Variety International Film Guide 1994**, ed. Peter Cowie; Hamlyn

**Variety Movie Guide 1994**, ed. Derek Elley; Hamlyn

**Vintage Monster Movies**, Robert Marrero; Robert Hale

**W. C. Fields – An Annotated Guide**, David T. Rocks; McFarland/Shelwing

**Walking Shadows – Shakespeare in the National Film and Television Archive**, Luke McKernan & Olwen Terris; BFI Publications

**Warren Beatty – The Last Great Lover of Hollywood**, John Parker; Headline

**When Hollywood was Fun – Snapshots of an Era**, Gene Lester & Peter Laufer; Robert Hale

**Willis O'Brien – Special Effects Genius**, Steve Archer; McFarland, dist. Shelwing

**Woman's View – How Hollywood Spoke to Women, 1930–1960**, Jeanine Basinger; Chatto

**Woody Allen Companion**, Stephen Spignesi; Plexus Publishing

# Awards and Festivals

We have always concentrated principally on the major established festivals and award ceremonies around the world. There are of course several hundred others which space does not allow us to include here; some are highly specialised events appealing principally to a small minority, while we have also – some may say unfairly – excluded many Middle and Far East festivals.

Nationality is stated only where films originate from a country other than that in which the award is given – though when this information would be unnecessary or repetitive, we have not included it.

### The 66th American Academy of Motion Picture Arts and Sciences Awards ('The Oscars') and Nominations for 1993, 21 March 1994

Best Film: *Schindler's List.* Nominations: *The Fugitive*; *In the Name of the Father*; *The Piano*; *The Remains of the Day.*

Best Director: Steven Spielberg, for *Schindler's List.* Nominations: Robert Altman, for *Short Cuts*; Jane Campion, for *The Piano*; James Ivory, for *The Remains of the Day*; Jim Sheridan, for *In the Name of the Father.*

Best Actor: Tom Hanks, for *Philadelphia.* Nominations: Daniel Day-Lewis, for *In the Name of the Father*; Laurence Fishburne, for *What's Love Got to Do with It*; Anthony Hopkins, for *The Remains of the Day*; Liam Neeson, for *Schindler's List.*

Best Actress: Holly Hunter, for *The Piano.* Nominations: Angela Bassett, for *What's Love Got to Do with It*; Stockard Channing, for *Six Degrees of Separation*; Emma Thompson, for *The Remains of the Day*; Debra Winger, for *Shadowlands.*

Best Supporting Actor: Tommy Lee Jones, for *The Fugitive.* Nominations: Leonardo DiCaprio, for *What's Eating Gilbert Grape*; Ralph Fiennes, for *Schindler's List*; John Malkovich, for *In the Line of Fire*; Pete Postlethwaite, for *In the Name of the Father.*

Best Supporting Actress: Anna Paquin, for *The Piano.* Nominations: Holly Hunter, for *The Firm*; Rosie Perez, for *Fearless*; Winona Ryder, for *The Age of Innocence*; Emma Thompson, for *In the Name of the Father.*

Best Original Screenplay: Jane Campion, for *The Piano.* Nominations:

*Embeth Davidtz and Ralph Fiennes in their star-making turns in Steven Spielberg's 1993 masterpiece, the Oscar-winning* Schindler's List

Gary Ross, for *Dave*; Jeff Maguire, for *In the Line of Fire*; Ron Nyswaner, for *Philadelphia*; Nora Ephron, David S. Ward and Jeff Arch, for *Sleepless in Seattle*.

Best Screenplay Adaptation: Steven Zaillian, for *Schindler's List*. Nominations: Jay Cocks and Martin Scorsese, for *The Age of Innocence*; Terry George and Jim Sheridan, for *In the Name of the Father*; Ruth Prawer Jhabvala, for *The Remains of the Day*; William Nicholson, for *Shadowlands*.

Best Cinematography: Janusz Kaminski, for *Schindler's List*. Nominations: Gu Changwei, for *Farewell My Concubine*; Michael Chapman, for *The Fugitive*; Stuart Dryburgh, for *The Piano*; Conrad L. Hall, for *Searching for Bobby Fischer* (aka *Innocent Moves*).

Best Editing: Michael Kahn, for *Schindler's List*. Nominations: Dennis Virkler, David Finfer, Dean Goodhill, Don Brochu, Richard Nord and Dov Hoenig, for *The Fugitive*; Anne V. Coates, for *In the Line of Fire*; Gerry Hambling, for *In the Name of the Father*; Veronika Jenet, for *The Piano*.

Best Original Score: John Williams, for *Schindler's List*. Nominations: Elmer Bernstein, for *The Age of Innocence*; Dave Grusin, for *The Firm*; James Newton Howard, for *The Fugitive*; Richard Robbins, for *The Remains of the Day*.

Best Original Song: 'Streets of Philadelphia', from *Philadelphia*, music and lyrics by Bruce Springsteen. Nominations: 'Again', from *Poetic Justice*, music and lyrics by Janet Jackson, James Harris III and Terry Lewis; 'The Day I Fall In Love', from *Beethoven's 2nd*, music and lyrics by Carole Bayer Sager, James Ingram and Cliff Magness; 'Philadelphia', from *Philadelphia*, music and lyrics by Neil Young; 'A Wink and a Smile', from *Sleepless in Seattle*, music by Marc Shaiman, lyrics by Ramsay McLean.

Best Art Direction: Allan Starski (art direction) and Ewa Braun (set decoration) for *Schindler's List*. Nominations: Ken Adam (art) and Marvin March (set) for *Addams Family Values*; Dante Ferretti (art) and Robert J. Franco (set), for *The Age of Innocence*; Ben Van Os and Jan Roelfs (art), for *Orlando*; Luciana Arrighi (art) and Ian Whittaker (set) for *The Remains of the Day*.

Best Costume Design: Gabriella Pescucci, for *The Age of Innocence*. Nominations: Sandy Powell, for *Orlando*; Janet Patterson, for *The Piano*; Jenny Beaven and John Bright, for *The Remains of the Day*; Anna Biedrzycka-Sheppard, for *Schindler's List*.

Best Sound: Gary Summers, Gary Rydstrom, Shawn Murphy and Ron Judkins, for *Jurassic Park*. Nominations: Michael Minkler, Bob Beemer and Tim Cooney, for *Cliffhanger*; Donald O. Mitchell, Michael Herbick, Frank A. Montano and Scott D. Smith, for *The Fugitive*; Chris Carpenter, D. M. Hemphill, Bill W. Benton and Lee Orloff, for *Geronimo: An American Legend*; Andy Nelson, Steve Pederson, Scott Millan and Ron Judkins, for *Schindler's List*.

Best Sound Effects Editing: Gary Rydstrom and Richard Hymns, for *Jurassic Park*. Nominations: Wylie Stateman and Gregg Baxter, for *Cliffhanger*; John Leveque and Bruce Stambler, for *The Fugitive*.

Best Make-up: Greg Cannom, Ve Neill and Yolanda Toussieng, for *Mrs Doubtfire*. Nominations: Carl Fullerton and Alan D'Angelo, for *Philadelphia*; Christina Smith, Matthew Mungle and Judith A. Cory, for *Schindler's List*.

Best Visual Effects: Dennis Muren, Stan Winston, Phil Tippett and Michael Lantieri, for *Jurassic Park*. Nominations: Neil Krepela, John Richardson, John Bruno and Pamela Easley, for *Cliffhanger*; Pete Kozachik, Eric Leighton, Ariel Velasco Shaw and Gordon Baker, for *The Nightmare Before Christmas*.

Best Animated Short Film: *The Wrong Trousers* (UK), by Nick Park. Nominations: *Blindscape*; *The Mighty River*; *Small Talk*; *The Village*.

Best Live Action Short Film: *Black Rider*. Nominations: *Down on the Waterfront*; *The Dutch Master*; *Partners*; *The Screw*.

Best Documentary Feature: *I Am a Promise: The Children of Stanton Elementary School*. Nominations: *The Broadcast Tapes of Dr Peter*; *Children of Fate*; *For Better or For Worse*; *The War Room*.

Best Documentary Short: *Defending Our Lives*. Nominations: *Blood Ties: The Life and Work of Sally Mann*; *Chicks in White Satin*.
Best Foreign Language Film: *Belle Epoque* (Spain). Nominations: *Farewell My Concubine* (Hong Kong/China); *Hedd Wyn* (UK); *The Scent of Green Papaya* (Vietnam); *The Wedding Banquet* (Taiwan).
Jean Hersholt Humanitarian Award: Paul Newman.
Honorary Academy Award: Deborah Kerr.

## The 35th Australian Film Institute Awards, 5 November 1993

Best Film: *The Piano*.
Best Actor: Harvey Keitel, for *The Piano*.
Best Actress: Holly Hunter, for *The Piano*.
Best Supporting Actor: David Ngoombujarra, for *Blackfellas*.
Best Supporting Actress: Judy Davis, for *On My Own*.
Best Director: Jane Campion, for *The Piano*.
Best Screenplay: Jane Campion, for *The Piano*.
Best Cinematography: Stuart Dryburgh, for *The Piano*.
Best Editing: Veronika Jenet, for *The Piano*.
Best Music: Michael Nyman, for *The Piano*.
Best Production Design: Andrew McAlpine, for *The Piano*.
Best Costumes: Janet Patterson, for *The Piano*.
Best Sound: Lee Smith, for *The Piano*.
Best Foreign Film: *The Crying Game*, by Neil Jordan (UK).

## The 44th Berlin International Film Festival, February 1994

Golden Bear for Best Film: *In the Name of the Father* (UK–Ireland).
Silver Bear Special Jury Prize: *Strawberry and Chocolate* (Cuba–Mexico–Spain).
Best Director: Krzysztof Kieslowski, for *Three Colours: White* (France–Switzerland–Poland).
Best Actor: Tom Hanks, for *Philadelphia* (USA).
Best Actress: Crissy Rock, for *Ladybird, Ladybird* (UK).
Outstanding Performance (Special Mention): Rosie Perez, for *Fearless* (USA).
Outstanding Single Achievement: Alain Resnais, for *Smoking/No Smoking* (France).
Cinematography (Special Mention): *Sparkling Fox* (Hong Kong–China).
Special Bear: Sophia Loren.
Blue Angel Prize: *Law of Courage* (Italy).
Wolfgang Staudte Prize: *Palms* (Russia).
International Film Critics' Award: *Ladybird, Ladybird*.
Children's Film Jury Prize: *No Worries* (Australia).
International Confederation of Art Cinemas Prize: *Pater Noster* (Finland).

*

Jury: Jeremy Thomas, Susan Seidelman, Morgan Freeman, Francis Girod, Maria Luisa Bemberg, Carlo Lizzani, etc.

## The 1993 British Academy of Film and Television Arts Awards, 24 April 1994

Best Film: *Schindler's List*, by Steven Spielberg.
Best Film (public vote): *Jurassic Park*, by Steven Spielberg.
David Lean Award for Best Direction: Steven Spielberg, for *Schindler's List*.
Best Adapted Screenplay: Steven Zaillian, for *Schindler's List*.
Best Actor: Anthony Hopkins, for *The Remains of the Day*.
Best Actress: Holly Hunter, for *The Piano*.
Best Supporting Actor: Ralph Fiennes, for *Schindler's List*.
Best Supporting Actress: Miriam Margolyes, for *The Age of Innocence*.
Best Cinematography: Janusz Kaminski, for *Schindler's List*.
Best Editing: Michael Kahn, for *Schindler's List*.
Best Score: John Williams, for *Schindler's List*.
Best British Film: *Shadowlands*, by Richard Attenborough.

## The 1993 Canadian Film Awards ('Genies'), 12 December 1993

Best Film: *Thirty-Two Short Films about Glenn Gould*.
Best Director: Francois Girard, for *Thirty-Two Short Films about Glenn Gould*.
Best Actor: Tom McCamus, for *I Love a Man in Uniform*.
Best Actress: Sheila McCarthy, for *The Lotus Eaters*.
Best Supporting Actor: Kevin Tighe, for *I Love a Man in Uniform*.
Best Supporting Actress: Nicola Cavendish, for *The Grocer's Wife*.
Best Screenplay: Peggy Thompson, for *The Lotus Eaters*.
Best Cinematography: Alain Dostie, for *Thirty-Two Short Films About Glenn Gould*.
Best Editing: Gaetan Huot, for *Thirty-Two Short Films About Glenn Gould*.
Best Art Direction/Production Design: Wolf Kroeger, for *Agaguk (Shadow of the Wolf)*.
Best Music: Simon Kendall, for *Cadillac Girls*.
Best Costumes: Olga Dimitrov, for *Agaguk*.
Best Overall Sound: Hans Peter Strobl, Richard Besse and Jocelyn Caron, for *Le Sexe des Etoiles*.
Best Sound Editing: Gael Maclean, Anke Bakker, Alison Grace, Ellen Gram and Maureen Wetteland, for *The Lotus Eaters*.
Best Feature-length Documentary: Aerlyn Weissman and Lynne Fernie, for *Forbidden Love*.
Best Short Documentary: Esther Valiquette, for *Le Singe Bleu*.
Best Live-Action Short Drama: Laurie Lynd, for *The Fairy Who Didn't Want To Be a Fairy Anymore*.
Best Animated Short: Lynn Smith, for *Pearl's Diner*.
Air Canada Award: John Dunning and Andre Link of Cinepix Inc.
Claude Jutra Award: John Pozer, for his first directorial feature, *The Grocer's Wife*.
Honorary Lifetime Achievement Award: Ken Heeley-Ray, for sound editing.
Golden Reel Award: *La Florida*, for top box-office performance.

### The 47th Cannes Film Festival Awards, 23 May 1994

Palme d'Or for Best Film: *Pulp Fiction*, by Quentin Tarantino (USA).
Grand Prix du Jury: *Burnt by the Sun*, by Nikita Mikhalkov (Russia–France); and *To Live*, by Zhang Yimou (Hong Kong–China).
Jury Prize: *La Reine Margot*, by Patrice Chereau (France).
Best Actor: Ge You, for *To Live*.
Best Actress: Virna Lisi, for *La Reine Margot*.
Best Director: Nanni Moretti, for *Caro Diaro* (Italy).
Best Screenplay: Michel Blanc, for *Gross Fatigue* (France).
International Critics' Prize: *Exotica*, by Atom Egoyan (Canada).
Prix de la Jeunesse: *Clerks*, by Kevin Smith (USA).
Palme d'Or for Best Short: *El Heroe* (Mexico).
Jury Prize for Best Short: *Lemming Aid* (New Zealand); and *Syrup* (UK).
Camera d'Or: *Coming to Terms with the Dead* (France).
Camera d'Or (special mention): *The Silences of the Palace* (Tunisia–France).
Grand Prix Technique: *Gross Fatigue*, by Michel Blanc (France).

Jury: Clint Eastwood, Catherine Deneuve, Kazuo Ishiguro, Lalo Schifrin, etc.

*Who would have thought two years ago that a John Travolta movie would snatch the Palme d'Or at Cannes? But here JT is – as hitman Vincent Vega – in Quentin Tarantino's* Pulp Fiction, *executive-produced by Danny DeVito*

### The David di Donatello Awards ('Davids'), Rome, 18 June 1994

Best Film: *Dear Diary*, by Nanni Moretti.
Best Director: Carlo Verdone, for *Perdiamoci di Vista*.
Best Actor: Giulio Scarpati, for *Law of Courage*.
Best Actress: Asia Argento, for *Perdiamoci di Vista*.
Best Supporting Actor: Alessandro Haber, for *For Love, Only For Love*.
Best Supporting Actress: Monica Scattini, for *Sentimental Maniacs*.
Best New Director: Francesco Martinotti, for *Abyssinia*; tying with Leone Pompucci, for *Mille Bolle Blu*; and Simona Izzo, for *Sentimental Maniacs*.
Best Producer: Aurelio De Laurentiis, for *For Love, Only For Love*.
Best Screenplay: Giovanni Veronesi and Ugo Chiti, for *For Love, Only For Love*.
Best Cinematography: Bruno Cascio, for *Father and Son*; tied with Dante Spinotti, for *The Secret of the Old Woods*.
Best Editing: Carlo Valerio, for *Father and Son*.
Art Direction: Antonello Geleng, for *Dellamorte Dellamore*.
Best Music: Nicola Piovani, for *Dear Diary*.
Costumes: Piero Tosi, for *Sparrow*.
Sound: Tullio Morganti, for *Stud*.
Best Foreign Film: *In the Name of the Father* (UK).
Best Foreign Actor: Anthony Hopkins, for *The Remains of the Day*.
Best Foreign Actress: Emma Thompson, for *The Remains of the Day*.
Career Achievement Award: Alberto Sordi.
Special Jury Prize: Stefano Dionisi.
Luchino Visconti Award: Manoel de Oliveira.
Franco Cristaldi Award: Alberto Lattuada.

### The 6th European Film Awards ('The Felixes'), Berlin, 4 December 1993

Best European Film: *Urga* (Russia), by Nikita Mikhalkov.
European Achievement of the Year: *The Crying Game* (UK), by Neil Jordan.
Best Young European Film: *Orlando* (UK), by Sally Potter.
Best Actor: Daniel Auteuil, for *Un Coeur en Hiver* (France).
Best Actress: Maia Morgenstern, for *The Oak* (Romania).
European Critics' Award: *Benny's Video* (Austria), by Michael Haneke.
Best Documentary: *Misfits to Yuppies* (Sweden), by Stefan Jarl.
Life Achievement Award: Michelangelo Antonioni.

### The 'Evening Standard' 1993 Film Awards, London, 30 January 1994

Best Film: *Raining Stones*.
Best Actor: David Thewlis, for *Naked*.
Best Actress: Emma Thompson, for *The Remains of the Day*.
Best Screenplay: Jim Allen, for *Raining Stones*.
The Peter Sellers Comedy Award: Les Blair, for *Bad Behaviour*.

Special Award for Outstanding Contribution to Cinema: Anthony Hopkins.

### The 19th French Academy (César) Awards, March 1994

Best Film: *Smoking/No Smoking*.
Best Director: Alain Resnais, for *Smoking/No Smoking*.
Best Actor: Pierre Arditi, for *Smoking/No Smoking*.
Best Actress: Juliette Binoche, for *Three Colours Blue*.
Best Supporting Actor: Fabrice Luchini, for *Tout ça pour ça*.
Best Supporting Actress: Valérie Lemercier, for *Les Visiteurs*.
Best New Actor: Olivier Martinez, for *Un, Deux, Trois, Soleil*.
Best New Actress: Valéria Bruni-Tedeschi, for *Les Gens Normaux N'Ont Rien d'Exceptionel*.
Best First Film: *The Scent of Green Papaya*, by Tran Anh Hung.
Best Screenplay: Jean-Pierre Bacri and Agnès Jaoui, for *Smoking/No Smoking*.
Best Photography: Yves Angelo, for *Germinal*.
Best Editing: Jacques Witta, for *Three Colours Blue*.
Best Production Design: Jacques Saulnier, for *Smoking/No Smoking*.
Best Music: Khaled, for *Un, Deux, Trois, Soleil*.
Best Costumes: Sylvie Gautrelet, Caroline de Vivalse and Bernadette Witta, for *Germinal*.
Best Sound: Jean-Claude Laureux, for *Smoking/No Smoking*.
Best Foreign Film: *The Piano*, by Jane Campion (Australia).
Best Short: *Gueule d'Atmosphère*, by d'Olivier Peray.
César d'Honneur: Jean Carmet.

### The 51st Hollywood Foreign Press Association (Golden Globe) Awards, January 1994

Best Film – Drama: *Schindler's List*.
Best Film – Comedy or Musical: *Mrs Doubtfire*.
Best Actor – Drama: Tom Hanks, for *Philadelphia*.
Best Actress – Drama: Holly Hunter, for *The Piano*.
Best Actor – Comedy or Musical: Robin Williams, for *Mrs Doubtfire*.

*Renaud and Judith Henry in Claude Berri's* Germinal, *the most expensive French film ever made, but which only received awards for best photography and costumes at the 1994 Césars*

Best Actress – Comedy or Musical: Angela Bassett, for *What's Love Got to Do with It*.
Best Supporting Actor: Tommy Lee Jones, for *The Fugitive*.
Best Supporting Actress: Winona Ryder, for *The Age of Innocence*.
Best Director: Steven Spielberg, for *Schindler's List*.
Best Screenplay: Steven Zaillian, for *Schindler's List*.
Best Original Score: Kitaro, for *Heaven and Earth*.
Best Original Song: 'Streets of Philadelphia', by Bruce Springsteen, for *Philadelphia*.
Best Foreign Language Film: *Farewell My Concubine* (Hong Kong–China).
Special Achievement Award: *Short Cuts*.
Cecil B. DeMille Award for Lifetime Achievement: Robert Redford.

### The 15th London Film Critics' Awards ('The Alfs'), 28 January 1994

Best Film: *The Piano*.
Best Actor: Anthony Hopkins, for *The Remains of the Day*.
Best Actress: Holly Hunter, for *The Piano*.
Best Director: James Ivory, for *The Remains of the Day*.
Best Screenwriter: Harold Ramis and Danny Rubin, for *Groundhog Day*.
Non-British Newcomer: Quentin Tarantino, writer/director of *Reservoir Dogs*, writer of *True Romance*.
Best British Film: *The Remains of the Day*.
Best British Producer: Kenneth Branagh, for *Much Ado About Nothing*.
Best British Director: Ken Loach, for *Raining Stones*.
Best British Screenwriter: Roddy Doyle, for *The Snapper*.
Best British Actor: David Thewlis, for *Naked*.
Best British Actress: Miranda Richardson, for *Damage*.
Best British Newcomer: Vadim Jean

and Gary Sinyor, producers/directors of *Leon the Pig Farmer*.
Best British Technical Achievement: Ken Adam, production designer of *Addams Family Values*.
Best Foreign Language Film: *Un Coeur en Hiver* (France).
Dilys Powell Award: Christopher Lee.

### The Los Angeles Film Critics' Association Awards, December 1993

Best Film: *Schindler's List*.
Best Actor: Anthony Hopkins, for *The Remains of the Day* and *Shadowlands*.
Best Actress: Holly Hunter, for *The Piano*.
Best Supporting Actor: Tommy Lee Jones, for *The Fugitive*.
Best Supporting Actress: shared by Anna Paquin, for *The Piano*; and Rosie Perez, for *Fearless*.
Best Director: Jane Campion, for *The Piano*.
Best Screenplay: Jane Campion, for *The Piano*.
Best Cinematography: shared by Janusz Kaminski, for *Schindler's List*; and Stuart Dryburgh, for *The Piano*.
Best Production Design: Allan Starski, for *Schindler's List*.
Best Score: Zbigniew Preisner, for *Three Colours Blue*, *The Secret Garden* and *Olivier, Olivier*.
Best Foreign Film: *Farewell My Concubine* (Hong Kong–China).
Best Documentary: *It's All True*, by Myron Meisel, Bill Krohn and Richard Wilson.
Best Animation: *The Mighty River*, by Frederick Back.
New Generation Award: Leonardo DiCaprio, actor, for *This Boy's Life* and *What's Eating Gilbert Grape*.
Career Achievement Award: John Alton, cinematographer.
Douglas Edwards Award for Independent/Experimental Film & Video: *Silverlake Life: The View From Here*, by Tom Joslin and Peter Friedman.

### The 1st Movie Awards, 13 June 1994

As voted by British cinemagoers and sponsored by Diet Coke
Best Film: *Jurassic Park*.
Best Hero: Liam Neeson, in *Schindler's List*.
Best Heroine: Meg Ryan, in *Sleepless in Seattle*.
Best Bad Guy/Girl: Wesley Snipes, in *Demolition Man*.
Best Male Body: Sylvester Stallone, in *Cliffhanger*.
Best Female Body: Robin Williams, in *Mrs Doubtfire*.
Best Haircut: Jimmy Workman, in *Addams Family Values*.
Sexiest Kiss: Daniel Day-Lewis and Michelle Pfeiffer, in *The Age of Innocence*.
Best Car Chase: *Jurassic Park*.
Best Chase on Foot: *The Fugitive*.
Best Shoot-out: *Demolition Man*.
Funniest Movie Moment: *Mrs Doubtfire*.
Best Soundtrack: *Aladdin*.

### The National Board of Review, December 1993

Best Film: *Schindler's List*.
Best Actor: Anthony Hopkins, for *The Remains of the Day*.
Best Actress: Holly Hunter, for *The Piano*.
Best Supporting Actor: Leonardo DiCaprio, for *What's Eating Gilbert Grape*.
Best Supporting Actress: Winona Ryder, for *The Age of Innocence*.
Best Director: Martin Scorsese, for *The Age of Innocence*.
Best Foreign Film: *Farewell My Concubine* (Hong Kong–China).
Best Documentary: *The War Room*, by D. A. Pennebaker and Chris Hegedus.
Career Achievement Award: Sean Connery.
Best TV Performance: Bette Midler, for *Gypsy*.
Best TV Series: *NYPD Blue*.
Special Awards: The Film Forum; Robert Rodriguez (for his exceptional directorial debut with *El Mariachi*); Ruth Prawer Jhabvala; the Tribeca Film Center.

### The 59th New York Film Critics' Circle Awards, December 1993

Best Film: *Schindler's List*.
Best Actor: David Thewlis, for *Naked*.
Best Actress: Holly Hunter, for *The Piano*.
Best Supporting Actor: Ralph Fiennes, for *Schindler's List*.
Best Supporting Actress: Gong Li, for *Farewell My Concubine*.
Best Director: Jane Campion, for *The Piano*.
Best Screenplay: Jane Campion, for *The Piano*.
Best Cinematography: Janusz Kaminsi, for *Schindler's List*.
Best Foreign Film: *Farewell My Concubine* (Hong Kong–China).
Best Documentary: *Visions of Light*, by Arnold Glassman, Stuart Samuels and Todd McCarthy.

### The 16th Sundance Film Festival, 30 January 1994

The Grand Jury Prize (best feature): *What Happened Was*, by Tom Noonan.
The Grand Jury Prize (best documentary): *Freedom on My Mind*, by Connie Field and Marilyn Mulford.
Audience Award (best feature): *Spanking the Monkey*, by David O. Russell.
Audience Award (best documentary): *Hoop Dreams*, by Steve James.
Filmmakers' Trophy (best feature): shared by *Clerks*, by Kevin Smith; and *Fresh*, by Boaz Yakin.
Filmmakers' Trophy (best documentary): *Theremin: An Electronic Odyssey*.

### The 50th Venice International Film Festival Awards, September 1993

Golden Lion for Best Film shared by: *Short Cuts*, by Robert Altman (USA); and *Three Colours: Blue*, by Krzysztof Kieslowski (France).
Special Jury Prize: *Bad Boy Bubby*, by Rolf De Heer (Australia–Italy).
Silver Lion: *Kosh ba Kosh*, by Bakhtiar Khudoinazarov (Taadzhikistan).
Best Actor: Fabrizio Bentivoglio, for *A Soul Torn in Two* (Italy).
Best Actress: Juliette Binoche, for *Three Colours: Blue*.
Best Supporting Actor: Marcello Mastroianni, for *Un, Deux, Trois: Soleil* (France).
Best Supporting Actress: Anna Bonaiuto, for *Where Are You? I'm Here* (Italy).
Volpi Cup for Ensemble Cast: *Short Cuts*.

# Index

*Page numbers in italic refer ro illustrations only*

*Video releases are listed separately between pages 132 and 144*